The Possibility of Progress

The Possibility of Progress

MARK BRAUND

SHEPHEARD-WALWYN (PUBLISHERS) LTD

First published in 2005 by
Shepheard-Walwyn (Publishers) Ltd
Suite 604, The Chandlery
50 Westminster Bridge Road
London SE1 7QY

British Library Cataloguing in Publication Data
A catalogue record of this book
is available from the British Library

ISBN 0 85683 226 X

Typeset by Alacrity,
Banwell Castle, Weston-super-Mare
Printed through Print Solutions, Wallington, Surrey

For
Annie and William

Contents

Acknowledgements viii

Introduction ix

1 Science and Humankind... 1

2 Evolution and Culture 23

3 Economics and Morals... 54

4 The State of the World 78

5 A Universal Ethic 106

6 Perception and Reality 129

7 Psyche and Society 155

8 Moral Development 184

9 A True Economics 202

10 Freedom and Justice 233

11 The Politics of Progress 261

Bibliography 285

References 292

Index 299

Acknowledgements

I AM GRATEFUL for permission to quote from the following: Random House Inc, *At the Dawn of Tyranny* by Eli Sagan, 1985 (extract on page 183); Blackwell Publishing Ltd, *Political and Apolitical Students* by Christian Bay, 1967 (extract on pages 195-6); McGill-Queen's University Press, *Karl Polanyi on Ethics and Economics* by Gregory Baum, 1996 (extract on page 199).

My thanks to Jessica Morris, Ed Pilkington and Julia Hobsbawm for their help with promoting the book; to Dave Wetzel for his illuminating comments on the manuscript; to Jean Desebrock for her expert work on the text; to Anthony Werner, my publisher and editor, without whose contribution this would have been a significantly lesser work; to Jeni Braund for fuelling my ambition; and to my wife, Henny, for her unfailing support and encouragement, for making my life complete, and for setting me a deadline.

Introduction

I N RECENT CENTURIES, the rate of human advance has been remarkable, and the pace of change shows no sign of slowing. Technological innovation constantly presents us with new discoveries, each apparently set to revolutionize our lives. Progress defines us; the achievements of our ancestors pale in comparison. But has all this progress led to an improvement in the quality of our lives, or does relentless change only present us with a tougher set of challenges and new anxieties to be overcome? Despite our achievements, are we really happier than our ancestors a hundred or a thousand years ago? How can we be sure if our drive for innovation has been of general benefit to humankind?

Need the material advantages conferred by a century of great advance necessarily have been applied so selectively among and within human populations? Why have certain groups, peoples and nations benefited so immensely while millions remain no better off than their forebears? Would this improvement have been possible in a form which was less selective and more embracing of all humankind, or is it only the selfish drive of ambitious individuals striving for their own material betterment that has enabled a fortunate minority to develop so rapidly in recent generations? If this is true, then what hope for the quarter of the world's people who still live in abject poverty, or the half that have access to the economy but no security within it; or even those lucky enough to have been born in the 'developed' nations, but where so many are troubled by the anxieties which spring from the gradual realization that the world they were brought up to believe was certain and secure is, in reality, anything but? Humankind faces many great, apparently insoluble problems: none has a simple solution and none has a solution in isolation from the others. All of them are a consequence of our failure honestly to appraise the motives and consequences of our relentless drive for progress.

Progress is a difficult concept to tie down. Archaeological evidence from the earliest societies suggests that humans have long been concerned with managing their communities so as to promote improvement on what has gone before. As a concrete idea, however, progress only came to prominence with the *Enlightenment* philosophers of the eighteenth century. Today it occupies a pre-eminent place in people's minds, but it is a concept about which we are strangely ambiguous: as often as we berate ourselves for not doing enough to improve society, we have nothing but praise for modernity. This confusion results from the absence of criteria against which to judge progress. Such criteria would enable us objectively to assess claims for progress, and also to make conscious decisions about future priorities. We need an explicit definition, one which provides clear benchmarks for the measurement of progress, and which is underscored by clear and recognizable moral values.

In the context of this book, progress has several elements: first, the creation of conditions in which growing numbers of people have access to economic opportunities sufficient to provide for their basic needs. Second, the improvement of life expectancy among those groups where it is lowest. Third, the provision of improved economic security for the poorest members of all societies, including the rich countries. Fourth, the achievement of these objectives through means which do not compromise the capacity of the planet to provide for future generations. Fifth, that whatever changes to social and economic arrangements are implemented in order to meet these objectives, they do not threaten the freedom and liberty of individuals. Finally, revised social arrangements should allow everyone to draw a measure of self-worth and creative satisfaction from their working lives and leisure time. The ultimate objective of progress is a reduction in the number of human beings whose lives are blighted by physical and emotional suffering, and lack of opportunity. To be concise, *progress*, in the context of this enquiry, is movement towards a more equitable, inclusive and sustainable global social order.

Philosophers, anthropologists, sociologists, economists, biologists and others regularly make claims for and against the possibility of progress. Occasionally, their ideas have a direct and rapid impact on society, but few thinkers any longer dare to attempt the broad sweep that the subject demands. Academic specialists tend to direct their attention at only one part of a very large picture, applying the criteria of one natural science or another, or focusing on a certain culture, or a particular time. Some writers have recognized the need for a broad approach and have successfully attempted to synthesize theory and evidence from diverse quarters, but few have been ambitious enough to attempt an integration of knowledge from all relevant disciplines, or been able to package the result in a format which is intelligible to ordinary people.

Problems of social organization and economic inclusion appear exempt from the demands of time for progress. If pioneers in physics, medicine and engineering had allowed their efforts to line the shelves of libraries, rather than become an integral part of our evolving society, we would still be waiting for the industrial revolution, and would not expect to live past fifty. But since the time of Socrates, ideas that could form the basis for fundamental changes in the way we organize our societies, and have a tangible impact on the quality of life for many people, have remained just ideas. Occasionally they enter a wider public consciousness, or elements are selected and applied in isolation, but they remain at the margins while we view developments driven by technology in pursuit of enhanced material benefits for a minority as evidence that we are constantly reinventing, improving and conforming to the ideal of progress. This book aims to explain the continuing gap between our hopes for humankind and the largely unchanging reality of existence for most people, and to seek solutions to the apparently timeless problems of suffering and social exclusion.

Just as our collective problems cannot be solved in isolation, neither can the solutions promised by different disciplines be applied without reference to one another. The following chapters draw from diverse sources in order to build an argument for the possibility of progress which addresses all potential criticisms and objections. Chapter 1 examines the history of ideas of progress and their entanglement with evolutionary science, to determine precisely what constraints human biology places on the possibility of progress. Chapter 2 broadens the debate to look at cultural evolution, how it differs from biological evolution, and the historical development of the mechanisms by which we provide for our needs through the economy. Chapter 3 asserts the unity of humankind in terms of our shared basic needs: if we are essentially all the same, are we not under a duty to organize the economy in ways that recognize the equal interests of all people? As a reminder of the pressing need for change, Chapter 4 examines the extent of misery and suffering in the world, and connects the hardship of the many with the comfort of the few. Chapter 5 seeks a philosophical basis for social change: unless we know why it is right to pursue progress, our efforts will be found wanting. Chapters 6 and 7 focus on the individual in society: what shapes us and makes us, and how the manner in which we are trained for life renders us powerless and accepting of the status quo. Chapter 8 looks at moral development in the individual, and uncovers evidence for an advanced level of moral awareness to which all humans naturally aspire. Chapter 9 investigates the ideas of classical economics, and unearths a long disregarded, but indisputable, explanation for our ongoing failure to build a more inclusive society. Chapter 10 applies this discovery to the challenge of reconciling the apparently opposing values of individual freedom and social justice though changes to economic arrangements which promise equity and sustainability. Finally, Chapter 11 assesses the arguments made in the book against the political and economic landscape of today's world, and considers the means by which a process of transformative social change might begin, and the likely implications of such change for our individual lives.

Many books have highlighted the miserable condition of humankind and the precarious state of our planet, but too many of these testaments fail to identify root causes, or to investigate the means by which we might stop the rot. This book attempts to discover what it is about humans as biological organisms, cultural players and economic agents which gives rise to our social problems, what we therefore need to change about ourselves, and how change in individuals might translate into wider social change.

If it is allowed a nurturing environment in which to develop, the human mind possesses a remarkable ability to absorb and assimilate information and evidence through observation and experience, to reflect on these, and to make considerable progress towards determining reality from unreality; to get some way towards knowing the truth. Widespread application of this capacity could set us on a course towards solving many of the problems we face. At present, for reasons we shall examine, not everyone, and not anyone all of the time, is able to engage this capacity consistently.

The means by which knowledge and understanding permeate the individual and collective consciousness, and the mechanisms by which such revelation is internalised and becomes motivation to action, are central to this enquiry. While I hope that what follows will prove inter-esting and stimulating, it is intended to make you think; to take the material here provided and do something with it: agree wholeheartedly, disagree vehemently, argue with colleagues, debate with friends, find common ground with lovers, but above all to think, to engage with and reflect on the most profound and challenging questions of our time. The only real obstacles to engaging with the issues considered here lie within each of us. Most of us are quite capable of deciding whether or not to join the debate, and whether to do so with an open mind.

Without a degree of certainty, a rootedness of belief, life would be very hard to negotiate. Once we begin to question anything, we can easily end up questioning everything. It is quite understandable that we seek some guarantees before we can give up firmly held beliefs and con-victions. This book provides no such guarantees; what it offers instead is an insecurity bypass, a vision of what might be, and an indication of the likely rewards for taking the biggest risk of all. For we have a choice, either to take the passive risk: to sit tight and see what happens; or to take the active risk, the one that gives us a degree of control: we can embrace both the validity and the possibility of building a world in which human beings live cooperatively and equitably. Although it may take generations, we can begin by accepting that it is a realizable and worth-while project, one which might ultimately produce a society which we would all choose over our current, rather troubled, world.

I

Science and Humankind

I T WAS OUR ANCESTORS' realization that the human mind is capable of understanding the forces of nature, and the human will capable of action to harness and exploit these forces, that set us on the path of progress. After millions of years as nature's subjects, human beings learned to take control. We became problem-solvers; we had discovered science. Our evolving scientific understanding has been the engine of human advance for ten thousand years, but latterly, as we have begun to apply scientific method to the study of human relations, it has proved a less than reliable guide. We have allowed our perceptions of the prospects for human society to be influenced by quasi-scientific claims for the limits to progress for which there is little evidence.

The principal gift of science to humankind has been certainty. Certainty makes life much more manageable for people. It is not surprising, then, that many social thinkers have turned to science in search of explanations for, and solutions to, the problems of human society. If properly conducted and applied, science can enable an idea, theory or claim about the world to be tested to the satisfaction of all but the most marginal sceptics. The best science is that which stands the test of time and survives the development of more sophisticated tools for evaluation. In physics and chemistry, even where bad science evades detection there are few consequences. While developments in genetic engineering may alter this assumption, if you misinterpret the mechanisms that drive the natural world, you will not have much impact upon it. As a rule, bad science will either fail to stand up to the test of observable evidence over time, or someone will offer an alternative which displaces the earlier theory. In the natural world, the only real cost of a bad theory, however long it survives as the dominant view, is to the reputations of its originator and proponents.

The quest for greater understanding of human social relations is not scientific in the sense that astronomy and molecular biology are. When speculative scientific method is applied to matters of society and economy, ill-conceived ideas are often taken up by people eager for evidence to support a pre-existing view of the world. Subjective notions about the way the world is, or should be, are then portrayed as having a sound basis in science. It is impossible to create laboratory conditions in which to test theories of human social relations, and unethical to conduct such experiments on people and societies in the real world. This should confine the contribution of science to one of theory only, but the history of the twentieth century suggests we are reluctant to accept this.

As we shall discover, when properly applied, scientific method can help us to appreciate the underlying causes of social and economic problems. It can help clear some of the obstacles to progress by improving our understanding of what it is about human nature and our historical cultural development that constrains progress. It can even give indications as to how we might create conditions more favourable to progress. But, just as when we identify certain problems within society, we do so by reference to values – we make an assessment of how we would like the world to be on the basis of what we think important and valuable, and what we think possible – so those same values must underpin any effort to apply science in the pursuit of progress. We shall investigate the philosophical basis for values compatible with our definition of progress in Chapter 5, for without a rational and informed value base, science-motivated attempts at shaping social advance will bring no progress whatsoever.

Efforts to establish a scientific basis for human behaviour and social relations have long been linked to arguments over the nature and possibility of progress. If we could prove through science that all humans possess an innate and invariable propensity for competitive attitudes and selfish behaviour then we might conclude that there is little point intervening and let nature run its course. Conversely, if science revealed that we were essentially altruistic beings whose cooperative nature had been corrupted by an identifiable cultural source that we could control, then we might see our way to a more equitable society. In either case, and in respect of any other scenario that science might reveal, we would have a blueprint for the future, some indication as to the likelihood of progress and the nature and extent of our role in promoting it.

While scientific method can help us along the path to progress, it will not provide any definitive prescription of possibilities and limitations. Terms such as social or political science should therefore be understood as the application of scientific method to the study of social or political relations. They are necessarily different from the physical sciences. By treating them as pure sciences, we assume that one day there will be nothing we cannot explain and predict with scientific confidence. This desire for simple, unarguable explanations for the world and its ways constitutes a massive threat to the integrity of human enquiry. While science has provided us with almost limitless potential for technological progress, the extent of our commitment to it compromises our ability to mediate its consequences. Science certainly enables us to work with nature on more equal terms, but in the social sphere it offers little in the way of indications towards progress.

Only if we articulate a clear moral basis for the application of scientific method to problems of social relations will the cause of progress be helped. Thus far, the general thrust of science-based attempts at improving our understanding of the social world has been to place strict limits on the possibility of progress: first, through an unfounded assertion that social injustice and economic inequity are the inevitable outcomes of a 'natural' unfolding which we cannot control, and latterly through the reckless misapplication of what we have learned about our evolution and the science of genes. This chapter aims to dispel the myth that the prospects for human society are necessarily constrained by our evolutionary heritage. We begin with a brief excursion through the history of social science, where we find its origins inexorably entwined with early biology.

Evolution is a word ubiquitously associated with science, but, before Charles Darwin claimed it for biology, it found common use among social thinkers. The ultimate gift of the word from philosophy to science is not simply a matter of historical record. The timing of the publication of Darwin's *On the Origin of Species* in 1859 ensured that subsequent debate about progress and the development of society would never escape the shadow of biology. The impact of the confluence of two spheres of thought around a single word cannot be overstated. We will return to Darwin, for we must accurately plot the boundary between biological and social evolution, and determine any overlap between the two. But first let us turn to the world of ideas in the decades before Darwin's birth.

In the mid-eighteenth century there was Europe-wide political upheaval. In England and The Netherlands a transition of power from the aristocracy to the commercial middle class was almost complete. France and Scotland lagged behind, and it was concern over how best to promote the political interests of the middle classes in these countries that gave birth to the philosophy of *The Enlightenment*. Before this sea change in ideas, philosophical thought had been limited by the absence of any concrete concept of progress or direction in social affairs. This precluded the possibility of either optimism or pessimism about the future; the question simply did not arise. Although, two thousand years earlier, Greek philosophers had speculated on how we should best live our lives and organize our societies, it was only two hundred and fifty years ago, with the publication of Montesquieu's *De L'esprit de Lois,* that

modern humans began seriously to consider the possibility of alternatives to prevailing structures of social organization and political control.
Up to that point, the idea of social change was usually associated with
degeneration and collapse.

The ideas of the Enlightenment philosophers were original and radical, revolving around the doctrine of *psychic unity,* which suggested that
there were no essential differences between groups or races of humans.
Nor were there any biological constraints on any group or individual
attaining *perfection.* Groups denied contact with others would, it was
thought, devise similar solutions to similar problems; and the very
observable differences between cultures were explained by the widely
varying environments in which isolated cultures had developed. People
were essentially good, and possessed a natural tendency to cooperate
with others. It was only the unwelcome intervention of certain social
forces which made people greedy and selfish. These ideas were summed
up in a belief that progress was the defining property of human history
and that it occurred continuously.

This new and optimistic view of humankind represented a major
change in a world of thought that had previously been dominated by the
less hopeful reading bequeathed by Thomas Hobbes in his *Leviathan*
more than a century earlier. Hobbes had suggested that conflict and the
resultant suffering were the inescapable destiny of humankind.
Enlightenment ideas quickly spread, and had considerable impact. Both
the French and American revolutions were influenced by the new thinking, and although marginalized in the first half of the nineteenth century,
the Enlightenment seed had been sown. Never again would the idea of
progress be absent from speculations about the origins of humankind,
or the future of human society.

As early as 1693 the German philosopher Gottfried Leibniz anticipated
the evolution of species in the sense that we now understand it. During
the eighteenth century, Montesquieu and Darwin's grandfather, Erasmus,
pursued the idea. But it was the French naturalist Jean-Baptiste Lamarck
who first suggested that all species were the product of a uniform process
of evolution. Lamarck believed that new species emerged spontaneously
to embark on a process of evolution towards perfection. He is most commonly associated with the idea that characteristics and behaviours
acquired by an organism during its lifetime are passed on through the
reproductive process to successive generations: *Lamarckism* is now
defined as 'a theory of evolution based on the inheritance of acquired
characteristics'. Lamarck was not the originator of this belief however,
it was a widely held assumption which survived well into the twentieth
century, but his original contributions were crucial to the development

of evolutionary biology. He was the first formally to advance the idea of an evolutionary transition of species over time, basing his belief on geologists' claims that the earth was far more ancient than most thinkers of the time allowed. Two hundred years ago, when Lamarck was struggling with evolution, anyone suggesting the world was much older than six thousand years or so, as the Bible implied, got very short shrift. By imagining a much older world, he was able to visualize a process of evolution slow enough not to conflict with the observable evidence of little change in the appearance or behaviour of species over time.

Lamarck's ideas met a frosty reception with the thinking middle classes of early nineteenth-century Europe. They were far too radical for a world still unready to discard divine explanations of human origins and a Christian moral basis for the prevailing social order. In Britain, that order, which had seen a shift in power and prestige to a growing but still small middle class, was under threat from the consequences of rapid industrialization and the movement of huge numbers from countryside to city. Just as the Enlightenment was invoked to protect the middle classes from an aristocracy unwilling to let go the reins of power, so a new maxim was required to justify and protect the comfort of the new ruling class against a backdrop of exploitation and poverty among the industrial working class. This was duly supplied by the philosopher Herbert Spencer, who did more than anyone to entangle the concepts of biological and social evolution.

The mid-nineteenth century in which Spencer lived and worked was a period of immense social change. Considerable wealth was accruing to the successful entrepreneurs of the new industrial age, but the plight of the majority, many of whom were faring worse than their pre-industrial forebears, was giving cause for concern. Politicians struggled to reconcile the obvious benefits of industrialization with its unforeseen social consequences. A successful economy meant allowing individuals the freedom to apply their entrepreneurial zeal in the pursuit of profit as an end in itself. Providing for the material needs of those who saw little benefit from industrialization belonged to a separate realm of collective welfare, to be funded by philanthropists and ultimately coordinated by the state.

Spencer's vision was of a grand evolutionary design. By way of a single process, plants and animals, then humans and ultimately the developing structures of civilized society were all the result of a seamless evolutionary process which took simple organisms and produced ever more complex species and social institutions. Spencer was motivated by a desire to reconcile advances in science with the moral teachings of Christianity, and he supported Adam Smith's *laissez-faire* approach to economic management which he considered essential to the unfettered course of evolution. He was convinced that the free market would grant access to the economy to all those excluded by the apparatus of state which acted principally in the interests of the established professional middle classes.

For Spencer, the emerging *entrepreneurial* middle class was key: once freed from the shackles of state intervention, he believed, these new entrepreneurs would better provide not only for themselves but for all they were able to employ. He advocated *laissez-faire*, individual freedom and the protection of property rights because he believed this was the surest route to a more equitable and inclusive social order. But Spencer was happy to suspend moral criteria along the way. He explicitly accepted the consequences of such arrangements: that some would be left to die. He opposed compulsory education as unhelpful meddling in the process of evolutionary improvement, and argued against colonial expansion on the grounds that it represented unwarranted interference in the development of other societies. He had a strong distaste for any action coordinated by the state, although it cannot have escaped him that, in securing colonies, the interests of both state and private enterprise were well served.

It was Spencer, not Darwin, who coined the phrase 'survival of the fittest' to describe a finite process which justified short-term suffering and loss of life in the pursuit of an 'equilibrium' society in which hardship would disappear and the needs of all be met. He thus provided a conscience-saving justification for the dreadful and very visible social consequences of industrialization. In the process he helped sell the idea of evolution to a previously reluctant middle class, further preparing the intellectual landscape for the publication of Darwin's theory of biological evolution in 1859.

Today Darwin is everywhere; no thinker is so revered and no reputation so secure as his. To criticize Darwin is to lay oneself open to accusations of intellectual naivety and even treachery. The reaction of Darwin's supporters to those who dare criticize him is akin to fundamentalist zeal. Darwinism has become the faith upon which not only the whole edifice of evolutionary biology rests, but upon which the prospects for human society are founded. There is a fine line between rational belief in sound scientific theories, and Darwin's are pretty sound, and an ideological belief in the same theory which is not circumscribed by a thorough understanding of its limits and how it can legitimately be applied in the pursuit of further knowledge. At his peak, Darwin was acutely aware of the boundaries of science, but towards the end of his life he found it impossible to resist the temptation to apply his theories more widely and controversially, reviving a trend for pseudo-philosophical speculation disguised as science which would come to characterize much of twentieth-century social thought.

A few mavericks have dared to question Darwin's contribution and to ask how much of his thought was truly original. He was certainly not the discoverer of the fact of evolution. Lamarck had proposed the evolution of species from primitive to more complex organisms while Darwin was still at school. Soren Lovtrup, in his analysis of the comparative contributions of Darwin and Lamarck, argues persuasively for Lamarck as the originator.[1] He is now largely discredited because he acquiesced in the notion that variation in species depended upon the heritability of acquired characteristics. Little mention is made of the fact that Darwin, always unsure of his own theories, supported the inheritance of acquired characteristics until his death.

In biology, according to the theory of natural selection, evolution occurs through the selection, in nature, of variations in the information stored in genes, the chemical units within biological cells which hold design specifications for species and ensure that established designs are passed on from generation to generation. But the mechanism by which genetic information is replicated during reproduction is sometimes subject to error: mistakes are made which lead to the substitution of slightly altered genes for the originals. Over the course of a few generations, such changes will have no discernible impact, but over many hundreds or thousands of generations, they will. This is because variations in genes are selected for, or against, depending on their impact on the *fitness* of the organism. Some accidental modifications to genes leave an organism with greater fitness and are selected for. These randomly mutated genes survive and multiply throughout the species group. Others reduce fitness and are selected out of the evolutionary process.

Fitness has two elements: the ability of the organism to survive to reproductive maturity, and its ability to reproduce successfully and so pass on its genetic inheritance to the next generation. The direction of evolution is influenced by both these aspects of the evolutionary process, which are called *natural* selection and *sexual* selection. Their interaction adds another variable to an already complex process.

External factors play a major role in setting the criteria for fitness: climate, environment, space and availability of food all interact with these accidental design changes to determine the order of selection. It is quite possible, especially in species which reproduce quickly, that the same genetic variation may be selected for during a cool summer but against during a warm one. This example begins to give an idea of just how uncertain the process of biological evolution is. However, whilst the mutation of genes is quite random and accidental, the process by which they are selected for and against is not. Only if it improves the fitness of an organism will an altered gene survive. It should be noted that Darwin himself had no conception of the mechanism by which variation entered the reproductive process; he knew nothing of genes. This description of his theory is embellished by a century of further thought and research.

Is natural selection sufficient a force to drive the entire evolutionary process? Darwin was unsure: not only did he fall back on Lamarckism, but he allowed the possibility of *macromutations*, major changes in organisms over a single generation. Alfred Wallace, who is credited with Darwin as the co-formulator of the theory, rejected Lamarckism all along, arguing for natural selection as the sole mechanism of evolution until 1869, when he concluded that it was not sufficient a force to have accounted for *human* evolution, and instead sought solace in eastern mysticism.

In contrast to Darwin's status today, the fiftieth anniversary of the publication of the *Origin* in 1909 saw natural selection universally opposed. Much of this early opposition was philosophical in nature, largely motivated by a reluctance to accept its implied lack of design. But the scientific arguments over the mechanics of evolution are of more interest, for they continue today. The debate provides a fascinating example of how poorly informed protagonists weighed down by preconceived ideas, guarding vested interests and assuming entrenched positions, can derail the process of human intellectual endeavour. Most damagingly, analogies have continually been drawn between the process of natural selection in biological species and the processes of social and cultural advance. Such analogies would have little merit if there was clear evidence that natural selection was the sole and exclusive mechanism for biological evolution; but, as John Maynard Smith, leading geneticist and proponent of natural selection, was happy to admit, even in biology natural selection remains a hypothesis.[2] While it certainly does occur in nature, evidence for additional mechanisms, ones that may play a more important role, may still emerge. Nonetheless, our attempts to understand developments in human social relations are under constant assault by analogy with an incomplete and possibly unprovable explanation for biological evolution.

Let us be clear: neither the fact of evolution, nor its tendency over time towards greater complexity, are in question. But, in addition to lingering doubts over its mechanisms, further concern centres on the issue of whether all species derive from a single ancestor. There are two main arguments for *common descent*. First, the intrinsic logic of Darwin's theory: on his five-year voyage around the world on *HMS Beagle*, he collected evidence that species evolve in a branching manner. Where species had become isolated it was possible to see how evolution had followed a particular path in one place and another elsewhere. Branch-like diagrams can be constructed to represent this process of *isolated speciation*. The human mind then only has to extrapolate these branch segments into one enormous and complete tree to determine a single origin for all species over all time.

The second piece of evidence for common descent is the fact that every living species has genetic material in common – but is this proof? We can be reasonably certain that, if common descent is a fact, then all species will share genetic material, but the reverse is not necessarily true. Consider a more recent theory, one that is rarely aired and not heavily featured in academic texts: that of Sir Fred Hoyle and Professor Chandra Wickramasinghe.[3] They point out that certain organic particles have been identified in dust clouds floating in space, and that these particles are not so different to those that form the building blocks of life on earth. Suppose these particles periodically find their way to earth, where, if encountering favourable conditions, they give rise to life. This may have happened many times in the history of our planet. It may have happened just once, but in many different places. It might mean that humans and chimpanzees share one common ancestor, but that snails and slugs share a different one. Both common ancestors may share a common origin in the space-borne particles in which the genetic markers common to all species are found. This would go some way to explaining the amazing diversity of life on earth. I do not know whether this explanation is more or less likely than the conventional theory of a single original life form emerging from a primordial soup of chemicals, but neither would I be persuaded by anyone who insists on the truth of either theory in the absence of conclusive evidence.

Biologists agree that the rate of evolutionary change in humankind is very slow. Over the last ten thousand years, only negligible changes in our biological construction have occurred. Social evolution, by contrast, can be very fast, and this is one of the reasons why analogies between the two are tenuous and unhelpful. This brings us back to Herbert Spencer, whose preoccupation was *social* evolution, but whose time was the time of Darwin.

Darwin drew from Spencer's view of the social world to illustrate his theories of the biological word, but he had done some rigorous science first, and knew its limitations. Spencer clearly did not; today he is a largely discredited theoretician. He survived Darwin by twenty years, dying in 1903, a sad and dispirited figure. The economic depression of the late nineteenth century revealed to Spencer immense problems which appeared to defy the power of *laissez-faire* to put society to rights. But the abject failure of his theories caused few to doubt Spencer, and in the early twentieth century his ideas were taken up with great enthusiasm. The impact of *social Darwinism*, as the popular interpretation of his philosophy came to be known, endures to this day.

Spencer himself never conceived of a social movement; there was no plan for social Darwinism. Some definitions are therefore useful. For John Greene, social Darwinism is the view 'that competition between individuals, tribes, nations and races has been an important, if not the chief, engine of progress in human history'.[4] For Howard Kaye it is 'the misapplication of the theories of natural selection and the struggle for existence to human society as a powerful and cruel apology for brutal exploitation both within and between societies'.[5]

Social Darwinism, although not yet so named, was the dominant idea in social thought in the mid-nineteenth century. Darwin's theories lent scientific credence to a Spencerian world view in which nature determined the direction of human social affairs. At the time of the publication of *On the Origin of Species*, Darwin was adamant that evolution had nothing to do with progress, and went out of his way to distance his theory from notions of moral value. According to Tim Megarry, 'Social Darwinism was little more than a rag-bag of contemporary preoccupations made into a pseudo-science by a misalliance of social observation with biological analogy.'[6] Mary Midgely argues that social Darwinism was adopted by people whose conscience was stirred by the plight of those who were victims rather than benefactors of nineteenth-century industrialization.[7] The new creed offered the possibility of enormous suffering and deprivation as a transient stage, representing the inevitable course of social evolution towards a perfect future.

Midgely makes the point that, in the analogy from biology to society, the meaning of competition is changed completely. In nature, two organisms vying for survival in a particular environmental niche are, in a sense, competing, but they have no choice in the matter and are in no way conscious of their actions. It is not possible for one of them to adopt a pragmatic approach and scuttle off to the next available niche. The competition between individuals at the core of social Darwinism consists of consciously directed behaviour which, often in the full knowledge of the protagonist, will lead to others being harmed. Social Darwinism excuses moral selectivism in the name of perceived collective progress. This may have been the way of things for much of human history, but it had never previously been articulated so convincingly, backed up with scientific 'proof', or disguised as an ultimate good.

Social Darwinism found its own niche in the United States in the 1870s when, in the words of Howard Kaye, social conditions represented 'a vast human caricature of the Darwinian struggle for existence and the survival of the fittest'.[8] Settler history comprised of pushing back the frontier, exterminating the indigenous population, and bloody disputes between the colonizers themselves. In two hundred years, American republicanism had defeated nature, marginalized an entire race, and emerged victor over competing colonial powers; a perfect environment, then, in which Spencer's philosophy could flourish.

William Graham Sumner encountered social Darwinism when Spencer's *Study of Sociology* was serialized in a monthly magazine. Sumner was already enthused by the Protestant work ethic and the pessimistic political economy of Thomas Malthus and David Ricardo; his immersion in Spencer completed his political philosophy. He wrote, travelled and lectured widely and with considerable impact on the emerging industrial economy of the time.

Sumner pulled no punches in his synthesis of the economic, political and natural worlds, arguing that 'democratic representation in the extreme was inappropriate given genetic differences in mental and moral sensitivities because intrinsically less capable voters will insist on having a voice in matters they are intrinsically incompetent to judge'.[9] He refuted, utterly, the spirit of Thomas Jefferson, and people listened to him. To this day, western, and increasingly global, political economy evokes Sumner and Spencer far more than it does the values of the *Declaration of Independence*. Lester Ward, who was the chief critic of Sumner and social Darwinism in the United States, suggested it was little more than a fresh dressing for the *laissez-faire* political economy of Smith, Ricardo and Malthus and that it had little do with Darwin.[10] But there is a difference between believing that general economic improvement will result from the free operation of market forces, and arguing, as Sumner did, that relentless competition between humans is not only a force for good but a prerequisite to a harmonious social order.

The contradictions of social Darwinism were visibly in evidence on the ground. John D. Rockefeller, founder of Standard Oil, and one of the greatest of American entrepreneurs, is often characterized as the leading exponent of the creed among business people. A close examination of his record, however, reveals a more interesting story. Rockefeller certainly believed in free markets and competition as vital to economic advance, and he explained business gains and losses as the consequence of natural laws. But the commercial world he encountered in the late 1870s was one of competition-fuelled chaos. Rockefeller quickly recognized the waste and inefficiency of prevailing arrangements and set out to bring stability and long-term solvency to the oil industry. This he did by acting the arch social Darwinist, by using every means possible to consolidate and extend his power and run all competitors out of town. He could see the obvious failings of open competition in the oil industry, and was fully aware of the dangers of monopoly, but he soon realized that the only way to sort out the oil business was to enforce a virtual monopoly. Not only did Rockefeller succeed in his project and provide an enduring model for large-scale enterprise, he also amassed an immense personal fortune which, in most undarwinian fashion, he promptly gave away.

From early in his career Rockefeller made it clear that beyond financing a suitably comfortable lifestyle as reward for his efforts, the rest of his wealth, which he saw as a by-product of his success in rationalising the oil industry, would be given away. He spent his retirement managing a charitable trust which dispersed $550 million to those in need – the very people whom Spencer and Sumner argued should be left to their fate.

Although social Darwinism suited a rapidly industrializing American society, once the full impact of industrialization and urbanization became clear and began to impinge on the quality of life of the emerging middle class – just as it had in Europe a century earlier – as an *economic* creed, social Darwinism fell quickly from favour. Whereas Britain had embraced it to explain and justify the horrors overtaking society, so America ditched it as the palpable cause of many new and intractable social problems. But Spencer's legacy survived its rejection by business and economics, with a change of direction away from competitive individualism towards a more insidious collectivized version through which Darwin was used to explain perceived differences between national, racial and ethnic groups. Darwin must share some of the responsibility for this turn of events. While discussing human evolution in *The Descent of Man*, he acknowledged that evolution had left no trace of any meaningful physiological differences between human groups, but went on to say, 'the intellectual and moral or social faculties must, of course, be excepted from this remark'.[11] Carl Degler argues convincingly that it is Darwin rather than Spencer who is responsible for the racist version of social Darwinism that grew rapidly in influence, especially in America.[12]

The 1900s brought a change in the pattern of migration to the United States, with many poorer people from southern and eastern Europe following in the wake of the earlier north Europeans. For many in the establishment, already fearful that industrialization was upsetting the established social order, the arrival of millions of individuals with little to invest, either in capital or skills, spelled disaster. And so Darwin was hoisted once again, this time in support of the arguments of those who demanded a more selective immigration policy.

As more was learned about the mechanisms of biological inheritance, those inclined to use Darwin as justification for dividing humans into groups on grounds of biology gained influence. Darwin's cousin, Francis Galton, coined the term *eugenics* in 1883, arguing that a better race of humans could be created through artificially controlled breeding programmes, echoing Darwin himself, who had earlier argued that weaker members of society should be encouraged to refrain from reproduction for the sake of improving the race.

Eugenics and social Darwinism were similarly influential, but they were quite different in nature. Social Darwinism was an argument and justification for the inevitability of a social situation which many found unbearably cruel and unjust. Eugenics was an attempt to attack the perceived cause of this injustice – genetic variation – by breeding a superior race of human beings. The United States, still struggling to come to terms with the fall-out of rapid industrialization, embraced the idea. By 1930, thirty states had laws sanctioning the sterilization of criminals and the mentally ill, whose contribution to the gene pool was deemed detrimental. Several European nations followed this lead, including Germany in 1933, *before* the Nazis came to power. There can be little doubt, however, that the eugenics movement played a role in Hitler's plan for the extermination of the 'lesser' races.

The phenomenon of social Darwinism is unmatched in its influence on the course of twentieth-century history. It took ten short years after 1859 for, as John Greene said, 'the idea of progress through competitive struggle to be elevated from the status of a principle of political economy to that of a law governing biological and social evolution'.[13] We have yet to rescind this law, but we could. Tim Megarry, following Thomas Huxley, suggests that, if we chose to, we could use our understanding of evolution to 'repudiate the gladiatorial theory of existence and the fanatical individualism of social evolutionary theory: society depends not on imitating nature but on ending its impositions'.[14]

Back in the scientific world, the *Evolutionary Synthesis* of the 1930s and 1940s amounted to a final reckoning on all the arguments over natural selection that had raged since Darwin's death. The synthesis comprised a number of works by leading evolutionists, notably Ernst Mayr, Theodisius Dobzhansky, George Simpson and Julian Huxley. They set out to move the debate forward by at least agreeing on the basics. Examination of the detail of their work reveals how incomplete the understanding of evolutionary mechanisms remained, and remains to this day. But the larger purpose was served and not for another thirty years was natural selection questioned as the principal mechanism of evolutionary change, by which time the theory had become virtually unassailable.

The period following 1945 held out the possibility of genuine social progress. Crucial to a short-lived revival of Enlightenment values, and a clear reaction to the horrors of Nazism, was the rapid emergence of a consensus that biology was of no value as a guide to ethics or social policy. In 1953, our understanding was enhanced by the discovery, by

Francis Crick and James Watson, of the chemical structure of DNA, the material from which genes are made. Unfortunately Crick, like many other great discoverers, was unable to confine himself to science. In 1964 he claimed that knowledge of DNA finally made eugenics a viable tool in the planning of human social affairs. Howard Kaye's discussion of this period summarizes the view of Crick and his followers as 'acknowledging the role of cultural evolution, but viewing mind and culture as regrettable rather than liberating, causing self-delusion, psychic pain and social instability by violating our true biological nature.'[15] As Kaye describes the opposing camps of the time, there were, on the one hand, the *biological humanists*, represented by Julian Huxley and Jacob Bronowski, on a 'value salvage project' to find a biological basis for the noble values of the ancient Greeks and Enlightenment thought. They argued that 'a Lamarckian process of cultural or psycho-social evolution has relegated biological evolution to a vastly inferior position'.[16] On the other side were Crick and his *philosophical biologists*, setting out to reduce philosophical thought in its historical entirety to basic laws of nature.

Nonetheless, the social and political world, anxious to be seen as having learned the lessons of the holocaust and two world wars, was able to resist arguments for a biological basis for human social affairs until the publication, in 1975, of Edward O. Wilson's *Sociobiology – The New Synthesis*.

Wilson has defined sociobiology as 'the systematic study of the biological basis of all forms of social behaviour in all forms of organisms, including man'.[17] The discipline originated in laboratory experiments on non-human organisms, generally less complex ones such as insects, which revealed evidence that the interaction between organisms – their 'social' behaviour – was heavily influenced by genes, and that certain social behaviours could be selected for through artificial breeding strategies. Wilson's book is a detailed exposition of this research and is generally acknowledged as an exceptionally rigorous piece of science. But he devoted his final chapter to the idea that, this gene-behaviour link having been established for fruit flies, it could be extended to humans. He further suggested that, ultimately, all human social behaviour could be explained in terms of our genetic constitution as shaped by evolution. He argued that our efforts should therefore be directed at unearthing the genetic roots of human behaviour, assuming that all behavioural traits were adaptive responses to changes in environmental conditions that were favoured by natural selection, rather than relying on traditional means of investigating human behaviour as pursued by the social sciences.

Critics of sociobiology assert that its mission is simply too ambitious to be realizable. To map comprehensively the nature and relation of links between biological, individual psychological and socio-cultural influences on individual and collective human social behaviour is impossible, and not necessarily useful. Whilst not as pernicious as the beliefs underlying social Darwinism and the eugenics movement, in the minds of many, the idea of a predictive model for human behaviour derived from an established natural science could easily be misapplied. Perhaps unsurprisingly, Wilson has steadily revised down his ambition for sociobiology in his subsequent writing.

Many sociobiologists were originally motivated by concerns over the growing separation of human biology from culture. They saw cultural evolution as creating a modern world for which human nature, the product of a much slower process of biological evolution, is quite unprepared. Sociobiology aimed to address this problem by determining precisely what kind of social structures the natural design of human beings equipped them for, so we could then set about constructing an appropriate social environment. This does seem ambitious: if the process of biological evolution is to be trusted as the indicator of the proper path of our species' development, why did it let us off the evolutionary leash? If we evolved the ability to make conscious contributions to shaping the future through culture, can it really be argued that something went wrong with the evolutionary process? Evolution just happens; it has no purpose or direction beyond that of creating more life. We are perfectly entitled to choose to reject the outcome and work to change it, and such a project would certainly be helped by improved understanding of our evolutionary heritage, but that is quite different from suggesting that solutions to contemporary problems are to be found by returning humankind to the 'natural course' of evolution, whatever that might be.

Sociobiology suggests that human nature is the result of natural selection acting on our species over an exceptionally long period when neither the environment, nor human interaction with it, changed very much. There is strong archaeological evidence to suggest that for about two million years, until only twelve thousand years ago, all humans, and our pre-human ancestors, pursued a hunter-gatherer existence. Sociobiology contends that our biological constitution was designed for a hunter-gatherer lifestyle quite different from the world which most of us now inhabit. The world of the hunter-gatherer is termed our 'environment of evolutionary adaptation'. It is true that we differ little from our hunter-gatherer ancestors in respect of our genes, but this does not make it impossible for us successfully to conduct our affairs in today's world. Our genes might not have changed, but they did not stop us from creating the modern world; what is to say it is not the correct outcome of the evolutionary process? Wilson himself admits that 'the cultural change involved in the appearance of civilization cannot be regarded as a result of any significant genetic change'.[18]

Sociobiologists have taken a particular interest in the topic of ethics, eager to find an explanation in biology for acts of altruism which fail to support the notion that only behaviours that guarantee personal survival and reproductive success will evolve. To this end, they modified the definition of fitness in the evolutionary sense, coining the term *inclusive fitness*. Fitness was no longer just about surviving to produce as many offspring as possible, rather it was about getting as many of your genes into the next generation as possible. As any organism shares a proportion of its genes with its siblings, cousins, nephews and nieces, its inclusive fitness will be enhanced not only by its own reproductive success but also by that of its close relatives. Altruistic behaviour therefore emerged, or so the argument goes, as a means to maximising inclusive fitness.

It is certainly true that genes are shared; some of my genes are making generational progress through my sister's children. It is also true that many humans show a preference for the well-being of their close relations over that of others. But there is no evidence that consideration of reproductive strategies for best propelling ones genes through time has ever played any role in the conduct of human social affairs, nor those of other species. There is, however, contrary evidence of the wholly unfit outcomes of regular episodes of sibling rivalry, fratricide and infanticide which do not support the theory of inclusive fitness as the source of altruistic behaviour at all. Sociobiologists have taken up the challenge of explaining many such theory-denting phenomena in terms of their preferred model, but other theorists have done the same, coming up with equally plausible explanations for social phenomena based on non-biological theories of social change, ones which do not imply that human beings are ruled by their genes, or by their evolutionary history. Over the last 25 years, there have been hundreds of pieces of research conducted to establish a basis in evolutionary history for various facets of contemporary human social life, many of which sound exceptionally plausible to an audience always grateful for concrete explanations of phenomena which do not always make sense. But none of these theories is, or can be, proven. As the anthropologist Marvin Harris argued, if we really want to understand the complexities of contemporary human society, we should be focusing our efforts on identifying the forces which have shaped human culture over the last ten thousand years, during which time, by the sociobiologists' own admission, our genes have barely altered, rather than investigating that element of our culture into which our genetic inheritance has had some input.[19]

The inclusive fitness argument is further compromised by too narrow a definition of altruism. For a sociobiologist, an altruistic act is one that ensures the progress of genes through generations. To a philosopher, or anyone who enjoys the prospect of mutual cooperation with others, an altruistic act is something quite different: it is about doing favours for people; occasionally putting the interests of others ahead of your own. Sociobiologists may argue that gene-free acts of altruism are simply an unanticipated evolutionary side-effect, but altruistic behaviour is now a fixture in the behavioural vocabulary of people of all cultures; it is liberated from any biological origin, and it is the most conscious form of human action. If we want to assess our true collective moral potential we should be investigating why humans exhibit such an enormous range of moral behaviours, from heinous crimes of genocide to unimaginable acts of self-sacrificing altruism. All sociobiology can tell us is that human genes permit as wide a range of behaviours as we are able to conceive of.

Much of the debate around sociobiology has centred on whether the discipline constitutes an attempt at a scientific defence of the social and economic status quo. If contemporary human society is the outcome of an inescapable evolutionary heritage, then our current situation, characterized by differing equality of opportunity and outcomes between genders and across racial groups and social classes, is unalterable: culture has no influence. Most serious sociobiologists do not take this line. In fact, a great deal of sociobiology-inspired research has been to identify universal traits among humans, rather than genetic causes of difference. The best sociobiology, rather than trying to justify class, gender and race divisions, attempts to illuminate the unity of humankind, and admits that the differences between people and groups are largely a result of non-biological interventions, that is to say the product of culture. Whether we need sociobiology to reveal these human universals is another question. As John Maynard Smith pointed out, if they exist, they will emerge via the observations of anthropologists and sociologists.[20]

Sociobiology has so far failed to provide any concrete examples of human behavioural traits which are immune to intervention by culture or reason. Clearly we exist under physiological constraints: we cannot jump more that a few feet in the air, for example, nor can we outrun a cheetah; but when it comes to behaviour, there is nothing among the collection of traits that sociobiology puts down to our evolutionary inheritance that we can not overcome through conscious choice. We need consider only one example to strike at the very heart of the argument: the fact that many individuals consciously decide to abstain from sexual, and therefore reproductive, activity. Furthermore, in seeking sterilization, or by using contraception, many others decide to deny their genes any possibility of generational progress. Examples abound of individual human beings deciding not to conform to behavioural norms and beginning, through culture, to define new ones.

If we are able to act, through reason and conscious will, against the dictates of our biological heritage, then, even if contemporary social ills such as racism and ethnic conflict can be partially explained in terms of our evolutionary origins, there is nothing to say they are inevitable. Whatever evolutionary origins can be identified for such attitudes, it is clearly their interaction with cultural advance that has brought out the worst in our innate behavioural armoury. It is the conscious acts of human beings, rather than nature, which determines cultural change. If this argument is rarely heard, it is because of a general but unfounded belief that, in biological evolution, *behaviours* which improve fitness are selected for. Whilst some behavioural traits have certainly been influenced by our evolutionary heritage, specific behaviours are not selected for or against, and no serious biologist or sociobiologist claims that they are.

The usefulness of sociobiology depends entirely on the proportion of behavioural traits attributable to biological evolution. It is reasonable to assume a watershed: a point at which culture began to play the dominant role in human decision-making processes, and when our ancestors development ceased to be driven solely by biology. Marvin Harris suggests that this may have occurred as long ago as five million years.[21] If so, he was right to argue that we should be looking to historical cultural explanations for our evolutionary development rather than biological ones. The problem that anthropologists and sociobiologists share is that conclusive scientific proof for their various hypotheses is unlikely ever to be forthcoming.

Perhaps to escape the shadow of so much criticism, sociobiology has now recast itself in popular form as *evolutionary psychology*. Popular science, as is to be expected, is less rigorous in its evaluation of new ideas than formal science. Not surprisingly, books about evolutionary psychology aimed at the lay person have been very successful. Despite the best efforts of serious writers not to make unrealistic claims for the new science, the message that permeates popular culture is that scientists have discovered that much contemporary human behaviour derives from our evolution and that we largely remain prisoners of our genes. Not only does this make us feel better about the horrors of war and genocide, especially in respect of so-called tribal conflicts that blight so many less-developed countries – the populations of which we mistakenly assume to be genetically closer to our barbarian ancestors – it also provides excuses for personal and individual behaviour about which we are not especially proud.

Evolutionary psychology has taken up sociobiology's interest in the evolutionary basis of mating and partner-selection strategies, and offers conclusions which are easily extended to justify unequal power relations between the genders, and even 'explain' acts of violence by men against women.

These criticisms should not be taken as an argument that socio-biology should be rejected out of hand. The discipline has clearly made a contribution to scientific understanding that is of value. As Georg Breuer argues, we need to be able to explain and understand social behaviour in terms that do not deny or contradict our best understanding of evolution.[22] But, as he also asserts, there is no value in reducing all of human social life down to biological components. Further, there is a role for sociobiology in piecing together the history of evolution as applied to human society in much the same way as anthropology has provided us with a historical view of sociology.

If sociobiology had set itself more moderate goals and used more moderate language, and if sociobiologists had been more consistent and less speculative in their statements, we would surely be closer to an accurate understanding of the role of evolution in human social behaviour. Science is at its best when it takes a small piece of observable reality and tries to explain it. Ideas emerge which can be systematically discounted until one remains which defies attempts to disprove it. It can then be tentatively extended to explain other related or similar phenomena. Sociobiology started from the premise that an explanation for all human social behaviour was available in biology, and set out to construct it. The project was doomed by its own ambition.

A rejection of the scope and ambition of human sociobiology does not constitute an attack on all social science based on genetics. The discipline of *behavioural genetics* stands in contrast to sociobiology in two notable regards. First, it takes as its subject matter observable differences in the behaviour of individual human beings. It acknowledges that differences among individuals are likely to be influenced by genetic factors, that is to say by biological heredity, *and* by environmental factors, the nature and type of social and cultural inputs to which the individual is exposed throughout life. In order to determine the extent of genetic influence, behavioural geneticists take as their subjects twins, both fraternal and identical, and siblings in adoptive families. By working with subjects about which the relative genetic inputs are known, it is possible to ascertain the extent to which genetic and environmental factors influence outcomes. They work closely with molecular geneticists in the hope of isolating genes or groups of genes that can be associated with particular behavioural traits. Behavioural genetics has enabled great advances in knowledge about, for example, the genetic basis for schizophrenia, and the relative influence of genes and environment on the development of general cognitive abilities in individuals.

Refreshingly, the texts on behavioural genetics are littered with reminders that a genetic basis for some aspect of human behaviour is neither an argument for the rightness of that trait nor its inevitability. They also point out that success in determining the degree of genetic relevance for a certain trait is the best argument for environmental influence: where genetic influences for behavioural traits have been identified, none is much greater than 50 per cent. They further stress that those traits where there is a significant genetic influence are rarely the result of a single gene, arguing that, where multiple genes combine to determine behavioural traits, behavioural genetics can only be partial in its explanatory and predictive potential. Practitioners of behavioural genetics appear to recognize the boundaries of their discipline. It is of little interest to them precisely how or why evolution left us with the genes we now possess. They focus on the genetic design of contemporary humans and what that means for the concerns we face today. They approach their task with a degree of value neutrality to which all scientists should aspire, and they fulfil the vital role of providing social science with pointers as to what consideration we should give biological factors based on current evidence.

Thankfully behavioural geneticists are more typical of scientists than some sociobiologists. It is not surprising that some scientists have difficulty remaining within bounds: they are usually ambitious, highly motivated individuals, eager to leave their mark. It is unfortunate that populist declarations stamp themselves on the public memory far more readily than does good science. Perhaps basic training for scientists should include classes on social and intellectual responsibility. As Georg Breuer suggests, scientists are largely responsible for the intellectual and popular world of ideas that their arguments create; they therefore have a duty of care.[23] History is littered with examples of the misapplication of semi-formed scientific theories in support of one ideology or another, and scientists must recognize their contribution. No one who volunteers an opinion, especially if he or she is recognized as an expert in a particular field, can hide behind a defence that science has its own value and cannot be responsible for any unanticipated outcomes which its ideas might inspire.

What contribution does this analysis of the history of evolutionary thought make to our enquiry? Is there any link between biological evolution and social and cultural advance? Does the fact of our biological evolution necessarily place constraints on our collective capacity to make progress towards a more equitable, inclusive and sustainable global society?

To describe evolution in terms of survival of the fittest as Darwin, after Spencer, chose to do, implies an element of value. It suggests that the process consciously selects fitter organisms for survival while others are permitted to fall by the wayside. It therefore implies that the process of evolution has a preconceived idea of what constitutes fitness, which it does not. As Tim Megarry describes it: 'Evolution by natural selection means constant undirected adaptation to an environment that is itself changing. It is nonsensical to claim that evolution produces superior fitness or complexity, it is simply a continual adjustment of the organism to its ecological niche.'[24] Nonetheless, Ernst Mayr did not exaggerate when he said, 'Every modern discussion of man's future, the population explosion, the struggle for existence, the purpose of man and the universe, and man's place in nature rests in Darwin.'[25] This is undoubtedly true today, but only because we make it so. We must reject Mayr's assertion and start thinking beyond the supposed constraints of our evolutionary heritage. Until we do, our ambition will be needlessly restricted.

It should be clear by now that evolution in biological species is quite different from evolution in culture and society. Indeed, the only advantage to be gained from drawing analogies between the two is to make obvious how great the differences are. This is not to suggest that we can make ambitious plans for transforming our world without reference to our evolutionary heritage, only that, over the last two centuries, the scope of our ambition has been unnecessarily limited by a tendency to overstate the constraints imposed by evolution. This unfoundedly pessimistic view of our prospects has most often been promoted by those whose privileged position in society it has helped to sustain.

We must conclude that the implications of the fact of evolution, and its supposed mechanisms, for the possibility of human social progress are neutral. Evolution is a prerequisite to progress in as much as it endowed the human species with consciousness and the capacity to conceive of progress. While we must be aware of the role of evolution in shaping the instinctual drives which influence the behaviours of all humans, our biological evolution places no insurmountable limits on the possibility of progress. Our genes may not give us much help in this project, but evolution's legacy in our capacity for reasoned reflection, and our ability, as individuals, to embrace behaviours which have little or nothing to do with evolution, most certainly will.

The principal reason biological evolution fails to explain, predict or determine the direction of human social advance is the fact of our consciousness. Evolution is an undirected process lacking in purpose beyond the survival of species to reproduce. Humans alone have developed the capacity for conscious awareness and for understanding the evolutionary process which made us. The evolution of species, including our own, happened without any consciousness on the part of its subjects. But our continuing evolution, biological and social, can no longer occur without our conscious involvement, for as long as we think about anything we do, as long as we take decisions in respect of the options presented us in our daily lives, we are actively directing the future course of our evolution.

Spencer's dream of a single process of evolution operating under universal laws is just a dream, one best left in the nineteenth century. That is not to say that our biological origins have no impact on the future direction of society, nor that our knowledge of them cannot guide us in mediating that future. There is no doubt that developments in human culture began to alter the direction of biological evolution long before we discovered its science, just a century and a half ago. If we can identify this bio-cultural watershed, the point at which culture began to outrun biology as the principal force in human advance, then we would learn a great deal more, both of the true constraints of our biological inheritance and the potential for progress through cultural innovation.

It is time to move on. We have seen that science and scientific method provide us with great opportunities, but can all too quickly become slaves to ideology. About evolution, the body of evidence points to a gradual process over many millions of years, but there are still huge gaps in our knowledge, and question marks hang over natural selection as its principal mechanism. The beauty of natural selection lies in its value neutrality, which is not to argue that our apparently purposeless evolutionary history condemns us to a future of meaningless existence – far from it. The sooner we take full responsibility for creating our own meaning in life, the sooner we will realize that the human mind and the culture it creates have always been the exclusive source of meaning. Without doubt, aspects of our future are prescribed by our evolution; but far from placing constraints on human potential, our recently acquired and still growing understanding of our evolutionary origins gives us greater power than we ever thought possible over our collective destiny. It is history itself, rather than the history of evolution, or even the history of ideas, that is likely to give us a more complete guide to the possibility of progress, and it is to our earliest history that we must now turn.

2

Evolution and Culture

DESPITE THE GAPS in our knowledge, the evidence points to modern humans being the product of a gradual process of evolution over millions of years. If we remain unsure of the facts of the early part of that descent, there is more certainty over our recent evolutionary history. Our investigation of human social development must begin at the point at which social relations emerged, and that requires us to delve a little deeper than the first human societies.

Around twelve million years ago, huge geological upheavals on the African continent led to the creation of the Great Rift Valley which created a natural barrier to animal migration in an east-west direction. This may have encouraged the separate evolution of human ancestors from the apes that populated central regions of Africa at the time. Newly isolated groups inhabiting areas of quite different ecology were subject to a series of new evolutionary adaptations which would eventually lead to the emergence of *homo sapiens*. As well as a new environment, human evolution was aided by an increased rate of reproduction. Apes produce one infant every four years; the ability of evolving humans to increase this rate probably resulted from the improved diet available in this new and favourable ecological niche.

Around 2½ million years ago, one line of the pre-human species, the *australopithecines*, evolved into what is now the first formally classified member of the genus *homo,* known as *homo habilis*. The earlier *australopithecines* continued to live along side the first true humans but became extinct around 1½ million years ago, possibly losing out in the competition for scarce food both to the faster evolving *homo habilis* and to the baboons which flourished during the same period.

Homo habilis made two great advances: learning the value of eating meat, and the benefits of using tools; each of which promoted an increase in brain size. Although the precise cause-and-effect relationship can only be guessed at, it is this unique evolutionary combination of meat eating, brain development and innovatory tool use which propelled the evolving species towards a far more ambitious model, *homo erectus*.

It was during the era of *homo erectus* that the proportionate brain size at birth for modern humans was set, the consequence of an interesting evolutionary trade-off. The advantages of walking on two, rather than four, legs meant that humans evolved a narrower pelvis, but this imposed limits on foetal brain development if childbirth was to remain viable. Ultimately, evolution struck a compromise which meant humans giving birth to much younger offspring, with brains only about a third of full adult size. This proportion has remained constant ever since. Evolutionary pressures caused human infants to be born earlier than the offspring of other species, and so human culture had to adapt and allow for more intense parental care of infants over a longer period.

Homo erectus represented a great leap forward. Not only the first strain of human to run, to use fire, actually to fashion stone tools rather than simply to use naturally occurring forms, they were the first humans to spread beyond Africa. The fossil remains of an *erectus* individual have been discovered in Java and dated at around two million years old. This is the best guide we have to the first great migration of humankind from Africa into Europe and Asia. The anthropologist Richard Leakey suggests that *homo erectus* may also have possessed language, consciousness and even a degree of self-awareness.[1] Certainly, the communication and organizational skills that such faculties provide would have helped facilitate the scale of migration required for *homo erectus* to have become established over such a wide area.

Humans continued to evolve for 1½ million years wherever communities were established. The global population during this period was no more than a few million, and remained below ten million until the emergence of agriculture around twelve thousand years ago. The earliest known remains of *homo sapiens* are dated at between 300,000 and 500,000 years old and are known as *archaic homo sapiens*, as they differed from modern humans in respect of the shape of their skull. During this period, different versions of archaic *homo sapiens* emerged in different places, and there may well have been further migrations among groups evolving in isolation.

Argument continues as to the means by which anatomically modern humans, known as *homo sapiens sapiens*, came to dominate the planet. This process was well under way 100,000 years ago, and there are two opposing theories. According to the *multi-regional evolution hypothesis*, modern humans evolved wherever archaic *homo sapiens* had become established. The opposing *out of Africa* theory argues that modern humans evolved exclusively in Africa and then spread throughout the inhabited world, gradually forcing archaic *homo sapiens* to extinction. There is now almost conclusive evidence for *out of Africa*. The alternative implies that only relatively recently would separately evolved groups of modern humans have come into contact. If this were the case, genetic markers indicating the lengthy evolutionary isolation of geographically disparate groups would be found. No such indicators are in evidence, in fact there is very little geographical difference in human genetic make up. Under these circumstances, for the multi-regional theory still to hold, there would have to have been a steady gene-flow, that is to say migration and inter-group breeding at regular intervals over two million years, which is most unlikely and not borne out by the superficial anatomical differences that have emerged among populations in different regions.

The other quite startling piece of evidence supporting the African origin of all modern humans is provided by the *mitochondrial eve theory*. Mitochondria is a type of DNA – the chemical compound from which genetic material is constructed – which is only passed through the maternal line. Once the existence of this unusual element was established, an American biochemist, Allan Wilson, set about analysing the mitochondria of many individuals of different racial and geographical origins to see if there was any evidence, based on the degree of variation in different populations and individuals, of a line of inheritance back to a common maternal ancestor. The evidence so far collected points to the existence of a woman, somewhere on the African continent, at some point between 150,000 and 300,000 years ago, in which a particular mutation, which is today present in all humans, first occurred. This is not to say that this woman was the first or only woman alive at that time, neither that this mitochondrial mutation gave her offspring some evolutionary advantage, only that circumstances were such that her descendants were able to establish themselves in the population and were present in the migrating groups of modern humans which set out on the second great colonization of the planet around 100,000 years ago.

This theory is corroborated by research into similarities among languages which have been analysed statistically to show a pattern almost identical to that found in the genes of different populations. Both genetic and linguistic variety result from the colonization of remote regions of the planet by migratory groups which then become isolated from others. The final piece of evidence for the *out of Africa* hypothesis is provided by the fossil record: remains of archaic *homo sapiens* unearthed in Africa are much closer to modern humans than those found elsewhere. Perhaps because of the same favourable evolutionary conditions that saw *homo erectus* emerge first in Africa and then spread over the old world, so evolution towards modern humans happened faster in Africa than elsewhere, until such a time that people virtually identical to ourselves set out once again to colonize the world. This new improved human was no longer content only to settle Europe and Asia: for the first time Australasia, around 60,000 years ago, and the Americas, via Siberia, about 20,000 years ago, became home to human beings.

Homo Sapiens Neandertalis was dominant in Europe until about 50,000 years ago, when they were quite rapidly displaced by modern humans. There have been no discoveries of Neanderthal remains less than 35,000 years old, so it appears that they became extinct around that time. Neanderthal physiology shows signs of being particularly well adapted to the harsh climate of Europe. It may well have taken modern humans, who seem to have become established in Asia before colonising Europe, some time to develop sufficient cultural advantages to attain dominance over their more robust cousins. Although there is evidence that the two types of human lived alongside each other, and speculation that inter-breeding may have occurred, the recent recovery of DNA from Neanderthal remains suggests that their contribution to the gene pool of modern humans was negligible.

Whether or not Neanderthals and other archaic *homo sapiens* possessed faculties we would today describe as uniquely human, they clearly lacked the adaptive advantages of modern humans. But these advantages were probably cultural rather than biological. For example, when modern humans spread into Europe from Asia, they may not have been as well adapted biologically to the harsher climate, but they may already have acquired the cultural equipment for dealing with it: better clothing, better techniques for constructing shelter and more expert use of fire. Certainly by the time modern humans became established in Europe, culture was paramount. Richard Leakey offers the following definition of modern humans as possessing 'a flair for technology and innovation, a capacity for artistic expression, an introspective consciousness, and a sense of morality'.[2] I can think of no better description of the qualities that have driven human advance.

Much of the argument about the evolution of early humans assumes natural selection at work on disparate groups over long periods. In the previous chapter, we had cause to doubt the claims of natural selection as the sole evolutionary mechanism. Those doubts persist, but observable evidence of the evolution of various human species strongly supports natural selection. Whether the same mechanism could have turned amoeba into amphibian reptiles, and gone on to produce the vast range of species that survive today, or the even greater number that have become extinct, is harder to know with certainty; but from around five million years ago, when our ancestors first stood upright, until the emergence of modern humans just 100,000 years ago, natural selection seems a plausible explanation for the means by which modern humans evolved as *biological* organisms.

Whether modern humans are all descendants of migrating populations from Africa 100,000 years ago, or the product of interbreeding between these groups and surviving archaic *homo sapiens*, one thing is clear: all humans share common ancestors, possibly twice over. The evolutionary conditions that gave *homo erectus* the impetus to colonize the old world were probably also responsible for the accelerated evolution of modern humans who spread from Africa more recently.

The differences in physical appearance between human groups are entirely the result of evolutionary adaptations to diverse environments. For example, the short stature of pygmies is an adaptation to the humid conditions in the tropical rain forests where they live. The effectiveness of perspiration as a cooling mechanism is compromised in conditions of high humidity: a high surface area to body volume ratio counteracts this problem. Genes that make for a short, squat stature have therefore been selected for. Variation in skin colour is an adaptation to the strength of sunlight to be found at different latitudes, and the ability of sunlight to convert elements in food into vitamin D. The melanin which determines pigment also regulates the amount of vitamin D absorbed into the body, as too much can be as dangerous as too little. Early humans in Africa needed dark skin to survive. After they migrated to cooler climes with weaker sunlight and less exposure to it, genes for lighter skin were selected for, as, under the changed conditions, these guaranteed optimal vitamin D absorption and therefore better health, survival and reproduction rates. The narrower nasal passages and consequent thin noses of Europeans are an adaptation to colder air which needs to be warmed before reaching the lungs if they are not be damaged. The adaptive advantage of narrow nasal passages to slow down the air on its way to the lungs were therefore selected for. Just three of many examples, all of which show that there is no intrinsic value or meaning in the contrasting appearances of different groups of humans. We have just evolved slightly differently in response to varying environments. And the difference is slight indeed: at the genetic level all humans are virtually identical. Genetic variation *between* racial groups is around 0.02 per cent, just about the same as the variation found *within* racial groups. As Luigi Luca Cavalli-Sforza, the world's leading evolutionary geneticist says,

> the genes that react to climate are those that influence *external features*. Adaptation to climate for the most part requires changes of the body surface, because this is our interface with the outside world. It is because they are external that these differences strike us so forcibly, and we automatically assume that differences of similar magnitude exist below the surface. This is simply not so: the remainder of our genetic make-up hardly differs at all.[3]

But when did these variations in physical appearance become established in human populations? Before the migration of modern humans, a hundred thousand years ago, you would have expected to find geographical variations wherever archaic humans had settled. But a recent theory suggests that nearly all human genetic diversity is the product of only the last seventy thousand years. About this time the eruption of Mount Toba in Sumatra caused a 'volcanic winter' which led to a most extreme ice age. The global human population may have been reduced to as few as fifteen thousand people. The possibility of such a recent evolutionary bottleneck matches the findings of geneticists who have attempted to time the rate of evolutionary divergence visible in contemporary human groups. Once the skies cleared, the potential for a rapid evolutionary spurt would have been enormous. Even a tiny surviving population would have retained the mental faculties and cultural practices necessary to apply technological solutions to rapidly re-colonising those parts of the world where populations were wiped out, and there would have been unusually little competition for resources. In respect of superficial appearances, natural selection would have had a field day. As Professor Stanley Ambrose, who proposed this theory, suggested, 'When our African recent ancestors passed through the prism of Toba's volcanic winter, a rainbow of differences appeared.'[4]

This theory is supported by analysis of contemporary languages which suggests that all modern humans are descended from around five thousand groups in which language developed in isolation. It takes only a thousand years for a language to evolve to such an extent that it becomes unrecognizable from the original. Even if all today's humans derive from a single group who survived a volcanic winter 70,000 years ago, that still gives ample time for isolated groups to evolve distinct languages.

We noted that the second great colonization of the planet was only completed relatively recently, when populations spread from Asia, via the Bering Strait, down through the Americas. Australasia also took a long time to reach. It is likely that not only the relative isolation of these continents, but also their inhospitable environments, were factors in delaying the establishment of permanent populations. The harsh and unchanging environment may also explain why there was little in the way of cultural innovation on these great continents once they were colonized. Australian aboriginals, Inuits in northern Canada, and the forest dwellers of the Amazon basin all adapted well to their respective environments, but in no case did they show the degree of cultural advance that occurred in Africa, Europe and Asia; a shortcoming which left them poorly equipped to cope once European explorers and then colonists arrived from the sixteenth century onwards.

Despite the geographic dispersion of human populations, the evidence for the biological unity of humankind is incontrovertible. With it comes the implication of a considerable degree of unity of potential. Human culture has emerged in concert with, and as an extension of, biological evolution, and whilst human social and cultural potential must to some extent be circumscribed by this biological inheritance, this condition applies universally and not selectively. The potential of *all* human beings is dictated by precisely the same biological inheritance. It is the cumulative effects of cultural advance that has given the appearance of varying potentialities among human groups.

For much of our evolutionary history, means of subsistence changed very little, and life was very rudimentary. We sought shelter in natural habitats like caves, and survived through the gathering of leaves, berries, nuts and roots, occasionally supplemented by scavenging the remains of the kills of predators. As we became more confident on our two feet, and learned of the benefits of using and then modifying stone for use as tools, we began to catch our own prey.

From what we have learned through archaeology, and the study of the few hunter-gatherer societies that survived into the twentieth century, all such groups were exceptionally well adapted to their environment. It may sound like hard work but, operating in small bands numbering about a hundred, four hours' work each day was usually sufficient to keep all members of the community fed. Such a degree of adaptation to the environment does not necessarily imply an optimal quality of life. Life expectancy and child mortality levels would have been poor by modern standards, and material comforts would have been few. There would have been no sense of progress or improvement, and there was little or no variation in social organization for hundreds of thousands of years. On the plus side, there would have been no sense of frustration at the lack of progress. There was far greater harmony between the experience of these early humans and their expectations. And this, perhaps, is the key to defining optimal cultural adaptation. The forms of culture and social organization were such that all members of society were equally secure, threatened only by major geological or climatological change, and people had no cause to think beyond the limits of their daily lives. This is not to argue for a return to primitive lifestyles as a solution to modern ills, but the idea of bringing experience and expectation back into balance is of interest.

By the time *homo erectus* set out to colonize the old world around two million years ago, evolution had endowed humankind with faculties which would forever distinguish it from other animals. The development of the human mind, with consciousness, self-awareness, intelligence and the capacity for language and conceptual thought, constitute the source ingredients for culture: the capacity to plan and to act in ways which transcend purely instinctual responses to biological needs, and to do so in concert with others. But is culture the exclusive preserve of human beings? Research evidence suggests not. Traces of culture, admittedly very elementary, are commonly found among our closest primate cousins. Observations of our nearest evolutionary relatives, particularly chimpanzees, to whom we are more closely related genetically than chimps themselves are to gorillas, have revealed that many of the traits we now use to emphasize the uniqueness of the human species were already beginning to evolve well before the human evolutionary line split from that of other primates. Some of Jane Goodall's observations of chimpanzees in Africa bear an uncanny resemblance to modern human society: 'Individuals rarely saw all of their community on a single day and patterns of interaction were governed by personal feelings rather than group pressures.'[5] More specifically, there are similarities in infant nurturing practices among all primates, including humans. Non-human primates demonstrate a propensity for environment-based learning strikingly similar to that of human children. Mothers have been observed to place their offspring in specialized learning environments and engage in lengthy non-verbal communication in order to teach them basic life skills. The quite different social behaviour of rhesus monkeys living near large cities in India to that of their biologically identical rural cousins suggests that very little of observed behaviour is genetically determined. Baboons isolated from contact with other baboons show virtually no sign of developing usual baboon behaviour beyond a few basic instinctual responses.

The case for a biological basis for social behaviour is clearly prejudiced by these observations. Interestingly, sexual behaviour among non-human primates shows very little similarity to that of humans, but then it shows little sign of any cultural mediation. Sex among chimps is purely instinctual, quite infrequent, and tells us little about the development of human sexuality, or the problems associated with it. We can only learn about human behaviour from non-human animals in respect of those animal behaviours in which a degree of basic culture has emerged.

So what does separate humans from primates? Vernon Reynolds suggests that humans were able to take a very basic culture inherited from primate ancestors and further develop it, principally through the advantages of language-inspired conceptual thought.[6] While there is evidence for consciously directed behaviour among non-human primates, there are no examples of action based on the evaluation of alternatives, and no hint of any capacity to retain ideas or concepts which can then be processed in conjunction with other pieces of information as they emerge. This ability evolved as brain size and function developed beyond the level of our pre-human ancestors.

It was Darwin's implication that we might not be quite as unique as we like to think that caused most opposition to his theories. But our evolutionary relatedness to other primates does nothing to compromise human uniqueness. In biological terms, humans are no more or less unique than any other species, but we possess traits that differentiate us from all other species to an exceptional degree. We may share 98.6 per cent of our genes with chimps, but in all other respects chimps have much more in common with all other species than we do with any of them. That we feel threatened when reminded of our primate ancestry is symptomatic of our lack of maturity as a cultural species. As we shall see, virtually every human trait with which we are uncomfortable, every act of premeditated brutality or 'inhumanity' that we often excuse as the legacy of our animal ancestry, is, in fact, a human cultural invention. Overwhelmingly, that which we perceive as unwholesome in human social relations derives from the adaptational advantage endowed us in the human mind.

Archaeology and social anthropology have helped enormously in piecing together the history of human evolution. The continued existence of populations living in less technologically advanced societies has provided helpful research material. Much early anthropology was entangled in Spencerian ideas of progress, and amounted to little more than attempts to affirm the position of European culture at the summit of human achievement. But, as the discipline evolved and research techniques improved, fascinating evidence emerged to plug the gaps in our knowledge of our social and cultural history.

Early anthropology tried to identify clear stages of development through which all societies passed with a view to elaborating universal laws. No such laws have been identified and, even if early societies had started out on an equal footing at a given point in time and developed in total isolation from one another, it is unlikely that a common pattern would have emerged. The recent history of humankind is one of diversification and differential development, although the last ten thousand years is characterized by continual and increasing population exchange, cross-cultural contact, imperial conquest and the rise and fall of empires. We can say with certainty that all humans once lived as foragers, but, once new forms of social organization evolved, never again did all humans live by the same social arrangements. As soon as difference emerged, difference became the norm. At the same time, the destiny of one group became increasingly connected to that of others – until the late twentieth century, when the destiny of all groups became perm-anently entangled with the destiny of *all* others.

By the time social anthropologists began to study 'primitive' societies, few of these subject societies were free from the influence of the outside world. Whilst customs and cultures showed little sign of having changed over millennia, it was already too late to examine these societies as *pristine*, untainted by the fall-out from imperial conquest and the inter-national trade in goods and slaves. Nonetheless, only a century ago, several remained sufficiently intact to yield useful information about our early social history, and help to answer two key questions: why did the universal form of human social organization remain unchanged for so long; and why did it then change so abruptly, in the process setting off an unprecedented chain of developmental events?

Foragers lived in small groups, usually less than a hundred people, often moving from place to place as food resources became exhausted, and taking shelter in caves and other protective spaces as the environ-ment provided. The size of these bands was determined by the avail-ability of food resources and the experience that groups of this size were able to secure optimal returns for all. Where resources were abundant, near the sea for example, groups would establish themselves in one place, but subsistence was still a matter of collecting the roots, berries, fruit and nuts occurring in nature, and of fishing or hunting down mammals for meat. There was no agriculture, no knowledge of the possibilities of seed planting or animal rearing. Generally, men engaged in hunting and fishing, while women collected food from the wild flora and cared for the young. As the main providers of nutrition, and as the only guarantors of something to eat, given the notoriously inconsistent yields of the hunt, the role of women in these early societies was often considered equal to that of men.

Forager bands consisted of extended families, although ties with other bands were cemented through intermarriage. This was the prin-cipal means of forging strategic alliances, which were essential given the fickleness of the environment. Many of the characteristics of, and changes in, band organization were linked to changes in food supply. During times of abundance, bands would consolidate into larger groups; as food became scarce, they would split into smaller bands and extend their range in the pursuit of nutrition. When times were good, band members would only be required to work between twenty and thirty hours a week. Although life was basic, it was not especially hard and there was plenty of time for leisure activities.

These early societies procured only what they needed to survive. With the exception of Eskimo communities, where the extremes of seasons demanded it, and natural refrigeration made it possible, there was no storage of surplus provisions. This was key to the longevity of foraging as a social system. Within and between bands, there was regular sharing of food, particularly the product of the hunt. It was obvious to all that successful hunting required an element of luck – even the best hunter was unable to bring back the goods every time – so sharing was the only means of ensuring that everyone was provided for. Among many such communities, quite elaborate and precise rules were established to govern the sharing of food. Few dared to offend against these norms for fear of being ostracized.

This economic egalitarianism was mirrored in the political sphere. Although alliances were forged, within groups there was no hierarchy, neither was there competition or warfare between bands. Episodes of personal violence did occur but these were not motivated by food scarcity as, depending on conditions, everyone was equally rich or poor. Neither is there any evidence that competition for political control was responsible for violence. There was often formal regulation of land tenure; land within the range of allied bands was not demarcated, but all bands submitted to agreements over who has access to which area and when. Tools were generally owned individually, but their use was shared. Beyond this there was no concept of rights over property.

There are interesting correlations between abundance, territoriality and cooperative behaviour among forager groups. When times were hard, rather than compete with each other for scarce resources, they tended to cooperate towards the well-being of all. Groups only became territorial during times of abundance: when they could afford to behave non-cooperatively and get away with it. When it is visibly and obviously in their collective interest to do so, human beings are quite able to behave cooperatively in the pursuit of the means to survival. Only when we perceive the possibility of personal survival in isolation from others, it seems, do we begin to consider self-centred, and other-excluding, solutions to subsistence.

The absence of social stratification and a political hierarchy refutes the common assumption that the present-day existence of these institutions is a legacy of our pre-human ancestry. While there is evidence among some primates of a degree of social stratification, this does not occur in ways which imply progression to the highly evolved forms of class hierarchies and politics among humans, and in any case it is far from universal. If modern inequalities have their roots in primate social organization, for several thousand generations we were able to transcend this supposedly innate tendency and live as equals with our forager neighbours.

For two million years our ancestors pursued a common lifestyle the world over, responding to different environmental pressures in similar ways. When conditions became too extreme for their limited range of cultural responses, forager groups had to migrate or perish. Biological evolution did not cease during this period: human physiology evolved through many versions; but this evolutionary process has been one of fine-tuning rather than rapid advance. Physiologically, we have barely changed in the last hundred thousand years, although it seems likely that the evolution of the human mind continued to the point, twelve thousand years ago, when we abruptly threw off the shackles of two thousand millennia and set off towards modernity.

All great evolutionary advances are sparked by some major ecological change. The change that occurred twelve thousand years ago unleashed pent-up adaptational energy in the form of a dramatic cultural revolution. Whilst we continue to live with the possibility of similar ecological upheaval which may forever change the direction of human advance, we have so far been spared such trauma.

The retreat of the last ice age, which began about thirteen thousand years ago, brought great changes in climate and sea level which decimated human populations and wiped out many of the mammals on which humans preyed. As a reduced human population re-established itself, probably growing relatively rapidly to colonize lands that had been laid waste for thousands of years, many groups began to practise agriculture. This was not a sudden and universal conversion to crop planting and animal husbandry, but a gradual process which occurred in certain areas where conditions suited. In others, where circumstances favoured the retention of traditional methods, they survived well into the twentieth century and, wherever agricultural communities did emerge, they did so alongside groups who stuck to the old ways: trade and other contacts between these new *horticulturalist* societies and forager groups was commonplace.

Horticulturalist communities were the forerunners to much larger and more complex agrarian states. In common with the forager system, food production, although now consciously planned and reliant on innovative technological inputs, remained for subsistence purposes only. Horticulture emerged in areas where population density increased beyond the capacity of the land to provide for all by simple foraging, but only if ecological and climatic conditions were favourable. It may be that improved reproductive success in groups where food was *most* abundant forced the change to horticulture as population growth outstripped the rich pickings of nature.

The change to horticulture was momentous, and its impact was not simply economic. Whilst the basis for collective labour remained the extended family, a form of political leadership began to emerge, and for the first time warfare became endemic. Although horticulturalists did not set out to create a surplus of food, such surpluses sometimes arose, and with them came a *prestige* economy. Humans now possessed the means to set themselves apart from other humans, to assert and enjoy superiority over others. This new prestige economy, combined with competition amongst men for reproductive access to women, which until that time had been moderated by the fact of material equality, led to violent disputes and inter-group warfare which was often extremely brutal. As people became dependent on agriculture they forgot their old foraging ways, and control of the best land became vital: another cause of conflict.

The unanticipated creation of economic surplus is of fundamental importance to the subsequent development of human society. Until these early horticulturalists happened upon a bumper crop of maize or manioc quite by chance, equality of outcome in economic provision was the way of humankind for millions of years. While there is nothing to prevent the peaceful trading of surpluses, once the first surplus was harvested, things were never the same again.

Surplus, a prestige economy, and competition for reproductive access to women all conspired towards the emergence of politics. Groups of horticulturalists set about minimising the risk of war by forging political alliances with other villages. Whereas among forager groups such alliances had been for the mutual benefit of all, it was now a case of strength in numbers in the battle against other alliances, rather than a battle of all against nature. This process saw the beginnings of the phenomenon that anthropologists refer to as *embeddedness*. Previously, economic activity had been a largely unconscious and unplanned activity. Little consideration was given to the means by which food was secured. But the newly introduced element of competition – a consequence of surplus *not* of scarcity – meant that, for the first time, the means by which food was produced became embedded in the political and cultural rules under which society operated. Just as today, scarcity did not necessarily mean an absolute shortage of food. It was the consequence of the adoption of systems geared to producing sufficient surplus for one group to demonstrate social and political superiority over another.

The emergence of political power – the dominance of a small group of people over a much larger one – fed off these changes. As production became more sophisticated, yields improved and chiefs were able to identify those crops which provided most surplus. They could thus manage output so as to provide themselves with greater surpluses to redistribute, and exert greater control over the wider population. Retention of, and control over, harvest surpluses constituted the first form of taxation. Over time, the proportion of output returned to producers was reduced. Small producers, who were now enjoying a greater sense of security and were unaware of the element of exploitation in these new arrangements, accepted them without question.

Inequalities in health and well-being followed quickly in the wake of centralized control over access to land and food. The taking and exploitation of slaves emerged with these changes. The realization that human individuals could be treated as economic instruments, put to work not in their own interests but in the interests of others, constituted an enormous advance in human perception. From what we know of forager societies, such relations were not previously conceived of, but the idea that the full value of a person's labour need not be returned to them, as long as their subsistence needs were met, came to be accepted as if it were the natural order of things.

As agriculture expanded, and dependence on hunting declined, co-operative strategies for food procurement were eclipsed, and blood relations, rather than community bonds, became more important. If certain individuals controlled most food production, then those most likely to benefit were their children and other close relations. Increasingly, to whom you were related dictated your access to strategic resources.

Around 3000BCE, early states emerged in places as diverse as the Mediterranean, the Middle East, South Asia and China. These centralized states depended for their foundation and maintenance on large and obedient armies for which a guaranteed food supply had to be available. The control that alliances of village chiefs had over agricultural surpluses was therefore key. Population density and constraints on migration also played a role. Even the best equipped army cannot control a populace which need only flee to new location and re-establish small-scale farming arrangements. When the choice facing a migrant is competition and warfare with others fleeing similar attempts to forge large and complex productive units, being a small player in a large state becomes an acceptable proposition.

The archaic civilizations of ancient Egypt, Mesopotamia, Crete and the Indus valley show clear signs of modern forms of social and economic organization. Large-scale agricultural production led to the establishment of large cities where, for the first time, many people played no direct role in food production. Surplus gave rise to the possibility of the division of labour and many individuals now devoted all their time to political or religious duties, craftsmanship, trade, or the planning of military expeditions. All such societies were characterized by economies based on trade, markets and taxation; but the importance of each varied from state to state. Society was divided not simply into a ruling elite and the rest, but into a hierarchy of classes and castes, each of which had differing levels of influence over the direction of economic activity. Given the lack of options faced by the average citizen concerned with economic security, it is unlikely that class divisions required much in the way of coercion to establish and sustain. They probably resulted from opportunistic advantage-taking by the few, the channelling of wealth and privilege through family ties, and the commitment of ruling elites to the construction of symbolic monuments: altars, temples, pyramids and the like which encouraged the belief, among a superstitious people, that benevolent rulers were committed to protecting them from supernatural forces. The nature of economic production further served to reinforce perceptions and furnish the accoutrements of class distinction. Artisans had a choice between the manufacture of utility items for the lower classes – pots, tools, basic clothing, from which they were able to generate relatively small incomes – or the more lucrative production of luxury items to satisfy the appetites and reinforce the prestige of the ruling classes.

Whilst the proceeds of taxation and the tribute of territorial conquests were certainly used to oil the wheels of economic production, such public-spirited objectives were neither the justification for taxation nor the motivation for citizens to pay up. If, as was widely assumed, the king owned everything in the land, then it was considered quite normal that mere citizens should have to pay, through taxation, for use of these assets. The accumulation of wealth in the hands of ruling elites provided a steady source of investment capital, but was primarily used to consolidate the position of rulers, through paying for bigger and better armies, financing military conquest, and enabling them to live the grand and elegant lifestyles to which they felt themselves entitled, and which, perversely, held the populace in thrall. Immense riches gave rulers the appearance of gods, and many assumed such status. This certainly made it easier to rule a society in which inequality, oppression and poverty were now the defining characteristics.

Little is known about the societies immediately preceding the archaic civilizations of the Mediterranean and the orient, but it seems likely that they were similar in form to the early complex societies of Buganda and Polynesia which were observed by anthropologists in the early twentieth century. It is unlikely that social systems in all parts of the world proceeded through a common sequence of development. It is more likely that primitive horticulturist communities had several stabs at forming a complex society, perhaps only becoming successful by merging with a nearby group where advances had already taken root. Likewise, the transition from complex state to archaic civilization is likely to have involved many failed transitions and reversions to earlier forms of social organization. Those who assumed greater power as a result of change, once aware of the advantages accruing to them, would have acted to consolidate their position, but there were no guarantees of success, or any awareness on the part of the ruling classes, or their new subjects, of a developmental process underlying change. In any case the process was so slow and subject to fits and starts, and life expectancy was so short, that people would have been quite unaware of change, let alone of the social forces acting upon them.

If the transition from forager bands to primitive horticulturalists was marked principally by changes in economic arrangements and relations, the main features of the subsequent move to complex societies were changes in social relations and the institutionalization of politics. For the first time the primacy of family ties as the bond between individuals was broken. It was replaced by a system of social networks, mediated by the state, which were quite inimical to the nature which humans had acquired over millions of years. Eli Sagan offers the following definition: 'the state is that form of human society in which non-kinship forms of social cohesion are as important as, or more important than, kinship forms'.[7] For millennia, all aspects of an individual's life had been determined by kinship: what counted in life was the people one knew intimately and could depend on completely. Imagine the shock to the human psyche when these bonds of security were torn apart. Without this psycho-social turmoil, all the benefits and advances of modernity would have remained beyond our reach, but humankind paid a high price for its great leap forward.

Again, it was not with any sense of progress that early rulers decided to grasp the nettle of *social* evolution, but there must have been some capacity within certain individuals to enable them to exploit opportunities for change when they arose. Sagan suggests that an innate drive for development, or a need to experiment with alternative forms of existence, resides within all humans.[8] Like all human qualities, it is more prevalent in certain individuals. This quality is not simply a desire to exercise power and control over others, although this is its most common manifestation. At the dawn of complex society, with a prestige economy already established, and the consequences of periodic famine exacerbated by the already unequal distribution of food resources, progress meant better methods of food production, which in turn depended on more centralized forms of social control over larger and more highly concentrated populations.

Quite why particular individuals emerged to lead this process is unclear. The question is perhaps best considered in terms of the psychological process of *individuation*, which today all humans have to endure as they emerge from infancy into childhood, but which, among early human communities based on collective identity, equality and unquestioning mutual support amongst kin throughout life, was never required. To become a fully mature and psychologically healthy individual independent of, but fully integrated with, society is an achievement which still eludes many people. Thousands of years ago, when the cultural forms which serve to ease this tortuous path were yet to be established, few humans would have possessed the psychological tools to deal with the breach of kinship bonds. Those that did were at a great advantage.

It was at this point in the development of society, possibly as a reaction to the replacement of family ties as the cement of the social order, that human beings lost the ability to recognize fellow humans as identical to themselves. Whether this conspecific myopia was a cause of the dreadful violence and aggression that rapidly consumed complex society, or a defensive reaction to it, is unclear; but as soon as humans began to organize their societies hierarchically, and inter-group conflict became commonplace, we lost the ability to identify other human beings as like ourselves, and to appreciate their interests as similar to our own. The inevitable consequence was tyranny, often of an omnipotent king over an awed populace. The creation of lower classes, or castes, and the subjugation of slaves, both of which were required to provide a flexible pool of labour to supply a hierarchical system of production, were unavoidable. But it is cannibalism and human sacrifice that mark out complex society from all other forms of social organization.

The evidence for human cannibalism is irrefutable, and is both as fascinating and discomfiting as our reaction to it today. It was just as Darwin was presenting his evidence of our common ancestry and the inescapable logic that all human beings are of the same species, that parallel evidence was unearthed of cannibalism and human sacrifice, not only amongst ancient societies, but within contemporary groups. We could embrace one reality or the other: for all races of humans to share common origins was just about tolerable, but only if we could deny or transform the fact of cannibalism. And so today, as Sagan points out, 'Proportionately, there is more cannibalism in the stories we read our children, than in the books of the anthropologists.'[9]

Why human beings turned to cannibalism, almost as a matter of routine, can only be explained by the impact on the collective psyche of changes in social structure. As Sagan suggests, even cannibalism amongst people living in such a society is not pathological, it is an inevitable symptom of a primitive level of cultural development.[10] Rather than indicating an absence of culture, cannibalism was, in fact, a feature of a more advanced form of culture than was necessary to sustain earlier social forms. Cannibalism was the outcome of the necessity to reconcile the opposing demands of the drive towards progress through individuation, difference and innovation, and the desperate need for security and certainty which remains at the heart of the human condition.

Cannibalism was dependent on the ability of individuals and groups to perceive others as 'not like us', and further served to reinforce this evolving perception. Once you had eaten your neighbours, there was no prospect of regarding them as fully human, for what would that make you? It also played a role in consolidating the power and mystique of kings and leaders. Not only were these individuals all-powerful, they were the only substitute for the loss of certainty and security resulting from the severance of extended family ties.

Cannibalism, with its connotations of absolute control and power manifest in the literal consumption of others, filled a gaping void. Its legitimacy lay in the approval of the king, who was all-powerful, and whose potency was further reinforced through this sanction. The people grew closer to their leader through the granting of permission to partake of this ultimate act of power. Cannibalism was an invention of culture in response to a collective psychological malaise that had no other solution. It was not a consequence of a shortage of protein, or a manifestation of an innate extreme sadism, it was simply the hideous downside of the onward march of social advance. Humankind could have avoided cannibalism, but only if social arrangements had remained at the level of small village communities with virtually no technological innovation in respect of food production. Cannibalism was the price we paid for civilization, and all forms of human-on-human violence through subsequent history are merely its moderated forms. Acknowledging our cannibalistic past, and our struggle to moderate our aggressive responses to the anxiety and fear inspired by new forms of social organization, is vital if we are to reduce the continuing suffering of humans at the hands of other humans.

Complex society was a fairly rapid transitory stage: cannibalism could not, and did not, last long. Although still practised by the Aztecs in Mexico at the time of the Spanish conquests in the sixteenth century, this late archaic civilization is the only one in which cannibalism survived. As other complex societies evolved, forms of cannibalism were revised. The practice became the preserve of the privileged classes, and ultimately was replaced by symbolic human sacrifice. In time human sacrifice was replaced by animal sacrifice, and subsequently, with the emergence of Christianity, the sacrifice of Christ on the cross amounted to a symbolic substitution of all forms of sacrifice. Christians still consume 'the body of Christ' as part of their ritual worship.

Although no longer part of the social fabric, episodes of cannibalism are frequently reported, and are interesting for the emotions they stir, and our continuing efforts to deny them. In the nineteenth century, British sailors, stranded at sea and short of supplies, regularly practised cannibalism as a means of survival, and even formalized the process with lots being drawn to find victims. While there is a difference between resorting to human flesh in order to survive, and doing so in the absence of necessity, our reaction to reports of contemporary cannibalism tells us a great deal about a deep-seated ambivalence in respect of our relations with others. And it holds lessons for conflicts that continue to plague the world today. We react with shock and disgust at reports of extreme brutality, especially when they occur as part of what are described as 'tribal' conflicts. Tribal conflicts, for some inexplicable reason, generally only occur among communities of Africans or Asians. The tragedy of the Balkans, no more or less tribal than any of those beyond Europe's borders, is described in terms that imply a form of barbarity possessed of greater humanity. 'Tribal' brutality fits with our image of cannibals and human sacrifice, and our misconception that their practice, historically, was the preserve of 'other' races. We write it off as a continuation of a long and distasteful tradition in distant lands, largely eradicated thanks to the best efforts of colonial powers, but occasionally resurgent when the natives forget their lessons. In fact, the reappearance of such brutality, wherever it occurs in the world, is usually traceable to the re-emergence of conditions not dissimilar to those that drove the inhabitants of early complex societies to cannibalism.

Rape has long been used as a weapon of war, but the reporting of it during the conflicts in the Balkans during the 1990s, and our reaction to the massive incidence of rape in a criminal context in post-apartheid South Africa, are indications of an increased willingness to face up to the horrors of human behaviour, and greater awareness and intolerance of rape across civilized society. When the social fabric breaks down, humans engage in the most frightful acts. Confronting this reality, and the nature and scale of the brutality involved, is the first step towards overcoming it.

This period of history is key to our understanding of all that followed, not just because it signalled the introduction of routine violence and brutality into human culture, but because it also heralded the systematic separation of people from the land. In fact, three great social upheavals are intimately linked: the replacement of kin relations by non-kin social structures; the tendency of human societies to practice internal oppression and external aggression; and the systematic separation of the people from the land. All first occurred during a rapid advance in cultural evolution around six thousand years ago. Subsequent human history is the story of our efforts to recover from this cultural earthquake, and it is in the matter of land that we have made least progress.

As political power and food production became more centralized, an early distinction was drawn between subsistence land and non-subsistence land. Those fortunate to reap the benefits of the new surplus economy were able to buy parcels of land on which to build fancy houses or to farm for further surplus. Control over large areas of land by a few individuals brought changes in the distribution of wealth among the population. As disproportionate wealth accrued to these new land-owners, they would lend money to buy seed when the previous harvest had been too poor to provide enough planting for the next season. Smallholders, who were forced to take out such loans, and whose pro-ductive capacity was limited by the moderate scale of their subsistence holdings, were often unable to repay their debts, except by signing over land to their creditors. In this way, most of the land fell into the hands of a small minority who were able to extract a slice of its product as rent. As a result, the former landowners, now reduced to the status of tenants, were further squeezed and their survival threatened. Through this process the concept of private property was established for all time, and great inequalities of wealth became the norm.

It was not without a struggle that equitable access to land was given up, at least not in Mesopotamia where the rulers, observing the periodic concentration of property and wealth into a few hands, and the deleter-ious consequences for the rest of the population, periodically made *clean slate proclamations* whereby land was redistributed and a degree of equity re-established. The policy was not entirely motivated by considerations of social justice, however: the major concern for political leaders at the time was the ability to raise an army to fend off invaders, or to furnish military expeditions. No one was prepared to lay down his life for a leader who presided over a state which systematically denied the means to subsistence to the majority of its population.

Michael Hudson argues persuasively that this process of economic polarization is the underlying cause of the rise and fall of all the great civilizations.[11] The three-way tension – between the requirement of the ruling classes for material wealth and self-aggrandizement; the resort to constant warfare, either in defence of established wealth, or in pursuit of yet more; and the reliance for warriors on a denuded underclass barely able to feed their families – was, ultimately, irreconcilable. There was no escape from a process driven by the unrelenting greed and envy of the ruling classes. The successful conquest of neighbouring states could only temporarily delay the collapse of the entire unsustainable edifice.

The ancient world appears remote from our modern experience; the history of economic development is not a direct progression from these early forms of surplus economy to contemporary capitalism, but their study reveals the emergence of social institutions that remain with us. The first stock market was established in the middle bronze age, when the temples that constituted centres of political and economic control sold the right to shares of future revenues. As a consequence, the ownership of resources became separate from their management for the first time. Contemporary advocates of the plight of rural populations in less-developed countries point to the use of subsistence lands to produce cash-crops in order to generate foreign exchange to pay off debts. But this is not new: the Romans devoted much of their best agricultural land to the production of grapes and olive oil, with the same impact on the lives of ordinary people as we see today.

What of the balance sheet of these great changes in the social and economic spheres? Hudson asks whether 'the emerging class of personal landholders developed a Protestant ethic, thereby pulling their civilization ahead to a higher plane; or did they indulge themselves in the traditional ethic of conspicuous consumption to the point of interfering with society's economic linkages and basic needs?'[12] Human society certainly changed immensely as a result of these developments. Whether this change constituted an improving civilization is arguable, but the form of progress had a sense of inevitability about it. Today, nobody is insulated from its effects.

For some, recent history is not the picture of anarchy and disorder painted by this progressive separation of people from the natural resources on which they depend for survival. Our reaction has been to redefine order as a system where the private ownership of property, especially land, is key to economic and social progress, and unequal access to the benefits that accrue, the unfortunate but inevitable price which has to be paid. But are economic polarization, and the denial of the means to subsistence to countless millions, the inevitable product of civilization? Perhaps not entirely: as Erich Fromm noted, 'there is a great deal of difference between cultures which foster and encourage greed, envy and exploitativeness by their social structures, and cultures which do the opposite'.[13] Our forager ancestors may have perceived no basis for economic advantage over others but, when that basis did appear, they were determined to make the most of it, and quite unable to mediate the consequences.

It is important to remember that these structural changes in social and economic relations and outcomes were not the result of any grand plan. No rational cost/benefit analysis was conducted by the leaders of the time which concluded that the price in human suffering was one worth paying for the technological and material advance which would likely follow. It is the origin of these developments in the unpremeditated course of social evolution which has left us with the conviction that a competitive, exclusive form of economic organization constitutes the natural order. If its development was not consciously mediated by human beings, it is suggested, then there is nothing that modern humans, despite many now having acquired the knack of conscious mediation, can do about it.

Only when ideas and theories about society, economy and politics were committed to paper in publishable form, after the invention of the printing press in the fifteenth century, did we acquire the ability to consider the way we live in a detached manner. By that time, norms of social, economic and political behaviour were so established and embedded in culture as to make them impervious to our enhanced rational and intellectual skills. The subsequent history of ideas has been to consider, with varying degrees of objectivity, the extent to which we are able to throw off the legacy of historical cultural development, and that process continues.

Eli Sagan suggests that acceptance of an economic system which involves the domination and exploitation of one group by another is a mechanism through which we are able to satisfy the same drive for power and control that forced our ancestors into cannibalism and human sacrifice.[14] This is not to equate a non-inclusive economic system with the horrors of cannibalism, but neither is it an overly pessimistic assessment of the human condition. If Sagan is right, then humankind has emerged from the dark days of cannibalism, through human and animal sacrifice, to a point where, notwithstanding regular lapses into warfare, we manage to deal with the trauma wrought by the collapse of the kinship structures that nurtured our humanity for millions of years, merely by advocating a less than equitable system for economic provision. This should be cause for some considerable hope: with our growing awareness of the psychological and cultural forces that drive social change, the path to progress may open up before us.

This brief analysis of the key points in the history of social evolution does not imply a universal progression in all parts of the world, and amongst all peoples, from an original forager existence, through primitive horticultural settlements, onwards to violence-ridden complex societies, before emerging into archaic civilizations. As soon as humans became territorial and acquired a taste for conquest, the main conduit for social evolution became exposure to alternative forms of social organization, from which ideas were absorbed and new ways of doing things learned. Such a question as, 'Did early humans in all parts of the world practice cannibalism?' is not easily answered. Cannibalism emerged where and when conditions determined. A better question would be, 'Are all humans descended from cannibals?', to which the answer must be, 'To some extent, yes.' Nonetheless, very different things happened in different parts of the world, and there must have been reasons for this. A number of theoretical approaches to explaining differential social evolution have been developed. Such explanations serve two purposes: firstly, they corroborate or refute perceptions of how and why the modern world turned out like it did, and these perceptions require validation, because they are often based on contentious notions of innate racial, ethnic or national superiority; and, secondly, because they give some pointers to future developments and remind us that today's world represents not the ultimate form of human society but one short stage in an unfolding process.

The anthropologist Marvin Harris advocated a research strategy which he called *cultural materialism*.[15] For Harris, the process of sociocultural evolution is directed by the choices of individuals as they strive to satisfy a number of basic objectives that govern their lives. The four most influential of these are: the need for food, and the preference for diets that promote health and longevity; the preference to maximize leisure and minimize work time; the need for sexual satisfaction; and the need for love and affection. According to this model, these needs are universal and apply to human beings throughout time. By analysing the likely consequences of changes in environment, and of changes in the relations between individuals and groups, on the ability of people to satisfy these core needs, Harris suggested it is possible to explain and predict the evolution of society through stages. This is not to imply a predetermined process, nor, for example, that the nature of twelfth-century Byzantine society could have been predicted by a cultural materialist working five thousand years ago. The Byzantine empire unfolded as it did because an infinite number of variables settled a certain way over the course of history.

Cultural materialism argues that this outcome can be understood as the result of a selective process through which decisions were made at the micro-level in response to the basic needs of certain individuals or groups. Harris stresses the primacy of culture over biology in this selection process, arguing that 'as a species we have been selected for our ability to acquire elaborate repertories of socially learned responses, rather than for species-specific drives and instincts'.[16] Instinctual drives remain the principal motivators for our non-human primate cousins and this is why, despite our genetic closeness, human society is so different from that of chimps. Harris's thesis is persuasive, and he provides many convincing examples of his model in action.

Columbus's discovery of the New World in 1492 was of a continent developmentally quite different from the Europe from which he had set sail. North America had yet to experience the emergence of complex society; foraging and horticulture were the universal order. We know from the fossil record that the Americas were the last part of the world to be populated by humans, as recently as 15,000 years ago. We also know that the North American continent has the most varied and unpredictable climate of any large land mass on the planet. This may have contributed to the continent's enormous evolutionary disadvantage in respect of land mammals. Those species of cattle that in Europe, Asia and Africa lent themselves to fairly easy domestication and employment for traction purposes, did not evolve in North America. Native Americans were therefore presented with no incentive to invent the wheel, so the cause of technological advance was irreparably compromised. Even among the great Inca civilization of South America, social networks were maintained by an elaborate messaging system that relied on a series of cross-country runners, each of whom would cover a short distance in relay with others. By these means, communications could be transmitted up to 150 miles a day. But the immense resourcefulness of the Incas in the absence of wheel technology was not shared across the Americas.

The evidence of history and anthropology reveals the paucity of explanations for differing rates of cultural evolution based on racial or genetic difference. Native Americans were close genetic relatives of the Chinese who, in immediately pre-Columbian times built the most advanced civilization on earth. Their different outcomes are simply products of the environment in which they found themselves, and not their biological evolution, which they share, intimately, with all other humans.

Cultural materialism explains differential development across continents and societies in terms of the means by which complex societies first emerged and the form they took. Interestingly, the head start afforded the ancient empires of Africa and Asia was precisely their undoing. Echoing Michael Hudson, we see the rise and fall of great empires predicated on their ability quite rapidly to centralize political control, intensify economic production and expand their populations. In all cases this was possible, due not to any innate advantage of peoples within particular regions, but rather to the geology and geography of their habitats, and in particular to the natural management of water resources. All of the great empires grew up around major rivers, the tributaries of which provided the framework for ambitious humans to turn their new-found technological bent towards irrigating areas of land which were not otherwise viable, but which, with the addition of water, proved exceptionally fertile. But the inhabitants of these *hydraulic* states were unable to exploit this natural advantage for the long-term benefit of all. In fact, the immense economic surpluses which the combination of geography and human technical ingenuity provided led only to the unsustainable concentration of wealth in the hands of the few.

Meanwhile, in regions where agriculture was dependent on rainfall alone, no such intensification of production was possible. This was the case in Europe, where it rains a lot, but where it rains everywhere. As Harris says, the feudal kings of Europe 'could not prevent the rain from falling on friend and foe alike'[17] No leader, however powerful, was able to marshal the most crucial productive resource of all, water, in the manner of the great emperors. If they had, they would likely have subjected Europe to the same crippling degree of economic polarization.

The reaction of the politically powerful and economically fortunate to conditions on the ground was identical the world over. But in Europe the consequences were moderated by the decentralization of power into many regional capitals – in contrast to the absolute centralization of the great empires – and the different relations this implied for the many smaller European and Mediterranean city states. Certainly, pressure on land increased, due to intensifying agricultural production and population growth, but wealth and power remained dispersed. By the fifteenth century, as Europe entered its era of great despotisms with the emergence of early nation states in Portugal, Spain, France and Britain, technology had advanced sufficiently to mediate the irreconcilable forces of population growth, intensification of production and economic polarization. And in contrast to the early empires, by the time Europe was threatened by the contradictions that destroyed earlier civilizations, organized religion had assumed an essential role as moderator of the social order.

But what of parts of Africa which were also home to feudal, rainfall-based economies quite similar to those of Europe? Again it was variations in environmental endowment which determined this great continent's degree of cultural and technological advance. Africa lacks grazing lands and is ridden with tsetse fly which carry diseases which kill cattle. Conditions did not exist to breed them to the extent necessary to base an agricultural system on their power. Preparing the land remained a manual process, far more intensive of human labour, and the rate of agricultural expansion was, therefore, heavily circumscribed. Nonetheless, until a thousand years ago, African society and economy, whether under hydraulic state or feudal system, was easily Europe's match. To that point, natural endowment working in concert with human culture possibly even favoured Africans over Europeans. But human culture never stops evolving, and the balance was about to tilt, overwhelmingly, in favour of Europe. As Harris concluded, 'the feudal polities of Africa were weaker, less centralized and more egalitarian than their European counterparts, and that's why it was ultimately the Europeans who developed capitalism and enslaved the Africans and not vice versa'.[18]

For four thousand years, China led the world in cultural and technological advance. The Chinese discovered gunpowder long before the Europeans. During the fifteenth century they built the largest fleet of ships in the world, using dry docks for shipbuilding a century before Europeans had the idea. China survived longer than any comparable empire and 600 years ago, shortly before Europeans set out to colonize the rest of the world, was equally well placed for global domination. But the Chinese failed to launch their fleets upon the world. A new emperor came to power, and the capital was moved from Peking to Nanking at considerable cost. Perhaps this reversal was as unplanned and lacking in logical foundation as the earlier orgy of shipbuilding. China had survived more than three millennia, it had suffered no serious external threat to its territorial integrity, and had been required to compete with no one. The Europeans, by contrast, had been under siege from the east until quite recently and, having contained that threat, found it impossible to stop fighting each other. They were therefore forced to look beyond their immediate surrounds. The Chinese, despite forever chasing the tail of a growing population struggling to feed itself, felt no such motivation. Ultimately, a shiny new nine-thousand-room palace in Nanking was more in keeping with Chinese aspirations.

The last thousand years also holds the key to current developmental differences between Europe and the Indian subcontinent. European-style decentralized rainfall-based economies characterized much of southern India for the last two millennia, but the region was subject to continual attacks, first from the hydraulic states that grew up around the Ganges, and subsequently from the plundering fleets of Arab, Portuguese and British expeditioners. Quite modern forms of capitalist economic activity were found in southern India: in the eighteenth century it was the largest exporter of manufactured goods in the world. Had it not been subject to continual attack, this region may well have developed as Europe did. The absence of a specific environmental cause for India's failure should not detract from the main point: it is the interaction of the natural environment and human culture which ultimately determines power relations between different peoples. All the evidence suggests that culture evolves uniformly in response to similar environmental stimuli. As a result, given the ecological and climatological history of our planet since the end of the last ice age, it was probable that a reasonably stable and sustainable centre of power would emerge in Europe. Further, the global domination that came with improved boat-building and navigational techniques, meant that only one such centre of power was possible.

How important a role has economics played in shaping the historical direction of human society? By economics, I mean the mechanisms, systems and processes by which people's needs and desires for material goods are met. For most of human history, for virtually all people, these have consisted, principally, of the food, clothing and the shelter necessary for survival. For the sake of clarity, and to distinguish this aspect of provision from other conceptions of economics, I shall term this the *needs economy*.

Humans seem to have a blind spot when it comes to economics. The mechanisms by which their material needs are met are anathema to most people. We work, we earn money, we buy what we desire and can afford, but there is little sense of any underlying system or process, or of the complex power relationships that direct the economy. People are even less able to equate what passes for economics in the media (stock markets, talk of speculation and capital flows, and the business cycle) with the means by which they secure their material needs. People know inflation is bad, and interest rate rises are also bad if you have a mortgage, but good if you have savings. But we rarely engage with economics, and this in the industrialized nations, where levels of education are high and information freely available.

Imagine how it must have been for our forager ancestors, whose entire existence was dictated solely by their capacity to engage, at the crudest possible level, with the natural environment. Conscious thought would have revolved around how best to maximize, quite literally, the fruits of their labours. But this process would have occurred within a context so rigidly confined and unchanging as to make the consideration of alternatives, and the introduction of innovatory techniques quite impossible. They may well have worked out that running faster and improved hand-eye coordination made for more successful hunting, and that the over-harvesting of berries and nuts from a particular area had a negative effect on yields the following season, but these observations would have been largely unconscious. The only conceivable world view for a forager was that she was slave to nature, and that nature alone set the limits to her enterprise. When nature threw up the first economic surplus and it occurred to humans that they could consciously direct their efforts to securing more of it, what an immense advance in human conscious awareness. It is the psycho-social basis for everything humankind has achieved, and for much of the suffering we have wrought. Intriguingly, despite the very real advances in human culture and conscious awareness, we seem no more willing than our ancient ancestors to contemplate the inequity of power underlying our economic relations, or its culpability for our social ills.

Does sustained economic insecurity contribute to the violence and warfare that feature so frequently in the history of human social relations? In order to answer the question, we must distinguish between individual acts of aggression and violence, and those Eli Sagan terms *social aggression.*[19] The relationship between the uncertainty arising from the subjugation of the needs economy and social aggression deserves attention. Changes in established social and economic relations clearly have an immense impact on the ability of human groups to coexist peacefully and cooperatively, even if it is often difficult to discern a direct causal link between threats to economic security and outbreaks of civil unrest or war. It is clear, however, that the insecurity that drives most social aggression has its root either in perceived threats to the institutions seen as having most to do with satisfying economic needs, or, less directly, in the inevitable inequality of outcomes of an economic system developed on principles which marginalize the objective of providing for the material needs of all people. The needs economy has become an adjunct of the wider economy, and whilst most people do not understand why or how this happened, they are all too aware of its impact on their lives.

There are, on occasion, clear examples of violence caused directly by economic threats. The food riots that punctuate civil society in less-developed countries are a spontaneous response to further price rises by people whose incomes are already insufficient to feed their families. Only when large numbers perceive a direct link between economic policy and immediate changes in their own situation does such explicit economic violence emerge. Ultimately, however, all collective human aggression is motivated by individual or collective insecurity and anxiety deriving from threats, real or perceived, to well-being and stability caused by the inability effectively to source material needs and to be reasonably confident of continuing to be able to do so. Often, an autocratic political leader may act as conduit and even catalyst for the realization of such reactions. The fact that despotic warmongers generally do not emerge in countries where economic security is good and perceived as improving, or where there is no enduring legacy of the inequitable outcomes of earlier conflicts or oppression, surely teaches us that the basic ingredient for stable, conflict-free society is economic security and the reasonably equitable distribution of wealth.

Some argue that we have neglected, indeed misplaced completely, the legacy of our ancestors who had cracked the problem of sustainable economics and equitable access to basic needs. As we have seen, in pre-agricultural societies, despite the lack of any surplus, there was an equitable distribution of all that could be collected and caught by the community, but this did nothing to guard against the regular decimation of entire societies when environmental conditions became hostile. While we certainly pay less heed to the consequences of resource depletion and other impacts on the natural environment than our forebears, we remain far better equipped than they to identify threats to our survival and to respond effectively to them. Of most concern is our inability to direct our collective rational powers to the solution of a problem as threatening as the damage we are doing to the environment. Our ancestors, apparently intuitively, were far more inclined to take measures to encourage a sustainable economy. They had little knowledge, but applied it rigorously; we have much greater knowledge, but most of the time we fail to apply it at all. There are very real lessons to be learned, but there can be no going back. By the standards of the modern world, the quality of life for those of our forebears who practised sustainable economics in an equitable society was rather poor.

There have been three types of influence on the direction of human advance: ecological, biological and cultural. For most of its history, humankind was subject to an ecological determinism that was absolute: we had no control over our environment. During that period, our biology was so tied to the ecology of the planet, the two were parts of the same whole. But once culture came along, not only did we encounter a force for change that possessed no innate direction, no element of determinism, we embraced a force that began to erode the determinism of the other two spheres. We were able to throw off the eco-biological chains of millions of years. The challenge now is to learn how, through culture, to make the most of this freedom.

There is a common perception that biological and cultural evolution each possess a different moral quality; that our biological nature makes us selfish and condemns us to aggressive and warlike behaviour, whereas cultural evolution acts as a restraining force. This is clearly wrong: the most peaceable humans were those who lived before culture took a dominating role in human social affairs. But again, this does not mean that culture, exclusively, is the root of all our ills. What we can say is that change through culture is now our only hope. Whilst a common genetic heritage shaped the lives of Adolph Hitler and Mohandas Gandhi, it was differing cultural inputs, personal experiences, and the social conditions that pertained during their lifetimes, that were key to the quite different impacts these two individuals had on the history of the twentieth century.

Acknowledgement of our genetic inheritance is crucial: there is, quite certainly, such a thing as human nature. It has many facets, but its one defining quality is its flexibility. Every life lived, every human act, is a product of the interaction of the hereditary make-up of an individual human being with the culture into which that genetically designed organism is born, nurtured, and released into the world to find its own, more or less, independent way in life. The most saintly acts and the most heinous crimes we can imagine of human beings are all the product of the same nature. Mother Theresa and Florence Nightingale shared virtually identical genes with Genghis Khan and Josef Stalin. That most human beings have far more in common with the former should give us cause for hope, and encourage us to discover what kinds of environmental inputs combine with human nature to produce a Mandela, rather than a Milosevic.

This chapter has followed a temporal sequence that began with the descent of early hominids from the trees, and concluded with a world on the verge of the colonial expeditions of the fifteenth century. I have presented an argument for the inevitability of the sequence of historical events which might suggest that history holds few lessons for anyone consciously working towards the goal of progressive social change. But this historical inevitability does not imply that we are similarly unable to take conscious control of our future. This is the most important lesson we can draw from history: we are quite different from our forebears. We have the capacity and knowledge to make decisions about the future which they did not. But we have to embrace the notion that we can act to influence the direction of social change and we must start by accepting our responsibility for what happens next.

Our failure yet to act has resulted in a world quite out of step with itself. It is a world in which parallel aspirations – individual, racial, national, economic, moral, political, spiritual, artistic, and technological – are all competing as if none impacts on the other, each one against a measure of progress couched only in its own terms. It is a recipe not only for fragmentation and alienation but also for social disaster. If we are going to bring all these aspirations back into balance, to be able to identify and anticipate the impact of changes in one sphere on the others, then we need to consider the limits of divergence and sustainability. How different we can all afford to be is one question, but how many views of the world we can afford to hold is the far more pressing one. The starting point of an investigation into the limits of diversity has to be what we have in common, and so we return to that supreme gift of the Enlightenment philosophers, the concept of the psychic unity of all human beings. Were they right, these ground-breaking thinkers, two hundred years ago? The evidence of the intervening two centuries suggests we were not prepared to accept their claims; but, until we are, there will be little possibility of progress.

We have a choice. We can take the position that all human lives are of equal value, and admit a duty to organize our affairs so that all people have a chance to make a positive and voluntary economic contribution from which they earn the means to satisfy their basic needs. Or we can assert that all human lives are not of equal worth: that some groups are more entitled than others, and that those which are most entitled can satisfy their desires at the cost of the less entitled. On the line that separates the most from the least entitled we can divide people into groups on whatever spurious grounds come to mind, much as Hitler did. Whilst we may not systematically set about the extermination of particular groups, we could simply stand by and leave them to the consequences of these consciously mediated exclusive economic arrangements. The situation of the many millions of people who today struggle to survive is inextricably linked to our own, not only by the fact that we are all players in a single global economy, but also by our common humanity. We can deny that common humanity, and hide behind the facade of an economic system erected and sustained for the benefit of a small minority, dishonestly professing ignorance of its complexity, or we can accept the gauntlet thrown down two hundred years ago, accept the unity of humankind, and do something about it. To the extent that it matters, we are all alike, we share the same hopes, fears, dreams and aspirations, and, as we shall see, we all have the same basic needs.

In the last chapter, we concluded that there was nothing in our biological evolutionary inheritance which precluded the possibility of progress towards a more inclusive society. Having examined the evidence of our cultural and social evolution, we can now add that here too, despite culture having evolved some of the most barbaric and harm-inducing forms of perception and institutions, there is nothing about culture itself which means it can not now evolve in a quite different direction to that of the last 10,000 years. The key to escaping the chains of both biology and culture is to increase awareness among individuals of the conditions set for us by our biological and cultural evolution. Armed with an awareness of prevailing misconceptions and their consequences, we can choose whether or not to take responsibility for our collective future. Accepting that challenge will surely be the sign of a mature humanity.

3

Economics and Morals

TO DETERMINE the prospects for a reordered global society which is more inclusive, which brings greater economic security and quality of life for more people, and which does not further compromise the ecology of our planet, we must consider four propositions. First, we need to establish the unity of humankind in terms of the basic needs of all people. If it turns out that different peoples have quite different basic needs, then mutual satisfaction of all needs may be impossible: the interests of certain groups may be irreconcilable with those of others. Conversely, if unity of basic needs is established, the argument for a collective duty to strive for their universal satisfaction is strengthened. Second, we need to establish that we have developed sufficient cultural and technological ingenuity to convert the resources of nature into the means to meet the basic needs of all people. Again, if this can be established, it further enhances the argument that we should, at least, try. Third, we need to determine if this can be achieved through arrangements which allow all people to make a contribution to the economy at least equal to the value of the benefits they derive. Finally, if current economic arrangements are not adequate to this task, we need to assure ourselves that movement towards new arrangements is realisable without causing increased suffering and hardship.

It is sometimes argued that attempts to define universal basic needs are futile given the cultural diversity of humankind. As we have noted, in terms of biology, with the exception of superficial differences which have no impact on individual potential, all human groups are identical. The impact of culture on our perceptions and psychology has been considerable, but our biological sameness is sufficient to yield a list of universal basic needs. To compile this list we need to distinguish material from non-material needs, and acknowledge the difference between needs and aspirations. This exercise is concerned principally with material needs, but these cannot be considered in isolation from other human needs: this was one of the great mistakes of the experiments in the Soviet Union and elsewhere where communist approaches to economic management have been attempted.

In assessing basic needs, physical survival is a prerequisite. If we do not survive as individual biological organisms, questions of quality of life do not arise. There is universal agreement on the ingredients necessary to guarantee physical survival: food of adequate nutritional value, clean water and hygienic sanitation, adequate clothing and shelter appropriate to the local climate. Further reflection suggests that reliable and responsible adult guardians to safeguard the interests of infants and children are also crucial, as is security from threats of violence or accident as far as possible. Protection from illness and disease through access to medicine and health care services is also important. Finally, education and economic opportunities which allow individuals to make a meaningful contribution to their own well-being are clearly beneficial.

This constitutes an adequate list of universal basic *material* needs: food, water, clothing, housing and health care, and three further *instrumental* needs: education, physical security and economic opportunity. I would add one further instrumental need: that of freedom of thought and expression, for without such freedom the value of education is compromised, and the conditions necessary to build the kind of society in which universal needs provision is achievable cannot exist. These needs are common to all human beings, regardless of race, culture or creed. I have separated out the instrumental needs only because they are not essential prerequisites to physical survival. Human beings can, under fortuitous circumstances, survive as physical entities without education, specific provision for physical security, and fulfilling economic opportunities; life would be precarious, miserable and unfulfilling, but it could be survived. Without food, water, clothing, housing and minimal medical inputs survival is impossible.

The list is complete and, as evidence of the unity of humankind, it is incontrovertible: as biological organisms we are identical. In terms of the material inputs necessary to sustain our individual lives we are all the same, and to the extent that education, security and fulfilling work opportunities could be foregone, then, in respect of these instrumental needs, what we want for ourselves over and above the basics of physical survival, we are all extremely similar. So, how realistic is universal provision for basic needs, and to what extent are prevailing economic arrangements suited to this objective?

Our list of basic needs provides a definition of the constituent elements of the *needs economy* we outlined in the previous chapter. The success of the needs economy, or improvements in its performance over time, can be measured in terms of the proportion of the global population to whom basic needs are supplied. Inputs into the needs economy include: natural resources – the land, minerals, flora and fauna occurring in nature; human know-how – our ability through cultural innovation and individual ingenuity to exploit and convert natural resources into the goods and services that constitute basic needs; and human effort – the labour committed by people in pursuit of their basic needs. But how can we know if these inputs are sufficient to meet the objective of universal, sustainable provision of basic needs? History gives few clues: for the last ten thousand years the goals of the needs economy have been secondary to other quite different goals.

It is difficult to assess, accurately, the proportion of the global economy accounted for by food, water services, clothing and housing because much of this activity occurs outside the formally measured economies of nation states. Also, for many people, the economic value of the basic needs they consume is considerably in excess of that necessary to provide an acceptable quality of life. This purposeful enhancement of necessities, their conversion into luxuries, is one of many ways we have succeeded in compromising the needs economy. We can, however, make some useful estimates.

The United Nations suggests that 2,300 calories per day are required for an individual to avoid malnutrition. World grain production alone is currently sufficient to provide every individual with more that 3,000 calories.[1] This is before counting the calorific value of vegetables, fruit, beans and pulses, seeds, nuts, fish and meat from grass-fed animals. In the second half of the twentieth century, the rate of increase in food production consistently outstripped the rate of population growth. There is no question of our not being able to produce sufficient food; we already produce more than enough. There is no shortage of food, but still a sixth of the world's people go hungry because of the way we organize agricultural production and distribute its output.

Looking at the wider economy, in 2002, the total value of global economic activity was estimated at $47 trillion,[2] a little under $8,000 per person: easily enough to provide for the basic material needs of all the worlds' people. And this is just the value of the formal economy; much basic needs production takes place outside the formal economy and is not counted in these figures. Again, our ability to create sufficient wealth to meet the needs of all people is not in doubt, only our priorities when it comes to distributing it.

Matching the supply of basic needs to demand depends on a number of variables: the size of the population and its rate of growth; regional differences in natural resource availability; constraints on our ability to convert natural resources into consumable form; the possibility of improvements in the rate and efficiency with which we are able to convert resources; and the means by which raw materials and finished goods are transported and distributed. The complexity of these and other variables mean there is no simple formula for the sustainable, long-term provision of basic needs. But if, as the evidence suggests, we already produce enough food and create enough wealth to meet the basic needs of the entire global population, and without directing our efforts specifically to this end, then a solution is well within reach. We can, should we so choose, achieve the goal of universal needs provision.

In failing to come to terms with the opportunities provided by economic surplus, the universal provision of basic needs was relegated to the status of a vague historical principle, one for which there was no place in a perpetually modernising economy. Feeding all the people, and assuring their well-being to the best of our collective ability, ceased to be the motivating force of social and economic activity. Productive endeavour was now the means to prestige, status, wealth, control over the majority by a minority, and the maintenance of elite power. And by excluding much of the population from the fruits of our new and dynamic economy, we also set the limits for that dynamism. Economic advance became a minority activity, one which drew the life-blood out of the needs economy on which the majority remained dependent.

With this transformation in economic activity came two particular changes, each of which had a huge impact. By turning land into an economic commodity, conditions were created by which, for the first time, it became possible that some might starve simply because they had no access to land. This *commodification* of land meant private ownership over the natural resources upon which all depended, and to which access had previously been considered the automatic right of all. Land ownership became the ultimate symbol of status and prestige, and it was not long until property rights over land were enmeshed in the legal codes of early states. Without access to land, everyone is forced to become part of the formal economy, usually by working land owned by someone else for only a partial return on their effort.

The second major change was specialization, or the division of labour. People were no longer exclusively responsible for providing for the needs of themselves and their families. Specialization was crucial to economic development and growth, but it removed from people a degree of independence and autonomy in respect of their economic security which had hitherto ensured the well-being of all in reasonably equal measure. Neither of these developments is necessarily bad, as long as the landless labourer has access to economic opportunities through which he can secure a just reward for his labour effort, which is sufficient to provide for his basic needs. If such opportunities do not exist, however, and if the landless labourer is denied access to land, then the outcome is bound to be less equitable than earlier forms of economic organization.

The history of economic development is not a continuous sequence. Many great empires have come and gone, and much knowledge and experience has been lost and relearned. But between 5000BCE and 1500AD, wherever societies became established around a reasonably high density of population, economic developments followed a very similar path. In fact, for nearly 7,000 years, despite gradual and sustained technological advance there was little to tell one society apart from another, at least in respect of their economic arrangements. All pre-industrial economies were characterized by inequitable distribution of resources to the point at which large numbers went without basic needs, concentration of land ownership in the hands of an elite, widespread use of slavery, and a tendency to territorial conquest in the pursuit of further riches.

Pre-industrial elites quickly learned that control over resources gave them control over labour. Labourers had little option but to work for rich landowners on their terms, and this led to a further concentration of wealth in the hands of the already privileged. It did not lead to any significant increase in production, but had a huge impact on the distribution of wealth in society. Between 500AD and 1500AD, the agrarian economy in Europe expanded only in proportion with population growth: *per-capita* output remained constant. In the absence of the technological innovation required for economic expansion, the only way for the privileged minority to ensure their continued material comfort was to expand the productive resource base of land and labour under their control. This was the motivation behind all the great conquests and empires. Genuine scarcity was rarely a cause of conflict: starving peasants have never started wars. It was the determination of wealthy elites to secure increasing benefits from surplus production that sparked conflicts. War-making has always been the prerogative of a privileged few in society, with the poor generally its victims.

The centuries preceding the industrial revolution in Britain saw clear signs of an emerging social morality. The feudal system under which land ownership was concentrated in the hands of an aristocracy was grossly inequitable, but it also featured a duty of care on the part of landowners towards tenants. Economic arrangements recognised that, where the majority of people survive through subsistence farming, everyone must be afforded access to sufficient quantity and quality of land. With time and advances in technology, more people entered specialized labour, and would rely for subsistence on payments derived from the surplus produce of others. To avoid disagreements over the relative worth of the goods and services being traded, money was introduced and markets developed. While the impact of new technologies remained slight, and scope for the production of surpluses quite limited, the market mechanism proved a reasonably equitable way of distributing output among the population, whilst doing nothing to threaten the privileges of the elite.

Life for the mass of the population remained pretty grim. Life expectancy was low, averaging just 30 years, and its quality poor. Untreatable illnesses claimed countless lives and caused immense suffering. But where feudal society differed from modern industrial society was in the fact that neither a redistribution of the wealth among the wider population, nor a restructuring of the economy on more equitable lines, would have had much impact on the general level of well-being. This is not to condone the excesses of the aristocracy, only to say that the general level of welfare among the population of pre-industrial Europe could not have been much improved. The limited technology of the time meant that the volume of economic output remained constant. The elite did secure a disproportionate share for themselves, but this was not the principal cause of the hardship of the peasantry. Cultural and technological advance was failing to match the rate of population growth. When harvests were poor, or epidemics struck, the aristocracy were slightly better able to insulate themselves from the consequences, but privilege provided few safeguards. It was only the rapid economic growth of the industrial revolution which provided the means for the improvement in material conditions of all people. But just as the realization of surplus revealed the greedy and selfish aspect of human nature, it was the realization of industrial advance which enabled the greedy and selfish to hammer home their advantage. The gains of the industrial revolution could have improved the lot of all people, but humankind was not yet equal to the challenge.

Prior to the industrial revolution, Britain was neither the most nor least developed of nations, but progress was being made, notably among the peasant population who were becoming more efficient producers of food. The aristocracy, unable to find the means to increase their wealth sufficiently to maintain their position of dominance over an upwardly mobile populace, turned increasingly to fighting among themselves over a shrinking pot of aristocratic wealth. The Church had emerged from the Reformation less inclined to support the notion that the prevailing social order was divinely pre-ordained; in some quarters it actively campaigned for a more egalitarian society. As the population began to grow at an increasing rate, more land had to be found for tenant farmers. The feudal classes were in crisis: the system that had sustained them for so long was on the verge of collapse.

Argument continues over precisely why the industrial revolution occurred first in Britain, and not elsewhere, for it was very much a unilateral event which, by the mid-nineteenth century, gave the British an apparently unassailable advantage. Whilst much of the land in Britain was parcelled up and worked by smallholders, compared with other European countries, fewer people lived exclusively by subsistence means. There was already a large cash economy. The majority of the population worked as labourers or servants, or were smallholders who sold a substantial amount of their time as labour. Eric Hobsbawm argues that the industrial revolution represented not just an acceleration in economic growth, but a radical transformation with consequences as great as the emergence of the first surplus economies. It hailed 'the start of self-sustained economic growth by means of perpetual technological revolution and social transformation'.[3]

Many of the causes often cited by historians for Britain's advantage are shown by Hobsbawm to be misguided. Climatic, geographic and resource endowments, the scientific revolution of the seventeenth century, the Reformation – none of these was exclusively British in character; they certainly helped, but they did not set Britain apart. But some things did. A rapidly growing population provided expanding domestic markets as well as forcing social transformation. There was no longer sufficient land for the food needs of all people to be met through traditional means. Interestingly, Britain's success may have been due, in part, to the relative inefficiency of its agriculture. In India, agricultural production was sufficiently developed to keep pace with a growing population. It was possible to feed enough people through the investment of surpluses in improved irrigation and so the conditions for industrialization were avoided, along with the trauma of the transition from an agricultural to an industrial economy. Many Indians are, instead, paying a heavy price today.

Nowhere in Britain is more than seventy miles from the sea and access to the ports that formed the hub of global trade, which Britain, through a combination of political nous and military might, came to dominate during the eighteenth century. To support growing international and domestic trade in the period prior to industrialization, there was massive public investment in transport infrastructure, especially the canals. This made investment in technology-based manufacture a more viable risk as there were now quicker and easier means for getting goods to markets and ports. The form of pre-industrial enterprise in Britain was a perfect model for the new industrialists. Small entrepreneurs and artisans were already employing staff for cash and had learned the basics of business management: how to calculate costs and determine prices; how to run a profitable business. Such knowledge and experience quickly becomes a part of the cultural mechanisms by which people learn to adopt successful practices and discard less favourable ones. Most important to Britain's ascendancy was the decision by political leaders to make economic concerns the sole and exclusive motive in foreign policy and military expansion. While other European powers were fighting amongst themselves, or embroiled in revolution, the British were picking up colonies – which provided profitable markets and were rich in raw materials – almost at will. Although the slave trade was so poorly managed and inefficient (at the cost of millions of African lives) that it failed to provide great direct financial returns, Britain's pre-eminence is demonstrated by the fact of its control of 50 per cent of the global trade in slaves by 1800.

Many factors contributed to Britain's advantage, but the establishment of colonies through military force, and the effective theft of land and natural resources from native peoples which this involved, were paramount. So rapid and total was Britain's dominance that the other nations were left trailing hopelessly. There could only be one industrial revolution, and it could occur only in one country. For a century the rest of the world would have to play catch-up.

At home the industrial revolution saw a re-run of the systematic separation of the people from the land. But this time its impact was far swifter and touched the lives of almost everyone. The psychological impact on individuals who, during the course of their lifetimes, were required to give up rural lifestyles and move *en masse* to the cities, must have been immense. And there would have been little consolation in terms of improved material well-being for most people.

Unlike earlier social transformations, the impact this time around might have been lessened had it been more carefully planned. It is true that population growth was outstripping the productive capacity of the pre-industrial economy; industrialization was possibly the only solution. But these circumstances arose in large part as a consequence of the enclosure, during the preceding two centuries, of large quantities of land. Such acts of enclosure may have improved agricultural output, and enabled the generation of surpluses for investment in new technologies, but the net effect was to restrict access to land to a privileged and increasingly wealthy land-owning minority. Accounts of the dreadful means by which land enclosure was achieved, and of the decimation of communities and widespread starvation which ensued, leaves little doubt that those who led the enclosure process cared little for the plight of ordinary people. The landless majority were disenfranchised. They had no choice but to head for the towns and provide the cheap labour required by the industrial revolution.

Whilst both land enclosure and industrialization played a role, a far older failing explains the deepening poverty of the period: the inability of human beings equitably to distribute the huge increase in economic surplus that often results from social transformation. As we shall learn in

Chapter 9, the *classical* economic theory which foreshadowed the industrial revolution provided an explanation for this failure, but at the time
nobody in a position of influence was able or willing to engage fully with
its teachings. Little progress has been made in this respect in the intervening centuries.

The era of merchant capitalism in Britain, from 1700 to 1830, saw
only modest per capita growth, averaging just 0.2 per cent annually.[4]
Although output grew considerably, so did the population; and whilst the
industrial revolution began to make a difference, if there was to be a
perceptible increase in material well-being, the economy would have to
find an extra gear. The biggest obstacle to economic expansion was a
shortage of capital, and this was compounded by the understandable fear
of risk-averse investors in a very insecure world. The Bankruptcy Act of
1861 reduced the risk to entrepreneurs virtually to nil. Whilst they still
stood to lose their investments if enterprises failed, there was no longer
any obstacle to starting again, and they were able to protect their
personal assets and safeguard the security of their families. Business
failure no longer meant destitution and social ostracization. In 1862
there followed the introduction of the device of *limited liability*, whereby
an entrepreneur could limit the extent of his liability for the debts of
a failed enterprise to the amount of his original investment. For the
ambitious businessman, these two innovations effectively removed
the risk from investment and brought a great deal of additional funds
to the economy. They also meant a great deal less circumspection in the
selection of investment opportunities and a great many more failed
enterprises, from which the capitalist could now recover, but against
which the poor wage labourer had no such legal protection. Further,
they encouraged investment in high-risk, high-return ventures which
took the formal economy even further away from the demands of basic
needs provision.

Until this legislation was enacted, growth had been largely dependent
on the ability of entrepreneurs to extract greater value from the effort of
those they employed. But the new injection of capital sparked a secondary, but no less significant, industrial revolution. In the 1880s, scientific
and technological innovation became the driving force for growth and
with it came a new paradigm: economic expansion was now possible
without having to engage excessive and costly quantities of labour. It was
the entrepreneurs' dream: through technology they could reduce their
profit-stifling dependency on wage-labour and find ever more lucrative
investment opportunities for their surplus wealth.

The economic history of the first half of the twentieth century is bound
up with the political geography of the period. Two world wars and the

depression that separated them caused death and suffering on an unprecedented scale. But the global struggle against fascism revealed a hitherto unseen potential for countries, regions and peoples to work together against a common threat. And that spirit of cooperation continued once peace came to Europe and Asia after World War II.

In 1945 Europe was in tatters, its infrastructure destroyed and its economy geared exclusively towards military production. No one had any money, a problem only mitigated by the absence of anything worth buying in the shops. But the economic opportunities presented by a population eager to build an inclusive society, one in which further war was impossible, was hamstrung by a crucial missing ingredient: investment. Help came in the form of the *Marshall Plan* through which, between 1948 and 1951, the United States *gave* the countries of western Europe the equivalent of 1.2 per cent of its annual economic output. This is equivalent to $250 billion each year at present value. Compare this with recent *repayable* loans to Russia to rebuild an economy of 250 million people which totalled only a few billion dollars and you get some idea of the scale of the investment Europe received. Marshall Aid was a one-off; along with regulatory measures to manage the world economy put in place at the Bretton Woods conference of 1948, it set up Europe for a quarter of a century. This period saw a dynamic economy, and for the only time since early humans discovered the double-edged sword of economic surplus, conscious progress towards a more inclusive society. In western Europe and North America, and in Japan, which saw similarly motivated US investment, the standard of living for most people improved considerably. Nearly everyone had economic security and access to basic needs. But then this was the only period in human history when moral concerns, rather than minority economic interests, were the dominating force in politics. Nobody could contemplate a return to the horrors of war and the holocaust, and it was obvious to the people, to politicians, and to economists, what was necessary to assure no such return: a global economy based on national sovereignty, stability, equity and improvement in basic needs provision across the board.

The motivation for the massive gift of development aid from the United States was not wholly altruistic. The Americans found themselves the main beneficiary of the war in economic terms. Although many American military personnel were lost, and it was US involvement that tipped the balance against Hitler, the continental United States was not subject to enemy attack. By 1945, the US found itself with a great deal of surplus wealth which required investment opportunities, and it needed to find new markets overseas in order to expand its economy. Americans were still enjoying the benefits of the massive programme of public works under President Roosevelt's *New Deal* programme, which

had been staggeringly successful in resurrecting the economy after the
depression that followed the Wall Street crash of 1929. The recovery and
sustained expansion of the post-war European economy, just like that of
the United States a decade earlier, was funded by a large, carefully
planned injection of public funds. The most successful period for the
world economy was built on a foundation of public investment, state
planning, international regulation and global economic cooperation –
not, as many economists suggest as a solution for today's ills, on free
markets, unfettered trade, intense international competition and
uncontrolled flows of capital.

Without aid and cooperation from the United States, the post-war
period of economic growth and stability would have been impossible.
Crucial to this stability was the *dollar standard:* the fixing of the value of
the US dollar to the price of gold. The exchange rates of other currencies were set against that of the dollar, and governments were free to
adjust the value of their currency to iron out any disequilibrium that
crept in. If, for example, the French found their balance of payments
went into deficit, they could devalue the franc so as to make French business competitive once again. As the benchmark against which all others
adjusted, the only economy denied this facility for adjustment was that
of the United States. The success of the system depended on the ability
of the Americans to keep their economy in order.

The *dollar standard* gave the world an effective way of assessing the
comparative value and performance of national economies. As long as
the United States was prepared to act as the bulwark, it afforded a degree
of stability which ensured that all participating economies could grow
steadily and in concert with one another. Domestically, governments
retained and employed a full set of *Keynesian* tools for economic management: as well as raising or lowering interest rates, they could alter tax
levels, restrict wage increases, even set prices, to ensure the economy
remained in balance, that growth was sustainable, that full employment
was maintained, and that more people were brought into range of the
benefits of a reasonably dynamic, carefully managed economy. Internationally, as a result of a unique consensus that the best way to economic success was via cooperation rather than competition between
nations, the system of fixed exchange rates and tight controls over the
flow of capital across national boundaries further ensured stability.
Whether this state of affairs, which William Keegan calls *enlightened capitalism*[5], could have endured is doubtful, but, compared with the problems facing the global economy today, it was stable, and worked for growing numbers of people throughout the non-communist world. In terms
of economic inclusion it constituted a massive advance on what had gone
before, and it paved the way for the social reforms of the last third of the

twentieth century, which brought greater equality for women and a grow-ing tolerance of racial and cultural difference. But although it heralded the creation of a large and satisfied middle class, and introduced univer-sal access to health care and education, even among the rich nations poverty remained a serious problem.

The age of enlightened capitalism was highly unusual, based as it was on cooperation between nations which had little in common save the desire to avoid a return to war, and to improve the lot of their peoples. But it was a rather false and partial achievement, and it was destined to fail because of its inherent exclusiveness. Once the memory of war and holocaust faded, the only remaining motivation for cooperation was the threat posed by Soviet communism.

Until after its fall, western observers had little idea of the fragility of the Soviet economy, and how culturally stultifying the constraints on personal freedoms really were. Except militarily – and here the threat was indeed real – the Soviet system was no match for the social and economic model of the West, but the United States remained convinced that it was. It indulged its paranoia through the prosecution of a war in Vietnam which cost far more than a global bulwark economy could afford. The inflationary pressure of the war was compounded by the cost of President Lyndon Johnson's *Great Society* programme. Johnson was appalled by the poverty still affecting many Americans for whom a successful period of economic growth had done little. He decided all citizens were entitled to a slice of the cake of economic success and launched a state-funded poverty reduction programme. The economy fell heavily into debt. The demise of enlightened capitalism was precipi-tated by American military spending to stave off a negligible communist threat, coupled with the recognition that even a carefully planned and regulated economy at home was unable to eradicate poverty. In August 1971, President Richard Nixon severed the link between the dollar and gold. Four months later he devalued the dollar; a second devaluation followed. The anchor which had kept the western economies steady for 25 years had been rapidly hauled in, and, in March 1973, the world awoke to a system of floating exchange rates for which it was ill-prepared.

This would have been bad enough, but then on 6 October 1973, Egypt and Syria attacked Israel in an effort to recapture land taken in the *Six Day War* of June 1967. Israel successfully repelled the assault. The Arab oil producers, acting in cartel through the Organization of Oil Producing and Exporting Countries (OPEC), responded by quadrupling the price of oil and plunging the world economy into deep recession. The effect of this move was to siphon off – and into the bank accounts of the Arab states – all of the investment capital from the industrialized economies. The cash which served to lubricate the world economy was extracted in a matter of months. The spell had been broken and the goodwill born of thirty years' international economic cooperation disappeared overnight.

For the industrialized nations, the 1970s were an unmitigated disaster. Unemployment became endemic, as did inflation. In a short decade, the carefully managed gains of the previous three were largely wiped out. The Keynesian economic policies which had underpinned stability for so long were written off as no longer appropriate. Many economists still refuse to acknowledge that the structural basis for Keynes-based economic success was demolished by Nixon in 1971, without any thought to the consequences. The death of Keynesian *enlightened capitalism* was far from inevitable; it was the actions of a new breed of politician which had killed it.

The post-war period of cooperation and stability was a one-off, a consequence of factors unlikely to be repeated. This period of unprecedented success in providing economic security, stability and expanding basic needs provision was the direct result of the intervention of politicians who were able to agree on what was best for all and to work towards it. There was a remarkable degree of balance between the demand for goods, our ability to produce them, advances in technology necessary to drive the economy forward, and the involvement of most who wanted to work. This was entirely the consequence of coordinated efforts by governments to manage the economy with a specific moral end in mind. If only we had realized the merits of our achievements and the reasons for them. The period since 1973 has given ample pause for reflection, but rather than strive to rebuild what, through our own neglect, we lost, we have instead set out in a quite different direction.

The ascendancy of the *New Right* under the leadership of Ronald Reagan and Margaret Thatcher brought in governments which set out to defeat the perceived evil of inflation, which was regarded as the greatest enemy of the capital accumulator. This may have been conducted with reference to a new economic theory, that of *monetarism* as expounded by Professor Milton Friedman and others of the *Chicago School,* but the policies pursued, in the United States and Britain at least, appeared designed specifically to remedy the losses experienced by the wealthy capitalist class in the 1970s.

On both sides of the Atlantic, economic policy featured a shift in the burden of taxation from businesses and high-earners onto middle- and low-income groups, coupled with the deregulation of markets, and the sale of public assets into private hands, usually at knock-down prices, and often with accompanying subsidies as incentives to the private sector to buy. Internationally a new, if much narrower, consensus emerged, one that served the exclusive interests of the rich nations. With floating exchange rates established as the new norm, proponents of *neo-classical* economics urged the abandonment of all exchange controls, and governments duly obliged. The under-regulation which had been responsible for the economic chaos and social disaster of the inter-war years, and which the institutions set up at Bretton Woods were designed to contain, was firmly back in fashion.

What does this whistle-stop tour through economic history tell us about the prospects for future progress? Could we have avoided the repeated tendency for societies to polarize into rich and poor, usually to the point at which they are no longer viable? We can divide economic history into three distinct phases. In the first, the period before the discovery of agricultural surplus, when economic activity was quite unconscious, the limitations of nature and a poorly developed culture at least ensured a degree of equity, even if the quality of life was poor by modern standards. In the second phase, which lasted from the dawn of agriculture until the Enlightenment, just 200 years ago, although society and culture evolved considerably, the methods and outcomes of economic activity were largely unchanging: rights over private property, the successful pursuit of excessive wealth by a few individuals, and the exploitation of the labour of others, were the defining characteristics of economic activity.

Only since the Enlightenment have we begun to accept the need to consider economics in moral terms, and to understand that the conditions we create for economic activity have a direct bearing on the ability of individuals to provide for their basic needs: principally, that conditions which facilitate the rapid accumulation of vast wealth by a few, inevitably lead to great poverty among the many.

It was this newly acquired capacity to see economics in moral terms which shaped the political consensus among western nations in the decades after 1945, when considerable gains were made. All too quickly, however, the link between economics and morals was forgotten as a new generation of politicians conspired in the dismantling of that consensus, and rapidly created a quite different context for economic activity. And so, today, we find ourselves living with economic arrangements which are supposed to be conducive to the spread of opportunity and a reduction in levels of poverty, but which appear to have precisely the opposite effect.

As we shall learn, the failure of current global economic arrangements is the result of a flawed understanding of economic laws; there is, however, an alternative form of economy which promises conditions more favourable to progress. But first we must investigate further our current malaise, and determine whether, unlike our forebears, we are ready to embrace the implications of a new understanding of economics and the revised social order that would flow from it.

Today, there is just one criterion by which the success of economic activity is judged: that of growth measured in financial terms. If the economy is growing, that is to say the value of productive output is increasing, then economic activity is successful. Growth, it seems, is all that business people and political leaders care about. Target rates for inflation are part of the same objective, because high inflation rates downgrade the real value of economic growth. Until the mid-1970s, full employment was viewed as an important measure of economic success. This is no longer the case. Today, if a successful, growing, economy provides jobs for all who want them, then well and good. If it does not, and no industrial economies any longer do, then this is the unfortunate price that society, and the struggling unemployed, have to pay for a successful economy.

Growth has to be carefully managed. If the economy grows too quickly, it will soon 'overheat'. Increases in output will reach unsustainable levels, and the economy will go into recession. More people will become unemployed, less will be produced and sold, business profits will fall and government revenues will be reduced, forcing the government to borrow money to fund public expenditure on essential services such as health and education, and to provide welfare payments for the growing army of unemployed. This further constrains the economy, because high and growing levels of public debt mean higher interest rates, which increase costs to business. At some point the debt has to be repaid, so, once the economy recovers, the government has to raise more revenue, again eating into business profits.

Most experts and governments estimate a sustainable rate of growth for an industrial economy to be between 2½ and 3½ per cent annually. Economic growth can be measured in two ways: growth in the value of the output of national economies, or the combined growth of all nations: the global economy. It is the global economy, the fact of all national economies being in competition with each other, that places the first limit on economic growth for individual national economies. If the global economy enjoys 5 per cent growth in a given year, this figure is the aggregate of the growth from all national economies. While it is conceivable for all national economies to grow by 5 per cent to give the combined global figure, in reality this never happens. Over the last thirty years, economic growth figures have incorporated immense disparities from country to country and region to region. While growth in the industrialized nations has varied between 0 per cent and 4 per cent with occasional lapses into contraction, and in some of the newly industrialized countries of South-East Asia has shot up, temporarily, into double figures, many of the countries of the Third World have seen their economies steadily contract; they have experienced long-term recession.

Growth requires increases in the production and sale of goods and services. Any product or service for which there is effective demand – that is someone prepared to pay for it – is, assuming the business activity is honestly reported to the authorities, counted towards the measure of output. Increased revenues are dependent on the ability of entrepreneurs to identify and exploit new market opportunities. This process is subject to obvious constraints: there are limits on the rate at which we can improve productive efficiency. Human ingenuity takes time to evolve, as does technological innovation. Further, as we seem to have settled on an economic model which excludes millions of people, which sets quite strict limits on the creative aspirations of the majority, and leaves control over resources and decisions over how they are to be used to a small minority, our ability to convert the natural endowment of the planet into viable economic output is somewhat constrained. Under these circumstances, at any given moment, the amount of wealth in the world is fixed, and its rate of growth, year on year, is very limited. The only variable is how this slowly growing pot of wealth is to be divided up among the world's people.

We are frequently told that an economy based on the private ownership of land, free markets and the unhindered flow of capital across borders will provide the people of the poorer nations – three quarters of the global population – with the opportunity to pull themselves out of poverty by pursuing the same approach to economic expansion pursued in the rich countries. These claims deny the reality of the obvious limitation on global economic growth in an economy where access to productive resources is denied to so many people. Ted Trainer, who has researched trends in economic growth in great detail, gives a couple of statistics to illustrate the point. The period 1965 to 1984 was the most successful for economic growth across the Third World. Poor countries averaged growth of 2.8 per cent during that time, compared with a rich country average of 2.4 per cent.[6] Even if this success had continued (poor country economies have since gone into steep decline, while rich countries have pulled away sharply) and a similar ratio was maintained, it would take 500 years for the Third World to attain rich-world standards of living. Adjusting for anticipated population growth, Trainer calculates that if rich-country economies continue to grow at 3 per cent, then, for the poor countries to catch up by 2060, world output would have to grow by 88 times.[7] Four per cent growth in rich countries would require output to increase by a factor of 220.

The poorest in the world are often described as having to survive on less than a dollar a day, but this is not the whole picture. In Mozambique, one of the world's poorest countries, the economy is required to grow at 5 per cent for the next 60 years simply to bring average incomes up to a dollar a day. And this is the average: before the economically crippling floods of 2000, the Mozambican economy, at 10 per cent, was the fastest growing in Africa, but the majority of poor rural inhabitants saw no benefits whatsoever of this miracle growth.

Given the impossibility of such growth under prevailing economic arrangements, and the fact that the benefits of growth are generally only felt by a minority, unless redistributed through welfare measures funded by taxation, why do economists and politicians continue to argue that the growth model and further deregulation is the only route to reducing poverty? Even the World Bank has realized that this approach is unrealistic: in 2002, recognizing that, on current trends, by 2050 world economic output will be four times current levels, its chief economist, Nick Stern, said 'The $140 trillion world of five decades time simply cannot be sustained on current production and consumption patterns.'[8] Looking fifty years further ahead, Edward O. Wilson suggests that if we 'continue on the current path, by 2100 we will need four more planet Earths to sustain life as we know it'.[9]

Before we proceed, it is worth reminding ourselves of the link between economic growth and the capacity to provide for the basic needs of more people. Under prevailing arrangements, there is no link. If growth is the sole measure of economic success, and if the quickest route to growth is via economic arrangements which exclude many people from economic activity, then there is no incentive to create conditions which lead to more people being involved in the economy, and so enabling them to work to provide for their basic needs. Growth depends on markets, and markets are constituted through effective demand, or purchasing power. As long as growth is the sole objective of economic activity, only those goods will be produced for which there exists effective demand. If there is greater demand for, and the promise of greater profits in, luxury consumer goods and non-essentials such as mobile phones, playstations, faster and more luxurious cars and the like, then these are the products that will attract investment, even where there is some, albeit less profitable, demand for basic needs. Investment will be attracted only to those activities which promise greatest returns. Unless the poorest people in the world, those who have insufficient to eat and can afford neither decent clothing nor adequate shelter, stumble upon large quantities of cash, the global economy will not make provision for their basic needs.

Once again, why do its promoters persist in arguing that the current model of capitalism is the solution? They seem still to rely on the notion of a *trickle-down effect* whereby the benefits of economic growth are assumed eventually to filter through to the bottom of society. Most academics have long abandoned *trickle-down*, but politicians continue to espouse it. In Britain, during the nineteenth century, wealth did spread down the social scale as a large middle class emerged, but this was a consequence of Britain's great success in securing both the natural resources and the market opportunities provided by the greatest empire ever seen. If you control half the world's resources and markets, you really should be able to improve the living standards of most of your citizens. In the period 1945 to 1973, people in many of the countries of western Europe enjoyed unprecedented, continent-wide growth, again with a considerable spread of wealth among the wider population, but this was a direct consequence of huge external investment in the form of non-repayable Marshall Plan aid and redistributive taxation.

There are clear explanations in economic theory for the inevitable failure of the growth model to address poverty and social injustice, but these explanations are routinely ignored, both by those who argue for a solution based on growth and trickle-down, and by those who argue for a solution through redistributing wealth from the better off to the poor through taxation. Under current arrangements, we can succeed in growing the economy, but the means by which we do so necessarily exclude millions of people from the economy, and actively prevent the equitable distribution of the wealth created. And, as we are increasingly aware, it has serious consequences for our natural environment.

The potential impact of our neglect of the planet's ecology has implications not only for our capacity to improve basic needs provision, but for the very future of humankind. There are three elements to the environmental question: the fact of a depleting and finite resource base; the harm we are doing through the destruction of ancient ecological resources such as the rainforests; and the damage we are doing the atmosphere through pollution.

In the 1970s and 1980s, much was made of the finite nature of world oil reserves, and the need to begin planning for the time when oil-based energy production was no longer possible. Since then, the discovery of unanticipated further reserves has knocked concern over oil exhaustion off the agenda. Nonetheless, supplies remain finite. Best estimates of global supply – and geological techniques have improved so that no further unexpected finds are likely – is about 2,000 billion barrels, just 80 years' supply at current levels of consumption, and only ten years' supply were all people to consume at the current rate of the average American.[10] Even with only moderate growth in oil use, supplies will be exhausted well before the end of the century. And, as oil becomes scarce, prices will increase, with serious effects for the economy. As George

Monbiot points out, 'the last five recessions in the United States were all preceded by a rise in the oil price.'[11]

The burning of oil, natural gas and coal for energy accounts for 95 per cent of world energy production, and constitutes the single largest source of harmful carbon emissions into the atmosphere, which, nearly all scientists now agree, contributes significantly to global warming. At the current rate of warming, it is suggested that the ice-cap that has covered Antarctica for 35 million years will melt over the next two hundred years, raising sea levels by up to seventy metres. This is the worst-case scenario, but, even with more moderate rises in sea levels, there will still be considerable devastation and loss of human habitats. It will not just be the paradise islands of the Indian and Pacific Oceans which will disappear. Major cities like London, New York, Miami, Los Angeles, Tokyo, Sydney, Jakarta, Cape Town, Buenos Aires, Shanghai and Bombay will be severely affected. Mass evacuation and resettlement of people from the threatened areas is quite beyond our capability. The government of Tuvalu has already put into operation plans to evacuate its entire population. This string of Pacific islands will soon disappear under rising sea levels. Global warming will have claimed its first sovereign state, its people's history and their culture. The population will be spread far and wide, the first of a new breed of refugee whose land has been lost to the ocean.

We still seem quite unable to contemplate the action necessary to tackle carbon emissions and reduce global warming. The first six months of 2002 were the warmest in the northern Hemisphere since records began in 1843.[12] The amount of carbon dioxide – the principal greenhouse gas – in the atmosphere has grown from 279 parts per million (ppm) in 1663, to 325 ppm in 1970 and 371 ppm in 2001.[13] By 2050, unless we take urgent action to curb emissions, it will have doubled in less than four hundred years, after thousands of years without much variation. Since the Rio *Earth Summit* in 1992, when governments were supposed to have agreed on the importance of addressing this issue, emissions have grown by 9 per cent, and between 1997 and 2020 they are expected to grow by a total of 75 per cent.[14] Michael Meacher, speaking as British Environment Minister in 1999, said that 'It is our firm intention in the European Union to stabilize concentrations at 550 ppm.' He went on to acknowledge that even this would require cuts in emissions 'five or six times higher than we agreed at Kyoto'.[15]

But we have not even managed to implement the reductions agreed at Kyoto: George W. Bush says it is not in US economic interests, even though his own *National Academy of Science* provides the most frightening warning to date. Their 2002 report argues that global temperatures could well rise between 1.5 and 5.9 degrees celsius by 2100, in which case we will see the most rapid period of climate change in the last 10,000 years. Global temperatures today are only 5.5 degrees celsius higher than during the last ice age. We know the impact that rising temperatures have had over such a long period. Similar changes condensed into just one century will cause enormous damage. Further, the report reveals that sudden changes in climate and temperature are not uncommon:

> On the basis of the inference from the paleo-climactic record, it is possible that the projected change will occur not through gradual evolution, proportionate to greenhouse gas concentration, but through abrupt and persistent regime shifts affecting sub-continental or larger regions – denying the likelihood or downplaying the reality of past abrupt changes could be costly.[16]

Reporting this discovery, Jeremy Rifkin concludes, 'If qualitative climate change were to occur suddenly in the coming century – within less than ten years – as has happened many times before in geological history, we may already have written our epitaph.'[17]

Growth as a strategy for expanding basic needs provision is, on its own terms, simply not viable. When we add the issues of resource depletion and pollution, not only does growth fail as a strategy, it threatens a scenario in which the possibility of progress is rapidly reduced to zero. Not only are we hitting limits for expansion in material provision because the economic mechanism we apply leads us into unsustainable investment decisions, we are also in danger of compromising the material well-being of the people of the rich nations. If the situation is this desperate, why are we not investing in renewable and sustainable sources of energy as a matter of priority? For one reason only: under current economic arrangements, market forces do not support such investment.

Renewable forms of energy such as solar, wind and wave power are expensive. Although the long-term potential for cheap, endless and pollution free power is immense, the investment in research and development of technologies to bring these sources on-line in sufficient quantity and geographical coverage, whilst not beyond the capacity of global financial resources, simply does not meet the markets' criteria for investment. Money is attracted to those investment opportunities which promise reasonably low risk and high rewards in the short term. Solar power, at a unit cost of 20 US cents (compared with 2 cents for conventional power and 3½ cents for wind power)[18] will only become viable with heavy investment in research and development. Once it gets that investment, it will quickly become as cheap as other forms, and could provide all our energy needs without any impact on the planet's ecology. In Denmark, where the government has made considerable public investment in renewable energy, it already accounts for 20 per cent of all energy production.[19]

The German scientist Wolfram Zeigler has carried out detailed analysis in which he calculates long-term sustainable natural resource usage based on population levels and energy expenditure.[20] His research suggests that we passed the sustainable level around a century ago. This was also the point at which the rate of extinction of biological species began to increase exponentially. We are now consuming and destroying the life-supporting resources of the planet at a rate ten times that which is sustainable over the long term. This gives an indication of the magnitude of change required: imposing marginal limits on the rate of growth in carbon emissions will have no impact whatsoever.

The ecological problem is not about one group of human beings benefiting at the expense of another: unless we address the situation soon and seriously, all human life will be threatened. For the current model of economy to sustain itself, it needs growth which demands ever greater exploitation of the world's natural resources, especially fossil fuels. This means industrial practices which undermine shrinking water resources, and large-scale agricultural enterprise which reduces the amount of cultivable land and destroys rainforests, but still fails to feed all the world's people. The environmental problem cannot be solved within the prevailing economic framework which is why politicians are unable to address it seriously. The framework must be replaced with one that gives us some hope of saving the planet.

The prevailing model of economy cannot create conditions in which the demands of progress, as defined at the outset of this book, can be realised. We have described a system which, although at times reasonably successful, very often fails even on its own terms. It is certainly not a system that in its current form could ever provide for the basic needs of all people. Nonetheless, we must not ignore the positive achievements of recent economic advance, many of which we must build on if we are to bring about a more inclusive world.

Had we not learned the knack of progressive reinvestment of returns from economic activity, growth on the scale experienced over the last century would not have been possible. Real standards of living for many people in the industrialized countries have improved considerably, and this has raised the benchmark to which people the world over now aspire. But capitalism has set itself an impossible task, for it is in the nature of the system that these benefits remain so selective. Had we pursued economic growth under economic arrangements which required the inclusion of steadily more people, then the benefits would have been dispersed more widely.

Perhaps the greatest gift of the capitalist phase is that of techno-logical innovation: human technological ingenuity knows no bounds, but only through the availability of huge quantities of surplus capital, and the willingness of some to forego short-term gains, have we been able to exploit this potential so expertly.

Although some of the consequences of recent economic advance would have better been avoided, at least we can now make informed judgments and practical compromises based on accurate assessments of economic and technological potential, environmental constraints and the value we place on human well-being. And nothing that capitalism has gifted us, especially in the technological realm, need be rejected just because it was born of an iniquitous economic system. Any knowledge or experience that can be integrated into a sustainable and equitable world order should be, regardless of its origin.

Capital has also funded progressive advance in the shape of medical breakthroughs. Unfortunately, investment is generally attracted only by the prospect of high medium-term returns, and so drugs are developed to treat rich-country ailments and save thousands of lives, rather than poor-country ones which could save millions. Nonetheless, the example of what we can do in terms of applying technology to improving human well-being has been set, and it would not have happened without capitalism.

Much technological advance has been driven by the demands of the military, and also by space exploration, neither of which have much to do with advancing human well-being; but again, we should not condemn the benefits in knowledge and capability that these dubiously motivated efforts have yielded: we just need to learn how to apply these wondrous technologies to more inclusive ends.

There is no doubt that the competitive culture on which capitalism depends does much to motivate many people to excel. It taps a pool of creative endeavour that may never have been revealed had our form of social organization been less ambitious. Progressive social change requires us to acknowledge the need for individual motivation and creative drive, and to understand the dynamics of the interface between the individual psyche and the form of social organization. Capitalism has given us indications of human ingenuity and potential, but we now need to adapt and build on this legacy in order to bring the talents and poten-tial of all people into the economy.

Whilst the capitalist phase may have introduced us to our full potential, save for a brief and untypical period after 1945, it has done so in ways that deny this potential to the vast majority of humans. Since 1973, when the post-war consensus was brought to an abrupt end, cap-italism has changed from a moderated force for social progress into an untempered monster, quite uninterested in the imperative of human collective well-being. Whether the pre-1973 position was sustainable is debatable. As the horrors of war and the holocaust passed into more distant memory, and as a new and differently motivated generation of political leaders came to power, the lessons of history gradually lost their power. But capitalism has, nonetheless, underwritten the possibility of progress. It has provided us with the means to build a better world; at the same time, by its very mechanisms, it has prevented us from applying them to this end.

The survival of capitalism in its current, self-defeating form is explained by a number of factors: the emergence of democracy as a moral check on its worst excesses; the greed and hypocrisy of many capitalists who are never too proud to accept public handouts when they over-stretch themselves; the success of its advocates in convincing people that there is no alternative; the noble motives of ordinary people who staff and fund charitable endeavour; and the adoption by governments of redistributive policies which have ensured a spread of wealth further down the social scale than would otherwise have been the case. What gains in human welfare we have enjoyed since the industrial revolution may not have occurred without capitalism, but they certainly would not have been achieved had the economy been left completely to its own devices.

Today's economic difficulties are not problems of production or technology. They are problems of allocation and distribution: they stem from the growing concentration of ownership of productive resources, and they persist because of the reluctance of politicians to seek a secure foundation in economic theory for their policies. Since the industrial revolution we have faced a choice: unreliable productive output with equitable distribution, or reliable and growing output with grossly inequitable distribution. As we shall learn, two centuries of industrial advance have brought us to a position where we can choose to feed, clothe, house and involve all humans beings in the global economy under a hybrid system which combines reliable output *and* equitable distribution. There need be no return to a pre-industrial economy. Communities will respond differently to the dual goals of reliable output and equitable distribution depending on their circumstances. Once we agree on the merits of a sustainable and inclusive global order, and recognize that we can set different objectives for the economy, we can begin to devise the structures required to fulfil our ambition. All we need do is decide that it is worth doing, and persuade the few who stand to lose financially that they have a moral duty to forego their ever-increasing wealth for the sake of the planet and all its inhabitants, including themselves.

It is, fundamentally, a moral question: several of the scenarios I have used to illustrate the consequences of a growth strategy for poverty reduction hypothesize a world in which the developing countries are miraculously assisted, through the power of the market, global trade and free enterprise, to catch up to the level of industrialized countries. Let us be clear, *under current economic arrangements this is completely out of the question*. It will not and cannot happen without fundamental changes in the way we organize the economy. This being so, any alternative strategy which is not governed by the dual imperatives of improved basic-needs provision and the sustainable exploitation of natural resources has huge moral implications. Once we are fully aware that the plight of the homeless and the hungry, and the fate of the planet, are as much a direct consequence of the 'success' of our economic system, as is the comfort and security of the fortunate few in the industrialized world, then we cannot avoid the moral aspect of any decision to support or accept the prevailing economic order. The nature of contemporary capitalism makes moral decisions for us which we cannot overturn until we reject the logic of the system itself. As long as we support it in anything like its current form, we condone worsening economic polarization, we condemn hundreds of millions to misery, and we guarantee that the human race can survive only a few more generations, as the means to life are exhausted and the environment destroyed. Under these circumstances, it will serve this project well to examine in detail the state of the world and the condition of its people.

4

The State of the World

IF PROGRESS means change then we need to be clear about what needs changing and why. We need to confront reality, however painful, and however much we would rather avoid it. One of the biggest obstacles to progress is the extent to which the scope and scale of human suffering is misrepresented and therefore underestimated by most people. We struggle to reconcile the received image of an improving and caring world with the reality of immense and widespread human suffering. The facility through which we avoid the truth prevents us from generating the moral will actively to pursue a more inclusive and equitable world. Just as psychologists have identified denial of the occurrence or meaning of personal experiences as detrimental to the health of the individual psyche, so denial of social reality hinders us from confronting the problems of the modern world. I make no apologies, therefore, for the fact that this chapter does not make easy reading. It is not intended to be depressing: rather, it should provoke incredulity and anger, and hopefully a determination to do something about the hideous social injustice that blights our supposedly civilized world.

The rate of population growth over the last century has been quite remarkable: the world's population currently stands at 6.3 billion, double its level in 1960, and it continues to rise by about eighty million people each year. Half of all humans are under 25; of these a billion are already adults, which means the next generation of parents is the largest group on the planet. Over the last thirty years, however, the predicted rate of population growth has fallen from 2.4 per cent to 1.3 per cent, and the United Nations has revised downwards its forecast for the global population in 2050 from 9.4 billion to 8.9 billion. Although reduced fertility is playing a part, one third of this reduction is due to increasing mortality rates – more people dying younger in Africa and the Asian subcontinent – as a consequence of the spread of HIV/AIDS, malnutrition, malaria, and the return of diseases such us cholera and tuberculosis which had previously been under control in many parts of the Third World.

Population growth in the industrialized nations has ground to a halt: only in the United States will the population continue to grow into the next century because of high levels of immigration, and the tendency of poorer immigrant groups to have larger families. In the Third World, population growth continues unabated. Africa has seen a threefold increase in just four decades, and continues to grow fastest. In Asia, the population has doubled in the same period. Over the last fifty years, fertility – the average number of children born per woman of child-bearing age – has fallen to just under three across the Third World, but only negligibly in sub-Saharan Africa, where poverty is greatest, from 6½ to 5½.[1] It is well established that people choose to have fewer children as they perceive an improvement in their economic security. It is not surprising, therefore, that the poorest region of the world continues to experience the highest rate of population growth. Lack of access to contraception continues to be a major factor: of the 175 million pregnancies occurring each year, 50 per cent are unplanned. Compared with boys, very few girls in poor countries get any education; where they do there is evidence that they are able to take more effective control over their fertility.

Is there a level of population, or a rate of change in population, that would, over time, enable a greater proportion to satisfy their basic needs? There is considerable evidence that individual decisions about the number of children to have is influenced by perception of the likely economic return. Among populations where children cost their parents more to bring up than they expect to get back as a contribution to their own welfare once their offspring have grown up, the number of children per family goes down. Conversely, where a larger family promises improved long-term welfare, people have more children. These strategies are disastrous when employed by whole populations. What is encouraging, however, is that people do appear to act on perceptions when they make reproductive decisions: human breeding is not a completely arbitrary process, although poor access to effective family planning for many women continues to add an unnecessary degree of uncertainty.

Some suggest that a growing population is evidence that things are in order. They often point to Thomas Malthus, the British economist who, in his 1798 *Essay on the Principle of Population,* argued that populations were self-regulating in relation to the capacity of the land to feed people. Contemporary followers of Malthus suggest that, if the population really was beyond the means of the planet, it would start falling towards an equilibrium level. But this argument ignores the huge advances in technology of the last two hundred years. The world of which Malthus wrote is not the world of today, and his theories were dubious even for his own time because he neglected to consider the mediating role of culture.

Advances in agriculture and the intensification of food production led directly to an increase in fertility, but, although more babies were born, the increase in food production was often insufficient to feed the growing population. Improved agriculture had the effect of worsening the balance between fertility levels and survival into adulthood. So the mechanism of Malthus' equilibrium model was forced out of alignment. Fertility and maternal health improved, food production increased, but so did mortality. Through our inability to distribute the benefits of economic progress more equitably, we created the conditions to bring more people into the world, only to fail to provide for their basic needs, and leave many of them to die as infants. Malthus was right: if people are denied the food they need they will die, but he was wrong about the causes of food scarcity. In the modern world, it is more often a problem of allocation than production. And he was wrong about the capacity of 'the struggle for survival' to keep the population at sustainable levels. There is a highly complex relationship between fertility, the political economy of food allocation, mortality rates and life expectancy, and population growth; and this before we consider the reproductive aspirations of individuals, and the biological and cultural factors which influence them.

Ernest Gellner suggested that it was the move from agrarian to industrial economies that broke the Malthusian ceiling on population growth.[2] With industrialization, economies could ensure productive output kept ahead of population growth. What we see today in poor countries is a quite different picture. Partial dissemination of the technology of industrialization to all corners of the globe has been crucial in raising fertility and improving maternal health. But it has not been extended to ensuring that the consequent acceleration in births is matched by a similar rise in the numbers of lives which remain viable beyond infancy. Poor countries receive only small quantities of the technological inputs that rich countries take for granted. Much of this is provided through the well-intentioned programmes of aid agencies, and motivated by a desire to reduce suffering. But the net effect, especially when so many resources are directed at pre- and post-natal health care, is to introduce more suffering by ensuring a population explosion which condemns many millions each year to premature deaths. Botswana provides an example of this one-sided Malthusian effect. Although a quarter of the population is infected with HIV and life expectancy has fallen from 62 to 40 in the last decade, the population will still double by 2050 as a result of high fertility rates.

Even though Malthus' nightmare vision was never likely to restrain human population growth, the gap between fertility and the means to survival has a tremendous impact on people's lives. Currently, around 30,000 children die each day from preventable causes.[3] Most of these young lives are lost in the poor countries of the southern hemisphere, where the routine experience of hardship and misery does nothing to moderate either the suffering of a dying toddler, or the torment of grieving, powerless parents. AIDS continues to devastate large parts of the world, with eleven people becoming infected with HIV every minute.[4] The provision of minimum standards of nutrition, health care and education could help reduce these problems. We have the understanding, the resources and the technology; all we lack is the collective will. Malthus got it wrong because he misconceived the relation between fertility and survival; but perhaps we should forgive him for failing to anticipate the capacity of modern society to bring ever greater numbers into the world and not bother to do anything about the quality or length of those lives.

Of the 6.3 billion humans alive today, 80 per cent, or 4.8 billion, live in poor countries, the majority of them in conditions that most westerners would find intolerable. Half lack basic sanitation, a third have no access to clean water, a quarter have inadequate housing, and a fifth have no access to health services. Half have no access to essential drugs, and a third of all children are undernourished.[5] These figures are not based on standards that might be applied in industrialized countries, they reflect expected levels of provision for poorer countries, and are assessed on what is considered possible and achievable, given the constraints of an agricultural economy.

Since 1945, the global economy has grown fivefold, but this growth has brought no reduction in poverty levels, which are now growing steadily, however and wherever they are measured. In 1960, the richest fifth of the world's population enjoyed incomes 30 times those of the poorest fifth. By 1998, the difference had grown to 78 times.[6] The richest 20 per cent now receive 85 per cent of all income, and average consumption among this fortunate group is 17 times that of the poorest *half* of the global population. The poorest 50 countries have seen their combined income decline to less than 2 per cent of the global total[7]: they are home to more than a billion people, most of whom survive on less than a dollar a day; 2.8 billion people survive on less than $2 a day.[8] In Europe, the average rate of subsidy for each *cow* runs at $2.20 a day.[9] This gives some idea of our economic priorities: we are prepared to pay more in agricultural subsidies to keep uneconomic cows alive than we are to feed, clothe and house nearly half of the world's people.

This widening gap is not a short-term trend, but it is accelerating: two hundred years ago, average incomes in the rich countries were only 1½ times those of the poorest; in 1960 they were twenty times, and by 1980 the ratio was 46 to 1. In 1800 per capita income in Britain was three times that of Africa. Today the per capita income of Switzerland is 80 times that of South Asia.[10] Average household expenditure in Africa is now 20 per cent less than it was 25 years ago.[11] In the same period Africa's share of world trade fell from 4 per cent to 1½ per cent.[12] The assets of the world's top three billionaires now exceed the combined incomes of the 48 poorest nations, which are home to 600 million people.[13] These extremes are illustrated in figures for private consumption, where the world's richest countries, with 20 per cent of global population, account for 86 per cent of total private consumption, whereas the poorest 20 per cent of the world's people account for just 1.3 per cent.

Of the 45 countries classified by the United Nations as least developed, 32 are in sub-Saharan Africa and it is the extent to which this region is drifting further away from the rest of the world that gives most cause for concern. Excluding South Africa, these countries are inhabited by 500 million people, but their combined income is less than that of Belgium, which is home to just eleven million. Living standards in Sierra Leone are at levels last experienced in Europe 600 years ago.[14]

Suffering in the Third World does not end when reports of famine drift out of the news. In fact, those who fall victim to these geographically concentrated disasters represent only a small fraction of the lives lost each year. More than ten million children die annually, most as a result of poor nutrition or lack of basic health care. This is the equivalent of a hundred jumbo jets full of infants crashing every day of the year. Most of these are miserable, lingering deaths, desperate experiences for the victims and their families. Three children die each minute from malaria. We know how malaria spreads, we know what is necessary to prevent it, but still there are half a billion cases each year worldwide. According to a study from Harvard University, if Malaria had been eliminated in 1965 (and it could have been) Africa's annual economic output today would be $100 billion higher.[15]

In sub-Saharan Africa there is one doctor per 18,000 people. This compares with a Third World average of one doctor per 7,000 people and a rich country ratio of 1 to 390.[16] More than a million children die each year from measles, which is easily prevented; and diseases such as cholera, tuberculosis and bubonic plague, which had been eradicated from many areas, are now returning to claim thousands of lives. Each year, half a million babies die from tetanus, mainly through lack of a sterile razor blade to cut the umbilical chord. The impact of AIDS continues to grow: of the forty million estimated to be carrying the HIV virus worldwide, 90 per cent live in the Third World, two thirds of them in sub-Saharan Africa; they include more than a million children. In 1994, the United Nations Children's Fund (UNICEF) predicted that, by 1999, five million African children would have lost their mothers to

AIDS.[17] In fact, by the end of 2000, thirteen million African children had lost *both* their parents to the disease.[18] Ten per cent of all AIDS orphans in Africa live in households headed by other children. Many of South Africa's 700,000 AIDS orphans are neglected, ill and starving according to a report by the Nelson Mandela Children's Fund.[19] A third of infants born to infected mothers are HIV positive; their life expectancy is just two years. Teenage girls are five times more likely to contract HIV than boys, largely because the virus is far more readily transmitted from male to female. AIDS currently kills two million and infects a further four million Africans each year. Worldwide, in less than 20 years, it has killed more than 22 million people, four million of whom were children.

In Botswana in 2001, 40 per cent of all adults, 45 per cent of pregnant women and 56 per cent of those aged 25 to 29 were infected with HIV. By 2010 life expectancy will have fallen to just 27 years, down from 65 in 1992.[20] In neighbouring South Africa it will be 41 years, down from 63.[21] In Russia rates of infection are doubling every year. By 2007, four million Russians will be infected;[22] and some forecasts suggest that infections in China could rise to ten million by 2010.[23]

The Caribbean, although home to many fewer people, has the second highest rate of infection after Africa. India has 4½ million people infected with HIV,[24] but with a dense and growing population, and uneven development across the country, this could grow rapidly. There is concern that a critical point will soon be reached, past which control of the epidemic will be impossible. One assessment forecasts that there will be 15 million HIV infections in India by 2015.[25] AIDS usually strikes people in the prime of life, with devastating effects on the economies of these already impoverished societies, as the disease removes many of the most productive young women and men from the workforce. Death from AIDS usually involves appalling, drawn-out suffering which is only partially alleviated by the most advanced drugs and technology. In the Third World, most of those who die with AIDS receive no professional care whatsoever.

The scale of death from AIDS likely in the early decades of the twenty-first century is unparalleled since smallpox wiped out the North American Indians in the sixteenth century and plague decimated much of Europe two centuries earlier. The impact of AIDS on life expectancy, the principle measure of long-term social and economic development, could well be to reverse the advances of the last 50 years in many parts of the world. The situation is not necessarily hopeless, however. In Thailand and The Philippines, where the governments have invested heavily and worked closely with non-government organizations to educate people and distribute millions of condoms, despite worrying signs a decade ago, the epidemic seems to have been contained. In Uganda a dynamic government campaign stressing the benefits of both abstention and safe sex is paying dividends. These successes come at a cost, however: Thailand spends the equivalent of 55 US cents per person each year combating the spread of AIDS; Uganda three times as much. India will have to find ways to increase its investment from the current 17 cents per person if it is to stave off social and economic disaster. A further 68 million lives will be lost to AIDS over the next twenty years.[26] We could stop the spread of AIDS in poor counties, but at present we seem unwilling to bear the cost.

Worldwide 800 million people lack sufficient and regular supplies of food; 500 million of them are chronically malnourished.[27] Many are victims of what experts term the *food security paradox,* whereby many children in poor countries grow up surrounded by surplus food production to which they have no access, the food growing around them being sold for consumption at the tables of Europe and North America. Developing country governments have no alternative: it is the only way they can generate sufficient funds to service the interest on foreign debts. In early 2002, India had a record grain surplus of 59 million tonnes, but half of Indian children remained malnourished.[28]

As populations grow, and poor environmental management leads to accelerating desertification, falling quantities of cropland per person are cause for considerable concern. But the food problem is not one of absolute scarcity, and it need not become so. We already produce enough food to provide everyone on the planet with an adequate diet, but we produce much of it in the wrong places, and we do the wrong things with it. We feed it to animals to produce meat, when an acre planted with cereals can produce five times the nutritional value of one devoted to meat production; half of all grain is fed to cattle for meat. If Americans reduced their meat consumption by just 10 per cent, the productive capacity freed up by the reduced demand for cattle feed would yield enough food for 60 million humans.[29] If they wasted a third less food each day, they could feed the entire population of North Korea.[30]

Current patterns of food production do little for the poor and hungry. The countries of the European Union import twice as much food from the Third World as they export to it. Much of this is cocoa to make chocolate, but of the money spent on chocolate in Britain each year, 15 per cent goes to the UK government in taxes whilst only 8 per cent reaches the cocoa growers.[31] In India, where the population has passed one billion and continues to grow at 1.6 per cent annually, 390 million people cannot afford enough food, and have to survive on a less than a dollar *a week*.[32] India has one of the world's most successful agricultural economies: reallocation of less than 10 per cent of its food production would end hunger.[33] This is all in stark contrast to the United States where a staggering 64 per cent of the adult population are overweight, and 30 per cent are officially regarded as obese.[34]

It does not have to be like this. In 1970 Africa fed itself, but by 1984 more than a quarter of Africans depended on imported grain. At base the problem is one of effective demand: the poor and hungry have no money to buy food, and an ever greater share of food production is being brought into the formal economy. Global capitalism sustains itself by commodifying more and more of economic activity, whilst at the same time excluding more of the population from involvement. This is nowhere better illustrated than in food production.

There are two types of solution on offer. One, advocated by multinational firms, involves high-tech inputs and the development and use of genetically modified (GM) crops. Were they to prove effective and not harmful to the environment, technological innovations like GM may, one day, have a role to play; but if the problem is not the volume of food produced, but rather where it is produced, and where control over the food economy lies, then strategies like GM, which may improve yields but which always cede control to multinational companies, are unlikely to help. *Sustainable agriculture* advocates a quite different strategy which already shows signs of success where it has been tried. It aims to increase yields in areas where food production falls short of demand by introducing cheap, low-tech innovations, which do not damage the environment. Of course, these new technologies have to be supplied to farmers at low cost. Indeed, the whole approach is quite antithetical to the thrust of global capitalism. It is a strategy that succeeds in feeding more people, in turn stimulating the local economy and building strong communities, and one that protects the environment for future generations.

Technology-based solutions like GM may increase food yields in some areas in the short term, but they can only widen the divide between the well fed and the hungry. We know the cause of world hunger: it is the inevitable outcome of current economic arrangements, and we have ample evidence that more of the same high-tech, capital-intensive, rich-country-controlled strategies are misguided. The solution offered by *sustainable agriculture* is an excellent example of progress through bringing the world and its people back into productive balance. As George Monbiot says, sustainable agriculture requires lots of labour, no debt, and no help from predatory corporations.[35] Only by such means can the world's poor maintain control over their food supply and protect themselves from technologies such as genetic modification. Current rich-country policy consists mainly of changes in the rules of international trade which favour agricultural producers in the rich countries at the expense of small-scale sustainable farming in the Third World.

The biggest threat to food provision in the coming century is posed by the shortage of water. 40 per cent of the world's people suffer serious and regular shortages.[36] In many poor countries the proportion of the population with access to safe drinking water is already falling. Across the planet, the rate of depletion of fresh-water ecosystems is 6 per cent per year.[37] This is the rate at which we are losing naturally occurring, self-sustaining sources of fresh water, which cannot be artificially recreated. Currently, about 7 per cent of people do not have enough water to survive.[38] Some forecasts suggest this could rise to 70 per cent by 2050.[39] As world population has tripled over the last seventy years, water use has increased at twice that rate, and is now doubling every twenty years. Although less than 1 per cent of the world's water is accessible and drinkable, there is still enough, on average, to meet the requirements of a global population forecast to peak at nine million in 2050. But its distribution is uneven: too much where populations are already falling, and insufficient where they are growing. In India, the rate at which water is drawn from natural sources is twice that at which nature is able to replenish it.

Most of the growth in water use is industry-related: it takes 25,000 gallons to produce one car; a nuclear power station can use up to thirty million gallons a day, and the United States computer industry needs 440 billion gallons a year.[40] There are concerns that disputes over water between countries which share access to rivers and inland lakes may turn into full-scale wars. Without a major shift towards cooperative and equitable solutions to economic problems, such conflicts seem inevitable. The Middle East is one of the most badly affected areas, and, as the struggle to bring peace to that region continues, the question of access to water will be paramount. Whether shortages of essential resources are due to a combination of absolute scarcity and poor management, as in the case of water, or a matter of relative scarcity resulting from an inequitable economic system, as with food, there can be no solution as long as the basis of political relations between nations is competitive and aggressive. Our leaders need to realize that common problems can only be solved cooperatively. Unless priorities are reassessed, people in most parts of the world, not just the poorest countries, will feel the impact of the global water shortage. But as leading water scientist Peter Gleick asserts, we have the capacity, through carefully judged, cooperative and sustainable efforts to bring clean water for drinking, food preparation and sanitation to 95 per cent of the world's people by 2035.[41]

Although Third World school-enrolment levels have risen over the last thirty years, 115 million children are still not in primary education, 70 per cent of them girls.[42] A further 150 million start school but drop out within four years.[43] Of those of secondary school age, 275 million are denied the opportunity to learn. In sub-Saharan Africa, the situation is deteriorating, with many fewer children in school at the end of the 1990s than at the beginning. One in three African children studies in a classroom with no blackboard.[44] For those in education, schooling is severely undermined by pupil-teacher ratios. The average class size in the Third World is 45 children; in Bangladesh it is 63, and in Chad 67.[45] Adult literacy rates are falling: more than a quarter of adults in poor countries, nearly a billion people, cannot read or write.[46] In Africa, one third of men and two thirds of women are illiterate.

Deteriorating long-term trends are one thing, but the global changes of recent years have seen a tangible reduction in the quality of life for many in these poor countries. For twelve years after gaining independence in 1975, the people of Mozambique found the cost of feeding the average family within their means. Today, average earnings do not cover half the nutritional needs of the same families, although the shops are full of luxury imported items. The requirements of the World Bank's economic adjustment programmes have exposed the frail economies of the poorest countries to competition in world markets, for which they are ill prepared, and have forced cuts in public investment which have hit health and education hardest of all. They have also brought rapid economic polarization: the richest 10 per cent in these countries now claim a third of incomes, the poorest 40 per cent less than a sixth, and the gap, once again, is widening.[47] Over the last twenty years the poorest 10 per cent of the world's people saw no increase whatsoever in their incomes.[48] Many African cities, where until recently crime against property was a rare occurrence, are now in the grip of an epidemic of banditry and burglary from which no one is safe. In South Africa, still a Third World country beyond the confines of its glitzy shopping malls and heavily fortified middle-class suburbs, levels of rape and other violent crime are the highest in the world. One in three South African women can expect to be raped during her lifetime, and three quarters say sexual violence is common where they live. Only 1 in 400 rapes lead to a conviction.[49]

The plight of the poorest, the majority among the five billion in poor countries, is often attributed to bad luck or misfortune. Many people believe that wealth and security come to those who merit it. In reality, the situation of the world's poor is closely tied to that of the rich: the political and economic factors that have delivered the goods so spectacularly to many in rich countries are precisely those that have condemned millions to misery elsewhere. The enlightened period that began in 1945 should, and could, have marked a new and hopeful beginning for the nations which constituted the empires and colonies of the European powers. Instead, no sooner had one form of subordination ended, than many of these states became pawns in the front line of the cold war, as the United States and the Soviet Union waged an ideological battle for the soul of humankind. This they did by supporting unelected and often despotic rulers who could be relied on to run their countries in the interests of their superpower sponsors in return for a blind eye being turned to whatever slice of the national wealth these autocrats felt themselves entitled.

Nonetheless, considerable advances were seen in many newly independent countries during the 1960s. For a while the spirit of cooperation that characterized the post-war period extended to many of the countries of the Third World. Notable improvements in maternal and child mortality rates, literacy levels and life expectancy were achieved very quickly. But, if the 1973 oil crisis had set the agenda for the reversal of 25 years of social gains in the rich countries, then for the poorer countries its impact was far worse.

After the hike in oil prices, oil purchasers had to liquidate assets to pay their bills, and the international banking system was soon awash with cash. Great amounts of wealth were creamed off the economies of the rich countries and into the bank accounts of Arab oil producers and Saudi princes. The blanket had been pulled from under the world economy, and it would be a decade before confidence was restored. The deep recession which followed meant there was no application to which this huge quantity of potential investment capital could profitably be put, and so it was lent to the governments and enterprises of the Third World.

The vast majority of these loans would not have been made under normal circumstances. There were no guarantees, and little evidence, that the beneficiaries would be able to repay them. It was always likely that much of the money would be poorly invested, or misappropriated by ruling elites, few of which were democratically accountable. Even without such concerns, the chances of these countries earning the foreign exchange revenues necessary to meet their repayments was compromised by the deep recession in the rich country markets into which they would have to sell their goods. Massive loans were nonetheless made under the principle of *Sovereign Debt,* the peculiar belief that loans to national governments were ultimately risk-free, as a country could not become bankrupt. There was no way this transfer of funds from the rich world to the poor world could have the effect of redistributing the capacity to create wealth: it was too rapid, unplanned and dubiously motivated. By 1982, there was a serious threat of loan defaults. If the poor countries were going to keep up their repayments, they would need further loans. To avoid a global financial meltdown these funds were provided. As a result, total Third World debt rose from $100 billion in 1970 to $600 billion ten years later, $1,600 billion in 1990 and $2,000 billion in 1997.[50] Much of this additional cash was lent under the auspices of the International Monetary Fund (IMF) and its structural adjustment programmes. These made loans conditional on domestic policies within recipient countries, which were intended to adjust their economies to reflect their true level of wealth relative to that of the rich nations. In doing this, or so the theory suggested, these countries would be put on a sound financial and economic footing from which they could assume an equal and effective role on the world economic stage. What the theorists neglected to consider was that, according to virtually all measures, these nations were way behind the rich countries in their economic development. A policy of levelling the global playing field, especially when most poor countries were heavily indebted to the rich, could only condemn the people of these countries to deepening poverty.

The policy was the reverse of that which had prevailed before 1973, when the thrust of development policy was to acknowledge the consequences of relative economic and industrial underdevelopment and to offer support in ways that would enable the gradual integration of these economies without further compromising the well-being of their populations. Under the new regime, in order to secure the loans necessary to service spiralling debt, Third World governments were forced to slash public expenditure, in the process destroying gains made in health and education, and to freeze public-sector wages at below subsistence levels, so that the best people would leave for better-paid jobs in the private sector, and the rest would be forced to take second and third jobs in order to feed their families.

A further feature of structural adjustment programmes is the privatization of state enterprises. Many of these firms were run for the benefit of a political elite, and were recipients of many of the original western loans, never repaid. However, in order to sell them to the private sector – often controlled by the same elites now divested of their state nomenclature – governments routinely take over responsibility for the international debt. The people responsible for incurring the original debts, mismanaging its investment and defaulting on loan repayments are now, thanks to the IMF, able to pick up the assets of these enterprises for a nominal sum, their debts conveniently relieved, instead to be shouldered by the poor taxpayer.

This *socialization of debt* is a growing feature of the global economy. It has been estimated that 95 per cent of Indonesia's $80 billion debt is owned, or was incurred, by fifty individuals. It is being repaid by the state, with the cost being borne by the general population, few of whom ever felt the benefits of the original loans. Under current economic arrangements, when investors lend money which is invested successfully, they get to keep the returns. When the investments go sour, the state, or the IMF, bails them out. Export credit guarantees are offered by all rich-country governments to private banks and corporations, by which the taxpayer underwrites the risk attached to loans for investment in poor countries. Big business, in league with politicians, now routinely appropriates the tax dollars of ordinary people to underwrite its risky investments. It is grossly unjust and undemocratic, yet it is regarded as a perfectly legitimate aspect of the economic system. By these means, it is the poor of the Third World, and the struggling taxpayers of the rich countries, who guarantee the economic security of the wealthy and privileged.

There is a growing sense of moral outrage at the injustice of the debt crisis, and many have signed up to campaigns to write off the debt. These campaigns have made reference to the *clean-slate proclamations* of ancient civilizations, arguing that governments today should be as enlightened as early rulers in recognising the consequences of the accumulation of wealth into the hands of a small minority. Such clean-slate proclamations fell out of favour around four thousand years ago, since which time the direction of political economy has been towards the justification, legitimation and protection of unequal wealth. But there have been some notable exceptions. As Noam Chomsky reminds us, when the United States took over Cuba in 1898, it cancelled Cuba's debt to Spain, arguing that the burden 'was imposed on the people of Cuba without their consent and by force of arms'.[51] Debts incurred by previous administrations came to be known as *odious debts*, and were routinely written off as colonies changed hands during the late colonial period. Not any more. Perhaps the most odious recent example is that of post-apartheid South Africa, where Nelson Mandela inherited $18 billion of debt from the apartheid regime, little of which was invested for the good of the black majority.

Even if the full amount of $2 trillion of Third World debt was abolished – and there is no sign of this: commitments so far amount to only a few billion, and these offers come with heavy conditions – it would be only the beginning of a solution. Cheap privatizations and the decimation of health and education services mean that poor-country economies are less prepared than ever to compete on the global stage.

The impact of debt, misdirected investments and structural adjustment have enabled multinational corporations to move into struggling economies and sweep up assets at prices way below their true value. The returns on the investments of multinationals in poor countries are mainly remitted back to the rich nations. Even where productive resources remain in local hands, and poor-country economies are able to develop efficient enterprises, there is still the problem of finding markets. At home there is little effective demand, and abroad, where there are potential buyers, trade regulations are weighted heavily in favour of the rich countries, so that access to the most lucrative markets is heavily restricted.

Many former advocates of *structural adjustment* now admit that as a poverty reduction policy it has failed completely. As Joseph Stiglitz, former chief economist at the World Bank, said of IMF policies towards poor country economies, 'Structural adjustment suggests they're out of kilter, that they need a nose job. My point is they're poor and they need more money to be less poor.'[52] Few experts, however, have dared to acknowledge what seems obvious to the impartial observer: that the entire thrust of global economic policy is geared to guaranteeing the privileged position of a small minority through the undermining of the economies of the poor nations. Whether this process was premeditated is impossible to know, but if the rich and powerful of the world had set out deliberately to secure an ever-increasing slice of global wealth for themselves, they could not have planned and executed a more effective scheme.

Whilst the political leaders of rich countries have dictated the terms of global economics to suit their own wealthy, many willing accomplices have emerged among the tiny privileged minorities of the poor countries. The starkest and most distressing disparities in wealth are to be found in many Third World capitals, where the conspicuous indulgence of the rich, and their gleeful ostentation amidst the dreadful suffering of their compatriots, is as galling as anything seen in Europe or the United States a century ago. It gives little hope that, even if the balance of economic possibilities was tipped in favour of the poor countries, those who rule them would be especially inclined to work towards reducing the chasm that separates the handful of haves from the millions of have-nots.

Compared with those of Africa, the nations of Latin America are in a different league and have enjoyed considerable economic growth. But still, a million children die annually from preventable causes and seven million remain undernourished. Rio de Janeiro boasts some of the most exclusive residential neighbourhoods in the world, yet slavery is a growing problem in Brazil: not just the employment of people under exploitative conditions, but of people being forced to work under threat of death.[53] Many thousands are so incarcerated, and transported hundreds of miles from their homes to clear forests and work the ranches of elite landowners who sell their beef for fast-food hamburgers.

Venezuela's natural endowment of oil and gas has generated income of $300 billion dollars over the last twenty years and the country now enjoys income per head of population equal to that of Greece, but 71 per cent of its people still live in poverty.[54] The boom years that saw many Argentineans increase their standard of living have ended abruptly and rudely deposited many thousands back into the ranks of the poor, with the added pain of their dreams shattered: 50 per cent of Argentineans now live below the poverty line. To the north, Mexico is able to boast the world's fastest rate of growth in billionaires; their combined wealth is equal to that of the poorest seventeen million of their compatriots.[55] Real wages in Mexico fell by 52 per cent between 1980 and 1994, *before* the currency collapse of 1995 which left millions destitute.[56] The scale of the problem in Latin America is small in comparison with those of Africa and Asia, but the inability of prevailing economic orthodoxy to countenance any alternative is absolute. And so the majority of Latin Americans will continue to slide deeper into poverty, and the semi-established middle class will never experience real economic security.

The crash of August 1997 exposed the economic miracle of the South-East Asian *Tiger* economies for what it really was: an example of how global capitalism can bring false hope to millions, and lead economists and politicians into acts of quite unbelievable self-delusion. No region, at any time in history, has experienced and survived an explosion of growth on the scale experienced by Hong Kong, Singapore, Taiwan and South Korea in the last quarter of the twentieth century. The 'miracle' began with massive cold-war motivated aid to Taiwan and South Korea in the post-war period. In the 1950s, aid to Taiwan was equivalent to 95 per cent of its trade surplus, whilst between 1945 and 1978 South Korea received as much in economic aid as the whole of Africa. This facilitated high levels of investment in industry and education, which, along with the protection of domestic markets from foreign competitors, and the employment of labour on terms and under conditions long deemed unacceptable in the West, brought dramatic results.

The countries of South-East Asia are quite untypical of the non-industrialized world: they all enjoy culturally homogenous populations, have benefited from a demographic shift to smaller families and a stable population, and, as city-states, Hong Kong and Singapore have been able to control the influx of migrants that plague other major cities. They simply take in workers from neighbouring states during boom times and expel them when they are no longer required. They have none of the responsibilities of a large rural population that characterize most less-developed nations.

It is remarkable to note that, in 1960, income per head of population in South Korea, at $230, was equal to that of Ghana; today South

Koreans are 90 times better off. But suggestions that this miracle represents an example to other poor countries do not stand up to scrutiny. As Paul Kennedy points out, if the poorest countries were somehow able to pull themselves up by their bootstraps and follow the South-East Asian nations down the road of rapid industrialization, the markets for consumer goods would be swamped.[57] Global absorption of new production is already very low and is likely to remain so. We noted how sustained growth at a level necessary to pull even half of the world's people out of poverty is completely out of the question. The rise and fall of the Asian Tigers illustrates the point perfectly.

Economic statistics hide the environmental costs of rapid economic growth. Taiwan saw its per capita income rise from $145 in 1952 to $9,805 in 1987 and employment held steady throughout the period. However, the country has streams so polluted they are combustible and only a fraction of its human waste receives primary treatment. Its farmers are among the world's heaviest users of agricultural chemicals, and cancer is the leading cause of death, its rate having doubled between 1960 and 1990.[58]

Rich-world environmental concern often results in problems being exported: since 1988, Japanese activists have succeeded in blocking plans for hundreds of new golf courses. They are built, instead, in neighbouring countries, where environmental legislation is lacking or not enforced. In 1994, Thailand experienced such an extreme drought that its farmers were prohibited from producing the usual second crop of rice, but sprinklers on the country's golf courses suffered no such injunction. The average Thai golf course consumes the same amount of water as 60,000 rural villagers.[59]

It might be argued that the undesirable social and environmental costs of rapid growth and modernization could be tolerated for the sake of economic advance, but they are all part and parcel of an unsustainable economic project which contains the seeds of its own failure. The base for economic development in Asia was built up slowly during the decades after 1945. Things only really started to go wrong once the region, like the rest of the world economy, became slave to the ideology of free markets and capital flows which came to dominate after the crises of the 1970s. It was political ideology that scuppered the stability and consensus of the post-war years, but it was the economic ideology it spawned that wrecked the lives of millions in South-East Asia.

It seems to be a law of applied economics that moderate success breeds overweening ambition. In Asia the systemic controls by which that ambition is kept in check were routinely overridden. Even in countries where the economy was not run for the benefit of the ruling family, state guarantees to business and support to the banking sector removed much of the risk attached to investments, and caused people to make poor investment decisions. This regularly led to over-investment in productive capacity for goods for which there was no market. But it was not only domestic governments that contributed to this *false* economy. International capital markets and western commercial banks were only too happy to pour billions of dollars into the currencies and stocks of these economies, only to withdraw their investments at a moment's notice, at the first sign that the unsustainable returns they were enjoying were under threat. If the enthusiasm for the Tiger economies was out of all proportion to their long-term prospects, then its reversal, and the decision to move out *en masse*, was quite absurd. Neither the scale of support for the region nor its sudden withdrawal were based on sound business or economic judgements, let alone consideration for the well-being of the peoples of the countries affected.

At the time of the collapse of the Thai currency in 1997, Thailand was in receipt of loans to the value of 125 per cent of its economic output. Two years earlier, when the Mexican economy collapsed, there had been deep misgivings that the Mexican ratio of loans to Gross Domestic Product (GDP) was as high as 45 per cent. The financial markets *never* learn from their mistakes, but not all the blame can be heaped on western banks and investors. The Asian economies, and the large business conglomerates they encouraged, were subject to appalling mismanagement, and afflicted by excessive corruption and cronyism. But, ultimately, it was foreign investors that provided the cash and raised expectations for the region beyond sustainable levels.

So who is to blame? Professor Milton Freidman, the leading advocate of free markets, blames the international community, which, through its agent, the IMF, routinely intervenes in times of crisis to protect the interests of western investors when their investments go sour. He points out that there is no risk attached to investment if investors see that the global authorities will bail out ailing economies. This, Friedman claims, is the principal reason investors go on making the type of misjudged investments which bring about problems in the first place.[60] Once a precedent is set, however, it is difficult to break the cycle. If the IMF had not intervened, the crisis would have spread to endanger the economic stability of the rich countries. Western leaders would not allow their economies to take the hit if, through an IMF funded by taxpayer's money, they could possibly avoid it. Only IMF bail-outs stand between the world economy and a repeat of the Wall Street Crash of 1929, but each time the IMF intervenes it spurs on the market to make even more ill-judged investments: the world economy digs itself deeper into a hole. By mid-1999, after some largely cosmetic political changes in the region and a few 'show trials' of disgraced businessmen, investment was flooding back into the region on a scale that world demand does not justify and cannot support.

Wherever there are losers, there are winners. After the Asian collapse, manufacturing industry in Europe and the United States became more competitive. For years it had hardly been worth bothering: companies like General Electric in the United States knew they could not beat their Asian competitors on price, and often on quality. Now they could; jobs that were lost in Thailand and South Korea reappeared in Detroit and Chicago. Further, as a condition of IMF rescue packages, Asian governments were forced to abolish restrictions on foreign ownership of enterprises. These ailing businesses were then snapped up, at a fraction of their true value, by western multinationals, another chunk of the global economy ending up in the hands of the already wealthy. Once again it seems as if the strategy of spreading free markets is not so much about assisting the less-developed world to catch up, it is a strategy for keeping it down. What better method could the rich nations devise than to invest in a country at levels that inexperienced and incompetent local business managers are quite unable to cope with, to pull the rug from under them at the first sign of declining returns, and then to rush in to relieve them of their few remaining assets when the economy hits rock bottom and has only one way to go?

Michel Chossudovsky has listed the benefits which accrue to western banks and multinational corporations as a result of what he describes as *global financial warfare.*[61] Not only are there bargains to be had in the assets of failed enterprises, but the entire foreign exchange reserves of struggling countries are transferred to the vaults of western banks. The prices of commodities on which poor countries depend for foreign currency earnings plummet, in turn reducing the costs to manufacturing enterprises in rich countries. After failed economies are bailed out by the IMF, interest rates are 25-30 per cent higher than those for comparable loans in rich countries. The entire process appears designed to transfer wealth from the hands of those most responsible for its production – the poor and hungry – into the coffers of those who struggle only to think up new ways to enjoy their immense wealth.

There is not a single example of short-term, market-driven economic growth pulling non-industrialized countries up to consistent and sustainable levels of economic output and national wealth comparable to those of the rich nations. The only truly *organic* free-market industrial economies were those which emerged in Europe in the early nineteenth century, and the United States in the latter part. But still, after the catastrophe of South-East Asia, where millions were thrown out of work with no safety net to catch them, these countries are held up as shining examples of how relatively poor, economically backward countries can

transform themselves into modern nations in a very short time, given the
right set of policies and a large helping of deference to the power of
the market-place. It did not work for them, and under prevailing
economic arrangements it will not work for anyone else.

It is certainly not working for the people of Russia. Since the fall of the
Soviet Union, the resulting social and economic chaos has seen male life
expectancy in Russia fall from 66 to 59 years in just ten years.[62] In a sur-
vey in 2002, the Russian Ministry of Health discovered that 60 per cent
of children were unhealthy.[63] Half of Russia's 18-year-olds were rejected
for military service on health grounds.[64] Since 1985, life expectancy
among men has fallen by ten years, principally as a result of widespread
alcoholism, but also due to the re-emergence of previously eradicated
diseases such as tuberculosis. Less than half of teenage boys in Russia
today will reach the age of 60.[65] Employment, virtually guaranteed under
the communist system, is no longer secure for many: 40 per cent of
Russians now live below the poverty line.[66] The country has an estimated
six million users of hard drugs out of a population of only 150 million.[67]
In many new republics, organized crime operates as a virtual shadow government, controlling a black market which provides for the needs of the
few, while the formal economy fails to meet the needs of the many. By
1994 murders in Russia were averaging 83 per day, or 30,000 a year; this
rate shows no sign of reducing and is way ahead of the United States.

The poorly planned move to a capitalist economy has had little
impact in the way of economic liberalization, or in reviving the economy
to feed, clothe and house the Russian people. The privatization of state
enterprises has led to oligarchic arrangements under which a tiny politically connected elite control much of the economy, in what has been
described as the *tycoon model* of capitalism. Profitable elements of the
economy are under the control of this political elite; non-profitable
elements, such as food production, are left to the people. Between 1991
and 1998, production within the formal economy almost halved.[68]
Millions of people have no money; they survive through subsistence
farming on small plots and by barter. The absence of traditional
agricultural planning, and the failure to develop adequate market-driven
mechanisms for food production, has left tens of millions of Russians
struggling to feed themselves. This experience suggests that certain conditions must hold in order for a market-based economy to provide adequate opportunities for all members of society. In Chapter 9 we shall discover precisely what these conditions are.

Despite Mikhail Gorbachev's attempts to prioritize environmental
concerns, the condition of the land, water and air in Russia is among the
worst in the world, and is deteriorating. Super-polluting factories which

were shut down for environmental reasons have been reopened in exactly the same condition. The quality of food and water available to the population is heavily compromised; people have neither the means nor the motivation to begin to put things right. As Vladimir Tsirkunov of the World Bank noted, 'If you are dying of hunger, what do you care if you are going to die of cancer in ten years time. Environment is an abandoned child.'[69]

Perhaps the most tragic aspect of Russia's situation is that since the fall of communism this huge county, rich in resources, and steeped in cultural tradition, has neither created nor invented anything of worth. The carcass of an exhausted economy has been divided up among a tiny minority, and that part of it on which the people depend for their basic needs, discarded.

The Russians have swapped the failings of the command economy, which deprived consumers of choice, for a desperately flawed attempt at emulating the market economies of the West, which seems likely to make them amongst the poorest and most deprived in the world. Whatever human rights violations were committed under the communist system, and they were many and very serious, virtually the entire population had its basic needs guaranteed for forty years following 1945. Under the economic reforms introduced by Boris Yeltsin and now taken up by Vladimir Putin, most Russians have seen their life savings become worthless as the currency has been devalued. John Gray suggests that western politicians are equally to blame. As he says, 'The crackpot policies that were foisted on Russia had little to do with the country's needs and everything to do with the neo-liberal hubris that had gripped western governments.'[70] The shelves that stood empty for decades may now be full of consumer goods, but few can afford to buy them. When the Soviet Union broke up, the fate of Russia was far from inevitable, but by forcing Russians to play by the rules of a game in which only a few can possibly be winners, the West ensured that it would be the direst aspects of the legacy of Stalin and Brezhnev which would emerge to lead the Russian people into darkness.

Much of the suffering and hardship that blights the modern world is of our own making, the inevitable consequence of our historical acquiescence in a process of economic development which has seen our ability to secure ever-greater material wealth from nature, outstripped only by our determination to distribute the benefits inequitably. But not all human suffering occurs at our own hands. We remain at the mercy of natural disasters: earthquakes, cyclones, hurricanes, drought-induced famine, and volcanic eruptions. While we have become better able to predict some of these, and to put in place measures to moderate their impact, our efforts in doing so are uneven and partial. We have a selective mentality when it comes to deciding what is, and what is not, within our control.

We know enough of the geology of our planet to predict where earthquakes will occur, but we are not yet able to predict when. We are, however, able to assess the relative impacts of earthquakes of similar intensity in different parts of the world. Residents of Los Angeles or Lisbon are far more likely to survive the same earthquake than their counterparts in Mexico City or Yerevan. Not only are emergency services better resourced, and effective contingency plans in place for managing such emergencies, but developed economies tend to have legal institutions with the foresight to legislate for building regulations appropriate to earthquake zones, and, most importantly, the power to enforce them. Richer nations are better placed to manage the consequences of earthquakes. The same applies to severe weather conditions. The Atlantic seaboard of North and Central America is subject to increasingly regular batterings from hurricanes. When these strike south of the Rio Grande, the dead are counted in thousands, and the homeless and dispossessed in hundreds of thousands. When they hit north of the Mexico-US border, deaths are usually counted in tens and homes lost in the order of hundreds. The impact of these climatological calamities is literally a thousand times greater in poorer countries. North Americans are largely insulated by their collective wealth and the institutions created to protect the social infrastructure.

Famine resulting from drought afflicts large parts of the Third World on a regular basis. The consequences are often catastrophic, and the capacity of national governments to soften the effects are negligible. Periodic fluctuations in the factors which determine agricultural output occur wherever crops are planted. Again, what separates the rich countries from the poor countries is the capacity to manage the consequences of these fluctuations.

The latest threat to populations in poor countries comes from the increase in average global temperatures. Again, it is the poorer countries who will be least able to manage the impact, just as they suffered most at the hands of El Niño, the change in sea temperature which affected the climate over large parts of the world in the late 1990s. El Niño wrought havoc wherever its impact was felt: in sub-Saharan Africa it deprived farmers of the rainfall on which their crops depend, in South America it caused the destruction of homes and crops through flooding, and in the United States it ruined the perfect summers which Californians consider their birthright. Experts are now convinced that global warming, deforestation and other human interventions are responsible for the increasing incidence and intensity of natural disasters, and for exacerbating the impact when disasters do strike. Natural disasters are responsible for a growing proportion of the world's refugees. One billion people now live in unplanned shanty towns which afford little or no protection from the elements; many of these are located in earthquake zones.

The number affected by natural disasters each year has grown from 740 million in the 1970s to two billion today.[71] The number of disasters has more than doubled. The economic cost has quadrupled to $629 billion. Insurance companies predict that, on current trends, economic damage from global warming will outstrip world economic output by 2065.[72] There are already 25 million environmental refugees worldwide compared with 12 million political refugees.[73]

Even where we cannot prevent natural disasters, we can moderate their consequences, and we do so quite successfully where we choose to. Were the poverty of countries unable to plan for the effects of natural disasters a consequence of some natural order, we might regard their plight with sympathy, and offer charity, but otherwise conclude that there is little we can do. If, on the other hand, their poverty is the result of an economic system biased in favour of the already rich nations, then our moral duty in respect of arbitrary threats from nature is surely quite different. Much of the suffering we have discussed is tied to systemic and structural inequities born of an economic system which confused its priorities as soon as humans started to manage it. The nature of that system also leaves us considerably less able to moderate the consequences of natural disasters than we otherwise would be. Only through a new approach to global economic arrangements will we be better able to protect all people from the often overwhelming interventions of nature.

Children and other civilians now account for 90 per cent of the victims of war, compared with 14 per cent in the First World War and 67 per cent in the Second.[74] Whether in the civil wars that rage in many African nations, or the more strategic wars in the Balkans or the Caucuses, or the inter-community violence in Indonesia, even the fragile arrangements for the protection of civilians under the Geneva Convention are now routinely disregarded by protagonists on all sides. The deliberate terrorising of civilian populations, the rape of women and the killing of children, have become premeditated tools of war. The mutilation of thousands in Sierra Leone, who had their hands or arms amputated, is just one example of the brutality of warfare as conducted by modern humans.

Killing, violence and persecution on the basis of perceived ethnic difference has become a recurring feature of modern warfare. People who for centuries have lived side by side, marrying each other and in the process breeding out any nominal legacy of historical racial difference, have, spurred on by the crazed rhetoric of political leaders, turned on their neighbours in ways unimaginably cruel. There is virtually no recognition of the complex web of causes and motivations that drive many of the conflicts which turn humans into ruthless killers. While there are no easy solutions, what solutions there are depend on our addressing the root causes, and we do not begin to do this at present. War and communal violence are extremely rare among communities and populations where economic security is good and where life provides stimulation and interest, and offers a sense of progress. The incidence of war, ethnic violence, even genocide, will rise or fall in proportion to the numbers of people for whom the experience of life can be improved. Superficial attempts to treat the symptoms of social breakdown are worthless as long as the gap between those with security and those without continues to grow.

The extent to which women and children are victimized through poverty and war cannot be overstated: 70 per cent of the world's poor are women.[75] The civil war in Sudan is sustained by the forced recruitment (kidnapping) of children as young as ten – they make obedient troops and are usually strong enough to handle a lightweight modern rifle. There are 120,000 child soldiers fighting in the civil wars of Africa, 300,000 worldwide, some as young as seven years old.[76] In the last ten years, two million children have died in wars, more than four million have been disabled, twelve million have lost their homes and more than one million have lost their parents.

Among the several hundred million people worldwide who have no local water supplies, the job of fetching and carrying falls firmly on the shoulders of women, who often spend five hours a day so employed. They also raise the children, prepare the meals and in most cases tend the crops. Women are responsible for most of the food production in poorer countries. In parts of west Africa, despite the practice being banned, many girls are married off before puberty, some as young as eight years old. Excused as an established cultural tradition, this practice is a mechanism to ensure girls are denied an education – and a childhood – and that power relations in society are tipped further in favour of men. The gains made by women in many of the richer nations during the twentieth century have yet to register with women in most countries of the world.

In many countries, child labour is the norm. Children are easily controlled and coerced, and, as long as they remain healthy, make more productive workers than adults. They often work very long hours and in dreadful conditions. Their parents often have no option but to send their children to work. In Pakistan, an estimated 8 million children are forced to work in sweatshop conditions under a system whereby child labour has become the principal means to the repayment of family debt.[77] The argument that all economies have to endure a period where the exploitation of children is commonplace, in order to advance, ignores current economic realities. If less-developed countries are to advance economically, they have to educate their young people at least as well as the rich countries. In sending their children to work before they can read and write, they condemn their economies to third-class status for decades to come. Child labour is not only a Third World problem. An estimated 300,000 children, some as young as ten, are in full-time employment in Italy, where many in the south of the country have yet to experience the benefits of modernity.[78] In Britain, 1½ million children work illegally: they are either under-age or employed in jobs which children are forbidden to do by law.[79] Like their Third World counterparts, the life-chances of these children are limited as their education is irrevocably compromised.

Even among the richer nations, tears in the social fabric have been appearing for some time now. The transfer of much manufacturing output to the Far East, and the effects of technological displacement, have left a legacy of unemployment for millions, and lower real wages and a reduction in living standards for many others. Among the industrialized nations 35 million people, more than 6 per cent, are currently seeking work, among the 15-24 age group the rate rises to 12 per cent.[80] A large section of the working population who, only a generation ago, were raised to expect lifelong employment have suddenly found their means to a livelihood, and the opportunity to make a meaningful contribution to society, removed from them. Among the older unemployed, cases of despair, depression, family breakdown and even suicide are commonplace. The young, for many of whom the education system has proved next to worthless, have a very uncertain future.

People are also finding themselves to be unemployable sooner. In 1970, 80 per cent of American men aged 55 to 64 were in work; by 1990 only 65 per cent had jobs. In the UK the percentage fell from 75 to 40 in the same period.[81] This trend is now well established, but policymakers are now so concerned that we will not be able to finance the cost of our ageing population that they are suggesting that we will all need to work beyond 70 in order to be able to afford our longer retirements. Clearly these two positions are irreconcilable without major structural change to the economy. Worldwide, the International Labour Organization estimates that over a billion people are unemployed or underemployed – wanting to work but unable to secure sufficient paid work to meet their basic needs.

Among the industrialized nations there are about five million people without homes. The problem is most acute in the United States, the richest country in the world, where an estimated three million people are without permanent shelter.[82] The pavements beneath the glistening sky-scrapers of downtown Los Angeles, through which millions of dollars are daily transacted, at night become home to thousands of people, their cardboard beds lined up shoulder to shoulder. The homeless of Los Angeles are lucky: they usually enjoy year-round warm weather. Elsewhere, freezing winter temperatures claim the lives of thousands of homeless people each year. In Britain, many of the homeless are young people, no longer welcome or no longer able to bear living with their families; sometimes they are the victims of violence or sexual abuse. Many are denied families altogether and find themselves on the streets, or the long-term residents of hostels, hopelessly ill-equipped to cope once institutional care ends and they are considered adult enough to make their own way in the world.

In Britain, homeless people are 34 times more likely to kill themselves than those with homes, eight times more likely to die in accidents and three times more likely to die of pneumonia or bronchitis. The average age of death among homeless people is 47 years.[83] The benefits of being born into an advanced industrial society are far from universal. Official efforts at resolving the problem focus on the removal of the homeless from the streets. They do little to rehabilitate people back into society, nor to counteract the conditions which ensure a continuing supply of new homeless. Homelessness affects all the industrialized nations but, rather than address its root causes, we have instead reclassified home-lessness as another unfortunate but inevitable side effect of economic advance.

The widening gap between rich and poor represents the reversing of a process through which increasing numbers were included in the econ-omies of the rich nations after 1945. One hundred million people now live below the poverty line in the industrialized countries.[84] Among the longer-standing member states of the European Union, where popula-tion increases have been negligible, between 1975 and 1988 the number living in poverty rose by a third to 52 million.[85] In Britain, the period since 1979 has seen considerable economic growth, but the poorest 30 per cent of the population has failed to see any of the benefits. Between 1966 and 1977, the wages of all male workers grew at a similar rate; how-ever after 1978 wages for the lowest paid barely changed, and in 1992 were worth less than in 1975.[86] During the same period, middle-wage earners saw their incomes rise by 35 per cent and high-wage earners by 50 per cent. In 1980 the top 20 per cent of UK earners took home four times the bottom 20 per cent. By 2000 the multiple had grown to seven times.

As a consequence of this growing divide, the richest fifth of households now receive about half of the country's total income, while the poorest two fifths receive only 12 per cent.[87] Debate usually begins and ends at the inequity of this situation; little thought is given to the reality of trying to support a family on as little as £6,000 a year.

In Britain, a strong correlation has emerged between poverty and child health. On the Easterhouse Estate in Glasgow, one of the poorest concentrations in Europe, the average height of children is several inches less than for their parents' generation – the consequence of chronic malnutrition.[88] Two in five children in Britain are born into households living on or below the poverty line, but it is in the United States, the most 'advanced' of industrial societies, where inequality is most severe. Although the economy grew by 20 per cent in the 1980s, an additional four million American children fell into poverty during that period.[89] Between 1973 and 1995, for the bottom 80 per cent of wage earners, the average wage fell by 18 per cent in real terms, while for the top 20 per cent real wages were 19 per cent higher before tax and 66 per cent higher after tax.[90]

Economic polarization, and the tendency for poverty to be geographically concentrated, has led to the ghettoization which is now a feature of most American cities. The relative abundance of space enables many Americans to avoid the realities of the poverty on their doorsteps, but a drive through any inner-city area, or the rural towns of the southern states, is an eye-opener of cosmic proportions. In South Africa, the white minority had to devise a political system to keep the races apart; in the United States, the task is left to the economy: the results are largely the same.

Perhaps Europe is fortunate to have inner-city America as a warning of what could happen. Widespread crime and violence have become a potent a symbol of American society. Its real causes are questioned only at the margins of the media and by academics; real solutions are never sought by politicians. Abetted by the peculiarly American notion that individual liberty extends to the freedom to carry firearms, there seems little hope of relief from the mire of crime, drugs and hopelessness into which a sizeable minority of America's young people now fall. Although, by the year 2000, murders in the United States had fallen below 16,000 (down from 24,000 in 1992), more than 90,000 cases of forcible rape were reported and nearly a million people were victims of aggravated assault.[91] More than two million homes were burgled and 1.2 million cars were stolen.

There has been a reduction in the incidence of violent crime, but this is explained principally by an ageing population – fewer angry young men on the streets means less violent crime – and, in many US cities, by a saturation level police presence. In 2001 there were only 15,517 murders, but there was an 11.7 per cent increase in murders in towns with less than 10,000 people.[92] The US capital, Washington DC, has the highest murder rate of any city in the world: 50.82 murders per 100,000 of population, compared with just 2.36 in London.[93] The failure to address the underlying causes of crime was demonstrated in the aftermath of the terrorist attacks of September 11, 2001, when, with police resources occupied elsewhere, crime levels in New York and London rocketed. To put these figures in perspective, compared with more than 216,000 murders in the United States in the 1980s, just 426 civilians fell victim to the sectarian violence in Northern Ireland during the same period. The United Nations defines a major armed conflict as one in which a thousand or more people are killed annually. By this measure, *Main Street, USA* constitutes a war zone of substantial proportions. No wonder eight million Americans now choose to live in secure gated communities.

The United States provides additional data that further confounds its claims to be an example to the world of the merits of the western model. In the 1988 presidential election only 51 per cent of those eligible to vote did so. George Bush Snr, with 53.4 per cent of the popular vote, was therefore elected by only 27 per cent of the electorate. The 1990 elections to the House of Representatives saw only a 34 per cent voter turnout. At regional level the situation is no better: fewer than 30 per cent turned out to vote Mario Cuomo Governor of New York State in 1990, and in Arkansas less than 40 per cent participated in the election of Bill Clinton to the State Capitol. A decade later things were little different. Voter turnout at mid-term elections to congress in 1998 and 2002 were 37.6 per cent and 39 per cent respectively. In the controversial 2000 presidential election, on a voter turnout of 51 per cent, George W. Bush, with only 47 per cent of the popular vote, claimed the presidency with the support of just 24½ per cent of the electorate – even less than his father.[94] Despite a record turnout in 2004, Bush won re-election with the support of just 30.6 per cent of Americans who were eligible to vote.

These figures are symptomatic of the way in which increasing numbers throughout the industrialized world are giving up their right to a say in the way their societies are run. It is true that the United States holds elections for more offices and on more issues than any other nation, but a large majority of the population pay no attention whatsoever.

In their book, *The Age of Insecurity*, Larry Elliott and Dan Atkinson describe the direct link between the disinterested advance of the economic system and its impact on people's lives. They point to a shift in the balance of risk: whereas, historically, risk was shared by entrepreneurs and the rest of society, today the risks associated with economic activity are shouldered exclusively by ordinary people. Under the traditional model, when the economy grew out of balance, adjustments were possible via inflation, exchange-rate adjustments and unemployment. Policy is now geared to keeping inflation at manageable levels and ensuring exchange-rate stability; the only adjusting mechanism left is that of unemployment. This model perfectly suits the interests of the wealthy, who are free to move their funds around the globe in search of the best short-term returns. As Elliott and Atkinson argue, 'the operations of the financial sector are effectively underwritten by the sacrifices of ordinary people.'[95] The wealthy minority, in league with economic ideologues and politicians too cowardly to call their bluff, have stacked the scales in their favour: they call all the shots.

In 1994, traders in London sold Government bonds and forced the authorities to raise interest rates – an action which benefited wealth-holders and damaged net-borrowers. Their action was in response to concerns over increased average wages, but ignored the fact that it was the traders' own bonuses which had been entirely responsible for the increase in earnings.[96]

If the privileged and powerful had set about designing a system to guarantee them maximum returns at the expense of ordinary people they could not have done a better job than the global economy as constituted at the start of the twenty-first century. The problem of economics is the ultimate moral question. It is not true that there is no alternative: more than any time in history, the mechanisms of the economy are purposely weighted in favour of the already privileged. The poor have no chance, and many middle-income earners in the industrialized nations now live in fear for their future. Until more people come to realize that our condition is a consequence of the power wielded by a small minority in defence of their selfish interests, and realise that the creation of a fairer economic system would be no harder to achieve than, for example, the abolition of slavery, there is little, if any, possibility of progress.

5

A Universal Ethic

BY NOW it should be clear that questions of ethics and economics cannot be considered in isolation from one another. At core, economics, the study of the production and distribution of wealth, and ethics, the study of moral conduct, are inseparable because every economic decision we make has a moral element – that is to say it impacts on other people.

Among the philosophy of the ancient Greeks there was little explicit reference to matters of economy and human material well-being. In both the ancient Greek civilization and the Roman Empire that followed, there was a much clearer division between city and countryside than exists today. Cultural, intellectual and political activities were centred on the city-states, while economic activity, almost entirely agricultural, occurred in rural areas. Mechanisms were in place to feed city-dwellers who specialized in all manner of noble activities, save that of making a personal contribution to the provision of their subsistence needs. Thinkers like Plato and Aristotle concerned themselves with matters of ethics, political organization and concepts such as what constituted the right way to live. But they were thinking and writing about, and for, a small and privileged ruling elite. The division of society into rigid social classes was considered a fixture and not worthy of examination, save for the occasional defence of the status quo, especially in respect of the practice of slavery.

It is the basis of the economy in slavery which kept economics out of mainstream philosophical thought. Slave labour, domestic and imported, was the engine of the economy, and enabled the fortunate to spend so much time pondering the nature of existence. Richard Dien Winfield suggests that in the thought of Plato and Aristotle, 'the good life begins precisely where concern with need and work ends'' This illustrates just how insulated the ruling classes in ancient Greece were from the struggle and drudgery of everyday life, and begs questions as to the relevance of Greek thought to today's world. It also helps explain why economics has been continually excluded from the realm of ethics. The easy answer is that, if the great thinkers of classical antiquity saw little need for economics within ethical thought, and if it is from them that we take our lead, then why should we consider economics in ethical terms?

Many contemporary thinkers apparently see little difference between ancient Greece and the modern world. Like the Greeks, they see an inevitability and natural order to the way things are. If the world seems impervious to any desires we might have to change it, why bother with an ethics-based approach to social problems? Why not save ethics for things where we can influence opinion and behaviour, such as animal rights, the medical implications of genetic science, or abortion and contraception?

The choice to exclude economics from ethics is one taken in protection of the interests of the privileged. As J.K.Galbraith says, 'Ethical judgement has a strong tendency to conform to what citizens of influence find it agreeable to believe.'[2] It is as true today as it was 2½ thousand years ago. In fact, things may be worse today. For Aristotle, notwithstanding the narrow confines of what could and could not be evaluated in ethical terms, at least ethics was the principal servant of truth, and rigorous philosophical debate the paramount criteria against which new ideas were tested. In ancient Greece ethics shaped politics, which in turn saw little value in, or scope for, meddling in economic affairs. In the modern world, a particular reading of economics determines the nature and quality of the lives of all people; politicians apply what sticking plaster to the social body they can afford, and ethics concerns itself with marginal issues. Economics is classified as a science, to which moral considerations do not apply.

The record of moral philosophers in respect of economics is ambiguous and ambivalent. Only since the formal separation and isolation of economic functions from the mechanisms of wider society have thinkers begun to consider economic matters in their own right. Historically, the inequitable distribution of the means to survival was seen as a function of natural constraints and unplanned cultural developments. What difference could philosophy possibly make? But once the extent of economic inequity was increased by transformative advances in technology, and reinforced through the conscious efforts of the wealthy to protect their advantage through political power, then it would become of concern to philosophers.

With the *Enlightenment* came a new breed of philosophy-inspired *classical* economists, whose principal objective was to identify essential laws of human social organization which would aid in the creation of a society where everyone had access to the means to provide for themselves and their families. As Reinhold Niebuhr pointed out, *laissez-faire* and rational self-interest were not the moral bases of the prescriptions of the Enlightenment economists, they were the means to the quite explicit ends of building a society in which all people have their basic needs met. 'Even when economic self-seeking is approved as in the political moral- ity of Adam Smith, the criterion of judgement is the good of the whole', wrote Niebuhr in his 1932 book, *Moral Man and Immoral Society.*[3]

Notwithstanding the shaky position of economics within the dis- cipline, there is much to be learned from the history of moral philosophy. It is the only source from which we might derive ultimate justification for a project to build a more inclusive society, and from which we might identify and articulate the values which must underpin efforts to redirect economic activity to more equitable ends.

There is evidence of ethical debate among the earliest discovered human writings, from the ancient civilizations of Mesopotamia and Egypt dating from the fourth millennium BCE. Principal among the concerns of these ancient peoples were systems of justice to reduce hostility and foster peace. The law code of Hammurabi of Babylon listed among its objectives the desire that 'the strong might not oppress the weak'. The earliest surviving literary relics of ancient Greece also contain evidence of lively ethical debate: the poems of Homer, written 800 years before the time of Christ, have a strong moral dimension, as do the plays of Aristophanes and Euripides. Across the Asian continent too, this early period contains a wealth of evidence of ethical concern. Unlike the Greeks, who in their ethical thought made an early break with religion, eastern ethical thought remained, as it does to this day, firmly inter- twined with religious belief. The Hindu vedas champion the virtues of truthfulness, giving and restraint. For Jainists, the most fundamental concept is the non-harming of other sentient beings. Buddhism urges the practice of conscientiousness, benevolence and self-restraint and empha- sizes the importance of concern for the spiritual and material well-being of others. And Confucius, whose dominance over Chinese culture lasted from the sixth century BCE until the early part of the twentieth century, conceived moral goodness as benevolence towards all humankind. It is perhaps surprising how ethical debate, born of different cultures, each with no knowledge of the others' existence, produced such similar out- comes. Or perhaps we should stop being surprised at what, for thousands of years, human beings have so obviously had in common, and focus instead on this shared tradition rather than on the cosmetic differences that set us apart.

As long as we have been thinking, it seems, we have been thinking about ethics, about how we should live and about the nature of our oblig- ations towards others. Early beginnings in ancient Greece sparked an enduring debate over the nature of human good. Whilst some argued that unrestrained self-aggrandizement was the embodiment of human achievement, there was greater acceptance of the view that self-interest is served not only through selfish ends, but that to be truly happy, and to live a good life, requires just behaviour towards others. This early period also marked the beginning of a debate over whether the virtues of restraint, temperance and justice constitute unwarranted restrictions on the freedom of the individual. Equally lively was debate about the source of moral knowledge. Protagorus, who was a major influence on Socrates, argued that the virtues central to living a good life (justice, courage, self-discipline, loyalty and, especially, wisdom) have their source in the human ability to reason. Any person who succeeded in developing powers of reason to a sufficiently high degree, claimed Protagorus, could learn what it is to lead a good life. This constituted a radical challenge to the prevailing social elite, the members of which had, until that point, been regarded as exclusively endowed with such knowledge.

Socrates believed that the exercise of reason, through sincere debate about the nature of truth was the sole means to moral knowledge. Through this process he became convinced of the rightness of the virtues outlined by Protagorus, and concluded that humans cannot do wrong knowingly and willingly. Plato took a rather more academic approach; whereas Socrates had championed public market-place debate, Plato obtusely concluded that knowledge of the good could only be achieved at age 50 after 15 years of highly focused study. He also differed over the motivation of human actions: Socrates held that we are motivated solely by our knowledge – correct or otherwise – of what is good, but Plato argued that our appetites and emotions also play a role, often working independently of, or even at odds with, reasoned judgement. He developed a theory of the interaction between reason, emotion and the various virtues. Wisdom, he maintained, is derived solely from reason, but courage is a product of the emotions which provides support for reasoned decisions. Temperance ensures that emotion and appetite yield to reason where necessary, and justice works to promote the appropriate contribution of each virtue to a person's actions. In his *Theory of Forms*, Plato secularized the idea that objective moral laws exist independently of human thought, and suggested that it is these laws which are learned through the exercise of reason in league with emotions and appetites.

In the second century BCE Greece was invaded by the Romans. The spirit of free enquiry that had characterized five hundred years of Greek civilization was extinguished, not to be resurrected in Europe for more than a millennium, save for a brief flurry of activity towards the end of the Roman Empire. By this time, Christianity was already beginning to exert a grip over Europe and the direction of ethics which would last a thousand years. The works of the Greek philosophers were lost. Saint

Augustine and others concentrated on the development of moral law in the Catholic doctrine based on the gospels. The doctrine was concerned almost entirely with matters of personal morality, eschewing more universal ethical and political considerations, and its unquestioned source was the will of God. But only a century after Augustine, Boethius initiated debate into the nature of human will, arguing that individual human freedom is inviolate and that it is entirely up to the individual to determine the right way to live. Although he placed a question mark over the dominant belief in the divine will, it was not until the late twelfth century, when the works of the Greek philosophers found their way back to Europe and prompted feverish attempts to reconcile their ideas with Christian doctrine, that ethics began to be prised from the grip of the theologians. A further six hundred years would pass, however, before European ethical thought was fully liberated from the straitjacket of Christianity. Nonetheless, the intervening period was marked by healthy argument over the nature of human will, the extent to which it was free, and its relation to reason. After a millennium of universal submission to belief in the divine will, these questions were quite momentous. In the thirteenth century, Thomas Aquinas went as far as to suggest that it was through passing the test of human reason that the moral precepts of divine law were validated. God's position was further undermined.

The Renaissance set free the spirit of enquiry which had been repressed for so long. In Italy, Greek thought, and the works of Plato in particular, was absorbed and incorporated by the *Humanists*. There was a subtle evolution of ideas, however: whereas Aristotle had suggested that the happiness gained by living a virtuous life could be enhanced by external bodily goods, such as physical well-being and material gain, the humanists thought that this addition diminished the value of virtue. They concluded that, although wealth has some moral value in its potential for allowing generosity, it was more often the root of pride and avarice. The ideas of the Stoics were also resurrected, particularly the belief that emotion has no role in virtuous conduct, and that only three emotions, joy, caution and will, have any rational basis. Petrarch advanced the case for a lifestyle in which the emotions were suppressed; others argued that it was unrealistic to expect such self-discipline from the ordinary mass of people. Grief, especially, was deemed beyond the control of even the greatest of Stoics.

During the seventeenth century, with belief in the divine will losing further ground, debate took on a more sociological slant. Less attention was paid to right and wrong, and how the intellectual elite came to know the difference. The focus moved, instead, to the forces that motivate the ordinary person to action. Thomas Hobbes, in *Leviathan*, asserted that human behaviour is motivated purely by self-interest. Hobbes may well have been stating an observable truth, but his ideas gave great fuel to the *egoist* movement that followed. Bernard Mandeville suggested that restraint in matters of food, sex and the enjoyment of luxuries would, in all likelihood, lead to unemployment and considerable suffering. It was through self-interested partaking of the vices, rather than benevolence towards others, that people were most likely to be kept busy and happy. These ideas were widely taken up, and the belief that the best chance of promoting the good of all is to strive to provide for one's self-interested desires gained considerable currency. The egoists rather complacently assumed that, if society was structured so that everyone could clearly see that morality pays, then individual self-direction would lead to morally acceptable behaviour. But society was not so structured and neither was it likely to become so.

Half a century later, and two thousand years after it was first postulated, Lord Shaftesbury resurrected Plato's system of interacting virtues and emotions, suggesting that we have a moral sense that enables us to arbitrate inconsistencies among our feelings. Francis Hutcheson further developed this view, arguing that this moral sense only approves feelings of benevolence. The merit of an action is therefore determined by the strength of benevolence in its motivation. This moral sense, together with feelings, which comprise benevolent desires as well as self-interested ones, enable us to be morally self-governing. Hutcheson still put our endowment with such equipment down to the benevolence of God, however.

David Hume was strongly influenced by Shaftesbury and Hutcheson, but set about constructing a wholly secular ethic of virtue. He saw virtues not as habits of compliance with natural laws communicated from above, but rather as internal responses to the needs of others, as reinforced by feelings of approval. Against Hume, Immanuel Kant set out to prove that motivation to moral action resides solely with reason. To this end he evoked the ideal of the perfectly rational being and argued that moral law is self-imposed by the truly rational individual. His mechanism for determining the moral acceptability of an action, *the categorical imperative*, was to test whether it could be willed and executed by everyone without contradiction. The test can be entertainingly applied to the contemporary world. Imagine the damage to the environment that would result were everyone of driving age to purchase and drive a new vehicle tomorrow. This hypothetical scenario prompts a more realistic question: if the planet can neither provide the means for nor sustain universal car ownership, how do we decide who gets to enjoy the privilege? It is as much an ethical question as an economic one, and it brings us to the point at which moral philosophers were no longer able to exclude consideration of economic matters from their domain. The branch of philosophy known as *economics* was born.

Kant's foray into economics is more implicit than explicit, a logical extension of his ethics, rather than a full recasting of his thought into the economic sphere. As Allen D. Rosen documents, Kant approached the subject by defining the concept of social justice as the link between theoretical ethics and the practicalities of social and economic policy.[4]

Kant, like many thinkers of his time, viewed the liberty of the individual as of paramount importance, but he was fully aware that the liberty of one individual was not independent of the liberty of others. Justice required the restriction of individual freedoms so as not to interfere with the like freedom of all others. The state was created as the guardian of individual liberty, a result of the general will to ensure the preservation of society, and necessary to avoid social breakdown and a return to a condition in which the liberty of no individual could be guaranteed. The state had a positive and important role in ensuring the stability of society so that, for example, it could impose taxation to fund provision for the poor. This was not to be seen as a restriction on individual liberty, rather the manifestation of one of the boundaries imposed by the categorical imperative on the liberty of individuals. Implicit in Kant's argument is that the 'right to live' is a prerequisite to the preservation of civil society. No individual can enjoy liberty without the means of physical and mental survival, and, as reason dictates that nothing can be willed by any individual which cannot be willed by all without contradiction, no individual can act in such a way as to deny those means to any other.

Kant's observations on social justice suggest that to separate economics and ethics requires us to dispense completely with his thought. He makes this explicit in his later work. As Rosen argues, 'Constitutionally guaranteed rights to a minimum level of well-being are, on Kantian principles, part of the structure of any just and rational civil society.'[5]

Although much of moral philosophy focuses on the source and nature of moral knowledge, the means by which individuals gain such knowledge, and the factors which motivate individual action, Kant shows us that ethics is predicated on our collective need to function as a society. If we all existed as independent entities, interacting only with nature in pursuit of the means to survival and satisfaction in life, there would be no need for ethics. But this is not the case: however much we might like to think we can live in isolation from, or independently of, wider society, we cannot. Given the social nature of our individual existence, if we prioritized our own well-being and had no consideration whatsoever for others, then, in an environment where resources are scarce, or where the means to convert them into basic needs are not available to individuals acting alone, social breakdown would quickly follow. This is the basis for Jean-Jacques Rousseau's conception in *The Social Contract.* The mutual interdependence of all members of society has clear implications for the way society is organized, especially the manner in which it is governed, and the means by which economic resources and opportunities are allocated. The Greeks were right: ethics and politics are inseparable; but, as we have now taken absolute conscious control over the means by which we provide for our physical survival, it follows that ethics can no longer be considered without reference to economics.

Politics is the tool applied by society in its management of the economy. If there is consensus on matters of ethics, on the proper form of relations between individuals in a society, and on the scope of moral obligation, then politicians can implement measures to ensure the moral basis of society is protected. If there is no agreement on the moral basis of society, politics would presumably allow an economic free-for-all. If, as in ancient Greece, there was full agreement among those with influence that half the population should be kept in servitude, then politics will pay little attention to economics, as the economic problem is essentially solved. The starting point has to be agreement on the moral basis for society, and full recognition of the implications therein. Kant has offered one such basis – that individual liberty should be safeguarded – and pointed out the implications for social and economic organization.

With the economic dynamic of European society radically altered by the industrial revolution, the direction of ethics was changed. In the midst of the social upheavals of the nineteenth century, Jeremy Bentham was concerned with combating growing social injustice. His axiom that 'it is the greatest happiness of the greatest number that is the measure of right and wrong',[6] and the utilitarian movement which he founded, had an enormous impact on the ethics and politics of the nineteenth century, and largely shaped the direction of progress in the twentieth. But his *utility* theory has a number of problems. How is happiness to be defined? Is it material well-being, physical pleasure, freedom from want or pain? Even if we agree on a definition, should the objective be to maximize total happiness or average happiness among the population, and what relative weightings are we to give to the contrasting experiences of human well-being and human suffering?

Many variants of the theory have emerged in response to these questions. In terms of judging the moral value of individual actions, utility theory says that an act is right if it does at least as much to increase happiness and lessen suffering for all those whom it affects as any alternative act. But it provides no obligation to act to reduce suffering, neither does it convey any moral duty to consider the consequences of inaction.

The motivating force for individuals acting under the doctrine was to be that of rational self-interest, the assumption being that, by and large, the interests of wider society would be best promoted through the pursuit of individual self-interest guided by the tenets of utilitarianism. But utilitarianism sets a modest limit to its own ambition, aiming to increase the welfare of the greatest possible number, rather than demanding minimum levels of welfare for all.

As Richard Bronk says in his book *Progress and the Invisible Hand*, utilitarianism 'reinforced the belief that the free market can itself guarantee a morally desirable economic outcome, and that the scientific pursuit of free-market efficiency should therefore be accorded the status almost of a moral goal.'[7] Today, scarcity is no longer a problem – we have developed the technology to provide for the basic needs of the entire global population – but, under an economic system guided by the utilitarian concept, we still find millions going hungry. It is inadequate to argue that universal needs provision is unrealistic, and therefore that a utilitarian approach to economic provision is best. In large part it is the utilitarian approach, which has come to identify happiness principally with material acquisition and value utility solely in monetary terms, that further entrenches in people the idea that universal needs provision is not possible.

The utilitarian position remained unassailable until the publication, in 1972, of John Rawls' book, *A Theory of Justice,* which saw the first serious attempt to reveal its moral fallibility. The book was lauded as an immensely important contribution to moral philosophy. It had less of an impact on the burgeoning global economic system. Rawls maintained that all individuals have the right to a minimum level of welfare which the utility preferences of others cannot override. To support his argument he suggested that, if a society were to be created from scratch by a group of people from behind a *veil of ignorance* as to what hand fate would deal them, any rational person would incorporate into this society mechanisms to ensure that the basic welfare of all its members is guaranteed. Nobody, he suggested, is consciously going to design a society in which they might end up starving to death on the streets.

In his advocacy of minimum basic rights, Rawls provided the philosophical impetus for the human rights movement which has grown dramatically over the last quarter century. The idea that individuals possess certain inalienable rights was first muted in the early seventeenth century by Hugo Grotius, but it took Rawls' book and the growing profile of the United Nations and its *Universal Declaration of Human Rights*, along with our growing knowledge of the restriction of political freedoms in certain countries, to place human rights at the centre of contemporary ethical debate.

It is remarkable how so much historical ethical debate reflects current concerns. If Grotius had known how long it would take for his ideas to come into vogue, he might have directed his efforts elsewhere. In the West, concern for animal welfare is commonly perceived to be a recent development, but it was high on the agenda of the ancient Egyptians, and is also an enduring theme in Hindu and Buddhist thought. And what of the status of women in society, nearly two thousand years since Seneca staked a claim for their equality? Perhaps most relevant to today's world are the ideas of the Stoics: the earth as a unitary living being with which we must live in harmony, and our duty to consider ourselves members of only one race, the human race – Zeno was the first environmentalist and the first internationalist, and he lived nearly two thousand years ago. Western civilization is having to relearn vast chunks of wisdom which it had put to one side, believing them an obstacle to rational scientific progress. Incredibly, many of these ancient ideas are still held to be ahead of their time.

Rawls and Kant both based their conceptions of ethics on the rational powers of human beings. A population of fully rational people, under both schemes, could not fail to recognize the logic that their actions must be determined by the imperative not to deny the option of the same actions to others. This implies that a rational person must accept the constraints of a system of rules which ensures that all people can make provision for the minimum requirements of survival; to ignore this injunction is irrational. Observation of the real world reveals that both approaches, despite their apparently undeniable logic, have had little impact on the way society has developed, or on how it now proceeds. Perhaps Kant's ambition for human rational powers is unrealistic; perhaps Rawls' conclusion about the self-preservation instincts of human beings is wide of the mark. It certainly seems that, given the option of ethical rationality offered by the philosophers Kant and Rawls, and the economic rationalism offered by contemporary followers of Smith and Bentham, human beings have chosen the latter. The great criticism of *neo-classical* economics is that it considers individual humans as purely economic agents, as rational maximizers. The sad lesson of recent history is that, for most of those who get the choice, economic rationalism and the blind pursuit of self-interest is the option with which they feel most comfortable. But Rawls' theory is still only 30 years old; it took more than a century to abolish slavery.

It is clear that advances in ethical thought have influenced the direction of social change, and helped shape our aspirations for a more just and inclusive society, but the link is not as secure as it might be. Whilst advances in ethical thought leave no doubt that economic matters must be considered in a moral context, this recognition has had only a partial and intermittent impact in the real world of political economy.

Reinhold Niebuhr argued that we cannot expect the moral transformation of society if we rely on the elevation and application of the rational powers of individuals alone. There are quite tight limits, he suggested, on the potential of human rationality.[8] Human rational capacities can be applied in pursuit of any end. It is quite rational for a businessman, whose objective is to increase company profits by 20 per cent annually, to pursue a ruthless policy of undercutting his competitors and driving them out of business, even if this means throwing hundreds of people out of work, and threatening the reputations and careers of his competitors. Rationality, or the application of human reason, is only as effective as the values which direct its use, and the ends towards which it is applied.

The leading contemporary moral philosopher, Peter Singer, has suggested that we are living amidst a revolution in ethics. He describes an *expanding circle*[9] of ethical awareness, spreading outwards from concern for one's own family towards concern for one's compatriots, then to include all human beings, and ultimately other species. It is certainly true that growing numbers of people are succeeding in extending the scope of their moral concern, but not necessarily in ways which are conducive to improved human well-being. For many the circle has extended to include the welfare of animals but has apparently bypassed concern for the wider community of human beings. At best, there is a growing gap between *some* people's perceptions of what is possible for the human race and current realities. One reason for this growing gap is that the capacity for extending the scope of moral concern is enjoyed by too few people for it to translate into practical social change.

Since Thomas More's *Utopia* was published in 1516, many have cherished the notion of a perfectly organized society of contented and cooperating human beings. The ideal may have been condemned as hopelessly unrealistic, but it has remained with us and, as economic advance has produced a better-educated populace, many more have recognized its appeal. The gap between human ideals and human realities has widened not just as a consequence of the elevated moral aspirations of some people, but also, as we have improved our knowledge of the condition of human existence throughout the world, in the way we have allowed reality to slip steadily further from the ideal. In our minds we aspire to a better experience of life for all people, but our collective actions result in an actual worsening of the situation of many. Despite centuries of ethical thought, hundreds of university departments producing thousands of philosophy graduates, a better-educated population in many countries and steady growth in moral awareness among many individuals, substantive progress towards a more equitable world still eludes us; and of late, what gains we have made, have begun to be reversed. We are failing to bridge the gap between what is and what could be, and we urgently need to understand why this is so. We need a strategy which is acutely aware of current realities but which can withstand the temptation to conclude that progress is impossible. To begin, we need to outline a workable ethic to guide us in our task.

In attempting to define a *universal ethic,* we are searching for a basis in ethics for the definition of progress outlined at the beginning of this book. Without a clear, convincingly argued ethical basis for change, progress towards a more inclusive society will lack moral force. A grounding in ethics will help keep the project on course.

The search begins with a simple question: is it wrong to kill another human being? If the question were asked of any group of people, the almost unanimous response would be: 'Yes, of course it is wrong.' If the same group was then asked: 'Why is it wrong?' the unanimity would soon disappear; a number of different answers would be given and many would have no answer beyond: 'It just is.' This failure to recognize and agree on the basis for the moral value we hold most dear is symptomatic of a fundamental weakness in our moral understanding. The problem lies in the way we come to believe that killing, for example, is wrong. We are taught that it is wrong, in the same way that we are taught the rights and wrongs of many aspects of human life: it is wrong to steal; it is wrong to commit adultery; it is wrong to torture a political opponent. We learn these *moral laws* from our parents, our teachers, in church and from various other cultural sources. In short, our path to belief in the rightness and wrongness of killing is a matter of social conditioning, most of which occurs very early in life. We learn the moral law by rote rather than by developing any personal understanding of the nature of moral value or by appealing to any innate ability to determine right from wrong. Our moral outlook, both individual and collective, is heavily shaped by age-old beliefs which change little from generation to generation. The process of moral education is conservative by its very nature.

Subjectivists argue that, in submitting to such *moral law*, we submit not only to what is valuable within in it, but also to the limitations it places on our ability to see issues as having a moral dimension. Moral law gives us a list of rights and wrongs: if we are confronted by a decision which is not easily assessed in terms of this list, we fail to treat it as a moral decision. Without moral law, *all* decisions have to be considered in terms of any moral implication they may have. As currently constituted, moral law puts us under no obligation to do anything to alleviate the suffering of the poor in distant lands. But it does give us security of belief, as without it all values are objectively equal: it is not possible to say that it is better to run to the aid of an elderly person who has fallen than to leave that person to be trampled underfoot. Without moral law, what is right depends entirely on the preferences and values of the individual. Nothing, and no act, possesses value until human beings, individually or collectively, apportion value to it. It is impossible to convince a despot that torturing his political opponents to death is wrong, unless we can convince him that there are other values, such as respect for the lives and well-being of his victims, which he holds more important than his desire to wield power. Most despots do not have their hierarchy of values so ordered.

Karl Polanyi pointed out that civil rights and the rule of law, which have emerged as society has evolved, have made it easier for individuals to live life without reference to ethical considerations. There is no incentive to love your neighbour when you know that the law will protect you from them, and anyone else who threatens your property or personal well-being. But what if there is no moral law, if we are all morally free to decide our attitude and actions towards others? In modern society the question is rather academic, as moral law has been encoded in statutes which are enforced to prevent violent or other antisocial behaviour, but the point is worth pursuing.

Jean-Paul Sartre developed the idea that we are morally free, but for him this freedom was a terrible burden. If there are no moral laws to inform us of right and wrong, how are we to know, asked Sartre, what is the right thing to do and when we have a responsibility to act? He had little faith in the ability of humankind to come to terms with its moral freedom and apply it constructively. To succeed in this task requires a painful assessment of the conflict between our selfish and altruistic desires; but such an assessment, honestly conducted among many individuals, is essential to progress. To ease Sartre's intolerable burden, we can either ignore his essential truth, which is only possible through psychological gymnastics which require consistent denial of reality, *or* we can learn to live with the dual challenge of moral freedom *and* moral responsibility. We can continue to live with a belief in moral law, and accept the limitations it imposes and the consequences that ensue, *or* we can replace it with a system of ethical belief and moral learning adequate to the challenge of building a more equitable global society.

To understand why Sartre's ethical nihilism need not imply social breakdown and a descent into chaos, we must consider the values which are most commonly found in human beings. Prime among these, I would suggest, is the desire to live a long and healthy life. This is something to which virtually all human beings give the highest value. It also tells us why it is wrong to kill: as individuals, we value the preservation of our own lives and are able to identify in others the same preference. I do not want to be killed; other people are like me; it follows that they do not want to die either. What is more, if I condone a state of affairs in which killing is accepted, then it is quite possible that I too will fall victim to a murderer. The argument can be extended: if I condone a state of affairs in which people are allowed to starve to death for want of an economic system which provides everyone with the opportunity to work to secure their basic needs, then I might also fall victim to its arbitrariness. This example illustrates the importance of the capacity to identify with others as being like ourselves in forming our moral beliefs. A stable society need not depend on the ability of its members to follow rules blindly. A better society would be built on a mutual capacity to identify common preferences and desires among the population and to organize society in a way that allows for these preferences to be met. This capacity for identification with the interests of others has to be realised in everyone. Even a small minority of non-identifiers, just like a small minority of non-submitters to the moral law, could lead to the break-down of civil society.

Essentially, we have arrived at the so-called *Golden Rule* of human conduct: 'Do unto others as you would have them do unto you.' It is perhaps the only injunction to human behaviour that is common to all the great religious traditions. But some versions of the *Golden Rule* fall into the moral law trap. Confucius stated the rule as: 'Do not do to others what you would not like yourself.' At first glance, the two appear the same. In practice they can be interpreted differently. The second provides only negative injunctions: we none of us want to die or have our houses burgled, so as a society we legislate against killing and stealing; but stated thus, the rule provides no obligation to take positive action. Like moral law, it leaves us free to ignore the consequences of our inaction and is, again, inherently conservative.

The contemporary philosophical expression of the golden rule is termed *the principle of equal consideration of interests*. As a basis for moral progress this principle is key, but it remains incomplete without a definition of the scope of its application. When making moral decisions, just whose interests are we supposed to consider as equal to our own? Those of our family and friends, people who live in the same town or country, people who speak the same language, people of the same gender or sexual orientation, people of the same skin colour, or *all* human beings? To answer the question correctly we must determine precisely what interests we can identify as being commonly held across these various groups. This is a re-run of the exercise by which we determined the universality of basic needs in Chapter 3. Those basic needs, material and instrumental, are prerequisites for a healthy, comfortable and fulfilling life, and are common to all people. If our moral decisions are to be guided by our capacity to identify with the preferences of others, and if that capacity extends to all human beings in respect of these universal basic preferences, then it is quite illogical arbitrarily to limit the scope of our moral concern to any sub-group of the human race.

The principal means by which we limit the scope of our moral concern is *relativism*. In ancient Greece, Protagorus was the first to suggest that the moral and political norms of any particular culture or society were necessarily correct. Some argue that the vast cultural differences that exist between nations and peoples preclude any attempt to define a universal moral standard which transcends national borders and cultural differences. But this position is not compatible with the suggestion that our moral concern should extend to all those with whom we can identify, or with the universality of common ethical concern we have already identified. Some multinational companies have been exposed for sub-contracting their manufacturing processes to Third World enterprises which employ children, pay below a living wage, and require their employees to work in dreadful conditions. Relativists argue that such low moral standards simply reflect the current stage of development in these countries:working conditions are the same as they were in Europe at the beginning of the industrial revolution. But this argument supposes that these countries will follow a developmental path similar to that of the industrialized nations, and that ultimately their moral standards, and business practices, will catch up. This is not only extremely convenient for firms looking for cheaper labour, but it ignores the fact that what has happened in Europe over the last two hundred years cannot possibly happen in most countries of the Third World. In any case, is it really necessary for these societies to repeat our painful learning processes – can we not pass on the benefit of our experience?

There are clear links between economic security and moral capacity: people are more likely to show concern for the well-being of others when they themselves feel economically secure. But the global economic order denies most poor countries the opportunity to promote widespread economic security. It encourages an inequitable distribution of economic goods which serves the interests of an elite minority, the same minority which is often the first to condemn the attempts of human rights groups to impose moral standards which they believe to be unnecessary and inappropriate. Increasingly, moral standards in poor countries are held back not by cultural and religious customs, but by the interests of big business. There is no point in trying to impose moral standards without allowing these countries the means to increase the material well-being of a larger part of their populations; history shows that this is the only path to moral advancement. With globalization, the argument becomes even more striking: a single global society cannot apply relative moral values to its members without deciding that some lives are worth more than others. When it is the privileged and wealthy who back such decisions, it should be clear that we are not witnessing the consequences of an inevitable and unalterable moral and social order. Through the use of relativism, those whom it suits to give different moral value to the lives of different individuals and groups have one objective in mind: to maintain the balance of power and privilege in their favour.

Universal application of the principle of equal consideration of interests could, under certain circumstances, impose an unrealistic duty on individuals in respect of the interests of others. It seems reasonable, therefore, that the rule should only be applied in respect of those on whom our individual actions have an impact. Thus, a peasant farmer, whose entire life is spent providing for the basic needs of her family through working the land, would have few obligations to others under the principle, except perhaps to her neighbours whose crops may be destroyed by her goat, if left untethered. In traditional, simply organized societies it is easy to set the scope for application of the principle. When society becomes as complex as it has in the industrialized world, and becomes globalized to boot, defining the range of impact of our actions, and therefore the scope of our moral responsibility, becomes a far more complicated task.

The currently preferred means for attempting to ensure a universal minimum ethical standard is the advocacy of human rights. But where do such rights come from? Are we born with them; do we acquire them as we mature; do they exist independently of our individual lives? The answer to these questions might provide some explanation as to why there is such widespread denial of human rights and why we tend to focus on cases where political rights are violated whilst largely ignoring the violation of the more basic economic rights of millions.

Rights can only be accorded to individuals by their peers in society and they usually reflect the moral beliefs of the individuals or groups who bestow them. If the United Nations, as it has done, bestows rights on all people which are patently unenforceable, we can safely assume that the moral aspirations of UN officials do not reflect those of world society at large as manifest through the actions of national political leaders, even if their governments are democratically elected and have signed the UN Charter. To return to the torture chamber for a moment: trying to convince the despot that, in torturing his prisoner, he is committing a flagrant abuse of his victim's human rights will do no good whatsoever. For the despot his opponent has no rights. Given that we have developed the means to produce sufficient food for all the world's people, the same could be said of the millions who suffer and die from malnutrition. Their right to life-sustaining nourishment is denied by those of us who could act to ensure they have sufficient to eat, but elect not to. To avoid personal implication in any widespread abuse of human rights, we tend not to consider death through malnutrition as a human rights issue. But Article 25 of the UN Declaration includes the right to food, and all of us, surely, can identify with the universal human requirement for nourishment.

It is interesting how human rights, as popularly defended, include those abuses which are opposable by national governments or international institutions without threatening the dominance or reputation of the economic system, whereas social and economic rights designed to guard against hunger and poverty are generally denied or ignored. As an apparently inescapable feature of our chosen mode of economic organization, they are excluded from the debate about human rights.

Only when sufficient numbers develop and apply the capacity to identify with the interests of others to its full extent, such that the political landscape is altered, will basic human rights for all become an enforceable reality. In the meantime we can only occupy ourselves with the very important, but numerically insignificant, human rights violations involving political prisoners and the like.

Rejection of the moral-law approach to ethics does not mean we should reject all of its injunctions; many of them are commonly held subjective preferences, confirmed by testing under the principle of equal consideration of interests. The injunction against killing should, and will, remain a universally held moral belief. But examination of the injunction against stealing illustrates the shortcomings of moral law. Under the principle of equal consideration of interests, it would be impossible to condemn an act of theft committed against a rich factory owner by one of his employees whose wage is insufficient to buy the drugs necessary to save the lives of his dying children. Here, stealing appears to be a positively moral action, but adherence to moral law would fail to produce a moral outcome: stealing is wrong, the desperate father is a criminal. In rich countries, consideration of mitigating circumstances might lead to a lighter sentence; in poor countries, where moral law functions in its purest form, this ultimately moral act may well result in a lynching. When applied to larger issues of humanity, this systemic failure in the moral law approach enables many of the most compelling moral issues of our time to be conveniently swept under the carpet.

Universalism is the term given by philosophers to the ethical principles we have been moving towards in this discussion. It represents a commitment and belief that all human lives are of equal value, and that no human being should take action, or participate in group actions, which compromise those interests which we have defined as universal to humankind, for any individual. What about personal freedom, the liberty of the individual to pursue his or her interests unhindered? Individual freedom was near the top of Kant's list of priorities, but he placed legitimate limits on the freedom of the individual; specifically, that it does not interfere with the like freedom of anyone else. For Karl Polanyi, the ultimate freedom was the freedom to live an ethical life, not simply to pursue whatever course of action one desired. Polanyi drew a distinction between collective and personal freedom, suggesting that collective freedom, freedom for all people, can only be achieved once people learn to subordinate their personal freedom to the demands of collective freedom.

It is worth reminding ourselves that, whilst there are many constraints and practical obstacles to movement to a more inclusive society, *human nature is not one of them.* As we have discussed, aspects of human behaviour are clearly influenced by our evolutionary heritage. The arguments of evolutionary psychologists find support in a popular culture happy to excuse selfish, arrogant and often violent behaviour, and by those desperate to justify prevailing economic orthodoxy and the social status quo. But the world is littered with evidence of millions of individuals, alone or in groups, overcoming the confines of 'human nature', and our supposed innate preferences for competitive and aggressive behaviour, and working cooperatively towards common ends in ways that strongly suggest the possibility of an innate preference for a world arranged on the basis of universalism.

Universalism does not call for sudden and absolute change in the social order: by its own definitions it cannot do so. Revolutionary change inevitably provokes discord and a forceful and violent defence of its position by any group which perceives a threat to its interests. A society based on universalism cannot emerge until it can do so peaceably and with the conscious and calculated support of the vast majority of people. Any attempt to impose such a moral order before these conditions pertain will fail.

Might it not be argued that the philosophy of universalism is not just another ideology? Critics of Karl Marx point out that the upshot of his theory of *historical materialism* was the replacement of traditional, theistic religious faith with an unreflective and unquestioning adherence to an ideology which was, in effect, just another *opium of the masses:* a set of beliefs which saved people the trouble of having to think about the world around them, their role in it and its effect upon their lives. Could not the same criticism be levelled at universalism?

There are two essential aspects of universalism which disqualify it as an ideology, and deny it the status of a potential religion. First, a universal outlook cannot be learned without being fully understood. Full understanding requires reflection and introspection, a reasonable standard of education, psychological health and emotional maturity. Ideologies and unquestioning religious beliefs are generally adopted by people who prefer not to think for themselves, who are happy to let others provide them with a ready-made world view and an implicit set of values. Second, religious faith, as framed by most of the major world religions, claims that the source of values and beliefs are extra-human, usually the word of God transmitted through the medium of a representative on earth.

Universalism is an explicitly human value and belief system. It may share certain values with institutional religions, which apportion responsibility for value to a non-human source, but universalism does not. It argues that only self-generating values, values sourced from within the psyches of human beings, are likely to be fully meaningful and succeed in motivating people to truly moral action. At the same time, the only human-sourced value system possible, given our psychic unity and commonality of experience and aspiration, is universalism. If individuals who succeed in internalising universal morality choose to look upon it as a replacement for traditional religious faith, then all well and good – such belief, of itself, can do no harm. The philosophy of universalism comes with a guarantee of authenticity; it can only be denied or contradicted by an alternative philosophy which suggests that all lives are not of equal value, and that we are under no obligation to organize society so that everyone is afforded the opportunity to live a decent and rewarding life.

This universal ethic provides a philosophical basis for transformative social change in pursuit of improved economic justice and the universal provision of basic needs, but in practice these goals remain a long way off. At the very least, there is no longer any question over the separation of economics and ethics: they belong together; it was to this end that Karl Polanyi dedicated much of his life's work. Aware of the role of philosophers and economists in the systematic separation of these co-dependent spheres, Polanyi focused on the practical implications of the split: the unconscious abandonment of ethical concern by ordinary people in their everyday lives, as the terms of their economic existence were altered by forces beyond their control.

In Britain, prior to the seismic changes of the early nineteenth century, which Polanyi described in his book, *The Great Transformation,* a more inclusive approach to economic relations within communities was the norm, not consciously enacted by individuals according to a particular set of ethical rules, but rather because for centuries survival had been dependent on mutual cooperation and neighbourly concern among ordinary people. With the systematic disembedding of the economy from established cultural forms and social structures, people and communities were left with no way to mediate their exchange relations. Not only did the economy cease to meet the needs of the people, but the social structures and cultural institutions of which it formed part also lost their principal purpose. And so people came to lament the collapse of traditional community structures, whilst at the same time bemoaning the failure of modernity to provide the economic security they once enjoyed. What they failed to identify was that this double assault on their well-being was part of the same inexorable process.

As Polanyi pointed out, the great failing of capitalism in its relation with traditional culture is its dependence for success on values like trust, honesty, diligence, and strong family and community ties, which, by its very mechanisms, it systematically undermines.[10] He thus argued that the process of disembedding the economy from culture would have to be reversed if we were to halt accelerating economic polarization and social breakdown. Today, a solution based solely on reviving a sense of community spirit seems quite unattainable. The process of globalization, of which Polanyi detected early signs, has so altered the perceptions and world view of so many people that calls for a return to traditional ways and means for economic provision are unlikely to be heeded. In any case, environmental concerns and population growth mean that small-scale, community-based systems for economic provision, whilst giving some pointers to new and sustainable forms of social organization, cannot in themselves address the problem of universal needs provision.

This brings us to another debate among philosophers, that between universalists and communitarians. The universalist position is that which this book follows: that the only way to assure minimum levels of well-being for all people is to promote widespread understanding of the moral imperative of identifying the kind of economic conditions in which universal needs provision is possible. It is often viewed as incompatible with the communitarian position which suggests that, given the limits of human rational powers, the only means to solving the problem of inequity in basic needs provision is through individuals learning (or relearning) to identify with the interests of those with whom they interact on a regular basis, that is to say the members of their immediate community. If they succeed in this, then, as a consequence of the obvious mutual co-interest and co-dependency that exists, they will be able to build and sustain social structures which guarantee the well-being of all members of that community.

There are two problems with this approach. Firstly, the power of individual members of local communities over the economic resources on which much basic needs provision depends is limited or non-existent. The vast majority of productive capacity is concentrated in the hands of those who control international capital, own land and the right to exploit the planet's natural resources, and wield economic power through multinational corporations. At best, a communitarian approach will bring about a second-class, informal local economy. It may be sufficient for the community-minded participants, and within itself may be environmentally sustainable, but it would leave most productive resources and wealth in the hands of a small global minority whose objectives are in conflict with initiatives of self-sufficiency, and whose lifeblood, expanding markets, will not be served by communities opting out of the formal economy. Unless the problem of concentrated ownership of economic resources is tackled, it will undermine any such attempts at communitarian provision – if nothing else by commodifying it: by turning communities into franchises.

The other shortcoming of the communitarian approach concerns the question of scope. Without an injunction not to act in ways which compromise universal needs provision, schemes for community-wide provision will be devised which, whilst quite equitable to all its members, actively deny provision to members of other communities. A world consisting of independent communities, all attempting to meet the needs of their own constituents, and competing with others for the requisite resources, will fragment and polarize: conflict between communities will be inevitable.

This is not to argue that there is no role for the type of community values supported by communitarians, just that those values should not be restricted to a limited group. Communitarians suggest that widening the scope of ethical concern to include all humans is too ambitious an aim; that people can only relate effectively to others with whom they have daily contact, or who they recognize as part of their community. This is not necessarily true. There is often intense antagonism among members of tight-knit communities. Conversely, great solidarity is found between townspeople on different continents who have formed a mutual bond through twinning schemes. And much Third World development work is funded by people in rich countries 'adopting' or sponsoring children or families in poor countries. Whether such initiatives make a great deal of difference is debatable, but they certainly provide evidence that many thousands of people draw a great deal of pride and satisfaction from the ability to make tangible their natural tendency to empathize and identify with the interests of people with whom they have no more in common than any member of the human race.

There is no chance of re-embedding economic systems within the social and cultural structures which determine the roles that individuals play in society; this would require all people, once again, to become quite unconscious of relations between economy and culture. But our response to this crisis is well under way: it is the development of a conscious rational ethic which acknowledges the consequences of this cultural dislocation and the need for explicit injunctions to ensure the economy meets its social obligations. This project is 200 years old: it was born of the Enlightenment. Along the way it was hijacked by the vested interests of minority wealth and elite power. It is about time it was won back for the interests of all human beings.

In 1932, Reinhold Niebuhr argued that the Enlightenment project was fatally flawed; that humankind was simply not up to the task of building a moral society on the basis of rational will. Niebuhr did not dispute the capacity of individuals to develop their rational powers to the extent necessary to adopt a universal ethic but believed that, when the rational wills of all people were aggregated into the collective will of human groups, something happened which not only crushed the moral aspirations of individuals, but also resulted in their absolute corruption.[11] There was nothing moral, or even morally aspiring, in the actions of collectives. In his 1960 preface to a new edition of *Moral Man and Immoral Society*, Niebuhr argued that his basic thesis remained valid: that those who argue for change towards a more inclusive social order 'fail to recognise the basic difference between the morality of individuals and the morality of collectives, whether races, classes, or nations'.[12]

The evidence of the twentieth century suggests that Niebuhr was right on the matter of collective morality. He argues persuasively that the individual will is corrupted when people decide to identify and show solidarity with a collective, and the selfish tendencies of individuals are projected onto the collective group and amplified many times. This thesis is borne out by the catalogue of wars between nations and conflicts between ethnic groups that scar our recent history. But we need to consider the limits of the collective, and identify by whom, and quite how, those limits are defined. Perceptions of race, ethnicity and nationhood will be considered in the next chapter; the only point to be made here is that, under a universal ethic, there is only one collective, that of the entire human race. To argue that we should all opt out of our current groupings and into one big group may seem unrealistic, but, as we uncover the artifice underlying current perceptions of ethnicity and nationhood, the argument to set the scope of our moral concern as wide as possible will gain more weight.

Problems of inter-group conflict arise from the tendency for those who have failed to develop universalistic moral aspirations to assume positions of power within our societies, and the failure of those who do desire a more inclusive world to be able to do anything to stop them. The way to progress is to identify the factors which limit the development of rational powers within individuals, which deny people exposure to the possibility of a better world, and which obstruct people in their desire to form an independent and objective world view. Currently, the moral limits for society are set low by those it suits to keep them there. The huge imbalance in economic power can only be overcome by a huge shift in the balance of moral power.

The one consolation we can draw from the immense success of the globalization project is its proof of just how similar people the world over are. If they can be so easily sold a system which not only wrecks their cultures, but promises the vast majority a rapid reduction in economic security, imagine how they might respond to the possibility of new ways of living which offer not only security, but access to similar opportunities as the rest of humankind.

Crucial values are the ones we all share, and these are the values targeted by our current economic system in its assault on human cultural value and creative potential. They are the values defended by a universal ethic, and the only values by which all humans can enjoy liberty and freedom from want. There is no compromise position between a universal ethic and some other ethical standpoint: rejection of the universal position implies that some human lives are of less value than others, and when that is allowed the whole ethic breaks down. A world based on a universal ethic may take generations to build, but we must hold on to its forming principle: that all human lives are of equal value.

Consideration of philosophical issues as they pertain to the real world must not be confined to the realms of academia. If they are to have any practical bearing, it is essential they gain a wider audience. In the millennia since philosophical debate moved from Socrates' beloved market-place to Plato's Academy, these issues have become the preserve of intellectuals who have brought us little nearer to solving the essential questions of human existence. We badly need to start making up for lost time, and we must begin by examining the myths and untruths which are promoted by those whose objectives are diametrically opposed to those of universalism, and which make it almost impossible for us to see the world as it really is.

6

Perception and Reality

THE NATURE of society is determined by a complex combination of many factors: the perceptions of individuals; the assessment by individuals of their rights, duties and responsibilities toward others; the actions of individuals motivated by these perceptions and assessments; and the power relations that mediate the impact of these actions. This description accommodates both sides of the question: do we shape society, or does it shape us? The answer depends entirely on the perceptions and actions of individuals, and the balance of power within society. To the extent that these components are fluid, individuals can shape society and bring about change towards any desired ends. If individual perceptions are fixed, and if there is something about society which dictates unchanging power relations which favour the interests of one group over another, then society will largely shape our individual perceptions and world view, and set very tight limits on the possibility for change. Encouragingly, there are many who refuse to allow their perceptions to be shaped by the dominant world view, but we need to identify the factors that frustrate our aspirations for a new social order, and the forces which keep too many people unwilling or unconscious participants in an economic system which is not in their best interests.

If securing essential economic goods is a high priority for all people, is there anything to be learned from historical changes in perceptions of how the economy shapes people's lives? Karl Marx believed that a growing awareness of the reality of social and economic forces among working people would prove a catalyst for transformative social change. Marx was too optimistic: in the last century and a half, the interests of wealth and privilege have proved equal to any increase in social consciousness among the masses. Although political economy is more complex than in Marx's time, its basic premises remain unaltered – yet our awareness of economics, and our perception of its impact on our lives, has barely improved.

Thinking about economics is not something that excites us, even though it determines almost every aspect of the way we live. Perhaps this is not surprising given that, after several million years of not thinking about how we came by our daily bread, decisions over economic matters quickly became the exclusive domain of a ruling elite. The idea that people could play a role in economic decision-making emerged only very recently with the arrival of democratic politics. But, just as we find ourselves at last poised to have our say, our leaders tell us that the economy is largely beyond political control. What a deadly combination: a population denied the chance to understand the economic basis for their material existence, and a political establishment who claim impotence over it.

If we are unable to think of our own security in terms of the larger economic picture, then we are not easily going to identify our situation as co-dependent with the situations of others, and certainly not that of all humans. We struggle to accept the possibility of universal needs provision because the economic system keeps us in its thrall by promoting an environment of fear, instability and insecurity. Just as it did with our bronze-age ancestors, the economy plays into the hands of our fragile, immature psyches. Real change requires an act of collective moral will. History predicts against this, but, just because we have so far refused to embrace the possibility of progress, does not mean we never can. Great leaps forward are marked by immense changes in the way we perceive and act, often in ways which would have been ridiculed or condemned only a generation before. A different kind of economy is well within our grasp.

The prevailing economic system and the political structures that support it need to be radically overhauled if the global economy is to be brought into line with our moral aspirations. Current arrangements cannot provide for the basic needs of all people and maintain the global population at sustainable levels. The present system showers material benefits on the privileged at the expense of the welfare of the disadvantaged. It creates conditions that encourage fertility at a rate which guarantees early death or a miserable existence to a third of all those born, and it leads to a diminution of cultural diversity which leaves people unable to find contentment without resort to further consumption of the same type which left them unsatisfied in the first place. We have a moral basis for change; we know the failings of the current order. What then stands in the way of progress? Simply answered: the apparent ease with which individuals are prepared to submit to beliefs engendered by others, by society and through the mass media, without questioning. We need to identify the source of this apathy and willing acceptance of the status quo.

History suggests confusion and ambiguity in our approach to values. We make considerable and genuine progress in some respects yet fail miserably in many others. The post-war consensus moved the economies of many countries in the direction of greater inclusion. More people had a bigger slice of a growing economic cake and most had their basic needs met. By the 1960s greater numbers were economically secure and had their needs for health care and education better provided for than at any time in history. But all was not well. Even happy and successful humans, it seems, need someone to demonize, and in the Soviet Union a target was found. The western powers, led by the United States, set about fighting the 'red menace' wherever the opportunity arose. Many newly independent African countries were destroyed by proxy wars fought by the two superpowers, but it was South-East Asia, and the war centred on Vietnam, which revealed the limited scope of the western powers' cosy consensus.

Ultimately, technological advance revealed the truth. Just as financing the war in Vietnam had led to the collapse of the economic mechanisms which had kept the western economies on a steady course, so improvements in communications technology, and the emergence of a commercially driven mass media, brought the world news of the dreadful events in South-East Asia. The image of an improving, progressive, inclusive world was shattered. Many in Europe and America, unable to express their opposition through democratic mechanisms, took to the streets in protest at the war for its futility, injustice and the immense loss of life on both sides. Such protest would have been impossible only a decade earlier. In terms of the numbers involved, the degree of organization, and the finesse with which anti-establishment arguments were articulated, the reaction was unprecedented.

Vietnam was a watershed in the development of independent human thought, and though a particularly hideous and unjust war was the focus, the conditions giving rise to such articulate opposition were wholly to do with the economic success of the post-war period. Once substantial numbers had less cause to worry about providing for their own families, more people became concerned with the plight of others: those at home and abroad who were excluded from the gains of economic success. The 1960s was not only a time of protest against Vietnam, it also saw the beginnings of campaigns against the arms race, against racial discrimination, against the oppression of homosexuals, and the launch of the modern feminist movement. Many people were, for the first time, able to express a latent concern for the interests of others, as the experience of improving economic security allowed a widening in the scope of their moral concern. It is a simple and obvious rule: people are more inclined to consider the interests of others when they feel their own position to be secure. But if greater economic inclusion means a broadening in moral outlook, it does not follow that reversals in economic progress imply moral regress. Once people learn the art of independent thought, it cannot be taken from them. At the very least, a new generation has to fail to repeat its parents' progress before all the gains can be reversed. Many of the moral gains of the 1960s continued through the economic meltdown of the 1970s, and despite the reconstruction of the global economy on less inclusive lines in the 1980s. It is the legacy of the post-war economic consensus, the cultural revolution of the 1960s and the rapid expiry of both that we now have such a gap between our moral aspirations and social reality.

When measuring progress towards universalist ideals, and the extent to which a society is becoming more or less inclusive, we can divide the world in two ways. We can set a quantitative threshold for economic opportunity and security, assess how many people fall either side of the line and then measure changes in the split over time. Alternatively, we can examine people's attitudes toward others, the extent to which opportunity and security is denied to certain groups on the basis of race, ethnicity, nationality, gender, sexuality or disability. It is insufficient to consider the position in society of so-called minorities solely in terms of the prejudice and discrimination they suffer. Prejudice is not simply a matter of opinion or attitude: the exclusion of people on the basis of their belonging to minority groups is an economic matter. It is impossible to imagine a scenario in which people from minorities have equal economic opportunity and security until they are afforded equal status as human beings.

The effect of prejudice and discrimination is to restrict the basic rights of members of certain groups and invariably this means access to the economy. We need to assess the link between general economic exclusion – the simple measure of haves to have-nots – and the extent to which minorities are excluded. If there is a proportionate spread of minorities above and below the economically included threshold, then we can conclude that prejudice against minority groups is not a contributing factor in economic division, and that the privileged have equal disdain for the interests of others regardless of their minority status. If, on the other hand, there is disproportionate representation of minorities among those below the threshold of inclusion, then we can conclude that prejudice and discrimination play a role in the distribution of economic goods in society. A cursory glance at the balance of economic wealth in the world today, both within wealthy societies and globally, indicates that belonging to a minority is not good for your economic prospects.

So which is more important: the tendency of humans to fail to identify with the interests of other humans *per se*, and so support economic arrangements which are divisive and polarising, or the tendency for humans to disregard the interests of those they identify as belonging to a group different to their own? And what does this tell us about the underlying causes of social injustice? Further, do both forms of the failure to extend the scope of moral concern to all people have a common solution, or are they quite different?

These are important questions because the last few decades have thrown up an interesting inconsistency. Divisive economic policies have coexisted with progress in respect of reducing discrimination. In many countries the position of women has improved. In the United States and South Africa, racist legislation has been repealed. In some countries homosexual men and women no longer feel the need to conceal their sexuality, and religious intolerance has eased in some regions. It seems that we care less about other humans *per se,* that is to say we are less concerned with poverty and deprivation, and at the same time we are more concerned with the plight of those whose exclusion is specific to certain traits or groups allegiances. We can identify two distinct but interrelated measures of moral progress: movement towards a more economically-inclusive society, and movement towards a more culturally-inclusive society. Overall, economic inclusiveness has worsened, whilst cultural inclusiveness, at least in the rich countries where more people enjoy economic security, has improved. It seems we are more inclined to fight for the rights of others when we perceive their disadvantage to be a result of unwarranted discrimination on racial or other 'minority' grounds than we are if we perceive them to be victims of an economic system which inevitably has winners and losers.

In order to identify any link between these two forms of exclusion and discrimination, we must examine each in turn, beginning with the pervasive tendency among all humans to place people in groups and afford them different status accordingly.

As we saw in Chapter 2, failure to identify with other humans as like ourselves is unique to our species. We are the only animals actively to apply variable standards of behaviour to our fellows on the basis of arbitrary distinctions. Interestingly, our capacity to differentiate other humans from ourselves arose, with culture, at about the same stage in human development that we learned of the value of amassing economic surpluses. There is no evidence of inter-group warfare before economic surplus. There is a deep historical and cultural link then, between our tendency to compartmentalize our species, and our desire to secure economic goods both for their prestige value and the perception of security they afford. The division of humans into groups was an essential and necessary part of the development of society. Long ago, it served the cause of progress well; without it there could have been no advance.

Ten thousand years on, however, our continuing commitment to such division threatens our collective existence.

There are many criteria by which humans divide themselves into groups. Among the most important are: race, gender, ethnicity, nationality, culture, religion, and sexuality. The first two of these are different from the others in that they are self-evident. Perhaps the most contentious and destructive division, the one that has been the focus for most prejudice, is that of race.

We have discussed the origin of differences in the physical appearance of people from various races as a consequence of the process of evolution. This is why some humans look different from other humans, but the difference is superficial and external. Natural selection takes thousands of years to create a population of distinct physical characteristics, and it requires three things: for humans to settle in different environments, for isolated groups to remain *in situ* for many thousands of years, and for periodic bouts of additional migration to new lands to take place, where once again populations become established for long periods. These conditions pertained on earth for two millions years until about ten thousand years ago, when migrations became much more frequent and involved many more people. At that point, the process was reversed: the boundaries between isolated races began to be broken down. There was greater mixing of historically isolated gene pools and previously stark distinctions began to be blurred. This process accelerated rapidly as new modes of transport were invented. Visit Brazil today and you will see the outcome of interracial procreation: a population which largely defies racial categorization.

Various attempts have been made to classify humans by their physical appearance. Early efforts were motivated by the need of anthropologists to find some quasi-scientific justification for the exploitation and mistreatment of the non-European races. Less politically-minded academics were interested to discover whether any intrinsic biological differences between races lay behind the quite different levels of social, cultural and economic development to be observed in much of the world outside Europe. We have identified the reasons for accelerated European socio-cultural advance, and seen how, until only five hundred years ago, China, West Africa and southern India were at least as well developed as Europe. We know, therefore, that rates of socio-cultural development are not racially determined. No serious evidence has been offered in support of this claim, but the idea has become established as if fact.

The development of genetics has provided genuine science-based opportunities to unearth the truth about racial difference and its implications for the organization of human society. The notion that race has implications for human potential, and is a justification for social inequity, is found in the work of those who have set out to provide a genetic basis, linked to racial difference, for differing levels of intelligence in humans.

The principal focus for debate about race and intelligence is Richard Herrnstein and Charles Murray's book, *The Bell Curve: Intelligence and Class Structure in American Life*. Herrnstein and Murray did not set out, explicitly, to formulate a theory of race and intelligence, but their approach to the subject, and the inevitability of the controversy that followed, suggests some intent on their part. They claim to have been motivated by the need to establish greater certainty about the underlying causes of human intelligence, because they feared that state intervention to assist those unable to support themselves was idealistic and futile. If intelligence is innate, they suggested, there is little point in society trying to reduce social injustices which are the product of genetic factors. The authors were also concerned about welfare dependency: that if people were paid not to work, they would be encouraged into 'dysfunctional attitudes and behaviours'. Further, they were worried that, if intelligence was heritable, society was likely to become stratified into a system of *cognitive castes* as people of lower intelligence intermarried and reproduced at a faster rate than those of higher intelligence. This would indeed be a concern if intelligence was profoundly determined by genetic factors, but in 850 pages the authors failed to provide conclusive proof.

Herrnstein and Murray argued that intelligence, as measured by IQ, is largely genetically inherited, and that there is a positive correlation between IQ and socio-economic success. They strongly suggested that socio-economic success and failure have a genetic cause. The first point to acknowledge is that there are measurable differences in IQ between different groups of humans; indeed, average IQ for white Americans is slightly higher than for African-Americans. IQ, or *intelligence quotient*, is a measure of ability designed early in the twentieth century which purports to measure abilities which are reckoned to give a reliable comparative measure of that human quality generally known as intelligence, and which is perceived to influence prospects in life heavily. Some argue that the only reason quantified intelligence is a useful guide to life prospects is that we arrange society to reward those with intelligence as we have defined it in our assessment of IQ. We have created a meritocracy based on a single measure; in the process we have defined the values that underpin society without considering other measures of value. Nonetheless, intelligence as measured by IQ is a consistent indicator of difference between individuals, and we have to begin with the observation that such difference exists.

There is considerable statistical evidence for a degree of heritability for intelligence; that is to say, a correlation between IQ in parents and their children. However, heritability does not imply *genetic* inheritance alone; it simply means a link between parents and children. The cause of this link may, in part, be genetic, but it will also be the result of environmental factors. In fact, it has so far proved impossible to determine accurately what part of the correlation between IQ in parents and children is due to genes, although many studies suggest it to be around 50 per cent. This only means that genetic inheritance is *likely* to be responsible for around half of the factors which influence and shape a child's IQ. It is only likely, we cannot be certain, because the process by which the parents' genes are mixed in the child is extremely complex and quite random. There is no single gene, or even a set of genes, for intelligence which can be isolated and measured. There are many hundreds of genes which may contribute to intelligence. Different genes may play a role in different children, depending on the environment to which the child is exposed and with which its genes interact. Certainly the genes that partially influence intelligence are inherited, but IQ in any measurable sense is not. We know this much from the science of *quantitative genetics* which uses statistical techniques that place proper boundaries on the extent to which we can legitimately infer a genetic basis for qualities and abilities in human beings. In 1997, a comprehensive study applied the techniques of quantitative genetics to the data used by Herrnstein and Murray to highlight a glaring deficiency in the statistical analysis underlying the latter's claim for a heavy genetic basis for intelligence.[1]

During reproduction, the child-to-be inherits 50 per cent of its genes from each parent. It will inherit some whole genes from either parent, and some genes which are a mixture of both parents' genes. The inheritance of mixed genes is know as *non-additive* inheritance and is useless as a predictor of traits in the child as it is impossible to know precisely how these genes were mixed from the source material provided by each parent. For this reason, a child could turn out to have more of the right kind of genes that influence intelligence than either of its parents. On the other hand, its parents may have much higher measurable IQ than their 'intelligence' genes suggest they should have because they were raised in an environment which was conducive to high intelligence. Herrnstein and Murray's theses is undermined by their failure to acknowledge the random nature of non-additive inheritance. Whereas their analysis suggests a heritability rate for intelligence of up to 80 per cent considerable and significant, the quantitative geneticists, who distinguish between *broad-sense heritability* (which includes non-additive inheritance, the scale and impact of which is unknown), and *narrow-sense heritability* (the only reliable measure), find a heritability rate of only 34 per cent.

This is all rather complicated, and the statistical methodology involved is beyond the scope of this book, but what is clear is that, according to the best science, genes, although contributing to intelligence, constitute at most half the picture. Environment plays an equal role.

So much for genes and intelligence – what about race? The authors of the 1997 study state, 'it is very unlikely that the IQ differential between races can be explained by genetics only'.[2] They reach this conclusion by assuming that the genes for intelligence, like all genes, are a product of natural selection working over thousands of years, and find no reason for intelligence to be selected for more in one racial group than another. The evolutionary cause of racial difference is environmental, and, whilst evolutionary environments varied, the reactions of our ancestors to them in their struggle for survival were similar wherever humans settled. Ten thousand years ago, humans discovered agriculture and began to apply new technologies with equal invention the world over. Only a thousand years ago did different groups of humans start 'developing' at different rates, and, as we have seen, this was largely for geographical and political reasons. Further, our genes have barely changed in ten thousand years. The genes that play a partial role in shaping intelligence in contemporary humans are identical to those possessed by our forager ancestors. The abilities and qualities we exhibit today are a consequence of culture. Certainly they are transmitted from generation to generation, but only partially through our genes, and there is no evidence to suggest that evolution left some races of humans with a genetic disadvantage. The final piece of evidence against a genetic cause for differences in IQ among people from different racial groups is provided by research into the IQs of people of mixed race, which shows no significant correlation between the proportion of white blood and rising intelligence.

If genes are not a reliable indicator of intelligence, and the intelligence-influencing genes are spread evenly across all human populations, then the differences in measured IQ between blacks and whites in the United States must have other causes. This suggests that social interventions to improve the environment for those human groups whose opportunities are necessarily limited by poverty, poor parenting and inadequate education are worthwhile. However, the net effect of the debate still resonating around *The Bell Curve* is an unfounded belief in wider society that intelligence is principally a matter of genes, and that black people are generally less intelligent and are therefore destined to remain on or near the bottom rung of the social ladder.

There is a further reason why we cannot be certain of the extent to which genes play a role in inheritance. Recent research suggests other factors have an impact on intelligence and other aspects of a person's character. There is considerable evidence that pre-natal maternal care and the environment to which the foetus is subjected in its mother's womb, are significant contributors to IQ. Poor nutrition and alcohol or drug abuse on the part of the mother all have a serious negative effect on brain development in the unborn infant, and subsequently on IQ. Similarly, inadequate nurturing and stimulatory input in the early months of life can lead to failures in brain development which are often irreversible. The quality and nature of education in the early years is also crucial. It has been shown that children who receive guidance in learning strategies, before they are required to accumulate the mass of knowledge and information we generally associate with education, turn out to be higher achievers and have higher IQs. These circumstances are much less likely to be encountered by the children of poor, less well-educated parents. Genes are the junior partner in the biology-environment dichotomy that determines intelligence; there is evidence that children from bad environments, if caught in time, can be assisted to catch up through teaching interventions which compensate for shortcomings in infancy. On this reading, if there was sufficient collective will to make the necessary investment, the differences in intelligence between racial groups could be wiped out in a couple of generations.

Whatever Herrnstein and Murray's motivation, their arguments are unfounded in science, and are devoid of any reference to morality. I set about my investigation of the race-IQ issue with an open mind. If I had found the truth to be that people of European descent have a genetic predisposition to higher intelligence, which gave them social and economic advantages in the modern world, I would have accepted this. I would then have argued for a moral duty to arrange society so that all people, regardless of genetic predisposition, were able to access their basic needs. But there is no substantive genetic predisposition for intelligence, or any other indicators of potential within or across human groups. The moral duty, therefore, is to argue for the truth. If we find ourselves living in a society where many people are disadvantaged, it is because some human beings have consciously shaped such a society, others have acquiesced in it, and the vast majority have been left to struggle for survival. Biology is no excuse for an economics which keeps many people poor so that some may prosper.

We often confuse ethnicity with race. We use the term *ethnic group* to distinguish races from each other as well as to delineate peoples who cannot be identified simply by reference to their physical appearance. So what are the criteria for membership of an ethnic group, and what is the link between ethnicity and race?

According to Richard Jenkins, racial differentiation is based upon observable differences in physical appearance, and our motivation in giving meaning to such differences stems from a general tendency towards group identification. Ethnic identification, he suggests, is much more specific, its principal basis being a shared belief among members of an *ethnic group* that they share common descent.[3]

Genetic analysis and investigation of migratory histories show little evidence for the shared descent of most professed ethnic groups in the world today. Only those populations that remained isolated until very recently and continue to marry exclusively within their own group can make such a claim with legitimacy. Nearly all contemporary ethnic groups have no actual common ancestry; they are a mix of populations from many migrations and conquests over the past two million years, a continuous process which has accelerated with modernity.

However, the belief in a shared ancestry is a very potent one; its impact as great as it would be were it based on historical truth. Max Weber was the first to write on this topic a century ago. He was concerned to identify the source of such erroneous belief, and how such a phenomenon could, apparently, be found in nearly all human populations. Weber concluded that it was a *consequence* of collective political action rather than the cause of it.[4] People found themselves to be part of an organized, geographically concentrated group – a society – and involved themselves in collective actions on behalf of that group. For Weber, the belief in shared ancestry arose out of participation in collective action, as if people needed an explanation for their preparedness to work with the group in pursuit of the wider interest. To find justification in the ideas of defending their ancestral history and continuing the traditions of their forebears was more exciting than the mere functional justification of organising and acting collectively for the betterment of the contemporary group. It proved an exceptionally good motivator of people and an effective tool for political leaders in shaping people's sentiments.

Roland Barthes extended the qualification criteria for ethnic groups beyond the biological. Common to most ethnic groups, he suggested, is a shared language, shared cultural values, and the fact that members see themselves as belonging to the group; membership was voluntary and uncoerced. Few would argue with such a set of definitions, but what this indicates, along with the absence of any basis in ancestry for ethnic groups, is that ethnicity is not fixed. Languages evolve all the time, and whilst it takes a thousand years for a language to evolve so as to be unrecognisable from its earlier incarnation, dialects can drift sufficiently to hinder clear communication between groups within a couple of generations.

Cultural values are even more amorphous, often serving only as a means to distinguish one group from another; likewise the voluntary nature of membership of an ethnic community. If ethnicity is fixed and permanent, and unchanging across generations, there can be no question of opting in or out of an ethnic group. Not only is a shared belief in ancestry usually a myth in the consolidation of an ethnic group, but assertions of common and unchanging language and culture, and of automatic membership, are human inventions. Ethnic groups do not exist in nature; human beings invent and reinforce them by promoting the idea that they are natural, pre-existing and independent of human culture and thought.

This is not to deny that for very many people ethnic belonging is an immensely powerful force in their lives. But why do we need to invent such artificial and arbitrary divisions; and why, currently, does the concept of ethnicity seem to exert so much influence?

The sense of belonging to a particular group, and the desire to label other groups as different, will have a varying impact depending on the nature of the differentiation. Other groups can be viewed as of equal status to our own, organized, like ourselves, into self-contained units in recognition of the social advantages this brings; or they can be viewed as inferior, which instantly makes them legitimate targets for aggression, exploitation and domination. There is evidence that early horticultural-ist groups were able to get the balance right for a short time, that humankind survived the transition to group life intact, and that different groups looked after their own, respected the autonomy of other groups, and worked together when it was in their mutual interests so to do. But this state of affairs did not last long. As early societies became more complex, they became less equal, and competition between groups, conquest and warfare became commonplace. Driving this process was the newly acquired cultural implement of ethnic identity.

The origins of the sense of ethnic identity can be traced to the psyches of those individuals who rise to the top of the political tree, and come to hold power over others. Whether securing a greater share of economic surplus is the object, or the consequence, of attaining power is difficult to know, but it is always an intrinsic part of the process of power expansion. The same cause can be observed for the inequity and injustice that characterizes all societies, ancient and modern. Ordinary people in all societies over the last ten thousand years have proved extremely susceptible to suggestions of the superiority of their group, and this mechanism has been used by rulers, first as compensation for the dreadful social and economic conditions that most people are forced to endure, and, second, to sustain and realize their lust for power and domination. But this is a symbiotic relationship: rulers would be powerless were they unable to manipulate their subjects with such ease, and ordinary people would experience their lives quite differently were they able to maintain a degree of independence of mind and action, and to ignore their rulers' injunctions.

For much of our history, the limitations of technology meant that, among competing groups, none had much advantage over others. All self-defining groups were reasonably equal, and so, in one sense, wars between them were just. Warfare between competing clans, tribes, city-states and empires was considered the norm. Inter-group relations were conducted principally through warfare, with occasional strategic alliances. Occasionally, one group would come to dominate a large area for a substantial period of time, but only in the last five hundred years did the battle become one for the whole planet, as successive European powers set out to secure new territories, resources and markets without geographical limitation. Distinct groups with roughly equal power may from time to time engage in warfare, but no particular outcome is inevitable; it is a fair and equal fight between adversaries, either of which may win. But when the balance of power, through better organization, more advanced use of technology, or sheer weight of numbers, gives one side a clear advantage over the other, then war will no longer be considered legitimate by both parties; the outcome will usually be a foregone conclusion, and the unilateral decision to make war by the more powerful aggressor will be viewed by the victims – and by most observers – as a calculated exercise to use pre-existing power and privilege to secure yet more, at the expense of the weaker group.

It is only when this form of unjust, or unequal, conflict occurs that people on both sides have cause to consider the nature of difference between competing groups, each for quite different reasons. The aggressor, if its action is not to be seen as gratuitous bullying, has to be able to justify itself. The only way to do this is to assert moral superiority over the victim. The act of aggression and colonization is thus transformed from an act of wanton greed and imperial domination to one of benevolent supervision. The innocent victim of an aggressive act will claim moral superiority simply on the basis of its innocence. It will attempt to demonize the aggressor, and will usually succeed in the eyes of its own people.

There is no doubt that the colonial project of the European powers did much to formalize notions of 'us' and 'them', and particularly to implant in the minds of white Europeans a sense superiority, and encourage the belief that all peoples could be categorized as more or less civilized on the basis of their cultural practices, and especially the degree to which they employed technology. The correlation between technology use and the physical characteristics of populations only reinforced ideas of white supremacy. Socio-cultural development is not determined by the physical characteristics of members of a society. The environmental factors behind the differentiation of physical characteristics may have conspired to help or hinder technological advance, but each process was quite independent. Relative rates of socio-cultural development today are determined by geographical and environmental factors and the political history of the last thousand years.

As always, the world of ideas played its part in the formulation of perceptions of ethnicity and race, and especially the more modern concept of nationhood. Enlightenment ideas of human universality and psychic unity hit the world at just the wrong time for the dominant political interests. How were they to justify imperial conquest and colonial domination, let alone the slave trade, if other types of human were essentially the same as 'us'? The reaction to the Enlightenment, in the shape of *Romanticism,* provided a useful counterweight and cemented the split between Enlightenment ideals, which continue to direct our moral concerns, and a political agenda which required the world to be divided up on distinctly unenlightened lines. Johannes Herder argued that differentiated cultures and nations were the essential units of which human society was comprised, and that the value of humankind lay precisely in the observable differences between peoples. In direct opposition to the ideas of the Enlightenment, the defining characteristic of global relations was not what humans had in common with each other, but rather those differences which set them apart, which Herder saw as immutable and intrinsic. Herder must take much of the responsibility for the notion that it is through our *roots,* our perceptions of ancient origins, that we derive the sense of identity which seems such an essential part of the human psyche. Until two centuries ago, little thought was given to such matters, but Herder's ideas found a ready audience among those seeking explanations for the observable differences between peoples, and justification for their brutal treatment of others.

Many people were very receptive to the idea of essential difference. These unfounded notions were given scientific credence by Darwin in his later, speculative work, and by others who used evolutionary theory to equate differences in physical appearance with different levels of socio-cultural development. It was accepted as fact that the evolutionary process equipped white Europeans with leadership qualities, especially with regard to commerce and technology, and left the rest lagging way behind.

Most of us grow up with a strong sense of a world divided into nation states, a notion which is reinforced by a perception that this constitutes a natural order, and that most national boundaries are permanent and well-established. It is only when we look closely at the history of the last two hundred years, and at the way in which the map of the world has been redrawn over the last decade or so, that we begin to question the assumption of permanence.

Is there a link between nationality, and race and ethnicity? Racial labels are usually imposed by people outside the racial group, and tend to be based on observable physical characteristics. Ethnic labels are voluntarily adopted by people who perceive themselves as having ancestry, culture and language in common. Each type of label is applied to groups of people; it has nothing to do with territory. Territory, or land, is the defining characteristic in the modern conception of nationhood, and is the principal cause of conflict between groups. It is also the principle measure, in the modern world, of distinguishing between groups. How did the tendency of people voluntarily to self-identify as members of *ethnic groups* translate into a world of territory-based nation states? Is the concept of nationhood new, and a specifically modern phenomenon, or is it simply a logical extension of ethnic division?

The answer lies in changes in the concentration and distribution of power over time, and especially in the concentration of technological advance in Europe from the mid-eighteenth century onwards. Ernest Gellner divided Europe into three zones, each with quite different 'national' histories.[5] First, and oldest established, are the areas ruled from the four great colonial capitals: Lisbon, Madrid, Paris and London, where culturally well-established and homogenous populations, territorially intact for many centuries, provided the prototype nation state. Over a long period they gradually defined, and thus satisfied, the criteria for nationhood, and provided a model for the rest of the world.

Britain is an interesting case. Many indigenous Britons – especially among the English – have a comparatively weak sense of ethnic identity. This is not because the British are a race pure bred from prehistoric ancestors who successfully repelled all invaders. Britain has suffered many conquests and been receptor to many migrations. But most of it happened a very long time ago. Indigenous Britons can trace their ancestry back to Romans, Saxons, Gauls, Celts, Britons and Normans, among others, all of whom arrived uninvited and with aggressive intent. Sufficient time has passed, however, and sufficient interbreeding has occurred, to have rendered ancestral blood ties quite meaningless. Britain's default status as an early-established nation has been reinforced by its enduring capacity over the last thousand years successfully to repel further attempts at conquest and, latterly, to consolidate its power in the world through the largest empire ever built. All these things make for a history in which ethnicity and internal differentiation feature only marginally in political discourse and in the psyches of many people.

In Britain, France, Spain and Portugal the two principal ingredients for nation-statehood were well established: unified culture and language and a strong centralized state with administrative power over a fixed geographical area. Italy and Germany, by contrast, whilst culturally developed and linguistically homogenous, lacked a centralized apparatus of state power. Today, Italy and Germany seem as established as any nation, but Germany did not emerge as a nation state until 1870, and Italy only ten years earlier.

Gellner's third zone comprises much of eastern Europe, most parts of which had developed neither uniformity of culture among strong, established populations, nor centralized political control. For the people of eastern Europe, the essential ingredients for a coherent territorial and political entity, a prerequisite to competing on equal terms with their western neighbours, were completely absent. The consequences are still visible in the Balkans. Whilst war and domination by the Soviet Union at least kept the lid on nationalist conflicts for much of the twentieth century, it did nothing to help the region catch up with its neighbours.

Why all the focus on Europe? Because what happened in Europe largely determined what happened elsewhere in terms of the dominant model of political organization. Beyond Europe, perhaps only China and Japan can claim to have followed a similarly independent route to nation-statehood. Sufficiently large and powerful to escape the shackles of colonization, and historically well-established entities, they can be compared to the four original nations of eastern Europe. What may have happened to the rest of the world can only be guessed at, for its destiny was shaped by the exploits of the European powers from the sixteenth century on. Before the Great War, although Russia was a reasonably centralized state, and had a degree of cultural homogeneity, neither of these attributes were sufficiently strong to ensure a smooth transition to nation-statehood along the lines of Italy and Germany. The political and economic condition of Russia and Central Asia at the beginning of the twentieth century left only one route to modernity, that of revolution. The consolidation of the Soviet Empire involved the wholesale obliteration of national identities. They would only re-emerge after the collapse of communism almost a century later. Chief among the casualties were the Armenians, a people who boast a cultural history as rich and enduring as any.

Elsewhere, the world map was first drawn by the competitive colonialism of the European powers, but methods and outcomes varied greatly. The indigenous populations of North America and Australasia suffered most, being virtually wiped out by a deadly combination of firepower and infectious disease against which they had no defence. The survivors were herded into reservations with little hope either of sustaining their cultures or emerging as viable economic entities to compete with the settlers. Colonizers, through war or political agreement, took control of subject territories and began to construct nation states on the emerging European model. Africa, the Indian sub-continent, South-East Asia and Latin America all eventually fell to colonial rule, although their indigenous populations remained the majority. While some colonial powers were more benevolent than others, their objectives were always to secure economic resources and markets, or to find territory on which to settle the overspill from an overcrowded Europe.

When, in the spirit of reflection that followed World War II, independence was granted to most of the former colonies, new nation states were created without any regard for the criteria essential to the construction of nationhood, and with little thought as to how these structural deficiencies might be compensated for. What would have been a difficult process under ideal conditions was made impossible by the cold war. The lesson is clear: successful nations states emerge over long periods, they cannot be constructed with a few signatures on a piece of paper. Over the last two hundred years, the process of nation construction has completely disregarded the conditions for viable nationhood. If colonial history had been different, then countries we take for granted like Brazil, Nigeria, Indonesia, Nicaragua and Tanzania may never have existed.

Where did we get the idea that we could design a world with no reference to history, culture or, in many cases, physical geography? It all began at the Vienna Conference of 1815, where the major European powers got together to divide up the spoils after the Napoleonic Wars. As an advance in diplomacy, Vienna was notable: for the first time, competing powers recognized that it might be in everyone's interest to divide up political control of territory over a map table rather than the battlefield. The carve-up may not have been equitable but it did provide Europe with its most peaceful century of the millennium, although, as Gellner points out, what happened post-Vienna was to have profound implications for the twentieth-century.

At Vienna the idea of the nation based on the coming together of culture, politics and territory was largely ignored. Much of Europe was divided up between the Hapsburg and Ottoman empires, with power to be wielded from afar; little or no reference was made to what potential for nationhood lay in any particular territory. In the meantime, the idea of nationhood gained considerable authority, with political philosophers such as Hegel and Nietzsche taking up the ideas of the Romantics. After the Great War, with the oldest-established nations victorious, and the exemplar created nation, the United States, as the ultimate power-broker, there was no question that the world would proceed along the model of arbitrarily defined nation states. And so at Versailles, Europe was carved up with an insensitivity to political realities which would condemn the continent to a century of discord, division, political conflict, war and mass killing, the like of which had never been witnessed.

To return to the question: what is the link between ethnicity and nationhood? Simply stated, ethnicity plus territory equals nationhood. Ethnicity without territory, or different ethnicities competing for the same territory, for example Serbs and Albanians in Kosovo, is a recipe for conflict. Ethnicity without territory describes the fate of the Jews until the establishment of the state of Israel in 1948, and reveals why the Jews, like the Gypsies, have a genuine claim to ethnicity that most groups do not. As Adrian Hastings says, an ethnic group denied a secure territorial base can only preserve itself by closely observing rules about marrying within the group.[6] Jews, almost uniquely, have a legitimate claim to the common ancestry on which most ethnic groups falsely base their own claims of recognition. But even Jewish ancestry only goes back so far. As Steve Jones points out in his book, *In the Blood,* Jews have far more genetic heritage in common with Arabs, their sworn enemies, than with any other group of humans.[7] At the other end of the spectrum, territory without ethnicity might well describe the British, or at least the English, and, more remarkably, white Americans, many of whom, whilst maintaining a fondness for their European origins, are American first and Irish, Italian or Polish second.

These examples give us a clue to the key of escaping the shackles of ethnicity: territorial and economic security. When large numbers of people within a society feel economically secure, and have no cause to blame others for their situation, thoughts of ethnic belonging rapidly disappear. The longer this cherished security endures, the less identity-conscious a society becomes. The sense of ethnic belonging usually moderates into less dangerous forms like patriotism. There is a clear link, then, between economic security and nationalist or ethnic feeling, but, until we extend the sense of long-term economic security to many millions of people the world over, there will remain a very fine line between benign patriotism and more harmful manifestations of group identity.

There are other key ways in which we choose to identify ourselves. Two of the most important are gender and religion. Like race, gender difference has its basis in biological difference, but, again like race, it has absolutely no implications in terms of value, merit or human potential. Certain physiological differences may make men better suited to certain tasks, and reproductive roles have some implications for culture and the organization of work, but the notion that men are intrinsically superior to women is as absurd, implausible and unsubstantiated as the notion that whites are intrinsically more capable than blacks, that the English are more civilized than the French, or that African-Americans have an innate tendency to criminality not possessed of their caucasian counterparts.

Considerable progress has been made towards equal status for women in some countries, but for most of the world's women conditions have changed little over the last century. In western countries, many of the women who enjoy successful careers do so largely on men's terms. Given the history of power in male-female relationships, and the way it has been absorbed into so many aspects of culture, genuinely equal status and opportunity for women seem unlikely to emerge without a massive change in attitudes and perceptions, particularly among men.

Of all the means by which humans satisfy their need for group identification, religious affiliation is, perhaps, the most challenging to anyone concerned with the exclusive nature of group identity. I am unable to make a categorical claim about the existence or otherwise of God. What I can state with absolute certainty is that the claims of different religions and denominations for gods of different names, natures and meanings are not compatible with one another: they cannot all be right; they cannot all be real. This gives me cause to doubt the existence of any extra-human power or transcendent source of moral authority. Not only are such competing claims incompatible with each other, they are incompatible with universalism. Not because divergent belief is of itself divisive, but because, when it becomes an integral part of inequitable power relations between human groups, it adds a further means by which one group may find cause to oppress, or justify war against, another. Religion is not the cause of war, but, like racial, ethnic and national identity, it is one more mechanism through which conflict is facilitated. Those who seek power and make war cannot do so alone. If the means through which they marshal and motivate support is based on religion, and on loyalty to a higher power, then all the more effective it will be.

The use of religion in war is at stark odds with the ancient wisdom on which each of the major religions is based, all of which, in their various descriptions of the *Golden Rule,* contain the seed of universalism. Widespread religious belief does, however, give cause for optimism. Many people sign up to religions in the hope of finding indications towards a more caring, loving and just world. But, given the prevailing social order, faith alone is insufficient. Further, the movement away from traditional faiths in favour of alternative quasi-religious belief systems, or the many self-styled denominations that litter the American religious landscape, is cause for concern.

For much of our history, formal religion was perceived by most people as the source of moral principles, when in reality it was a vehicle through which we could formalize our moral desires in a world which was poorly understood compared with today. Formal religion, of whatever creed, acts for many people as a constraint on independent thought and the ability for moral generalization. Despite the ecumenical efforts of many religious leaders, the mere existence of competing religions, and the importance of religion in the lives of so many, especially the less-educated, is a major obstacle to moral progress. This does not mean that belief in a god or gods, or some other non-tangible source of moral authority, is necessarily incompatible with universalism, but the moral capacity of an individual or group must be judged first against the principles of universalism, not against the doctrine of any organized religion. Under universalism, all people are free to believe what, or in whatever, they like, but use of this freedom does not of itself make them morally mature human beings.

The motivations, attitudes and world view of many who profess religious faith suggest that it has evolved in response to unfulfilled psychological needs: the requirement to make sense of a complex and painful world and the need to feel positive about one's place in it. Religious faith fulfils a very real need in people, but that does not mean it is based on reality, and it should not prevent us from identifying aspects of religious belief and practice which are divisive, exclusive and anti-universal.

There are many ways in which humans identify themselves with others, as part of a group, but few such assertions of group uniqueness or superiority have any basis in fact or reality, and none gives justification for preferential treatment in the allocation of economic goods and life opportunities. Most perceived differences are artificial and arbitrary, and incompatible with universalism. Universalism does not call for the disbandment of a guild of craftspeople who meet to exchange new design ideas or techniques, neither does it require those who profess an absolute preference for Mozart over Bach to keep quiet about their taste. It does, however, require the erosion of group identities based on imagined differences between people, especially those which foster an attitude of superiority. As those perceptions have been part and parcel of human history for ten thousand years, this is a huge obstacle to be overcome.

To return to our original question: is our failure to arrange society so as to extend economic security and opportunity to all humans primarily caused by a general tendency to accept the exclusion of some people, whoever they may be, or by the tendency to divide people up into different groups, to which we accord different status? Over the last thirty years we have seen considerable progress in respect of prejudice, but this has coincided with a growing gap between rich and poor. Many people are no longer happy to allow social and economic exclusion of people based on the specifics of race, gender or sexuality, but there is comparatively little concern that the majority of humankind is suffering a reduction in economic security. Whereas before it was acceptable to exclude because some groups were considered less worthy than others, today it appears acceptable to exclude as long as we practise exclusion on the basis of equality: anybody is a candidate for exclusion. Perhaps we now reject race as a criterion for exclusion for the same reason we embraced it in the first place: it is easily identifiable. When our aims were exploitation and political domination, race was an easy excuse; now we have higher moral aspirations, racial prejudice strikes us as the most arbitrary and unjust human construction and so we determine to dismantle it.

It certainly seems that the tendency for human beings to disregard the interests of others has been reinforced by a parallel tendency to discriminate against certain groups. Such discrimination is not primarily motivated by selfish economic concerns, but it has the effect of reinforcing antipathy towards others. It provides us with categories which help us to make sense of the world. Movement towards a more inclusive world order requires a two-pronged strategy, against specific exclusion and against general exclusion. It is possible to imagine a world where discrimination on the basis of perceived difference is absent but where many people, for no specific reason, continue to be excluded. Nonetheless, an approach which recognizes the equality of interests of all human beings would necessarily incorporate the end of group distinctions.

In his book, *The True and Only Heaven,* Christopher Lasch argued that the gains of minorities are 'problematic because they are viewed as isolated ends in themselves'.[8] He continued, 'The manner in which they are secured is far too much centred on the rights of the individual to unlimited choice and freedom; but these gains do not necessarily ensure that society becomes a better place – except for those previously oppressed individuals who are now empowered.' Lasch has a point. Given a society based on competition, in which only so many can achieve economic security, any change which allows improved economic access for members of previously excluded groups, can only achieve a reordering of the social hierarchy in which some slide down the ladder as others move up. This helps us to see why it is wrong to discriminate against minorities: not simply because it is wrong to discriminate on the basis of difference, but because it is wrong to discriminate against anyone. We already see the consequences of opening up opportunities to all-comers in a competitive society. The newly displaced find easy culprits for their predicament and the cycle of ethnic hatred starts over again. Prejudice can only be ended when a transparently inclusive economy is in place.

The gains we have made in respect of prejudice are positive, but they constitute a partial victory in the struggle for an inclusive society. Ultimately, the replacement of tyranny and oppression based on prejudice with a new form based simply on political and economic power and individual good fortune, constitutes little genuine progress.

The common thread in these discussions is the difference between perceptions and reality. Much of what drives us, most of the bases for cultural advance and social organization, are founded on false perceptions or partial truths. This is not a new problem. In recent times, we have been getting better at separating myth from reality, or at least replacing older myths with new, more plausible ones.

Myth has long been the principal means through which humankind protects itself from the dismal reality of life. The pain, hardship and misery that has characterized most human lives is only made survivable by recourse to myth: commonly held and celebrated beliefs about how the world may one day be, about the causes of hardship, or the promise of a better life in the next world. Myth makes life tolerable, but, in playing such a crucial role in shaping human belief and sentiment, its impact goes far beyond sustaining the individual. If, as myth suggests, our suffering has meaning and purpose, then why take the risk of positive action to change things?

Whether our history of allegiance to myth is the cause of our present difficulty in separating reality from fiction, or each are symptoms of something innate to the human condition, I am not sure; but in western culture, where many people have given up on traditional religious beliefs, we have embraced other equally potent, but erroneous, beliefs about the structure of society and the forces that shape it. These modern myths, just like ancient ones, are constructed to help absolve individual human beings from responsibility for the problems of wider society. The forces which shape our lives may no longer be supernatural, but we seem determined to believe they remain beyond our control.

Perhaps the strongest contemporary myth concerns the necessity of a competitive society; the idea that only by competing with each other as individuals and groups can we collectively advance. Competitive and aggressive behaviour has been the defining feature of human society since our ancestors discovered agriculture, and with it the value of land and property. But, until recently, it was accepted that cooperative activity towards collective ends was the only way to keep society intact. Competition still fails to deliver economic security to the majority of the world's people, and therein lies the key to the success of this great modern myth: it does deliver the goods to just enough people to maintain an acceptable degree of social order in the rich countries. Further, it holds out hope that everyone might achieve a share of the cake if they succeed in playing the system expertly enough.

An economy which relies exclusively on competition can never provide for universal basic needs. Nonetheless, we are all compelled to cultivate the competitive aspect of our personalities to the maximum, and in the process reinforce the belief that a competitive society and economy is the model that best suits human nature. Humans compete with each other because they feel insecure. There is a widespread perception of scarcity which leads us all to conclude that, unless we compete for economic security, we will be left with nothing. The myth of scarcity is deliberately cultivated by those who stand to lose from movement to a society based on equity and cooperation. And this myth is reinforced by one with a deeper and more enduring history: that divisions between rich and poor are inevitable; that they are either part of God's complex and unknowable plan for humankind, or they at least represent the natural order of things.

Another myth which must be firmly rejected is that surrounding the essential goodness of humankind. We inhabit a world of misery and suffering, the vast majority of which is inflicted by humans upon other humans. We must not underestimate the capacity of the morally corrupt human, and especially of morally corrupt groups, for inflicting pain and suffering. It is only a small step from civilization to barbarism; we must improve our understanding of what causes individuals and groups to act with such barbarity. In order to begin this process, we need to accept the scale and the intensity of such horrors and the historical evidence that barbarism is more typical than atypical of human behaviour. We have to acknowledge the potential for evil in all people, and come to understand how that potential can be healthily suppressed. We could start by not referring to all such behaviour as inhuman. The reality of human brutality requires brutal honesty.

The final misconception to address is belief in the importance and inevitability of *cultural difference*. We need criteria to distinguish between expressions of difference which add richness to human lives and are compatible with universalism, and claims and expressions which are divisive, competitive and inherently anti-universal. Belief in cultural uniqueness is an important psychological base for many people, but the degree of cultural attachment felt by an individual is a function of particular social and economic circumstances and varies from time to time, and from place to place. It becomes less important for people as they perceive their economic security to be improving. Indeed, wherever in the world pockets of wealth emerge, the population divides into those who seek to counter destabilising social change by promoting the importance of traditional cultural practices, and those who, no longer dependent on myth and tradition to make sense of the world, embrace western values.

Many people fear change for the threat it poses to cultural traditions and local values, but there is confusion over the source of cultural values, and the direction of the process of cultural globalization. If economic advance has the impact of dislodging cultural traditions, then we must conclude that it is the impact of wealth and perceptions of economic security that changes people's thinking, in that order. People do not make a conscious decision to reject local traditions and then go off in pursuit of wealth. With global access to western media and images, people the world over aspire to the material lifestyle they see on their satellite TV screens. But this is not a conscious rejection of their own culture, merely a manifestation of a universal aspect of the human psyche whereby all individuals, given the choice between an ancient and prosaic culture which helps them deal with poverty and the misery of their lives, and one offering the perception of economic security, would aspire to the latter, whatever the accompanying values. The process is not an implicit substitution of western values for traditional ones. It works through the adoption of certain values already held in parts of the world where a consumer culture is well established.

The experience of the last century is that cultural changes follow economic developments in an almost identical fashion wherever they occur. If economic change leads to a rapid polarization in society, where none existed before, the beneficiaries will throw off their cultural traditions, whilst, for those who find themselves worse off, traditions will take on added importance. It follows that, if economic advance occurs in ways which do not polarize a society but rather lift the entire population out of poverty and provide security for all, then the impact on cultural traditions will be somewhat different. Those traditions and practices which are symptomatic of poverty and suffering, and which project the reasons for them onto a higher power, will fall away. Those which celebrate human creativity, love and inclusive difference will be retained, although they may evolve to suit the new conditions.

Such a transition has yet to occur organically, that is to say through the collective desire and action of most people for progressive social change. No wonder humankind retains a bewildering array of cultural traditions and supposedly unique value systems, and no wonder there is such confusion about their origins and meaning. Where cultural transitions do occur, they generally involve the substitution of a value system designed to sustain, support and reconcile an entire population to poverty, with one which argues for the wealth and privilege of the few as the only possible path to collective improvement. The problem with the current project of globalization is not simply the imposition of alien, external values, rather it is the imposition of an exclusive economic framework and its attendant value system. Rich countries, with established social, economic and political institutions which have evolved over centuries according to the requirements of such a value system, can just about survive its inherent injustice, as long as they keep moving, and holding out the hope of improvement. In poor countries, where no such institutions exist, the outcome of change for most people will be, at best, no discernible improvement in economic security or quality of life.

If you remain sceptical about the speed with which traditional cultures can embrace and adapt to a new value system, the situation in many African capitals, where only two generations ago Africans made up a tiny minority of the urban population, illustrates the point. The attitudes, values, aspirations and lifestyles of the wealthy urban professional class are strikingly similar to those of their counterparts in western capitals. The only difference is that a few miles beyond the city perimeter the bulk of the population is still living in the iron age. It is encouraging, however, that people are able to embrace transformative economic and cultural change when they perceive it to be in their interests to do so.

The obstacles to progress are not cultural; they are political and economic. Cultural difference is at once the most important and the most impermanent form of differentiation. It offers progressive and inclusive aspects that make the world a richer, more diverse and interesting place: these can and should be preserved. It also provides obstacles to progress which can be removed once we understand their true nature. The current globalization project seems intent on replacing one set of bad values with a new set of bad values and crushing the positive aspects of traditional culture. Unless we wake up to this very soon, it will be too late.

If difference remains the defining characteristic of human populations, how are we to reconcile this fact with the demands of universal morality? Even for many who argue for an end to prejudice and discrimination, the perception of difference as the defining factor remains paramount. In their efforts to be inclusive, liberal thinkers confuse the issue: resisting discrimination and prejudice is not the greatest good in the hierarchy of values we draw from a universal ethic. Under universalism, the interests of all individuals must be given equal consideration. Social or behavioural norms which are grossly unjust or discriminatory are often justified as an integral part of a culture. If acceptance and promotion of cultural difference is the guiding ethic for progressives then it is difficult to question traditional practices such as female genital mutilation, the treatment of low-caste people in India, or the practice of forced marriages. If, instead, the guiding principle is the equal consideration of interests, then there need be no conflict between the values of safeguarding valuable cultural differences and protecting the interests of all. Cultural practices should be protected and promoted in so far as they do not promote the interests of some at a cost to others, that they do not reinforce prevailing imbalances of power between genders and groups, and that they do not cause physical and emotional harm to the victim, or compromise the capacity of certain groups to provide for themselves and their families. All human beings, regardless of culture, should be subjected to the same moral standards.

Perversely, many of the most strongly held beliefs regarding the intrinsic nature of differences between groups of humans are shown to have little basis in reality. Most of them are just arbitrary cultural constructs reinforced by the passage of time. But it is the persistence and universality of these misconceptions that largely shapes the modern world and sets limits on the possibility of progress. The key to progress is reconciling individual perceptions of identity, belonging and difference with historical reality and moral relevance. We perceive difference because we set out to create a world based on difference. In reality what unites us is far greater than what separates us. We must get to the root of what it is that causes us to embrace such exclusive identification. We must investigate why so many people are unable to separate truth and fact from myth and fiction. We need to look at how the individual human psyche is shaped by society, and work out how society can begin to be shaped by a new conscious, rational and moral human psyche.

7

Psyche and Society

KARL POLANYI disliked the *structuralist* theories that dominated sociology in the first half of the twentieth century, and which suggested that society had a predetermined structure into which people fitted, and which they could do nothing to change. Polanyi argued that if many people's view of society seemed to fit reality, this was only because effective social conditioning had persuaded them of the fixed nature of society and the futility of attempts to challenge social convention. Polanyi believed that every individual human action has some social consequence, and that every power structure within society derives from the actions of individuals.

Two pieces of empirical evidence back up Polanyi's claims. First, the varied and diverse nature of social structures and institutions around the world. Second, the flexibility observed in all societies, especially over the last century, as technological advance has driven immense change. Only a century ago, the universal democratic franchise had been achieved in not a single country. Now it is a feature of most, and an aspiration for the populations of all. So much for people having no power to change society, or to oppose and erode the power of wealthy elites.

Society will not change itself, neither is it under the control of some extra-human authority. It does not conform to structures laid out in some book of ancient designs. It is the expression of collective human action, not necessarily a collective process, and certainly not one in which all humans are pulling in the same direction. Nonetheless, the construction and development of society is a human enterprise, and if that enterprise seems to be failing in many essential respects, then we need to identify the roots of this failure within individual human beings.

Sigmund Freud developed *psychoanalysis* as a tool to heal the neurosis and psychological trauma he found in his patients, and which he linked to their childhood experience. His explanatory framework for certain individuals growing up with childhood-related neuroses did not identify fundamental problems in nurturing and parenting, but instead relied on divergences from a rather arcane and symbolic sequence of events in the relationship between parents and children on which, he believed, healthy psychological development depended. Psychoanalysis, by reference to this framework, would enable able people to put back together the broken parts of their personal experience, and resume a normal life. For Freud there was nothing essentially wrong with the general environment in which children were brought up.

This was a core assumption of practitioners of Freudian psycho-analysis until John Bowlby outlined his quite different ideas. It was Bowlby who introduced the idea that environment plays an important role in the development of a healthy psyche. His *Attachment Theory* is still the single most important theory of human psychological development.

Attachment Theory suggests that a child who is securely attached to her parent or parents, that is to say feels secure, loved, cared for, and engaged with, is more likely to grow up free from neurosis and other psychological problems. Bowlby came to this conclusion through a great deal of clinical research. Many of his patients were deeply troubled; all had suffered extended periods of parental deprivation. They had been unable to develop secure attachments to parents or other principal carers because such access had been denied them. As Bowlby said: 'Thus I was alerted to a possible connection between prolonged deprivation and the development of a personality apparently incapable of making affectual bonds and, because immune to praise and blame, prone to repeated delinquencies.'[1] Although Bowlby's prime concern was the mental anguish of children and the need to find ways to avoid and alleviate it, it was also immediately obvious to him that large numbers of attachment-deprived children would have consequences for wider society. Such children, he suggested in 1953, 'are a source of social infection as real and as serious as are carriers of diphtheria and typhoid'.[2]

Bowlby was concerned that in post-war Britain, where a nascent welfare state was promoting comparatively inclusive social conditions, many children were still failing to get adequate parenting. As he suggested: 'In a society where death rates are low, the rate of employment high, and social welfare schemes adequate, it is emotional instability and the inability of parents to make effective family relationships which are the outstanding cause of children becoming deprived of a normal family life.'[3] He saw an inescapable cycle of deprivation characterized by 'the neglected psychopathic child growing up to become the neglectful psychopathic parent ... a self-perpetuating social circle'.[4]

Attachment is not about overprotecting children. As Jeremy Holmes says in his assessment of Bowlby's work, 'attachment requires a secure base, the essence of which is that it provides a springboard for curiosity and exploration'.[5] Children must feel safe enough to test boundaries, take risks and expand their own environment by giving vent to their natural inquisitiveness. The good parent has to tread a fine line. Being over-anxious may hinder a child's natural development, with consequences as harmful as those caused by the neglectful parent whose child suffers acute anxiety and feelings of abandonment. Providing an attachment base of the right quality is very difficult. One of the key issues is the ability of the parent to allow children to express feelings of aggression and frustration in ways which do not cause serious destruction or harm to themselves or others. Bowlby suggested that such a faculty is 'one of the greatest gifts that parents can give to their children'.[6]

Bowlby identified two coping strategies in children who were unable to form secure attachments. First, *avoidant* attachment, whereby the child attempts to minimize the needs for attachment and pretends that everything is all right. Second, *ambivalent* attachment, whereby the child submits to the parents' inconsistent or abusive care and often becomes very clinging. In his investigation of these pathological forms of attachment, he discovered just how strong the need for attachment is. Many children would secure for themselves any form of attachment, however unhealthy.

The quality of a child's attachment clearly has implications for the subsequent development of its personality. Bowlby was able to identify how different patterns of attachment were the result of different patterns of interaction with those to whom the child was more or less successfully attached. It was reasonably easy, with hindsight, to investigate the nature of a child's attachment and make predictions about his or her psychological well-being in adolescence or adulthood. Bowlby therefore concluded that environment was the principal factor affecting the development of personality.

Quality of attachment is not the only factor affecting a young person's psychological and personality development. Some securely attached infants will experience other negative environmental influences in the course of their development which may leave them with neuroses or other psychological problems. Conversely, it is possible that some individuals whose experience of attachment is poor will, nonetheless, emerge into adulthood as reasonably healthy, well-adjusted people. It was of great interest to Bowlby how it was that humans respond to diversity and deprivation in such contrasting ways. While, as a general rule, environmental interaction is the key factor in a child's psychological development, some individuals appear to possess a resilience to such deprivation which is able to compensate. This may be a consequence of other more positive environmental inputs, or of some innate predisposition which favours the faculty we often call 'strength of character'. The key to greater numbers of psychologically healthy individuals remains, however, the creation of conditions in which far greater numbers of parents are able to provide the secure attachment base that every child needs.

Bowlby also identified that poor attachment is not class-specific. There is no over-representation of poor attachment in children among people of low socio-economic class. Poor attachment is not simply a function of poverty or poor education. This suggests that there is no solution to the problem of attachment in economics alone. This was one of Bowlby's key findings in relatively affluent 1950s Britain. The economy was more inclusive than at any time in history, yet many parents were still failing in their obligations to their children.

In 1949 Bowlby wrote of 'the vicious circle of neurosis in which insecure parents create insecure children who grow up to create an insecure society which in its turn creates more insecure parents'.[7] He believed there was a need for 'one great therapeutic endeavour: that of reducing tensions and fostering understanding cooperation between groups of human beings'.[8] In order to prevent harm to the next generation, the current generation of children need to be the beneficiaries of secure attachment relationships. Further, the ongoing need for secure attachment in adult life needs to become the experience of many more adults. It is a herculean task, but Bowlby pointed the way by unearthing the root causes of many of the problems that affect society today.

We know what needs to change: we now need effective strategies to make it happen. A resolution to the problem of attachment will not follow directly from improved economic justice. The flow of cause and effect is in the opposite direction. A world peopled by secure, well-attached individuals is the only place in which a more inclusive society can evolve.

Towards the end of his life Bowlby became increasingly concerned with the societal implications of attachment theory. In 1988 he wrote: 'man and woman power devoted to the production of material goods counts a plus in all our economic indices. Man and woman power devoted to the production of happy, healthy and self-reliant children in their own homes does not count at all.'[9] Drawing a similar analogy, Jeremy Holmes suggests that 'in an unequal society, there is competition for security. Security becomes a commodity to which the rich cling.'[10] We need to increase the supply of security and ensure it is freely accessible to all.

If the consequences of poor attachment were that individuals suffered psychological problems alone, then there might be hope for them in therapeutic treatments. But there is mounting evidence to suggest that the damage wrought by poor parenting and inadequate nurturing in the first months and years of life can also be physiological, that is to say it affects the physical development of the brain, and may, therefore, be irreparable.

In his book, *Mind Sculpture*, Ian Robertson summarizes research which provides quite frightening evidence of the impact on the physiological development of the brain, of poor early nurturing, poor emotional engagement from parents and carers, and poor educational inputs. The human brain does not develop physically according to some genetically predetermined pattern which grants everyone a minimum level of intelligence or cerebral potential. Whilst the mass of grey tissue will assume a similar dimension in all humans, the neurons which connect the many billions of brain cells together and which determine how effectively the brain works, only grow as a consequence of environmental inputs. If the requisite inputs are lacking or misdirected, then the brain will not develop as it could and much of this developmental failure will be irreparable.

The process of stimulation-driven brain development begins at birth, and for some infants things start to go wrong when they are only minutes old. As Robertson says: 'Children who are deprived of cuddles and a close emotional relationship to one or more adults show brains and bodies that are stunted.'[11] But brain development is not just a matter of positive emotional inputs. Whereas Bowlby had found that problems of attachment were equally distributed across socio-economic groups, statistics show that inputs that help build the brain's capacity for intelligence and academic learning vary depending on social background. As Robertson quotes: 'By the age of three, the average child of a professional family in the United States will have heard approximately thirty million words addressed to him or her. This contrasts with approximately twenty million words heard by children of working-class families, and ten million words by children whose families are on welfare.'[12] There is a clear correlation between these figures and size of vocabularies possessed by school-age children. It is one more way in which ability and potential are inequitably meted out to children early in life; it creates differences in ability which are not innate and could be avoided. It now seems that such early loss of advantage cannot be remedied later in life.

Dispositions that last throughout life are also shaped by experiences in the first six months. People who turn out positive, engaging and optimistic about life can trace their outlook to a comfortable, secure and happy first six months. A negative, pessimistic outlook often begins with the wrong type of inputs during infancy and can significantly affect life chances. The formal learning environment of the child is also crucial. As Robertson concludes, 'Schooling and education without doubt physically changes the brains of children. It matters enormously how, and how much, children are taught.'[13]

The quality of teaching is key. Individual tutoring is found to be the most effective means of academic learning. The average individually tutored child performs better than 98 per cent of children taught using the standard classroom method.[14] For many reasons individual tutoring for all children is not possible, and not even desirable; learning in a classroom environment can teach other equally valuable life skills. However, this does tell us something about class sizes and the need for individual feedback which is essential for remedying learning deficiencies. If learning affects physical brain development, it is crucial that all children get adequate amounts of teaching attention.

Although emotional intelligence requires a quite different type of learning, the effectiveness of emotional learning has similar consequences for brain development. The impact can be serious not only for the life prospects of the individual but also for wider society. As Robertson states: 'Insufficiently educated emotional brains contribute to the epidemic of psychological problems that is plaguing the industrialized world.'[15] He goes on to say:

> Unfortunately, in undemocratic countries that lack a free press and appropriate political balances, it can be impossible to curb the rise to power of psychopaths. Their brutality can become sewn into the very fabric of society, woven into the brains of the most susceptible children of that society. So not just individuals but whole cultures can become infected by this emotional programming which may engender casual cruelty and a lack of concern for others on a disturbingly wide scale.[16]

Even in more advanced cultures, there are plenty of examples of antisocial attitudes passing from parent to child in ways which resist all attempts to change them through therapy or reasoned argument. Robertson writes: 'If his father is prejudiced against some racial, social or religious group, so the boy will have this prejudice embroidered into his trembling web.'[17] And often such cultural or parental transmission is irreversible because it happens unconsciously. Unconsciously learned attitudes are virtually impossible to reverse through conscious reflection. This is why racist, homophobic and sexist attitudes in some individuals are hopelessly immune to reasoned argument. It also explains why otherwise reasonable, well-educated individuals sometimes reveal the most appalling and stubborn prejudices.

The extent to which poor brain development can be reversed through positive inputs later in life depends on the nature and severity of early years' damage. However, the fact that so few subjects of therapy or counselling appear fully to 'recover' from the consequences of their initial deprivation suggests that therapy as a wide-scale solution to the consequences of a deprived environment for brain development is not viable.

We have neither the resources nor the understanding successfully to mount a universal programme of therapy to reverse the damage. We do know, however, the kinds of environmental deprivation that lead to problems in the first place, and we could therefore act to ensure that future generations are spared such harm.

We need to be clear that differences in intelligence, emotional capacities and individual potential are influenced at least as much by environment as they are by genes. It is environmental inputs which foster or inhibit brain development and this happens at a physiological level. Certainly there are limits to each individual's intelligence which may be genetically determined, but the only way to determine these limits, as Robertson points out, is first to exhaust the resources of environmental stimulation. We must do everything possible to ensure the best possible socialization and education experiences for all children. Thus far no government, society or culture has come remotely close to realizing this ideal, or even acknowledging its validity. If the intelligence gap could be reduced to 'natural' levels – that determined by genes – then considerable impact would be made on the distribution of opportunities in life. This in turn would impact on the perceptions, world view and values of many people. But the prospects are not good. As Robertson says: 'The recent rise in genetic explanations of behaviour has made us forget quite how important learning and experience are in moulding the connections of the brain.'[18]

The evidence for the impact of early-years nurturing and socialization on the formation of the adult character is overwhelming. It is now possible to assess the character of an adult and make reasonably reliable predictions about the early-years environment of that individual. Scientific evidence backs up commonsense observations about good and bad parenting. An adult who is able to love, show affection, trust others, and form durable and equal relationships will, on the whole, be found to have been a beneficiary of devoted, loving parents or other full-time committed carers, and vice versa. The rule may not apply in every case, but it does apply often enough to indicate that attention to providing a favourable environment for infants and children is likely to produce a happier, more trusting and psychologically healthier adult population, and, ultimately, a society more inclined towards cooperative rather than competitive behaviour.

We have already rejected the argument that human cooperative potential is circumscribed by genetic factors, or that a competitive society is inevitable because of the constraints of human nature. At the same time, and in order to help us determine the best possible environment in which to raise our children, we must acknowledge that our evolutionary heritage does contribute to a range of the drives that influence our behaviour, most notably negative ones such as greed, jealousy, hate, lust and aggression. When considering the roots of such drives in evolution, it is crucial to remember that the process by which certain genes were selected for began long before culture emerged, and before the human mind developed consciousness. In such an environment, genes that caused certain physiological responses – increases in testosterone, adrenalin, or other state-altering chemicals in the blood – would have proved useful in aiding survival and reproductive success. Today, such responses, and the behaviours they engender, are generally socially destructive.

There are no genes for jealousy, greed or aggression. The motivation for these behaviours is a complex series of chemical changes within the brain, the strength of which is determined by an even more complex arrangement of genetic material, combinations of which were selected for millions of years ago. Further, the emerging science of *epigenetics* adds another level of complexity. It suggests that certain genes are switched on or off depending on the environment to which the developing foetus or infant is exposed. Superimposed on this now apparently flexible genetic inheritance are the processes of brain and consciousness development which are also shaped by environmental inputs, resultant perceptions of how the world is, and social rules, cultural norms, moral aspirations and powers of reason, all of which vary in strength from person to person.

Biological psychologists emphasise the difference between saying that behaviour is influenced by changes in the chemical balance in the blood, which is managed by the brain in response to external and internal stimuli, and saying that such chemical changes are genetically determined responses fixed into our DNA as a result of the adaptive experience of our pre-human ancestors. Evolution has shaped us, but culture has made us human, and it is culture which offers us solutions to the problems bequeathed us by evolution. The evidence for this lies in the vast behavioural differences among genetically similar individuals. Most violent, aggressive, jealous, selfish reactions today are the result of a sceptical, envious, suspicious and untrusting world view which is largely the product of environment. People who are unable to love, to trust, or to show compassion for others in adult life are often so constrained because they were shown no love, trust or compassion during their own early life, not because of some genetic defect.

We are all capable of selfish, exclusive behaviours, but it is not these behaviours that are genetically coded into us, only the drives which fuel such behaviours can be blamed on our genetic inheritance. The answer to the question, 'Where would such drives find their outlet in a cooperative society?' is the same as the answer to the question, 'What happens to the terrible temper tantrums we witness in virtually all two-year-old infants?' The drives continue to reside within us, but their influence on our behaviour is tempered as a result of the socialization process. We learn to punch a cushion, when we are frustrated or angry, instead of our little brother's nose. But we do not refrain from such behaviours simply because we have been told they are wrong. We refrain because we sense they are at odds with the values of an inclusive society, even if those values are not fully realized within us. The path to full internalization of universal, inclusive values is a long one; the progress we each make is reflected in the extent to which those values colour our individual behaviour. That many of us refrain from violent, aggressive, blaming behaviour is evidence of our considerable progress along this path. We refrain because we want to.

The negative drives that reside within us are activated and accentuated by the environment to which we are exposed, both during our formative years and in adult life. Negative drives will be dominant in individuals – and among groups – where nurturing and socialization processes are harsh, inconsistent and unloving, and will become very damaging if such individuals grow up in a society where there is little economic security, or the rule of law is weak. Positive drives will be dominant where the reverse is true: for those who have been well cared for throughout childhood and adolescence, and for whom, in adult life, the world is experienced as secure, cooperative, respectful and just. It is the social and cultural environment which determines which side of a human's nature will dominate.

It was a key proposition of the Enlightenment that measures to improve human intelligence were the route to reducing social injustice. To this end, improved standards in education, and extending its provision to the entire population, were considered crucial. Since then, universal education has become the norm in many countries, and has been one of the driving forces for economic advance, but it has not had the desired effect in terms of spreading the benefits of economic advance as widely as Enlightenment thinkers had hoped.

Education gives individuals the opportunity to make an active and productive contribution to society via economic and cultural mechanisms which supersede those of traditional subsistence. The current trend in education is towards producing young adults able to excel in economic terms. This should mean that more individuals can look forward to the economic security that comes with a career, and it should be of benefit to the national economy in its competition with other national economies. But however good the quality of education, and however wide its coverage, if its principal focus is on turning out economic agents, rather than moral citizens, the economy will be successful only in the terms it sets for itself. As we have seen, successful economics today is not about universal needs provision, or the equitable distribution of wealth: its objectives are steady growth and maximising short-term gains. Despite great investment in education, access to the economy remains far from equitable or universal. Save for experiments in comprehensive education which accompanied the moral ambition of governments in the post-war period, education continues to be highly selective, if not as elitist as in the nineteenth century. The Enlightenment experiment in education has not so much failed in its moral ambition as been usurped by the rational-economic ethos born of the same movement. Education will make a difference to the structure of society only when it is designed and executed to that end. Education that focuses on turning out good citizens in the terms of the dominant world view, however much it may improve and enlarge the pool of 'intelligent' individuals, will only serve to reinforce prevailing inequities.

As currently constituted, formal education is about differentiation. It takes children with poorly formed innate and environmentally-induced inequalities, many of which, at age five or six, could be compensated for by carefully targeted educational interventions, and proceeds to rein-force these differences through a system which values rank and order, and which provides considerable motivation to those who start out with an advantage and very little to those who do not. Very early on in life, children get a firm impression of their position on the ability hierarchy, and this soon shapes their perceptions of life prospects, and influences the amount of effort they put into their schoolwork. It is a process which turns minor and manageable inequalities into huge and unbridgeable ones. In the process it guarantees the perpetuation of a polarized and exclusive society.

The object of the education system is inextricably linked to the values and structure of society. The current economic order depends not only on a pool of reserve (unemployed) labour at the bottom to keep wages down, costs low and prices competitive. It also requires a stratified output of differently qualified individuals to provide the labour the economy requires: some must have leadership qualities; others must be more technically-minded; some need the skills required of middle-management; many should possess the aptitudes which suit the growing service sector; yet others require the dexterity and application to become expert in a skilled trade; and a sizeable number must be prepared to do unskilled manual work. In a high-tech economy the streets still need cleaning and the dustbins emptying. But there is a problem: economies are more dynamic and faster-changing than education systems and the values that underpin them. In many countries, the education system is still turning out people in the proportions demanded a generation ago. Education is failing to cater for the very real and rapid changes in the economy and the world of work, and it leaves growing numbers ill-prepared and insecure. By producing a stratified population of young adults whose career opportunities and earnings potential are largely determined at age 16, 18 or 21, education inevitably reinforces existing divisions and inequalities in society.

Those who determine education policy give little attention to the question of what we should educate people to do. The emphasis is on getting more young people into higher education, regardless of the quality of that education. Richard Sennett notes that by 2010, 41 per cent of 25-year-olds in the United States will have a four-year college degree, whilst only 20 per cent of jobs will require a college degree.[19] Millions of Americans will be stuck with jobs for which even their dubious qualifications overqualify them. The sad reality of late capitalist society is that it is as stratified and hierarchical as ever: it does not create sufficient opportunities for large numbers of clever, initiative-showing, responsibility-taking individuals. Cosmetic exercises in extending educational opportunities will neither give young people a better chance in life, nor increase the effectiveness of the economy as a vehicle through which more people can attain economic security and personal satisfaction through work. Genuine, inclusive, progressive, high-cost, value-based socialization and education are key to progress. What we have at present can only undermine it.

Education falls into the same trap as the economy. Both claim to create conditions in which opportunity is available to all. The explicit objective of any course of education is to enable each student to gain the best possible preparation and qualifications for adult life. But adult life is about surviving in a competitive society where, by definition, only a few can excel, some succeed and many struggle. Such a society would not be well served by an education system which enabled all young people to qualify at the level currently attained by the top 10 per cent. Looked at another way, it is in the interests of those who gain from the current social and economic set-up to ensure that such universal excellence in education is avoided.

The kind of education currently provided by state schools in many industrialized nations is increasingly formulaic. Generally, the same method and approach is applied to all children; it is one which assumes that every child exists in a value-common, democratic, supportive, caring environment outside school. Although special-needs classes are provided for children with particular difficulties, there is little recognition that the home environments of children vary considerably, as do other formative influences outside school. It follows, therefore, that a broadly similar education will have a quite different outcome on different children. Even if the quality of formal education is not good, children from a secure, supportive and encouraging home environment will do relatively well. Children without those benefits will struggle. Such an education fails both advantaged children, through a lack of individual attention, and less secure children, because it is unable to identify and cater for the different experiences they bring with them to school. Children learn about life from all their experiences, not just what happens at school. The capacity for education to promote inclusive values and inspire curiosity and interest in the world is limited by the child's experiences outside school. This is why progressive educational initiatives usually fail: they cannot succeed in a social vacuum.

The ingredients for the kind of education likely to aid the individual in attaining a progressive outlook – moral integrity and independence of mind – do exist, but they extend beyond the usual scope of formal education. Such an education demands a favourable, secure, out-of-school environment. It would take some elements of the best education currently on offer, but it would encourage independence of mind and would expose older pupils to social, political and economic issues, rather than just equipping them with vocational or academic skills. The ideals of inclusiveness, sustainability, social justice, and individual happiness and fulfilment, would be offered as alternatives to the values that currently dominate society – values which, although not explicitly taught, generally succeed in infecting the school environment as effortlessly as they do all arenas of social learning. Young adults would be encouraged to consider the world at large, the forces that shape it, and the possibility of alternatives. Such an education must be made available to large numbers across all societies. Many of the values that inform such an education will be the values that inspired the traditional classical education: encouraging independent thought; learning for the sake of learning; acquiring general problem-solving and abstracting skills; developing the ability to identify quality, or value, beyond that determined by money and material excess; and an emphasis on learning from history, from literature, from philosophy and from art, to gain insights into the way the world works. In short, education could and should be about the establishment of an independent and autonomous mind.

Teaching methods, and what is taught, clearly impact on the social learning of young people. The classroom and playground environment can be more or less competitive, depending on the degree to which teachers are concerned with extracurricular activities and the general school environment. In Britain today, many teachers are so poorly paid and motivated, their schools so poorly resourced, and many of their pupils denied the benefits of a structured and nurturing home life, that it is very difficult to create a healthy and comfortable school environment. A largely unguided social environment will probably be a more competitive one, not because all children are innately competitive, but because competitive behaviours and aggressive individuals will usually win out in an unmoderated environment. The teaching process itself can be more or less reinforcing of competitive values. We learn at a very young age that the world is divided into clever and not-so-clever people, and that in later life this tends to determine levels of success and security. We learn nothing of the complex reasons for this, nor that the education system is shaped by the assumption that these conditions are constant and unchangeable. The status quo is bound to be reinforced by an education system which does nothing to question prevailing assumptions.

Educational change is a vital prerequisite of social change, but it will require considerable investment and new thinking. Smaller class sizes, investment in quality materials and technology, and raising the status of the teaching profession, so as to retain the best teachers and encourage exceptional people into the profession, are all key. Equally important is social agreement on the merits of an inclusive education strategy. Education is worth investing in because it promises positive economic outcomes, but only if those positive outcomes are spread among the entire population and do not serve to reinforce pre-existing inequalities. The provision of high-quality education to all children would broaden access to opportunities; not all children would attain the standards of the highest, but the successes of lower achievers would not be so far behind as to fatally compromise their economic prospects and quality of life in adulthood.

The quality of children's home environments heavily influence their prospects for making the best of whatever educational opportunities they are presented with. For a child, poverty is not just about poor diet, no holidays and not having the toys that other kids have. It is often about having only one parent or several siblings close together in age. In such cases, the quantity of attentive parenting is rationed and invariably the quality of nurturing is compromised. Few parents can be accused of not wanting the best for their children, but circumstances often prevent them from providing the conditions necessary to enable their children to get the best from their education. Many poor parents have not, themselves, benefited greatly from the education system, and are cynical as to the merits of education, with some justification. They are less likely to give their children the support and encouragement to excel at school. Further, many poor families live in exclusively poor communities and attend schools where the majority of pupils are similarly underprivileged – again, not an environment likely to foster academic excellence.

Generation on generation, not only does the economic system mitigate in favour of a steady increase in the gap between those included and excluded, but this division is compounded by social conditions which leave a sizeable chunk of the population in rich countries with no escape from grinding poverty. That some children from such backgrounds do break out is testament only to the fact that most children, at the moment of birth, have such potential. That potential may be extinguished in the first few months of life by poor environmental inputs, but few, if any, healthy children are born without hope. It is the social environment they encounter that takes hope from them, and it is that social environment which can be changed for the better.

A more inclusive world requires greater equality of opportunity for children as they set out on the precarious path to adulthood. Adolescence is tough enough with all the advantages of a secure home life and a decent education. It is virtually impossible if your chances have been reduced almost to zero by the time you are out of nappies. Economic security at home, loving and attentive early nurturing, and a well-resourced and supportive educational environment, are essential for children to grow into active, contributing members of society. By rationing these inputs, we ensure that existing divisions are deepened.

The economic pragmatism and social vision of the post-war period went a long way to breaking down the barriers responsible for these divisions, but for the last thirty years we have been busy rebuilding them. Looked at in global terms, the problems and underlying causes of poverty and exclusion are magnified. In newly industrialising countries, and even in those Third World countries where economic liberalization is creating highly concentrated pockets of wealth, the gap between haves and have-nots, especially in respect of access to education and formal employment, is enormous. In many of the poorest countries, IMF-imposed restrictions on public-sector wages, and the inability of the authorities to collect taxes from the emerging wealthy minority, deny the rest of the population the public services on which civil society depends. Many people are still excluded from meaningful economic participation in rich countries; there seems little hope for the people of poor countries which are having to follow harsh economic prescriptions without any of the social infrastructure necessary to offset the inevitably polarising effects.

Wherever in the world you are born, the strongest indicators of your prospects for survival and success in adult life are the social and economic status of your parents. Until the trend towards polarization in wealth and advantage is reversed, more people will be excluded from the global economy, and more human potential will be sacrificed at a time when we can least afford to be wasting our most valuable resource: human effort and ingenuity.

Even for the educationally advantaged and economically included, the world of work is becoming noticeably less secure. In his book, *The Corrosion of Character*, Richard Sennett reminds us of the difference between having a job and having a career. A career, he suggests, is 'a life-long channel for one's economic pursuits'[20] It provides the individual with a sense of place, of belonging, and of having a useful role to play. It also provides a context in which people can take responsibility for building their own skills. A career forms a lasting and constant element of your life, and, whether or not it becomes the most important thing, it can contribute to a strong sense of self-worth. Whereas in previous generations a lifetime of work meant just one or two jobs, today, for many people, a job is a short-term engagement which provides little scope for individual creativity or career-building. Few jobs offer any long-term security and, as Sennett points out, even supposedly permanent jobs are becoming rarer: the fastest-growing sector of employment is of people signed up with agencies which find temporary work.

Sennett laments the consequences of workplace and economic short-termism for wider society. 'How', he asks, 'can long-term purposes – the objective of family – be pursued in a short-term society? How can a human being develop a narrative of identity and life history in a society composed of episodes or fragments?'[21] As he points out, war, famine and other disasters are a constant feature of human history. 'What's peculiar about uncertainty today,' he continues, 'is that it exists without any looming historical disaster; instead it is woven into the everyday practices of vigorous capitalism. Instability is meant to be normal.'[22]

Among people with jobs, the nature of work is becoming increasingly routine for many, and this now includes well-educated people, who, thanks to their advanced learning, often hold aspirations and expectations way beyond the possibilities and opportunities provided by the routinized work of modern capitalism. Technology leaves many humans having to behave as robots in order to operate machines which take the place of other humans. Overly routine work can make people depressed and unproductive. Even the routine work of the production line has more tangible outputs than much of the paper-pushing, number-crunching, service-sector jobs of today. At least the factory worker sees automobiles trundle out of his factory – things which people want. The modern service-sector worker has no such visible sign of having produced anything except, usually, additional wealth for an anonymous client. A sense of having little or no control over your life has been identified as a major cause of stress and depression. How many of us end up having to make do with jobs we would really rather not be doing? How few of us succeed in working at what we really want to do?

Change itself has become the agent responsible for the difficulties people now face: the loss of security and the absence of work opportunities which afford job satisfaction. Instead of attempting to identify the source of change, we simply accept that change is an inevitable fact of life. But responsibility for the growing instability we are now experiencing can be laid firmly at the door of changes in values and political priorities which are designed for the benefit of a minority of wealthy, powerful and privileged people. Insecurity, flexibility, and disruption are the staples of the new capitalist elite, because they allow large quantities of wealth to be accumulated very quickly.

One of the consequences, as Sennett remarks, is that, after two centuries of expansion, 'the shrinking size of the elite makes achievement more elusive. The winner-take-all market is a competitive structure which disposes large numbers of educated people to fail'.[23] It is a cruel system. Not only does it urge young people to study hard as the only way to success in adult life, it fills them with ambition and aspiration which by definition can only be enjoyed by the fortunate few. Throughout history, a sizeable majority has ended up poor and miserable, but at least they expected little else. Today, growing numbers are encouraged to excel with a promise of success and well-being. They do exactly as they are told, but for many the reward is insecurity and broken dreams.

The changing nature of work is a consequence of increasing competitiveness across society, but in the economy in particular. The current economic order depends for its success and survival on the willingness of sufficient numbers of individuals to behave competitively: to pit their wits and resources against one another in order to drive the economy forward. But this does not imply that today's economy is the necessary or inevitable product of a primarily competitive human nature. Rather, as it has evolved and been continually refined in the interests of minority privilege; the economic system has forced many individuals who, given a choice, would not base their social relations on competition, to do so.

Here we confront one of the great contradictions of the modern world: we are brought up to believe that considerate behaviour towards others is the cornerstone of civilized society and that it is only through self-sacrifice and cooperation that the social order is sustained. At the same time, we are instructed that our own interests, and ultimately the interests of progress and improvement, can only be served by competitive behaviour. Our governing philosophy urges that the interests of all are best served by the self-regarding behaviour of each of us as individuals. How are we to reconcile these two positions, to remain true to either one without deep psychological conflict?

We could attempt to separate society from the economy, to argue that society is dependent on cooperation and concern for the interests of others, whilst the interests of the economy are best served by competitive and individualistic behaviour. But this is to deny the primacy of the economy, the means by which we make provision for our basic needs. People come together in society because they cannot survive in isolation. Society takes on many functions, but its first function is to facilitate the provision of basic needs. Currently, a competition-based economy fails to deliver security in basic needs provision to two thirds of the world's people. Society has no non-economic alternative for making up the shortfall. The economy cannot be separated out from society, and society and the economy can operate only on the same values. Competition cannot be the sole basis of economic activity if the primary aim of society is the universal provision for basic needs.

A competition-based economic system is not a democratic creation: its foundations long predate democratic ideals. Modern global capitalism is a direct descendent of the economic order that emerged in pre-industrial Britain, one which was based on a grossly inequitable distribution of land, and which was exported to much of the rest of the world through force of arms. The original model assumed a world divided into competing territorial units, or nations, which mirrored the competitive relations among those with power. The modern world was shaped by those among the wealthy and privileged who most easily succumbed to the greedy, selfish and competitive drives which are common to the nature of all humans. The result is a framework for social and economic relations which draws out those very same divisive and exclusive qualities in everyone who aspires to success or security in life.

In his book, *Democracy versus Socialism*, Max Hirsch described two forms of competition: one in which there are fewer prizes than there are competitors; another where there is a prize for all who play, but where the prize value varies depending on performance.[24] Under the first arrangement, if the prizes represent economic goods, then competition will leave the losers destitute. Under the second, even the lowest-placed competitors will get a prize. Universalism has no problem with this model as long as the prize awarded to last-placed competitor is sufficient to secure his basic needs, provide him with some incentive to improve, and not leave him with a sense of injustice. But this seems unlikely given the nature and outcome of competition, where, generally, the rewards to the most successful tend constantly to increase at the cost of the rewards to the least successful. Universalism demands a mechanism to ensure that the least successful, as long as they are prepared to give of their labour, have their basic needs met.

To Hirsch's forms of competition, we may add a third: that of competing against a standard to which we all may aspire. Instead of measuring our individual achievements against the achievements of others, let us instead set targets for collective achievement, moral and economic. There is no need to compete with each other: our evolutionary heritage, our rapidly growing population, the ecological limits of our planet and centuries of compounded historical injustice surely provide us with plenty of challenges to take up.

Competition in the economic sphere is undoubtedly a force which motivates human beings, but it is a motivational force which appeals to fear and insecurity and which induces great anxiety. The consequences of failure in a competitive economic environment are all too visible; they undermine the potential of many individuals and, in an environment of artificially created scarcity, a competitive economy leaves millions to starve, or to die of cold or easily treated diseases. Competition only serves the interests of those who come to the game with a pre-existing advantage. Most of the winners come from this group; they leave with yet greater advantage extracted entirely at the cost of the losers. But if the scarcity which fuels competition is purely a function of the way we organize our economy, and if an alternative model of economy were discovered which removed this artificially created scarcity, then the need to compete would be diminished. In later chapters we will learn of such an alternative model, and of the means by which it has come to be assumed that only through competition can economic success be achieved.

Is there a place for non-economic competition in an inclusive society, and is there a link between economic competition and non-economic competition? Sibling infants compete with one another: for their parents' love and attention, for the lion's share of whatever treats are on offer, and, in some cases, to prove they are better at competitive games and sports. This early competitive behaviour is the product of an innate predisposition to self-centred behaviour which defines the social relations between the infant and other humans from the moment those relations begin. The jealous and competitive behaviour of the two-year-old is not a conscious act against siblings, parents or other children. It is an unconscious act in defence of the self. It might appear that an infant enters social relations predisposed to competing with all-comers for attention, but the child is competing with no one, only with the inner torment and vulnerability that is part and parcel of the emerging consciousness.

To suggest that this early self-centred behaviour is the natural form of human social relations, and can only be partly moderated with good parenting, education and socialization, is to misinterpret its causes. It is as if to say that, as we start off so bad, we can only improve a little, and therefore a competitive-aggressive society is the best we can hope for. This is nonsense: self-centred behaviour is the natural condition of nearly all two-year-olds. Some of these grow into caring universalizers, and some into competitive-aggressive individuals; most of us end up somewhere between the two. Philosophically, it seems, we are far readier to accept the aggressive-competitive individual as the prototypical human, and the compassionate universalizer as the freak of nature. Because we misunderstand the nature of infant selfish behaviour, and what it takes for a mature individual to outgrow it, we are prepared to excuse the failure of many individuals to reach moral maturity. Further, we are quite prepared to base our society on this failure. If adult human beings are competitive, it is because they are encouraged to be so, and because they grow up in an environment which accepts such an outcome as inevitable.

Different socializing environments have different impacts on children. Some children tend to become more competitive as they mature, others less. Some feel quite alienated by the concept of competitive sports at school, others take it in their stride. All children have considerable exposure to the culture of competitiveness which pervades modern society from very early in their lives. Every parent, every influential adult or other role model has the choice to reinforce the values of competitiveness or to gently steer a child in the direction of contentment and satisfaction without resort to competitive behaviour. Few parents have the independence of mind or the moral courage to take the second option. If they did, then the raw material for a competitive economy would quickly be eroded. The projection of competitive values from generation to generation is responsible for sustaining a competitive economic order and reinforcing the perception that it is both natural and inevitable.

From the day we begin school, we are subtly introduced to the paradox: to be good we must show concern for the well-being of others, but to survive we must compete. We have to study hard, and do well in exams. As young children we are not aware of the inevitable exclusiveness of such an approach, but we certainly are aware that some of our peers score better than us at spelling and others much worse. Only because we are protected from the harsh reality of the adult world do we fail fully to equate poor educational performance with bad prospects in adult life. By the time we do make the equation, for most of us the die is cast. There is little chance of redeeming a poor early-years education.

If it is the nature of the socialization and education processes that shape people for life in a competitive society, then changes to those institutions are vital if progress is to be made. Many academics, educationalists and teachers already question the value of a system based on competitive achievement. At the same time, the trend in many countries is towards standardization in measures of academic ability, the use of league tables to rank school and individual performance, and a focus on vocational education at the expense of pure learning. How are the objectives of education going to be altered when those who determine policy are apparently fully committed to the inevitability of a competitive society? Change may take many generations, but, where we can identify forces against progress, the seeds of change need to be sown now. Those with power and influence must be persuaded to take the lead in a process to encourage reflection on, and revision of, the values that shape society. Prime among these must be a move away from a belief in the merit and inevitability of a competitive society and towards valuing and believing in the possibility of a society based on values of cooperative endeavour.

Psychologists have identified many needs of the human psyche, the absence of which leaves individuals unable to negotiate life successfully and happily. Independence, respect, autonomy, affection, recognition, praise, sympathy, discipline, attention and understanding are all recognized as essential to the development of a healthy, rounded, emotionally mature human being. Not only do shortcomings in these inputs lead to the formation of individuals without the capacity or motivation to contemplate and embrace progressive social change, they also leave many people quite unable to negotiate today's competitive world.

For most people, the development of a healthy psyche is far from complete as they enter adulthood; for few adults is it ever complete. The most mature and stable human beings are usually the first to acknowledge how much they still have to learn about life, and about how best to relate to the world and the people around them. But, for all people, the time when these inputs, which collectively we might term *love,* are most important is during infancy, childhood and adolescence.

Erich Fromm, in his short book, *The Art of Loving,* wrote of five quite distinct types of love, all of which play a crucial role in the construction and maintenance of a mature psyche. First is *brotherly love*, which Fromm defines as 'the sense of responsibility, care, respect, knowledge of any other human being, the wish to further his life'.[25] This he suggests is ' the most fundamental kind of love, which underlies all other types of love.'[26] Second, Fromm identifies *motherly love*, which is described as 'unconditional affirmation of the child's life and needs'.[27] However, as well as protecting the child and preserving its life, Fromm asserts a second function of motherly love, which is to instil the feeling that 'it is good to be alive, it is good to be a little boy or girl, it is good to be on this earth.'[28]

Then there is *erotic love*, 'the craving for complete fusion, for union with one other person'.[29] As Fromm says, 'It is by its very nature exclusive and not universal', quite unlike brotherly love, which is love for all humans and motherly love, which implies love for all one's children and, by logical extension, for all children. Even when occurring between two psychologically healthy individuals, erotic love invites us to fall into the trap of self-obsession, or obsession with our relationship. But such relationships do provide an excellent personal training-ground for brotherly love. If we can practise true love towards an individual to whom we are committed, with all the compromises involved, then this can only help develop our capacity for brotherly or universal love. There is no better illustration of both the pleasures and difficulties of human relations, than the personal experience of a committed relationship. If we can commit to live with one other human in a just, equitable and mutually beneficial way, and come to realize that our lives are enriched as a consequence, then we can learn the value of the same relationship, albeit not at the level of personal experience, with all human beings.

Fromm's fourth type of love is *self-love*, although it is quite different from Freud's narrow definition of an unhealthy, narcissistic self-love which precludes the love of others. Fromm argues for an alternative healthy form, in which the positive, nurturing and equal feelings of love towards others, expressed in brotherly, motherly and erotic love, can be turned upon oneself. Fromm is describing a sense of self-worth, self-esteem or self-confidence which is found in all psychologically mature individuals. An acceptance of oneself and one's value as being equal to that of any other. All these forms of love, Fromm argues, result from the need to overcome the anxiety of separateness, the feeling of isolation which often results from a lack of love during childhood. Many adult relationships fail because the experience of love, and thus the capacity for love, in one or both parties is so poor that the relationship has to take the weight of so much expectation that it is doomed to failure. Only the well-loved learn to love well, and too few people are granted this privilege.

Fromm's final type of love is *love of God*, which he again emphasizes is a function of the need to overcome the anxiety of separateness. Throughout human history, God or gods have fulfilled this role in may different ways for people. The role of God has evolved as humankind has matured psychologically. And, Fromm hoped, it would go on evolving until a truly monotheistic God is accepted by all humans and comes to be regarded as 'the unity underlying the phenomenal universe, the ground of all existence; God becomes truth, love and justice.'[30]

Fromm's definition of love comes full circle. In beginning with brotherly love, he challenges us with the assertion that the love of all humans is the most fundamental of all loves. The types of love we recognize more readily, motherly and erotic love, he suggests are unlikely to be properly expressed without first recognising the fundamentality of brotherly love. They are components of the larger brotherly love. True self-love, in Fromm's terms, is also impossible in isolation. How can one love oneself as a human being of equal value if one is unable to value the lives of all humans equally? Finally Fromm turns to love of God. Whether or not a symbolic belief in God is a necessary bedrock for the development of brotherly love, and all the other forms, is open to question. Some people who achieve the ability for brotherly, or universal love, clearly do so through a process in which a conception of God figures prominently – although this is usually not the conception of God pedalled by the established, formalized religions; others do not. Many who term themselves atheists or humanists, or who refuse all labels, also achieve the capacity for universal love. The best we can say about the God method is that it helps some people, but it could be called something else and still be equally useful. In his book, *Stages of Faith*, James Fowler describes a model of psychological and spiritual development which avoids reference to the kind of fear-inducing other-worldly idea of God which leads so many believers astray. Perhaps *faith* is a better word for the driving force behind the thrust of humankind towards universal love. It is essential that we begin to project that faith back onto ourselves, and away from a God-like external focus.

In western societies, increasing numbers are opting not to have children, and many more people are choosing not to commit to long-term relationships, but to live alone. None of these trends is necessarily bad; none of them is intrinsically incompatible with universalism. But, given other developments in contemporary society, it seems likely that they are symptomatic either of an increase in social alienation – the involuntary failure of individuals to identify with others, and to build relationships based on a sense of common interests and aspirations – or, more worryingly, the logical consequence of an ethos of individualism taken so far that it condones an amoral attitude to human relations. This *postmodern* approach to life frees the individual from any obligations to society, whilst allowing him to enjoy all the benefits of membership. Erich Fromm believed the practice of love as observed between partners in an equal, committed and authentic relationship, and the successful practice of unconditional love towards children, were great contributors to the rational development and emotional maturity necessary for an individual to embrace universalism. If contemporary society is characterized by the kind of atomization that statistics on cohabitation and parenting seem to suggest, then we appear to be losing one of the mechanisms through which individuals learn to identify with the interests of others. We should be focusing on the value of genuine, mutually committed and beneficial relationships, and creating social conditions in which such relationships can successfully be enjoyed by many more couples.

The need for love is an essential and necessary requirement for successful psychological development. What of the need for roots, the sense of belonging to one particular human group? Little consideration has been given to the compensatory nature of the need for roots, that it is greater in individuals who perceive their life experiences as being short on love. The experience of love in infancy, childhood and adolescence, and the resultant ability positively to experience loving relationships in adulthood, leaves people much more likely to extend positive sentiments towards others, and even to all other human beings. The opposite experience, that of not receiving love, and the consequent lack of empathy and trust it engenders, renders people unable to give or receive love as adults, and leaves them grasping for alternative means to identify with other humans. The absence of love drives people back on a corrupted form of selfless expression: the identification with some largely artificial and invented sub-group of humankind, which manifests itself in varying degrees as patriotism, nationalism, xenophobia, racism, ethnic hatred or outright fascism.

In the previous chapter, we looked at the immense impact on society of the largely artificial and arbitrary imposition and adoption of group identities. Perceptions of group difference are incompatible with a society built upon the values of universalism if they involve differential treatment to individuals on the basis of prescribed or professed group membership. Universalism does not call for the repression of all feelings of group association, only for an end to the differential treatment and behaviour such divisions usually imply. There are many examples of group associations which humans enjoy which do not have such implications for justice and equity.

Group identity is not an essential human need: it is a product of historical inequity and the domination and exploitation of some groups over others, and it is compounded by negative personal experience. Christian Bay reminds us that much of the need to adopt a group identity results from failures in infant nurturing:

> The most fundamental obstacle to the freeing of intelligence is the active presence of ego defence motives. Severely repressed anxieties about one's worth as a human being, which may well be the result of a childhood starved of affection may predestine a person to become a true believer – a person who seeks a new collective identity because he cannot live with his own self. This type of person is not psychologically free. His views may keep his anxieties and fears manageable, but contribute no realistic understanding to the external political world.[31]

For Bay, people do not seek out group identities or adopt racist beliefs because they necessarily hate others. They do it primarily because, as a result of the way they were brought up, they have learned only to hate themselves.

I once heard an expert social commentator discussing concerns over the question of identity in a multi-cultural society: 'How,' he asked, 'is someone to form an identity for themselves in the face of such cultural pluralism?' The question implies a need for children to develop a particular ethnic or cultural identity by which they can come to see themselves as different from their peers. But is there really such a need? There is no problem with a child developing a particular view of itself in relation to other children or groups of children. It is the content of that identity that matters. Most importantly, it is the notion that the particular group identity developed by each child implies an element of moral or cultural superiority over other groups.

The principal source of such a sense of superiority is adults in positions of influence over the child. It ought to be quite possible to inculcate a sense of respect and genuine feeling for the historic rituals and traditions of a particular culture without imbuing such a divisive sense of superiority. The problem is that, in most cases, the influencing adults themselves hold the sense of superiority to be the most important aspect of their cultural identity, and believe their value system to be superior to all others. There is only one measure of the relative merits of competing value systems: the extent to which they conform to the ideal of universalism. It is not worth assessing any of the value systems forced upon children by devout parents against the criteria of universalism because they all visibly fail the test of inclusivity. Belief in the superiority of any value system means it cannot be inclusive or universal. It is not possible to believe in the equality of interests of all human beings and subscribe to a faith which claims cultural or moral superiority.

Claims for the importance of separate cultural identity indicate a desire on the part of many influential adults to implement culturally separate environments in which children are denied the chance to learn for themselves the equal value of all human lives. Young children know only one identity: that they are all alike. If you doubt this, take a look at any group of four- or five-year-olds in a school playground. They may be selfish, they may throw tantrums and occasionally even punches, they are certainly aware of gender differences and differences in skin colour – but this awareness comes with no innate prejudice or sense of superiority. Prejudice is learned, and the process is started by those adults of all cultures who insist that their children be directed towards forming a particular identity for themselves, one that sets them apart from other groups. At a stroke it imbues a sense of superiority and directs the innate tendency of children for irrationality and aggression onto gender, racial, class and ethnic differences which are entirely the constructs of human culture and the obsessions of influential adults.

The need for roots is very real. Those for whom membership of an exclusive group is the most important value, and who are often prepared to give their lives for their beliefs, are not imagining their need to identify. They are not suffering a mild neurosis which is easily cured. It is a reaction to an absence of love and an unremitting feeling of insecurity. The degree of patriotic, national or ethnic belonging felt by an individual is largely proportional to their direct experience of relations with the people closest to them. It can also be a reaction to profound social change, or the consequence of the whipping up of nationalist or ethnic sentiment by political leaders. A combination of all three factors usually lies at the root of the impulse to seek security in a sense of nationalistic or ethnic belonging.

It would be nonsensical to suggest that all Germans born in the early twentieth century experienced an equal and profoundly damaging lack of love and parental affection, and so, thirty years later, Germany embraced Nazism. However, as Eli Sagan asserts, a century ago attitudes to parenting were quite different from today. The children of the better-off were usually entrusted to nannies or packed off to boarding school. The children of working-class parents suffered a similar lack of parental care by today's standards, their parents often so poor and hardworking that they had little time for childcare. This comparatively poor standard of parenting (and I am not suggesting that it was any worse in Germany than in Britain or France, or anywhere else), whilst in no way the cause of the rise of fascism, meant that Germans were more readily persuaded in sufficient numbers to follow Hitler than might be the case today. The situation of Germany which, after the Great War, suffered a profound sense of loss of national identity and power at the hands of the victors, and then suffered more than most countries from the fall-out of the great depression, helped create the conditions for what happened subsequently. Germany's ultimate misfortune was to come under the spell of a charismatic leader with immense psychological problems of his own. These are well documented, and begin with poor parenting and socialization experiences. In the case of Germany, a combination of historical circumstance, rapid and damaging changes in social and economic conditions, a population which shared a common standard of parenting which would be considered inadequate today, and a deeply disturbed leader, conspired to lead a nation, and the world, into chaos.

Encouraging sentiments of separateness, uniqueness or difference, however well intentioned, is a recipe for greater conflict. To suggest that what an individual has in common with those who share his physical appearance, language or territory is more important than what he has in common with all humans, pushes us further away from the ideal of universal understanding. We all have a legitimate interest in, and a right to knowledge of, our roots – to understand where we come from, who our ancestors were, their relations with other groups, and the impact of their time on the historical development of our society and culture. This is quite different from arguing that it is a fundamental human need to label ourselves as different from our fellow humans. Carl Schmitt suggested: 'Having an enemy is our principal means of acquiring an identity.'[32] Johannes Herder claimed: 'nationalism fulfils a deep need in human beings to belong to a society that provides them with a complete form of life'.[33] Judith Litchenberg pessimistically opines: 'humanity is too large and indistinct a group for people to identify with'.[34] Each of these statements fails to recognize the root causes of ethnic and nationalistic sentiment.

Most human beings do have a need for roots, a sense of belonging and group identity. Much of the time this is benign, but all too often it becomes magnified and corrupted, and the cause of much conflict and suffering. We all need security, affection and love as a consequence of how we enter the world: unaware, powerless and acutely vulnerable. It is only because of failures in the way these needs are met that we later project our insecurities onto the need for a sense of identity and solidarity with a close group of our fellow humans. The need for roots is a consequence of failures in our nurturing and socialization experiences. If these were addressed, what is currently a very real need would be hugely diminished in importance.

We have noted that it is consciousness which singles out humankind from other sentient species. It is the basis for our conception and understanding of everything, including our own psychology. It is also the foundation for all we create through culture. The nature of consciousness is explored by Stanislav Grof, Peter Russell and Ervin Laszlo in their book, *The Consciousness Revolution*, in which they assert that only through a massive revolution in consciousness among millions of people can humankind be saved from itself.[35]

They discuss the means by which such a widespread shift in consciousness might come about, and, unconvinced that it is possible by conventional means, explore the likelihood of consciousness changes through metaphysical means – means that cannot be understood or predicted in terms of physical science. In a very strong sense, metaphysics is the opposite of reason and the enemy of science. It suggests, in ways that strike fear into many, that there are things we do not yet, and may never, understand about the universe and our place in it. That said, metaphysics has long been of interest to philosophers, and the suggestion that it could contribute to a widespread shift in consciousness deserves consideration.

Russell, Grof and Lazslo explore two themes that are of particular interest here: the idea of the collective unconscious, and the benefits of transpersonal experiences and non-ordinary states of consciousness.

The idea of the collective unconscious originated with Carl Jung. It suggests that the consciousness experienced by the individual is drawn from a common pool of potential consciousness to which all humans somehow have access. This may sound crazy but, as the authors argue, our understanding of how consciousness works is so poor that, as a theory, *the collective unconscious* is impossible to disprove. Further, there is not inconsiderable anecdotal and experimental evidence for its existence. The question is, even if it does exist, can it be relied on to deliver the huge and widespread change in consciousness which progressive social improvement demands? It is a question which cannot be answered without much more research into the nature of consciousness.

In their discussion of *transpersonal* experiences, the authors examine individual revelatory experiences, often associated with religious belief, by which individuals quite rapidly and unexpectedly come to adopt a radically different world view. There are many documented cases of this and, encouragingly, they seem always of the progressive kind whereby people come to reject prevailing orthodoxies in favour of ideas that place collective human well-being at the summit of their value hierarchy.

Grof describes the results of experiments he conducted: 'When people get involved in self-exploration using non-ordinary states of consciousness', he says, 'it is not necessary to teach them ecology or ethics; when they have transpersonal experiences their system of values changes automatically and they develop deep ecological awareness, tolerance and compassion.'[36] This is extremely interesting. Whether or not it affirms the existence of a collective unconscious, it certainly suggests that when freed from the constraints of conventional consciousness shaped, as it is, by the demands of survival in a competitive, insecure world, human beings commonly adopt, without direction, the values and world view that we have been discussing in this book. Encouragingly, such experiences do not push people in the 'wrong' direction, they cause them to question current orthodoxies and to believe in the possibility of a better world.

The kind of non-ordinary states of consciousness Grof refers to are those brought on by certain types of meditation, breathing exercises or psychedelic drugs. It would be impractical and unethical to impose these regimes on people, but what these catalysts appear to do is roll back the stultifying effects of conventional, ordinary states of consciousness, and provoke rapid and radical changes in attitudes and values. This is an extremely positive discovery. It identifies a moral corruption of consciousness which must have potential remedies not only in meditation and psychedelic drugs, but in less invasive and more subtle changes to the social environment in which consciousness develops.

There is evidence that many people come to a clearer and more enlightened and progressive world view, and adopt progressive values, as a consequence of changing consciousness after various spiritual experiences. This area needs much more research in order that we may gain a better understanding of its possibilities. At present the conditions and motivation to seek the means to raise the level of consciousness, whether by means of reason and study, or through alternative techniques, are denied to most people. The opportunities for personal change indicated by the evidence described by Russell, Grof and Laszlo should not be ignored.

There is immense dissatisfaction with the prevailing social order, and the current direction of social change. At the same time, many people feel deep frustration and anxiety within their own lives. Few people, however, seem able to see a link between the two. Never have so many sought the help of counsellors, psychotherapists and the peddlers of various alternative lifestyle solutions. But the anxiety and frustration felt by many, even among those who enjoy considerable material benefits, lacks direction and focus. If few people are able to make the link between social injustice and personal feelings of anxiety, it is because such notions are too threatening. Imagine if large numbers of consumers became aware of the causal link between the economic mechanisms by which they sustain their lifestyles and Third-World infant mortality. Such recognitions are extremely painful: the sense of guilt, responsibility, vulnerability and insecurity that full engagement with social reality provokes is beyond the capacity of most people to survive psychologically intact – and so their psyches begin to let them down. Frustration and anxiety is directed onto more tangible targets – dissatisfaction with relationships, problems with colleagues at work; or onto invented targets – the notion that a breakdown in parental discipline is exclusively responsible for the ills of modern society, for example.

Many people turn to so-called experts to help them, but few counsellors or therapists bring to their work a fully informed world view with which they might support and encourage their clients in locating the source of their anxiety in the competitive, high-pressure society we have created. As John Ralston Saul suggests, psychotherapy has not brought people closer to reality.[37] Many therapists today fall into the trap that Carl Jung warned against: confusing narrow self-knowledge with full conscious awareness of the social world. As a consequence, many people pay 'experts' in good faith for solutions to their problems, but the therapeutic process they are offered fails even to acknowledge the true source of their anxieties. Therapy could be a potent force for change if large numbers got off the couch with the message to go out and change the world so that it fits with their inner needs. Instead, most people leave therapy having been expertly adjusted to suppress or redirect their anxiety and to continue ignoring the unavoidable truth: that personal contentment is hard to come by in a world which fails to value all human life. As Saul says, 'It is as if our obsession with our individual unconscious has alleviated and even replaced the need for public consciousness. The promise, real or illusory, of personal self-fulfilment seems to leave no room for the individual as a responsible conscious citizen.'[38] Eli Sagan places the problem in its full historical context:

> The enormous push for individualism in the West which began in the twelfth century and came to full flower in the reformation – a movement that has given us capitalism, liberalism, democracy and the reign of science and technology – was an antithetical negation of conglomerate medieval Christian society. In its exaggerated form, it created an ideal of the individuated person capable of living with almost no sense of community, almost no sense of obligation to his or her society – a pathological individualism. The next great developmental advance will surely restore the sense of community without making us regress to medieval times, or give up all the legitimate gains of freedom that three centuries of intense individualism have brought us.[39]

The gap between our perceptions and reality is a result of failures in the nurturing, socialization and education processes to which the majority of the population are exposed. Many other social and cultural factors reinforce the consequences of this failing and serve to ensure that we continually fail to address the problems underlying our inability to produce more people who feel secure, are fully aware of the forces which shape society and dictate their place within it, and are able to develop the capacity for moral consistency. We know we have to change the nature and quality of the early-years environment, but we also need to examine the content of that environment, and look at the specific issue of moral development in individuals as the single most important element of psychological development, and the prime indicator of psychological health.

8

Moral Development

IN THE CONTEXT of this enquiry, morality refers to the means by which individuals come to consider the interests of others, and how these considerations inform their actions. Under the principles of universalism, questions of morality concern not just our considerations and actions in respect of those with whom we have direct contact, but extend to anyone on whom our behaviour, actions or lifestyle has some impact. Today, for many of us, this means all human beings. As we cannot insulate ourselves from an increasingly complex and interdependent global society, we cannot reasonably deny our moral responsibilities. We can choose to ignore them, but this is the province of the irrational, the lazy or the damaged human being.

Issues which are the more usual focus of debate about morality – sexual behaviour, pornography, abortion, adultery, and questions raised by advances in medical science – are quite clearly moral issues by our broader definition, but they remain a small subset of the universal moral domain. That they consume such a disproportionate amount of our moral energy is symptomatic of our inability to get to grips with the big moral questions. It is a tragedy that so much suffering is caused through the termination of pregnancies, but this is as nothing compared with the vast numbers of already born infants who die needlessly through want of adequate and affordable nutrition and medical provision. The human cost of our moral distraction is enormous.

Historically, discussion of moral issues was the preserve of philosophers and theologians. In more recent times, some have attempted to address moral questions with science. Many of these efforts have been controversial and unhelpful, as we noted in Chapter 1. But the subject does lend itself to scientific as well as philosophical treatment in a way that is perhaps unique.

Over the centuries, key ideas about moral development in children have foreshadowed the science to come. Saint Augustine alluded to the moral development of children through his interpretation of original sin, arguing that children are naturally sinful, and can only find redemption through the harsh intervention of adults. John Locke saw the child as morally neutral – a blank sheet of paper – out of which would emerge a more or less moral human being dependent on the quality and content of the child's training and its experience of early life. Rousseau believed children had an innate purity, and that the emergence of immoral behaviour was a consequence of the corrupting influence of adults and the world in which they develop. Already, these thinkers were addressing questions which would become central in child psychology and the study of human development.

Although Freud gave some attention to moral issues in his psychoanalytic theory, it was Jean Piaget who made moral psychology a discipline in its own right. Piaget's principal interest was in the developmental origin of knowledge: how we acquire knowledge and the link between this process and the means by which academic disciplines evolve. He turned his methods and ideas to the study of moral learning in his 1932 book, *The Moral Development of Children.*

The way Piaget framed his studies is interesting as it draws on two parallel threads of human advance: First that, generally speaking, humankind is developing in terms of its culture, scientific advance, technological capability and intellectual growth; and second that, despite this generation-on-generation advance, all new-born humans have to do their individual learning from scratch. Piaget was fascinated by this dual process: a duality which applies equally well to the concepts of collective human moral advance and individual moral learning in all new humans.

Piaget believed that the development of cognitive structures – the framework of physiological brain development which is a prerequisite to any learning – are innate, invariant, hierarchical and culturally universal. That is to say, the development of those parts of the body which we use for learning and thinking are, under the same conditions, the same for all people. He also believed that cognitive and moral development proceed hand in hand; one is not possible without the other, although the outcomes of each could be quite different. For Piaget, 'Development is not the result of maturation alone, but of a constant interaction between the maturing organism and the environment.'[1]

Freud had believed that the growing child's perception of the social order, of acceptable behaviour, and its acquisition of values, were almost exclusively determined by the influence of parents and other key adults. Piaget regarded parental and other adult influence as secondary to the influence of peer interaction.

Environmental influences were important for Piaget, but they were filtered through a complex series of universal developmental stages from which children emerge more or less well equipped to develop through the next stage. 'Knowledge is neither innate nor the result of learning,'[2] he said, rather it is the product of a developing mind interacting with the environment.

Piaget identified four stages of cognitive and moral development in children. The first is the *sensorimotor stage*, from birth to two years, during which a child's actions are determined completely by physical needs and changes, and by reactions to whatever sensual inputs it encounters. Next comes the *pre-operational stage*, from two to seven years, in which the actions are driven by egocentric considerations, and the child remains largely unable to see the needs and viewpoints of others. The third is the *concrete operational stage*, from seven to twelve years, when children learn some independence of mind and are able to free themselves and their actions from immediate perceptions, becoming aware of certain unchanging realities which they cannot influence. Finally, there is the *formal operational stage*, from eleven years on, when children become able to reason formally, to consider ideas, to form opinions and to base their behaviour on these considerations.

Piaget rejected the suggestion that universal stages of development implied that child development was somehow predestined or programmed into us. Such a stage process does not imply equality of outcomes, but it does provide a framework for others to study child development further, especially its moral component.

Piaget's theories, which were founded upon a great deal of practical research, led him to the firm belief that thinking about social problems was central to the way people made moral decisions. People did not just take inherited values and behavioural norms at face value and apply them in their own lives. Individuals had the potential to use their independently acquired powers of reflection and reason to determine whether or not the course of action set out by social convention was morally correct. They could act morally if they chose to, even if such action went against social convention. The relation between social convention and the means by which it is enforced, and the freedom of individuals to make independent moral decisions, was crucial.

If young people learn in reasonably universal concrete stages, then what about adults? The social, psychological and emotional development of human beings is not confined to childhood and adolescence. For many of us, our greatest period of learning and advance comes in adult life only when we find nourishing, mature relationships with partners. Lawrence Kolhberg took Piaget's nascent theory and turned it into a stage-based model of moral development which blurred the lines between children and adults, and acknowledged that psychological, and especially moral, development was a process which could continue throughout life.

We must acknowledge that Kohlberg is a friend of the idea of moral universalism. As Daniel Lapsley puts it, he was concerned with 'the possibility of articulating a conception of moral development that was adequate to the task of defending moral universality and defeating moral relativism'.[3]

Kohlberg wanted to prove that there was such a thing as universal morality and that it could occur and be applied in the real world. He set about researching the way human beings developed morally, hoping to establish that this development was universal in order to show that, given the right conditions, all humans might grow towards common moral aspirations which were universally compatible. He was also aware that any conclusions he was able to draw from his psychological research would be meaningless without a philosophical context. He needed criteria against which to judge moral development in individuals, and moral philosophy – what humans think and have thought about morality – provided the only possible context. Further, he recognized that no humans, however limited their moral capacity, make moral decisions in a vacuum. All moral decisions are made within a framework of social convention, exposure to religious teachings on morality, and a rich and diverse heritage of moral thought filtered through various cultures. He therefore gave as much attention to moral philosophy as he did to the psychology of moral development.

Kohlberg was moved and appalled by the revelations of the holocaust at the end of World War II. Like many at that time, he wanted to know why it had happened, what had gone wrong, and, most importantly, what could be done to ensure it could never happen again. He was most concerned at efforts to explain it in terms of moral relativism: the holocaust happened, some alleged, because human beings have no shared ultimate moral purpose. In the absence of any clear, knowable, source of moral authority, one morality becomes as good as any other. The values and standards of a particular society are seen, in relativists' eyes, as the inevitable product of unique cultural experience; whilst they may not appear palatable to people of other cultures, nor indeed to many members of the culture which espouses them, objectively they are of equal worth. According to the doctrine of moral relativism, a moral norm which stated that one group of human beings was sub-human and had to be eliminated, even if it led to the murder of six million Jews, was as valid as any other. Kohlberg saw how dangerous this was: not only would it allow for the emergence of another Hitler, but it denied any grounds for the rational criticism of one morality by proponents of another. But he knew no amount of philosophising would defeat it. Only rigorous science-based research evidence could build a case for moral universalism, and it was to this object that Kohlberg dedicated his life.

He began by extending and elaborating Piaget's stage theory of child development, in respect of the moral development of humans through and beyond childhood. His model has six stages which he grouped into three levels.

The first level, which Kohlberg termed *preconventional,* is divided into the *heteronomous morality* stage and the *instrumental morality* stage. Heteronomous morality, often referred to as the obedience and punishment orientation, is the stage at which most small children operate. Here there are concrete rules, which are given by some authority figure. Actions and behaviours are seen as either right or wrong; no consideration is given to why this is so. In fact no thought is given to moral decisions save recalling what is the correct course of action when confronted with a particular situation. Here, the only thing that encourages particular behaviours is the threat of punishment.

At the instrumental stage, morality, justice, or what is right, is seen to be determined by the instrumental exchange of goods or favours. Appropriate behaviour is that which is likely to gain some benefit in your relations with others. Conversely, where you are the victim of some disbenefit, it is seen as right to inflict the same harm on the perceived culprit. Here, good behaviour is encouraged by the prospect of similar goods being received in return.

Level two is termed *conventional,* and within it lies stage three, the *interpersonal orientation.* At this stage, individuals have an awareness of shared moral norms. They become aware that others think like they do, and that there are prescribed roles to be played which carry with them an obligation to certain behaviours. It is important to fit in; the threat of ostracization dictates against errant behaviour. Good behaviour is encouraged by the desire to seek the approval of others.

Stage four is *social system morality*, often known as *the law and order* orientation. Here society takes on the role of providing the norms for behaviour and the sanctions for non-conformity. Individuals perceive society as the instrument which determines what is right and wrong; as society is made up of institutions created by groups of people, the members of which identify with each other. At this stage, the individual learns that it can be wrong to give preference to the interests of someone close to you over other members of society. Good and right behaviour is dictated by the rules, norms and laws established by institutions to which members of society are expected to subscribe.

The third level Kohlberg termed *post-conventional* or *principled,* and stage five is termed the *social contract* orientation. Here the individual begins to hold ideals about the value of liberty and human dignity and starts to believe that 'in an ideal world' all people would like to be able to share these values. Stage five individuals begin to think in terms of people being able to reshape society by redefining its values, rather than those values being given by society. Good and right behaviour begins to be determined by the optimistic possibility of individuals changing society by adopting non-conventional behaviours.

Stage six, called *universal morality* or *principled conscience*, is the highest moral stage that Kohlberg found in humans, albeit in relatively few individuals. At this stage, it is the conscience of the individual which determines moral decisions, and conscience operates in accord with self-chosen ethical principles of logical consistency and universalizability. The individual is guided by thought that echoes Kant's *categorical imperative* and Rawl's *theory of justice* among other ideas. In stage six, concrete or prescribed rules become almost irrelevant. Someone thinking at this level would refrain from killing another not because the Bible says it is wrong, or because she is likely to spend the rest of her life in jail, but because it would be a gross violation of her conscience. Good and right behaviour is dictated by what could and should be possible in a world where the interests and well-being of all people are treated as equal.

At stages five and six, people begin to think in terms of the inherent value of life. For people at lower stages, life and their existence is a given, rarely warranting a second thought. They may well feel differently from day to day as their mood changes in reaction to events around them, but they do not reflect on the value or meaning of life itself. This ability is crucial to high-level moral decision-making: an objective perception of life as inherently worthwhile is necessary if you are going to be able to appreciate the interests and viewpoint of others. Further, the ability for such reflection helps develop ideas about the potential for improving the experience of life for all people. This added level of perception parallels the realization at the principled level that individuals can devise ways of encouraging wider society towards changing values. The ability to see that life has value of itself, and that the experience of life can and should be positive and fulfilling for all people, is a key ingredient in sustainable and progressive social change.

Once Kohlberg had identified his six stages, if his theory was to be taken seriously, he had to prove they existed. This he did with numerous studies in which he measured the moral development of many individuals over long periods. He was able to prove beyond doubt that the stage process is sequential and that there is no regression. People move from stage to stage, they never skip a stage, and once they reach a particular stage there is no going back. As part of this process, he found that people understand and are able to relate to the stage above their own before they move to it. Sometimes people gain an understanding of the next stage without ever fully making the leap.

The research found no correlation between the attainment of moral stages and IQ, although it did find a link to educational experience and social class. Some experience of higher education was necessary in order for people fully to attain stage four, and no one was found to have attained stage five without having completed a course of higher education. This is not to imply that higher education teaches moral development, or that such formal education is necessary to attaining the higher stages, only that the kind of mental activities and stimulation routinely encountered in higher education are conducive to high-stage moral development.

There have been a number of critiques of Kohlberg's theory which require careful consideration. First, there are the problems implicit in using what appears to be a grading scheme to classify people. Many have argued that, by assessing and labelling individuals at a particular stage, and by arguing that stage six is a higher level of attainment than stage five and so on, that Kohlberg's scheme makes value judgments about the adequateness of individuals, and implies that some are more moral, and therefore of greater worth, than others. Kohlberg replied that, although he cannot prevent people from misusing his model, his research was not devised as a tool to classify people or make judgments about their worth. His objective was to discover whether moral development occurs in stages, and if there was an ultimate and realisable stage of moral reasoning. Kohlberg was always very careful to avoid any such judgments. Nonetheless all such schemes do lend themselves to abuse by people with agendas not as noble as Kohlberg's own.

Kohlberg is also criticized by philosophers for committing the *naturalistic fallacy:* the deduction of ought from is, an act of philosophical blasphemy for more than a century now. In his research, Kohlberg has demonstrated an ultimate stage of moral development which can only be reached by passing through each of the others. A few people succeed in attaining it and this implies that the attainment of higher stages is desirable. Kohlberg is taking a view on what *ought to*, or *could*, be for most people, based on his observations of what *is* for a few. He countered that his act of philosophical barbarism is permissible in this case, his conclusions being based on the incontrovertible evidence of rigorous scientific research. If he has proved that moral development does pass through sequential stages in all people, and that an ultimate stage is evident and attained by some; if he has also proved that once people attain a particular stage they are happier there than at earlier stages; and if it is also true that the highest level of attainment broadly echoes the highest moral ideals of philosophers, then perhaps we should not be arguing about esoteric points of philosophical good practice, but instead take a closer look at what factors influence the attainment of successive moral stages in individuals.

The third principal criticism of Kohlberg's work is that he approaches his subject from a very masculine point of view, and that he underrates the moral potential of women by failing to take into account other factors which influence moral thought and action beyond the capacity for rational reflection. Research suggests that, while the majority of adults studied are found to be in stages three or four, at the conventional level, there is an over-representation of women at stage three relative to men. Carol Gilligan criticizes Kohlberg for suggesting that women are better suited to stage three[4]. But Kohlberg also argues that fewer women made it to stages four and five because, at the time most of his research was conducted, the type of educational and life opportunities that are conducive to development beyond stage three were denied to most women.

Carol Gilligan's work, and in particular her book, *In a Different Voice,* are of especial interest. She argues that the different approach to life and to conflict situations of women mean that they generally act beyond the moral stage at which Kohlberg's reason-based measures categorize them. According to Gilligan, women focus on the values of caring for, responsibility towards, and avoidance of harm to others. They seem to have an innate ethic of empathy and compassion which men generally lack. Women focus on interpersonal responsibility, the way one behaves towards the people with whom one comes into contact, whereas men think about moral issues far more in terms of rights, duties and reciprocal arrangements. Women think and act at a personal level, whereas men allow their actions to be determined, and excused, by the tenets of social convention.

To what extent these differences are innate, and to what extent they result from the socialization process, is an important question, for it seems that if more women were able to complement their innate empathy and reasonableness with a greater degree of reasoned judgment (and, conversely, more men were able to learn a little empathy and compassion), then society would benefit and relations between people would improve. That said, it is clear that more men have more to learn from women. These female moral traits seem to be prevalent among the vast majority of the female population, whereas the positive contribution that reason can make to moral decision-making and behaviour seems poorly developed in the majority of men. Gilligan's ideas do cast some doubt on the usefulness of Kohlberg's model. Certainly women are under-represented at the higher stages of Kohlberg's scale, yet observable evidence of the world around us suggests that men are more often responsible for immoral, violent, aggressive, selfish and brutish acts. Women aspire to be peacemakers despite their relatively poor moral standing in Kohlberg's terms.

Others criticize Kohlberg's theories as not sufficiently proven to be cross-cultural[5]. It is true that, in one piece of research in Turkey, Kohlberg failed to find any examples of stage six. However, *culture* is a difficult concept to tie down when it comes to classifying subjects in a piece of research. Are all Turks members of the same culture, and is there likely to be some particular cultural influence on Turks which prevents any of them from reaching stage six? There is clear evidence that moral stage correlates strongly to educational opportunities and achievement. It is also abundantly clear that educational opportunities are restricted in countries like Turkey. This, along with the difficulties experienced by researchers in obtaining representative samples of subjects in such places, may well go some way to explaining the anomaly. It is true, however, that a disproportionate number of stage five and six subjects are found in urban areas of western industrialized countries. This does not mean that Kohlberg's model is applicable only to westerners who live in big cities, only that those conditions most favourable to attaining the higher stages are found in such places. The challenge is to create those conditions elsewhere and everywhere. Rather than criticize the model for being culturally biased, perhaps we should grasp the implications of Kohlberg's honest reporting of the way things are, and begin to make links between the social and cultural environment in some less-developed countries and the poor showing in Kohlberg's model of many people in those countries.

Critics of Kohlberg neglect the general value of his work. As a consequence of his disgust at the holocaust, he succeeded in elaborating a framework which survives close scrutiny and provides us with an ultimate collective moral goal. He has backed up centuries of philosophical belief in an ultimate level of moral attainment with empirical evidence that proves not only that such a level exists, but also that it is attainable by many people. None of his doubters have provided any evidence that the higher stages are not attainable by many more humans given the right conditions. Until and unless someone does, then Kohlberg gives us considerable cause for optimism.

Of all Kohlberg's critics, Carol Gilligan has the strongest case, but her work should be seen as adding to the pool of optimism that Kohlberg has started to fill, rather than undermining it. If Gilligan is right, then we must approach the ongoing development of Kohlberg's ideas and their practical application with added consideration given to the uniquely female, but non-Kohlbergian, factors that influence positive moral behaviour. We must also consider the gulf that exists between measured levels of moral reasoning in men and the behaviours that follow. Perhaps the higher-reasoning male is unable to translate his reasoned moral judgment into appropriate action because he lacks some of the traits which push women toward moral action without the need for a higher level of moral reasoning.

Professor Kohlberg died in 1980. His students and others have continued his work, but their impact has been slight. Why has Kohlberg and the topic of moral psychology fallen so rapidly from favour? In the 1970s his theories were a staple part of many social science undergraduate courses, especially in the United States. There is no evidence of any campaign to silence Kohlberg's followers, or attempts to suppress his work by rival academics. Indeed, there continues to be vigorous academic debate among a small band of Kohlberg's students, successors and critics, nearly all of which is valuable and constructive.

Kolhberg was never popularized, perhaps because of the confusion and misunderstanding around the term *morals,* but perhaps also because a few key opinion-formers had the foresight to realize the radical implications of Kohlberg's discoveries. The main reason for Kohlberg's disappearance from the radar of ideas is that, in the decades after he published his findings, when his ideas might have spread beyond academia, the world fell under the spell of a quite different approach to morals and social responsibility – the antithesis of Kohlberg's universalism, peddled by the architects of the New Right agenda. The other reason for Kohlberg's failure to gain a wider audience is the fact that his subject matter remains outside the frame of reference of most people: we are simply not encouraged to consider the world or our position in it in Kohlbergian moral terms. Until that changes, Kohlberg's ideas will remain firmly out of mind.

Kohlberg's work strongly suggests that many more people can, given the right environment, attain the higher stages of moral maturity and understanding, but, if his ideas are to have any practical long-term impact, then the link must be made between the requirement for post-conventional moral stage aspiration and attainment, and progressive change in the social order. Moral development is not about producing model citizens whose behaviours reflect the established values of the contemporary world neither is it about preparing people to survive in an imperfect world. It is about changing that world through spreading awareness of its immense problems, accepting the possibility and desirability of change, and finding strategies to bring it about. As part of a strategy underpinned by a universalist moral philosophy, widespread knowledge of Kohlberg's discoveries could play a valuable role in the struggle for progress.

How do Kohlberg's findings tie in with the idea of conscience? An act compelled by conscience is different from any other act. When we act in response to the demands of conscience we feel, and think, differently from the way we do when acting under any other motivation. A conscience-inspired act usually occurs after a period, sometimes very brief, of reasoned thinking. At other times clear acts of conscience seem to come from nowhere. We do things because we know we must, and because we know they are right, but we are not quite sure how we arrived at that conclusion so quickly. Acts of conscience take two forms: the *positive* form, where we take action to prevent harm, or to provide additional good, to others; and the *constraining* form, where we are set on a particular course, only to be thwarted by pangs of conscience as we realize that some potential harm might come to others as a consequence of our actions.

The mechanism is linked to reasoning, but is not the same. Sometimes conscience help us turn the demands of reason into action. At other times, conscience can stop us from acting where we have failed to consult reason, or where reason has been found wanting, perhaps because it has been guided by values which fall short of universalism. If this is true, it points to some link between conscience and universal morality which does not require the intervention of reason. But, as we see all too clearly in the world around us, conscience does not always work to prevent harm. In some people it works much of the time, in others hardly ever. In no one does it work consistently and without fail. Much research remains to be done on the nature of conscience, its development in individuals and its link to moral reasoning.

Conscience tends to be less reliable when the object of our actions is far removed from our own lives. Just as we have discussed the need to enlarge the scope of our moral concern, so we must find ways of extending the power and consistency of our conscience. Conscience clearly has a heavy emotional aspect to it. It bolts into action when we see images of starving children on television and we are motivated to donate money to help them. It does not really help much when we are considering the complex web of causes and effects that link our material aspirations and patterns of consumption to economic failure and social breakdown in the countries where children go hungry. Conscience fails us because all too often we fail to listen to it. It is only as effective as we permit it to be. As part of the project to create the conditions for more people to attain post-conventional levels of moral reasoning *and behaviour*, we need to find means of enhancing the consistency, effectiveness and power of the mechanism of conscience. In many people, conscience remains active but unconscious. How can we bring conscience into the consciousness of more people and with greater power?

Eli Sagan considers the role of conscience in relation to his belief that all humans 'are born with an ultimate capacity for moral reflection that goes beyond values'.[6] He argues that basic love, the love given by parents to their children, is not a result of conscience, but rather its foundation: 'Parents love their offspring, first, because it fulfils a biological necessity: a completely unloved child, if it does not die, would become a psychological catastrophe.'[7] He makes a link between healthy psychological development – the product of a loving and secure environment – and the development of moral faculties. Sagan continues: 'Conscience is the primary mechanism in the psyche whereby conflicts between basic love and aggression are resolved in a moral (that is, loving) manner.'[8] So, for Sagan, conscience is born of the necessary love that psychologically healthy parents show for their children, and the developmentally positive impact this has on the infant. But positive experiences in infancy are not enough. 'It is identification with other human beings that enables conscience to generalize concerns of love and nurturance to those who are not kin,'[9] continues Sagan. The obstacles and constraints to our capacity for identification with others, and the consequent impact on the development of conscience, are many; but identification is crucial to progress, both individually and socially. Sagan is in no doubt of the link between childhood experience and the sorry state of the social world:

> The experiences of infancy are ultimately played out in Hiroshima and Auschwitz, and antithetically in the lives of moral leaders such as Gandhi and Martin Luther King. So much of the world's misery results from the fact that when politically empowered, he who cannot identify with his fellow human being becomes a killer. The capacity to make these crucial identifications is fundamentally dependent on the quality of the nurturing that a child receives.[10]

Christian Bay confirms this thesis in his analysis of research conducted in the mid-1960s, which reveals a link between the individual's attitude to progressive social change and neuroses. These findings, detailed in the *Journal of Social Issues*, would probably be unpublishable today for they assert a link between conservative, right-wing political views and neurosis and other psychological problems. The implication is that a psychologically healthy and secure individual is likely to hold more liberal, tolerant views, and be more embracing of the possibility of progressive social change, even if not active in its pursuance. I will quote Bay's summary at length:

> The more secure and sheltered a person's infancy and childhood, and the more freedom that educational and other social processes has given to him to develop according to his inner needs and potentialities, the more likely that a capacity for political rationality and independence will develop simply because the likelihood of severe anxieties is relatively low. The better the individual has been able to resolve his own anxieties the more likely that he will empathize with others less fortunate than

himself. A sense of justice as well as a capacity for rationality is, according to this theory, a likely development in relatively secure individuals
whose politics, if any, will therefore tend toward the left – toward supporting the champions of the underdog, not the defenders of established,
unjust institutions. Every new human being is potentially a liberal animal
and a rebel; yet every social organization he will be up against, from the
family to the state, is likely to seek to socialize him into a conveniently
compliant reformist."

It is our shared psychology which is the source of universal morality. Just
as our shared physiology enabled us to identify universal basic needs, the
fact that the same environmental inputs tend to have the same impact
on the development of the individual human psyche regardless of
culture, points to the unavoidable conclusion that our common moral
aspirations and potential are an essential part of our humanity. To ignore
or deny this can only mean continued suffering for the excluded majority
and considerable psychological anguish – however much it is repressed –
for those of us fortunate to enjoy a degree of economic security.

Kohlberg and Sagan show that the idea and the ideal of a universal
ethic is not simply wishful thinking. Some people attain an ultimate level
of moral development and many others aspire to it. The environment
into which many people are born severely reduces their potential for
moral attainment at an early age; but most newborns constitute viable
source material for post-conventional moral reasoning. But can we be
sure that progressive social change will follow from large numbers of
individuals attaining higher-stage moral reasoning? Is there a concrete
and identifiable link? Certainly, at present, far too few people attain
the post-conventional stages, and most of those that do are found in the
urban centres of western countries. There need to be more higher-stage
attainers and they need to be more widely spread across cultures and
regions. Social change is usually dependent on the attainment of a critical
mass. It is impossible to know how many post-conventional moral reasoners would be required to tip the balance in favour of progressive social
change, nonetheless, as part of a wider strategy, increasing the numbers
of post-conventional reasoners would make a critical contribution.

In his book, *Rethinking Ethnicity*, Richard Jenkins describes how ethnic
identity can be an element in the primary socialization process and that,
where this is the case, the chances of reversing it are remote. Primary
socialization includes all those essential things that one learns from
others in the early years of life. It normally and healthily includes the
incorporation into the psyche of recognition of one's humanity, gender
and selfness. We all learn at a very early age that we are human, unlike

cats and dogs, that we are a boy or girl and that there is a difference, and also that we are Annie as opposed to William. But sometimes the identification process goes further. Jenkins states that 'there is no necessity that ethnicity will feature explicitly in primary socialization; much depends here on local circumstances and histories'. But, if it does, the sense of ethnic identity will be 'deeply rooted in first encounters and the ego-centric taken for granted constitution of the social world' and will be 'resilient to easy transformation'.[12] If you begin life amidst a belief that you and your group are different from others, then you are likely always to believe it. Further, as we have seen, belief in difference encourages perceptions of superiority. Anyone who perceives himself a member of a sub-group of humankind is unlikely to be able to avoid the implication that his group is superior to others.

Kwame Anthony Appiah describes a 'cognitive incapacity' in respect of racism.[13] He suggests people are unable to overcome their racial and ethnic prejudices because they are so deeply conditioned into the psyche that it is cognitively impossible for them to do so. If this is true, it means that attempts in adult life to change some people's attitudes to race and ethnicity are bound to fail. We need to strike at the root causes of ethnic identification in individuals if we are to avoid future generations of people who are immune to the merits of universalism.

It seems reasonable to extend Appiah's logic and examine the possibility of a more general cognitive incapacity in respect of recognising and valuing the interests of others. Some people are routinely selfish, and seem quite unable to recognize the interests of others, sometimes those within their own families. This kind of rigidly anti-universal attitude is usually born of experience. It is as hard to reverse in adult life as ethnic or racial prejudice. If some people are cognitively incapable of changing their perceptions and beliefs, then there is no point trying to change them. In Kohlbergian terms, they have become irretrievably stuck at pre-conventional levels of moral reasoning. All we can do is identify the root causes of such incapacity and create conditions to ensure future generations do not suffer the same fate.

Whether overemphasis on ethnic identity lies at the root of the limitations on the scope of our moral concern, or is a product of it, is an important question. If there is some innate limit on moral scope, then the ideal of universalism is certainly unattainable. But there is ample evidence – in the form of individuals who are able to hold and live by universal values – that there is no such innate limitation. This strongly suggests that our moral scope is determined by what we are taught and learn through life experience, and the messages we receive from those around us, and the environment in which we grow up. For Eli Sagan the essential question is: 'Why do some adults extend their experience of good nurturing to the whole of mankind, and others stop this process of generalization short, at the boundary of religion, or race, or class or country?"[14] He affirms that:

> Everyone has that morally generalizing capability to some degree or other, but it is enormously vulnerable to the pressures of parents and the society in which one lives. It may be encouraged or discouraged, encouraged in some areas and discouraged in others. Without the keen support of parents or of society, for most people any desire to generalize moral experience ends up as one factor in some ambivalent compromise formulation.[15]

Sagan agrees that a conducive environment is crucial, but he also suggests that moral generalization is a skill that can be compared to sporting ability or musical flare, an ability that is naturally more developed in some people than in others. Although this may explain why some do attain high levels of moral generalization without a particularly supportive environment, it also suggests that, just as not everyone can be a Mozart or a Pelé, neither can everyone be a Gandhi or a Mandela. This argument is flawed, however. The measurement of accomplishment in the fields of sport or the arts is inevitably competitive: individuals are compared against each other in order to identify the best. Moral generalization, as a capacity, has none of these competitive elements: in fact its principal measurement is how uncompetitive an approach an individual is able to take to life. All individuals, in the measurement of their ability for moral generalization, are assessed against a single – admittedly very high – standard. In short, there is room in the world for billions of Gandhis and Mandelas, and they would be able to live harmoniously together; there can only ever be one Mozart or Pele.

Sagan suggests that an individual's moral progress can be seen as the abandonment of defence mechanisms. If, through our experience of adult life, we learn the true nature of the defensive reactions we use to protect ourselves from the memory of difficult childhood or adolescent experiences, then we can start to let down those barriers, learn the benefits of trusting others, and restart the process of moral development which was halted by immersion in a poor environment. It is possible for adults to catch up – and when they do they rapidly increase their ability for generalization. It might get harder to learn the piano as you get older, but, with the help of life experience, and with a reasonably undamaged psyche, it is possible to make rapid progress in moral generalization.

Progress towards full moral generalization, the ability to extend the scope of our moral concern to all humans and use this to shape our everyday behaviour, requires levels of transparency and understanding which are unusual in the complex modern world. Gregory Baum, in his analysis of the work of Karl Polanyi, explains the demands of transparency and understanding so eloquently that I shall quote him at length.

> In a simpler society, Polanyi argues, people knew the impact their actions had on others: they knew the farmer, the miller, the baker, and the other craftsmen and merchants with whom they dealt. They could estimate whether their interaction with them was just or unjust. Their society was transparent. But because of increasing complexity, modern industrial society has become largely 'opaque'. We realize that our actions have an impact on others but most of the time we do not know what this impact is. We are aware that our participation in society makes us co-responsible for the good and for the evil done by society but we do not know with any precision what these good and evil actions are.
>
> In this situation, Polanyi suggests, the civil conscience is deeply anguished. People desire to be ethical and assume responsibility for the consequences of what they do, but in an opaque society they cannot know what these consequences are. Complex society is largely ignorant. The ethical longings of the bourgeois, Polanyi argues, cannot be satisfied within bourgeois society. The longing of the bourgeois conscience transcends the possibilities of bourgeois society. What this conscience calls for is the creation of a transparent society that allows its members to estimate the effects of what they are doing and thus assume ethical responsibility for their actions.[16]

Whether Polanyi's view of the bourgeois conscience is consciously articulated in many individuals, I am not sure. But it is self-evident that, in order to make informed moral decisions and to be able effectively to extend the scope of our moral concern to all humans, transparency is crucial – along with a thorough understanding of the ways in which social, legal and economic structures work. Having the right information to make informed moral decisions is vital. For example, if you don't believe greenhouse gases contribute to global warming, which in turn affects sea levels and rainfall patterns, a consequence of which is many people losing their homes and many others going hungry, then excessive or unnecessary car use will not occur to you as immoral or anti-universal. Universalism in action is not just about selflessness and allowing for absolute equality of interests, it is also about acquiring sufficient information to make decisions that support these principles. Full information assists in correctly identifying which behaviours and actions carry a moral dimension. In the modern world virtually all acts of spending and consumption have such a dimension.

Beginning with Kohlberg, we have outlined a framework for individual and collective moral development which is key to the social progress which this book advocates. We have taken Kohlberg's basic premise, but acknowledged that there is more to moral development in individuals than a highly developed capacity for reason. We have accepted Carol Gilligan's argument for other types of moral motivation which are more commonly, but not exclusively, found in women. We have considered Sagan's claims that humans possess an ability for moral abstraction which requires support and nurturing if it is to flourish, and we have emphasized the importance of a positive socialization and educational environment. Finally, we have noted Polanyi's observations about the complexity of the modern world and the need for transparency if we are to satisfy our urge to be more moral. We have quite an elaborate, if rather informal, theory then. But how does our theory lend itself to a practical framework for improved socio-economic justice? We must resist the temptation to convert the theory into a practical programme for political and economic change. Such change can come only from the collective conscious will of very many people. Any attempt by a few right-minded people to force the theory into practical action is bound to fail. We need to address the obstacles we have identified in order to extend the opportunity for attaining moral maturity to greater numbers, and see what happens.

A particular form of conscience, *universalized social conscience*, forms the conduit between high-stage moral reasoning and progressive social change. A fully active social conscience, underpinned by a universal ethic, will help individuals to identify the means by which progressive global social change can be effected. We are fortunate that, in the democratic and liberal political and legal systems in place in many parts of the world, there is general acceptance of the legitimacy of allowing the entire adult population to decide how best to organize society and the economy, and thus whose interests should be served. So far, liberal democracy has failed to deliver on its promise, but there is no reason why it should not be used to effect progressive change by a population among whom social conscience becomes an increasingly important determinant of political and economic priorities.

We need an exercise in realism, and in reconciling the moral aspirations of the modern world with its dreadful reality. Only when our leaders start to entertain the possibility of a quite different social and economic order, and start nudging us in that direction in an inspired but unthreatening way, will enough people consider it worth investing the requisite effort in their own moral development. We can begin to create the necessary conditions and to talk up the possibility of progress, but this is the extent of the political programme we can draw from our theory of moral development. Anything more would constitute an exercise in social engineering of the kind tried so disastrously in the Soviet Union. One of the reasons that western capitalism has come to dominate the world is the incremental nature of its imposition: the gradual changes and tweaks over generations, the passing of legislation, the consequences of which few were able to foresee, and the confusion of the ideals of liberty and freedom with a system which provides security for so few. Our project must reject the deceit and hypocrisy of the capitalist one, but it could learn something from its stealth – the way it plants seeds and lets them grow in people's minds – and particularly from the aura of inevitability with which it surrounds itself. The widespread promotion of ideas, and one idea in particular – the possibility of the better world – is the most effective tool at our disposal.

We have made little mention of the concept of community. For nearly all of us, most of our direct contacts with others are with those we are geographically close to. People we live near, work with; people whose children share the same school as ours. Universalism argues that we should treat everyone equally, and consider their interests as equal to our own. Needless to say this still applies to those to whom we are geographically closest. Further, in respect of such proximate relations, Polanyi's obstacle of opaqueness should not apply. There are very few excuses for not behaving with ultimate morality towards those with whom we have direct contact. But the value of community in contributing to an increase in the scope of our moral concern is dubious. It should guide us by reminding us that, where we do succeed in moral behaviours within in our small communities, these are the very same standards of behaviour we should apply in our dealings, however indirect, with all people.

That said, it is clearly the case that, as Reinhold Niebuhr argued back in 1932, 'The failure of even the wisest type of social pedagogy to prompt benevolences as generous as those which a more intimate community naturally evolves, suggests that ethical attitudes are more dependent upon personal, intimate and organic contacts than social technicians are inclined to assume.'[17] This is true, and explains why morality cannot be explicitly taught. Equally true, however, is the fact that the power of community to generate such benevolences is diminished greatly in the complex modern world, and so, while we can look to the best examples of community spirit for indications of how we should behave in general, the power of community is not sufficient to foster widespread progressive social change. Communities will always have a role – few of us will ever be true global citizens, equally at home anywhere on the planet – but the management of relations between these communities, under a global framework for mutually beneficial governance in accordance with universalist principles, is crucial.

9

A True Economics

I N RECENT TIMES our moral aspirations – what we want for the world – have progressed at a rate far in excess of our ability to transform those aspirations into reality. This is why we struggle to make sense of the world and why it frequently disappoints us. We fail to understand it because we fail to grasp the complex web of causes and consequences that colour human social relations. We dream of a better world and we know what it is about the current order that we dislike, but we remain unable to take collective action to bring about a new inclusive social order, or even to set the process in motion.

Our successes, though considerable, remain piecemeal. They are reactions to legitimate but isolated moral concerns; they are not part of an overall strategy for social change, and they are not driven by reference to universal moral principles. Such islands of progress may one day form part of a comprehensive strategy for change, but they do not indicate that any such strategy yet exists. It is the central thesis of this book that progressive social change requires not only the internalization of universal moral principles by many people, but also that they behave in accordance with those principles, and find the collective strength to overcome the many obstacles to change. Thus far, too few people have succeeded in this difficult task, leaving those that have largely unable to realize their ambitions. Society is never static, and in terms of the measurable experience of people's lives it can move in only two directions: towards greater inclusion, or towards greater polarization. The challenge for the twenty-first century is to determine how we reconcile growing moral aspirations for greater inclusion with the reality of a world which is being torn steadily further apart.

We have never been better equipped to tackle the problem of social injustice and the growing threat to our planet's capacity to support life. There is no biological impediment to many more people attaining the psychological maturity and moral awareness necessary to generate the commitment to work for a better world. If the obstacles to progress are principally a consequence of cultural advance, and if culture is the aggregate of the attitudes, perceptions and behaviours of all individuals, and the power relations which mediate their impact, then none of them are necessarily immune to resolution through conscious cultural intervention.

Globalization provides a great opportunity. For the first time, a single economic philosophy is being imposed or adopted in virtually every country of the world, its attendant value system squeezing out more inclusive values which for centuries have been the only thing uniting otherwise disparate cultures. It matters little whether the globalization project is a conscious plan by a wealthy elite to safeguard their privilege, or the result of the misguided efforts of otherwise honourable people to spread the benefits of wealth creation more widely; globalization demonstrates how quickly and easily changes to social institutions and economic arrangements can be introduced. And this with a system which delivers few improvements to the disenfranchised, which visibly exacerbates the plight of many of the worse off, and which makes no reference to the democratic wishes of the majority of those whose lives it affects.

Most of the supposed obstacles to progress are erected by people with an interest in keeping things as they are. Although they represent a tiny minority of the global population, their disproportionate power can only be neutralized if many millions find the moral motivation, courage and determination to oppose them. Substantive change to the social order will require a political movement which recognizes the central importance of economics, and is aware of the way in which politicians and economists encourage the false belief that immutable economic laws constrain our capacity to tackle poverty and inequality; and how, in the process, they have allowed the balance of wealth and power to be skewed in favour of a small minority.

In this chapter we shall discover that the current order is based on a false understanding of economic laws, and that this false understanding is responsible for our failure to extend the benefits of economic advance more widely. We shall learn of a true reading of economics which supports the possibility of a more inclusive world; an economics which reveals the causes of our lack of progress, and offers a prescription for change which demands neither revolution nor the dismantling of prevailing political structures; a new understanding which indicates a solution to the problems of the creation and distribution of wealth, which promises fair shares for equal effort, and which provides opportunities for all who wish to work; an economics which brings the ideals of the socialist within range, but allows us to retain and build on those aspects of capitalism which have helped transform society and have delivered immense material benefits to some.

Although the period after 1945 gives clear indications of the potential for collective moral action in the example of a generation's determination to avoid a repeat of the circumstances which led to war, it offers little assistance on the economic front. The requirement to rebuild the economies of western Europe, almost from scratch, and the emergence, virtually unscathed, of an economic powerhouse in the United States, created conditions for a period of sustained economic growth. This, aided by an international economic framework to which all western nations signed up, led to improved living standards for millions.

After the post-war consensus was dismantled in the 1970s and the western nations suffered deep recession, the 1980s brought a right-wing backlash which saw national economies re-formulated on a model of deregulated free markets, uncontrolled capital flows, the privatization of public assets, and a tightening of public expenditure on services such as health, education and transport. Whilst these measures helped put western nations back onto the path of steady growth, they had other consequences: the distribution of wealth was further skewed in favour of the already wealthy, permanently raised levels of unemployment became the norm, economic security was reduced across the board, and the promise of universal access to essential services was undermined.

In the 1990s, with this extreme economic liberalism failing to meet aspirations for a more inclusive society, and with a growing perception of a deterioration in the quality of life, left-leaning governments were elected, promising a *third way* of organising society and the economy. Under this approach, the benefits of additional wealth arising from deregulated markets and conditions designed to enhance the productivity of private enterprise were to be distributed among the wider population through careful economic management, well-judged investment in public services, sensitively levied taxes, and the use of public money to underwrite private investment in infrastructure projects. Nearly a decade on, the third way project appears to have failed. More than at any time in recent history, politicians are distrusted, and faith in democracy as the defender of majority interests has largely disappeared.

Elsewhere, most of the United Nations' development goals for reducing poverty, which were set at the turn of the millennium, are already well off-course; in some cases things are getting measurably worse. World Bank President, James Wolfensohn, and British Finance Minister, Gordon Brown, wrote in early 2004 that 'we must act, not only because it is morally right, but because it is now essential for stability and security. It is only by tackling poverty that we can shape the better world we want our children to inhabit.' I am prepared to give Wolfensohn and Brown the benefit of the doubt. I think they genuinely desire a more inclusive world in which the problems which follow in the wake of poverty are mitigated. They are unusual among people of power and influence in seeing a moral dimension to the economics of wealth and poverty, but they appear to believe that a solution is possible without a wholesale revision of our understanding of economics, and the policies that flow from it. They still cling to the belief that, simply by creating the conditions for steady economic growth, the additional wealth generated will filter down to all levels of society, relieving poverty and creating economic opportunities for all. This will not and cannot happen. There are, indeed, immutable laws of economics which prevent it, but these laws do not prevent equity under all conditions, only under the conditions which we have created and allow to prevail.

Although a growing number of academic economists and journalists are beginning to reject the current 'autistic' state of the discipline,[2] political leaders appear deaf to calls for a new understanding of economics. This being so, the only way forward is for a critical mass of people committed to progressive change to engage seriously with the economic question as the basis for a popular movement. Only when large numbers have a clear understanding of economic realities will it become possible, though the ballot box and other mechanisms of a vibrant democracy, to make a difference.

Let us be clear: neither current economic arrangements, nor any minor variation in them, can bring progress towards improved social justice or ecological sustainability. We have been reasonably successful at promoting growth, but these gains are mainly confined to the richer nations; they generally prove unsustainable in newly industrialized countries, and they make little or no difference in the poorest parts of the world, where most people live. As a strategy for tackling poverty and social injustice, growth on its own does not work. Of course, an alternative form of economy which did address these issues would still require growth in economic activity and output, at least to the point at which all people were sufficiently engaged in productive activities to provide for their basic needs. This requirement frames the fundamental question we must ask of economics: can it offer a model which enables us to order the economy to meet the needs of all people, which involves the productive effort of all who wish to work, which promotes the equitable distribution of the wealth so produced, and which ensures the life-sustaining capacity of the planet is preserved for future generations?

There are two forms of economics which must be considered here: both are academic disciplines which demand a great deal of attentive study. Both, ostensibly, have the same *raison d'etre*: to help the rest of us understand what it is about the way we exploit the natural resources at our disposal that determines who gets what share of the goods produced, and how changes to the rules and conditions we impose on economic activity affect the creation of wealth and its distribution over time. Both forms of the discipline assume there are fixed laws which govern wealth creation. One of these disciplines, which has come to be known as *neo-classical* economics, is an outgrowth of the other, *classical economics*.

Neo-classical economics emerged in the mid-nineteenth century when the motivation of many economists changed. No longer were they concerned with identifying the principles which govern the creation and distribution of wealth; instead, they turned their efforts to promoting and justifying the greater efficiency of the new industrial techniques, ignoring the issue of distribution, and implying that the poverty of the majority was somehow due to the scarcity of the resources of nature.

This new breed of economist made a single assumption which appears to have set the parameters of the discipline ever since: that an industrial economy driven by capital accumulation, the private ownership of all economic resources, including land, and the determining of prices and output by the market mechanism, was the only viable economic model. They developed a 'scientific' version of economics by introducing complex mathematical techniques which caused its practitioners to forget its origins as the *worldly philosophy*, and encouraged the conclusion, among ordinary people, that there was no alternative to this 'scientific' model to which economists now devoted all their energies. Only by referring back to the ideas of their predecessors, the great classical economist-philosophers of the Enlightenment, will we discover that there is indeed an alternative, one that promises a solution to social injustice, and suggests mechanisms to safeguard the environment.

Perhaps best known among the classical economists is Adam Smith. Smith is especially interesting because his name has been appropriated by modern day neo-classical economics in defence of its claims. But the neo-classical position is based on a very partial reading of Smith's rigorous thought. For Smith, the objectives of political economy were: 'First, to provide a plentiful revenue of subsistence for the people, or more properly to enable them to provide such a revenue or subsistence for themselves; secondly, to supply the state or commonwealth with a revenue sufficient for public services. It proposes to enrich both the people and the sovereign.'³

Smith's classic work, *The Wealth of Nations*, published in 1776, reveals much about his motivation which sets him apart from his modern-day counterparts. As a moral philosopher first, and an economist second, his primary aim was to identify principles of economics which would promote the equitable distribution of wealth among the population. Smith believed in economic justice for all, and sought out economic laws which he hoped would encourage the view not only that economic justice is morally desirable, but also that it is quite achievable, given the resources of nature and the creativity and ingenuity of humankind. Although he did not describe the challenge of equitable distribution in terms of a class struggle, he wanted to discover why the economy was failing to provide for the needs of so many. He recognised that the plight of the poorest in society had deep moral implications, and went as far to say that, 'Civil government, in so far as it is instituted for the security of property is, in reality, instituted for the defence of the rich against the poor, or of those who have some property against those who have none at all.'[4] As we shall discover, it is the ownership of one particular type of property, land, and the natural resources to which it gives access, that largely determines the distribution of wealth among the population.

Smith is best known for his assertion that only through the free play of markets will the wealth generated through economic activity be maximized. Less well known is his belief that the free market has dual objectives: to maximize wealth creation, certainly, but also to address the problem of its inequitable distribution. Through constantly adjusting prices, he suggested, the market mechanism could balance the supply of, and demand for, goods and services, so that all members of society could satisfy their needs by exchanging the product of their own economic activity for that of others. The idea of the market as a self-adjusting regulator of supply and demand is extremely persuasive. It is quite true, as Richard Bronk says, that 'central planning appears incapable, no matter how big the civil service, of allocating resources with anything like the efficiency of Adam Smith's *invisible hand*'.[5]

It is clear from Smith's writing that the efficient functioning of the market mechanism requires a certain self-discipline on the part of individuals. He believed the market could only fulfil the objectives he set for it if certain rules were observed and certain standards adhered to, although he was rather vague about what those standards were. This is at odds with the modern conception of Smith's achievement. As Bronk points out, today it is widely assumed that Smith had 'demonstrated the possibility of a morally acceptable economic outcome without the need for moral motives', and described a 'mechanism for delivering human progress without the requirement for the moral perfection of man as a precursor to the establishment of a better world.'[6] Not only have loose interpretations of Smith's ideas encouraged the view that the free market permits us to dispense with ethics, but they also suggest we can do without rational thought. As Bronk continues, 'Gone too was the requirement that human reason should be able to plot and plan the way forward and develop a perfect system of government capable of promoting the public interest.'[7] It is unlikely that Adam Smith, the accomplished moral philosopher, believed in the possibility of a positive and moral economic outcome without recourse to either ethics or reason on the part of individuals, but that appears to be his legacy.

Today, it is widely believed that Smith's conception of a market economy enables the reconciliation of the self-interested pursuit of individual ends with the greater good of all; but there is a clear difference between self-interest and unrestrained greed. The first is legitimately pursued by anyone wishing to achieve economic security for herself and her family. The second generally implies the seeking, by an individual, of economic benefits far in excess of his basic needs in a fashion which denies the opportunity to secure basic needs to others. Smith wished to discover economic laws which facilitated the legitimate self-interested pursuit of economic benefits by all members of society without impeding the same pursuit by others. He did not suggest that the unrestrained pursuit of wealth by some would necessarily lead, thanks to the magic of the market, to a general improvement in welfare – although many contemporary peddlers of free-market ideology appear to make this claim in Smith's name. As we shall discover, an equity-promoting model of economy more in keeping with Smith's intentions does exist, but creating the conditions in which it can function successfully requires a grasp of classical economic theory not possessed by most of today's neo-classical economists.

Smith was clear that progress, which he rather vaguely defined as an improvement in living conditions for the whole population, depended on increasing the wealth-creating capacity of the economy. He saw the market mechanism as a means to increasing efficiency, maximising wealth generation, and, in promoting the equitable distribution of wealth, reducing prevailing inequalities in well-being. He was among the first to point out that economic expansion required increasing specialization among the workforce. He was also aware that this ongoing process of the *division of labour* required constant increases in opportunities for market exchange, and that this, in turn, required free trade between regions and nations. He attacked the protectionist policies that framed the *mercantile system* of his day, and which, in denying many people the freedom to apply their labour as they would like, amounted to the formally sanctioned restraint of trade. The effect of these policies, like many of the time – and like many pursued today – was to rig the market in favour of the already wealthy minority, and deny society the equity-promoting benefits of a free-market economy.

In part, subsequent developments have proved Smith right; his model has certainly delivered the goods in terms of economic growth, but it has failed badly in respect of his hope that it would narrow the gap between the richest and poorest in society. In order to explain this failure, and to discover why, even today, we are no more able to crack the nut of equitable distribution, we must examine further the theory of classical economics, as bequeathed us by Smith and his contemporaries.

Under classical theory, economic activity draws on three 'factors of production'. First, *land*, which can be thought of as everything not man-made. Today we include in 'land' all the resources of the natural environment, including those which had not been discovered in Adam Smith's time, such as the spectrum of radio waves. The second factor of production is *labour*, which comprises the physical and mental effort expended by human beings in their pursuit of economic goals. In this context, labour includes the effort, expertise and experience of the entrepreneur as well as those he employs. The third factor is *capital*, the product of previous economic activity, which generally includes the tools, plant and machinery, buildings, technology, and even such things as secret recipes which, when combined with human effort, make economic exploitation of the natural environment more productive and efficient.

There is no overlap between the three factors; they are mutually exclusive. Each of the elements applied in economic activity counts as land, labour or capital, but only one of these. In classical theory there is nothing which can be contributed to economic activity which is not land, labour or capital. Cash is not capital, it is merely a means of exchange through which the various factors of production can be valued relative to one another, and traded. Cash can be used to acquire capital, as in the hiring of a crane for the duration of a building project, but it can also be used to employ labour, and to secure land, or raw materials extracted from it, which are required to furnish an enterprise.

For its contribution, each of the three factors of production receives a return. The whole product or output of the enterprise is divided up among the owners of the land and capital contributed, and the labour applied. In the language of classical theory, the landowner is rewarded with *rent*, the supplier of capital is rewarded with *profit* (sometimes called *interest*), and the labourer is rewarded with *wages*. As David Ricardo pointed out in the preface to his *Principles of Political Economy and Taxation*, published in 1817, at 'different stages of society, the proportions of the whole produce of the earth which will be allotted to these three classes will be essentially different; depending mainly on the actual fertility of the soil, on the accumulation of capital and population, and on the skill, ingenuity, and instruments employed in agriculture'.[8] That Ricardo writes of an agriculture-based economy does not alter the validity of classical theory for the modern world. The object of economics has not changed in two centuries. As Ricardo put it, 'to determine the laws which regulate the distribution of wealth, is the principal problem of Political Economy.'[9]

Following the enclosure of land in Britain from the sixteenth century on, and with changes in economic activity driven by the industrial revolution, it became clear that the distribution of wealth was altering rapidly, with the poorer majority losing ground to the wealthy minority. Smith had identified the means to increase the size of the pot of wealth, but not a solution to the problem of its distribution. The significance of Ricardo's work was not appreciated at the time, but, if he failed to provide an explicit solution to the problem, he did at least give an explanation as to how, with economic advance, the distribution of wealth is skewed in favour of one particular class, the owner of land, and against the providers of capital and labour.

Ricardo's *law of rent* is little considered by practitioners of the neo-classical economics which holds sway today. Perhaps modern-day economists find it too difficult to get to grips with; or perhaps they prefer to sacrifice their intellectual integrity, rather than confront an essential law of economics, the implications of which are profound and far-reaching, directly threatening the balance of wealth and power in the world. The law of rent is not difficult to understand, but it is essential to understanding how the economy works, for it precisely explains why the free market consistently fails to distribute wealth equitably as Adam Smith had hoped it would.

Before we examine the implications of Ricardo's discovery for the modern world, it will be helpful to consider the problem of rent in the agricultural terms which applied in his time. Let us imagine an uninhabited island, the land of which comprises four different grades or qualities, three of which are suitable for agricultural use, the fourth of which is not. Sea-faring migrants happen upon this land and, noting its economic potential, decide to settle it. At the outset, the population is confined to a few hundred people and there is more than enough first-grade land available to provide for the needs of all.

In this early condition, each individual or family farms their own plot with the few basic tools they brought with them on their voyage. Although there is plenty of land to go round, in order that everyone knows which produce is the result of which farmer's sewing, hedgerows are planted to separate plots. Given the plentiful nature of high-quality land, *de facto* ownership of each plot is assumed by those who occupy it.

As the first harvest is gathered, the farmers begin to make advance payments, in the form of food and clothing, to a group of specialist tool-makers among their number who have knowledge of extracting iron from ore to manufacture tools. This ore is easily mined from caves in the mountainous region of the island which is unsuitable for agricultural use. These advance payments tide over the toolmakers while they manufacture the first batch of much-demanded new tools. Here we see the first signs of the specialisation of labour, and movement from an original condition in which each person is responsible for producing his own food, to a more advanced form of economy, in which mutually beneficial market exchange is practised.

As well as the application of labour in the form of farming, mining and toolmaking, we already see the presence of capital at work, both in the basic tools that the settlers brought with them, and in the application of manufacturing techniques passed down by previous generations of toolmakers. Under these very simple economic arrangements, most of the product of economic activity is distributed to labour as wages, but a portion is counted as profit payable to capital, both for the extra output generated by the application of the old tools, and the capital investment made by the toolmakers as they set up their enterprises. The distribution of wealth between farmers and toolmakers is determined by the market mechanism, and will depend on the supply of tools for sale, and the amount of their surplus output that farmers are prepared to exchange for the promise of improved yields next season, should they invest in new tools. Once a farmer 'buys' a new tool, although it remains the product of the toolmaker's labour, it becomes part of the farmer's capital. Indeed, in classical theory, all capital derives from the combination of labour with land. It is a durable form of value, but one which is subject to a reduction in its value over time; all capital depreciates.

While working on the first year's crops, all the settlers live in makeshift accommodation constructed from materials found on the island. Fortunately, the surplus provided by the first harvest is sufficient to provide for a sizeable team to work full-time on the construction of more robust dwellings. Capital, in the form of equipment provided by toolmakers to construction workers, along with their inherited knowledge of house-building techniques, is once again at work.

We already see evidence of the key requirements for the successful division of labour: trust and cooperation. Without them, there is no possibility of economic development. All members of society realize that their common interests are served by making advance payments to toolmakers and house-builders. They hand over a proportion of the food they produce because they can see that such cooperation will lead to an increase in wealth creation and collective well-being. It is only because people recognize that cooperation is key to collective improvement as society becomes more complex, that the market mechanism is able to work its magic. Here, recognising the preference of islanders for better homes and access to new tools, it allocates a part of this year's produce to enable future work which will benefit the entire community. Without such a spirit of cooperation, nobody would give up farming and enter a specialized trade for fear of not being able to feed himself.

Over the long term, the market will work to determine an optimal ratio of farmers, toolmakers and house-builders so that the desires of all for adequate food and shelter are met. By giving equal value to the preferences of all economic agents, or members of society, the market determines the relative prices of various agricultural products and manufactured tools, and the amount of labour which can be freed up for home-building. In subsequent years, farmers will place more advance orders for the tools they think they will need. If the original toolmakers cannot meet this demand alone, then others, who had supposed themselves farmers, will opt to be apprenticed as toolmakers, lured by the promise of higher wages. Once the optimal ratio of farmers to toolmakers is established, seasonal adjustments in the demand for tools will be reflected by changes in their price. Likewise, if agricultural output in the second year is sufficient to accelerate the rate of house-building, more will enter the construction trade.

It is important to remember that the market brings no assumption of value to its task; it is morally neutral. It simply provides a means, in the price mechanism, through which the preferences of all those active in the economy can be reconciled. As long as the strength of these preferences, as indicated by the relative wealth, or purchasing power, underlying them is reasonably equal, then the market will distribute economic benefits equitably. If, however, the strength of these competing preferences becomes unequal, if some individuals secure exclusive access to certain economic resources, for example, then the market will no longer work in favour of equity.

At this point in our island society's development, with sufficient first-grade land to meet the needs and ambitions of all, and where the resources necessary to manufacture tools and build houses are freely available, the market divides up the product of economic activity equitably among the entire population. Equity does not imply equality; it means a fair reward for the effort and application of each individual, and that everyone who is prepared to work has access to opportunities through which they can provide for their basic needs. It may be an oversimplified example, but it shows that, where populations arise or choose to settle, at the outset at least there is no reason in economics why all should not be able to satisfy their basic needs. The market mechanism works in favour of equity, but it also provides incentives to people to improve their skills, or learn a new trade: it helps to drive the economy forward.

In time, as farmers learn that the fertile land will produce several harvests each year if crops are rotated, they realize that there is little point in buying tools with crop-specific uses which are only employed for three months of the year. Far better to hire tools for short periods when they are needed. The toolmakers are so busy trying to meet demand that they have no time to manage a tool-hire business – all except one, who decides to sell his foundry to a competitor and use the proceeds to buy a large stock of tools to hire out. This new entrepreneurial capitalist still applies his own labour to his tool-broking business, but his labour is a lesser proportion of the factors applied, the bulk being the capital in his stock of tools which he has acquired in exchange for the land he originally settled, and the capital he had built up in his foundry business.

This tool-broker has changed from being a producer of goods to the provider of a service, and is a capitalist in the sense that we might understand it today. But, other things remaining equal, there is no reason why his entrepreneurial zeal should compromise the ability of those who continue to labour as toolmakers, builders or farmers to make a living. His income may be higher than others', but all are welcome to try their hands at tool-broking and secure a part of the additional wealth this new specialism affords. The market will determine how many tool-brokers the economy can support. If one too many ambitious individuals sets up as a tool-broker, his business will fail and his wage will fall below that which he could earn as a farmer, toolmaker or builder. He will return to his original occupation, little the worse for his experience. If newly qualified toolmakers turn out to be more successful than those who trained them, then the original toolmakers might also opt for a change of trade.

Now this is really interesting. Those who blame free-market capitalism for poverty and social injustice usually argue that it is the accumulation of capital by self-interested individuals and the pure functioning of the free market which keeps so many in poverty. But our example appears to demonstrate that the emergence of pure capitalists, people who do little 'labour' in the traditional sense, has no discernible impact on the capacity of the entire population to secure adequate economic opportunities. In fact, the addition of capital to the process of production increases the wealth-generating capacity of the economy in a way that may benefit all.

The tool-broker is not the only capitalist entrepreneur, and shopkeeper, to emerge on the island. Several other specialist businesses become established including a bakery, two dairies, a butcher, a tanner, a blacksmith and a tailor. Initially, they each operate from their original plots of land, but this does not make them especially accessible to their customers, so in time each exchanges his large plot of agricultural land on the periphery for a smaller, but more centrally located, plot. They now occupy less land, but the land they do occupy is a far more valuable asset to their newly established businesses. Thus, a small town quickly becomes established; it provides a focal point through which agricultural produce is more efficiently traded, and from where all who set up in business can more profitably ply their various trades. Location has become an important factor in the emerging economy.

Let us fast-forward a few generations. The population has grown and new settlers have arrived on the island so that the population is now ten times that of the original settlement. There is no longer sufficient first-grade agricultural land to meet everyone's needs so many people have no choice but to occupy the second-grade land. Not only is this land less fertile, therefore producing lower yields, but it is also quite a distance from the town. It takes farmers in this part of the island a day to get their produce to market – and a day spent on the road is a day lost working the land. On the second-grade land it is more difficult to make ends meet. By contrast, the descendents of the original settlers, all of whom are farming inherited first-grade land close to the main town and its busy market, are doing extremely well. They have the best land, highest yields and lowest market access costs, and are therefore able to generate the most revenue to invest in new tools and equipment, further reinforcing their advantage.

It is population pressure that has forced people to settle on second-grade land, but it is the fact that land varies in fertility or locational advantage which is the important economic factor. Those on less favourable land will either have to work harder to compensate for the disadvantage of their site, or accept a lower income. The advantage enjoyed by those on the better sites is not of their own making: it is the increase in population which has made the variable productive capacity of land significant. Were the settlers on the second-grade land to depart, there would no longer be any advantage in having first-grade land, and the community would be poorer for their departure. Once land of varying productive capacity is brought into production, the economy changes fundamentally.

This process describes the effects of the *law of rent* in operation. In purely agricultural terms, the law of rent states that, where two plots of land of identical size but differing fertility are each subject to the same application of capital and labour, then the difference between the yield from each constitutes the rent on the more productive plot. The rent of a plot of land is the additional amount of output, or wealth, that can be extracted from it, given the same inputs, compared with other plots of land of the same size but of differing quality. If all land was of the same quality, yields would be identical given the same inputs, and the product of each plot would be divided between the labour and capital applied to it: there would be no rent. It is only the fact of the variable productive capacity of land, and that land of differing productive capacities is brought into production by the growth of population, which gives rise to rent.

At the outset of our island economy, when there was ample first-grade land to go around, the land attracted no rent. But once population pressure forced second-grade land into use, the first-grade land began to command rent at an amount equal to the difference in yields obtained from the two grades of land when subject to the same application of labour and capital. The key point is that rent is solely a function of the differing productive capacity of land; it has nothing to do with the quantity of capital or the quality of labour applied to land.

The law of rent assumes greater importance as society and the economy develop, as population grows, and as the division of labour intensifies. Its effect is steadily to increase the proportion of the reward from economic activity which goes, as rent, to the owners of land. The wealth earned by labour and capital is not necessarily reduced in absolute terms, but its proportion compared with that of rent steadily declines as the claim of land to rent increases.

The fact of the variable quality of land coupled with the inevitability of population growth, is the first factor which determines levels of rent. But, as economic development proceeds, a second factor, location, becomes as, and ultimately more, important. Whereas the rent earned by plots of agricultural land is determined by its natural endowment, rent arising from the preferential location of one site over another is a function of cultural and economic advance. The early entrepreneurs on our island soon realised that running a business from their own plots of land did not make for easy access to customers. A commercial centre was quickly established as they each exchanged their prime agricultural plots for land in what soon became the island's first town.

The emergence of towns has nothing do with a desire on the part of individuals to live cheek by jowl with their neighbours, it is a function of economic advance. The costs of trading agricultural goods and the products of manufacturing businesses are greatly reduced if that trading all occurs in one place. Land in these commercial centres soon takes on a considerable rent-earning potential, because it promises conditions which make for a more profitable business. The creation of a commercial centre as the focus for trade and manufacture takes the economy to a new level of complexity and efficiency; it enables the generation of more wealth. But, in the very process, because of the operation of the law of rent, the proportion of the product that goes as rent, rather than wages and profit, will increase to the landowner's benefit, even if he has contributed nothing to the process of wealth creation.

On our island, the rent earned by a tiny plot of land near the market square will become greater than that earned by a much larger parcel of high-quality farming land. As rent increases, the proportion remaining to be divided between labour and capital is reduced. In the modern economy, where agriculture contributes only a small share of total economic output, location is the principal factor in determining rent. The more successful the economy, the greater the share of wealth that goes in rent.

Society gets richer, but if most of the best land is owned by a small minority, few people feel the benefit.

Our island society, which afforded equal economic opportunities to all citizens while there was sufficient first-grade land to go around, now sees the population divided into more and less wealthy. Those who were fortunate enough to inherit first-grade land now claim exclusive rights over it. In time, the island's parliament decides that, if the trading of land is to be transparent and fair, legislation is required. Under these new laws, the established occupants of land are able formally to register their claim for ownership, and title is granted to claimants with full entitlement to farm, rent or sell the land, and to keep the proceeds. With land formally under private ownership, the market gets to work reconciling its fixed supply with steadily growing demand, through the price mechanism. The most expensive land is that in the town, where most of the entrepreneurial specialists find themselves able to generate incomes far in excess of that they would have earned had they continued farming the best land. Then comes the first-grade agricultural land, followed by the second-grade land, which is most cheaply priced, and all of which is now occupied.

Although society is becoming stratified into richer and poorer, everyone still enjoys a degree of choice. The fortunate owners of first-grade land can expand their operations by buying more land, or use their relative wealth to buy shop premises and start up specialized businesses. Poorer people also have a choice, albeit a more restricted one. They can work as farmers, where even the second-grade land is good enough to provide them a reasonable living, or they can take up an apprenticeship in one of the specialized businesses, although this means renting a small room on the edge of town, some distance from the shops and factories. Life is becoming more of a struggle for the poorer members of society, and their comparatively poor quality of life is a direct consequence of their not having access to the best land.

Another few generations on, and the population has grown to such an extent that all of the third-grade land has been brought into use. This land is considerably less fertile and crop yields are very poor. Many people have no choice but to farm these poor lands, even though yields are insufficient to fund investment in the tools and fertilizers they require to improve output. The third-grade land earns no rent because it is only just possible to extract from it sufficient produce to feed those who work it; it generates no surplus whatsoever. The absence of any further land to bring into production, and the fact that population pressure continues to increase, means that second-grade land now earns rent, as represented by the difference between its yield and that of the third-grade land, given the same application of labour and capital. The rent earned by the first-grade land also increases by the same amount, as it retains its productive advantage over the second-grade land. The rent earned by a plot of land in the town is now so great that only the really wealthy can afford to live there, or to acquire preferentially located business premises.

The law of rent operates progressively as population grows, with the effect of increasing the disparity in wealth enjoyed by the occupiers of the best and worst land. Again, this is not because of any special effort or expertise on the part of the occupier of the best land; it is simply a consequence of his fortuitous occupation of the best land, and the fact of population growth.

A situation of competition now exists between the capitalist and the wage-labourer for whatever wealth is left after the landowner has taken his inflated share in rent. Once all cultivable land is brought into production, the landless wage-labourer no longer has the option of subsistence farming; his earning potential is determined entirely by the labour market. During the course of the development of the island's economy, many have already become wage-labourers, working for toolmaker-capitalists, or the various tradespeople who have started businesses. Historically, those who chose such employment could demand a fair wage for their effort because they always had the option of returning to the land, and providing for their own subsistence. But now, with growing numbers denied any such choice, wages are forced down to whatever level that desperate, competing, landless labourers will accept, even if that level drops below the requirements of subsistence.

Although the rent enjoyed by landowners also reduces the return to capital, the supplier of capital benefits in other ways. With all land now *enclosed* and under private ownership, the capitalist assumes great power over the labourer whose level of wages he can dictate. This position of relative power is not of his own making, but one which he is nevertheless able to exploit. His situation may not be as advantageous as that of the landowner, but he is much better placed than the poor wage-labourer.

The market mechanism is still functioning, but it now produces an inequitable outcome. Those with plots on third-grade land have to work the longest hours simply to ensure their families are fed, and the landless wage-labourers have no choice but to work for minimal wages in whatever conditions their employers deem suitable. Where the ownership of land and the right to its rent are enjoyed by only a small number or people, it is inevitable that these people will get richer, simply as a consequences of their ownership of land, and regardless of how hard they work. At the other end of the economy, those without land, or with access only to marginal land, will get poorer, again regardless of how hard they work.

In the early days of our island society, when there was still plenty of first-grade land, nobody among the original settlers had any particular advantage. There was no call for competition because there was no perception of scarcity. It was clear to all that the best way to drive forward economic advance was mutual cooperation. Only through cooperation could the division of labour take economic activity beyond the purely agricultural, and promote social and economic progress, the benefits of which would be shared by all, according to their contribution. Nobody starved because he had no access to land, or was too poor to pay for food in the market. However, once population pressure brings land of varying quality into production, and ownership of the best land becomes concentrated into the hands of a minority, there comes a point past which economic advance actively discourages cooperation and destroys the bonds of trust which had previously held the community together. When certain individuals obtain exclusive access to a key economic resource like land, they quickly discover that their own position of wealth and privilege is best protected, not by cooperating with others, but rather by exploiting their labour as cheaply as they can.

With economic advance and the inevitable polarization that follows when an increasing proportion of economic output accrues as rent to landowners, an artificial scarcity is created which makes the consequences of losing out in a competitive economy very serious for those with no access to land. Under such conditions, people have no choice but to compete or starve, and the pitting against each other of opposing human interests becomes an inherent feature of the market economy. The beneficial effects of allowing the market to allocate wealth among the population are reversed: it becomes the mechanism through which an ever-widening gap between rich and poor is effected.

To sum up: rent arises as soon as land of differing quality comes under cultivation. Once increases in population force all viable agricultural land into production, the variable quality of land causes rent to arise on all but the most marginal. With economic advance and the division of labour, specialist tradespeople emerge, and, quite rapidly, a commercial centre is established from which businesses are more profitably run. Ultimately, proximity to centres of economic activity, that is to say *location*, takes over from the variable quality of agricultural land as the principal determinant of rent. As the proportion of the return on economic activity going to rent increases, so the rewards to capital and labour are reduced. Battle is joined between the capitalist and the landless wage-labourer for whatever wealth remains after rent has been paid. Denied any land to farm for himself, the desperate wage-labourer has no option but to take whatever paid work he can find, in the process undercutting the wages of other landless labourers, and so forcing the general level of wages down. The capitalist employer is quite happy to exploit this situation, and thus achieves an absolute advantage over the labour he employs.

Ricardo explained how and why, with economic advance and the growth of population, rent arises and inevitably assumes a growing proportion of the wealth produced. He also recognised that, as a consequence, the share of wealth remaining for wages and profit inevitably diminishes. This persuaded him to accept the view of Thomas Malthus, who argued that population growth ultimately exceeds the capacity of the land to feed all the people. For Malthus, the only solutions were birth control, or for nature to take its course and for those excluded from the agricultural economy to starve to death until the population stabilized at a level which could be supported by the land. We now know that Malthus was wrong. Today, thanks to technological advance, we produce more than enough food for six billion people; yet millions still go hungry. But Ricardo's pessimism left Adam Smith's hope that the free market would address the problem of inequitable distribution quite forlorn.

It was left to an American named Henry George to point out that the implications of the law of rent were not necessarily as negative as Ricardo had thought them to be. In the latter half of the nineteenth century, George became curious as to how, with rapid economic development in the United States, the extent of poverty seemed only to worsen. He set out to determine why, and in 1879 published his conclusions in a book entitled *Progress and Poverty*. As he observed in his introduction, 'Where the conditions to which material progress everywhere tends are most fully realized – that is to say where population is densest, wealth greatest, and the machinery of production and exchange most highly developed – we find the deepest poverty, the sharpest struggle for existence, and the most of enforced idleness.'[10]

Like Smith and Ricardo, George believed free markets and free trade were essential to sustained economic expansion and the creation of conditions in which individual freedom could flourish. Like them, he sought an understanding of economics which would allow the reconciliation of the requirement for individual freedom with the moral imperative for universal access to the economy. In six hundred pages of closely argued analysis, George showed that, although the law of rent always operates, and although its effect accelerates with economic development, it is not inevitable that economic advance leads to extremes of wealth and poverty.

George explained that, as the share of wealth which goes to rent inevitably increases with economic advance, it is commercially advantageous, for those in a position to do so, to enclose or otherwise assert ownership over as much of the land as they can; not necessarily to use it for themselves, but to ensure they enjoy the benefits of the rent it earns and, in the process, to create a pool of landless labour and so drive wages down. In Britain, this process of land enclosure took place over several centuries, but in the United States it happened much more quickly. The emergence of trade unions and collective bargaining had a mitigating effect, but it did not alter the fundamental imbalance. If a relatively small number of individuals are permitted to own most of the land, and if ownership of land confers the right to treat rent as private income, then the operation of market forces inevitably makes already wealthy landowners richer; and means that, among landowners, those who own the most favourably located land become richest of all.

Under these circumstances, the introduction of new technologies which facilitate great increases in productive efficiency and output, and generate increased general prosperity, has little impact on poverty. As the economy advances, the wealth-creating benefits of the introduction of new technology serves principally to increase rent with the inevitable result that the rich get richer at the expense of the poor.

For George, the key point was that the reward, in rent, to the owner of land is not the result of his work, but is a consequence solely of his ownership. It is a completely unearned income. Should the owners of land be entitled to the unearned share they receive in rent? They are certainly entitled to any profits and wages they might earn as a result of their application of capital or their own labour to their land, but the rent they enjoy is neither a consequence of any work they have done, nor any risk taken. The land and the natural resources it contains existed long before human beings came along; ownership of land is not won on merit, and there is certainly no basis in ethics for some individuals being bestowed land while others are not, or for the gross inequality in land ownership we see today. The distribution of land is a consequence of cumulative cultural, political and economic developments, many of which involved violence and brutality.

If landowners are allowed to treat rent as private income, they can use this unearned wealth to secure further land, and they can use the inflated value of their landholdings as collateral to borrow capital which further enhances their position of dominance. Given the limited extent of land and the tendency for population to increase with economic advance, it is inevitable that, once land is enclosed and rights to private ownership are enshrined in law, the more successful the economy is in terms of wealth creation, the greater will be the gap between rich and poor, and the deeper will be the poverty into which the poorest fall. This being so, there is a compelling moral case for suggesting that all land and natural resources should belong, in common, to the entire population. No one can survive without access to land or the resources contained within it.

Why should we allow a tiny minority of people to own and control the right to use them?

George showed that the problem of free-market capitalism is neither the accumulation of capital into few hands, nor private ownership over the means of production, distribution and exchange; it is the concentration of land ownership, and the effect of Ricardo's law of rent under such conditions. By the same token, the cause of poverty is not that the population grows beyond the capacity of the land to support it, as Malthus suggested; it is that, as the ownership of land becomes concentrated (initially as a consequence of enclosure, and subsequently as a result of a tax regime which encourages landowners to expand their ownership of land), not only is access to natural resources restricted, but also an increasing proportion of the wealth generated by the combination of labour and capital with land goes to rent and is reflected in rising land values.

Poverty is not caused by scarcity, or because some people are intrinsically less capable of earning a living: it arises because, under such conditions, so much of the wealth generated through economic activity goes to rent. The free market has been transformed from a tool to promote economic growth and distributive equity into a mechanism which generates only moderate growth and sends most of the wealth created into the bank accounts of the already wealthy. It can only work in favour of greater equity, as Adam Smith hoped it would, if we can find a way of addressing the issue of rent as private income.

Henry George believed that the role of capital in the economy was to enhance the efficiency of labour. The addition of capital – tools, machines and other such products of the efforts of earlier labour – enables the output achieved by a given quantity of labour effort to be increased. The development of the pneumatic drill, for example, dramatically increased the quantity of coal a miner could extract from underground seams. The miner's new tool is capital: it represents the earlier labour effort both of its inventor and the factory workers who produced the drills, and the miners who extracted the metal ore from which the drills are made. The application of capital is essential to economic development: without the help of tools, machines, buildings, transport infrastructure, methods and techniques, which are the legacy of the labour of others, human effort cannot drive the economy forward. Capital makes its contribution to the economy through its ability to improve the productivity of labour. Labour makes use of capital to enhance its productive capability. However, labour benefits from economic advance only when it controls machines and determines the uses to which they are put. Under such conditions of equity, capital would be the servant of labour.

Under present conditions, instead of capital serving labour, the situation is reversed: labour becomes the servant of capital. Instead of capital enhancing the efficiency of labour, and enabling all members of society to generate more wealth for themselves and their families, as rent consumes a growing proportion of the output of the economy, wages are forced down and the capitalist entrepreneur is able to employ labour at a lower cost to his enterprise. He puts this cheap supply of labour to work increasing his share of the output. In these circumstances, a greater proportion of the wealth generated by the effort of labour is retained by the owner of capital as profit. Labour has become the servant of capital, and employers dictate the terms under which the majority are forced to work, and the uses to which capital is put.

If capital exists to enhance the productivity of labour, but labour is denied this facility, then the only remaining function of capital is to increase the wealth of those who own it. Labour, in combination with land, can generate some wealth without the aid of capital, but capital without labour is useless. The natural and just relationship between the two is for capital to serve labour, but just as concentrated land ownership has become a device through which the landowning minority consolidate their position of wealth, so capital becomes another means by which the wealthy protect their advantage. In the process, the poor wage labourer is turned into an economic resource to be exploited by capitalists in their pursuit of additional riches.

A hierarchy of economic power has emerged: those who own land are best placed; those who own capital are well placed, but those who have only their labour to sell can only expect minimal reward, possibly below that required to survive. In its very workings, the economic system protects the interests of the minority who own land, and works against the interests of the majority who do not. This completely ignores the equality of interests which is the basis of universalism. Until a mechanism is found to counter the effects of the accumulation of rent in private hands, and return capital to its rightful place as the servant of labour, economic advance will do nothing for the disenfranchised majority.

The impact of the law of rent is all too visible today. Traditional agricultural land use may contribute only a small portion of the output of modern industrial economies, but all enterprise requires land or makes use of the resources of nature. In recent decades, with the deregulation of markets and the sale into private hands of state-owned assets, the consequences of economic advance have come to reflect George's description more than at any time since the industrial revolution. Output grows steadily, spectacularly in some cases, but poverty deepens, and the social fabric is stretched to breaking point. The economy fails so many people because no attention is paid to the rent question, and state intervention in the free functioning of the market mechanism, intended to ameliorate market failures, only undermines economic efficiency. Rich and poor both feel the consequences of inefficient markets, but the position of the rich is protected by their assumed right to appropriate rent. An inefficient, interfered-with market still distributes a disproportionate share of whatever wealth is created to landowners.

The principal way in which the accumulation of rent in private hands is manifest in the modern economy is the steady increase in the value of land. Whenever there is a sustained period of economic growth, it is the value of land which increases at the fastest rate, just as the law of rent predicts it will. And land which is preferentially located, and therefore most highly valued, necessarily increases in value the most as the economy grows. If you doubt that the law of rent accurately describes the market distribution of wealth among the three factors of production, you only need compare increases in land values with declining real wages and the complaints of entrepreneurs that their activities are too often constrained by a shortage of investment capital.

It is through increasing land values, and their impact on the price of residential property, that the growing gap between haves and have-nots among ordinary people is most tangibly realised. A home has two elements in terms of economic theory: it has a capital element and a land element. Every home is built on land which generally appreciates in value with economic advance because of the operation of the law of rent. The house itself constitutes capital, and the value of the capital element depreciates over time. The capital value of a home can be maintained if additional labour and capital are applied to it by way of maintenance, and can be enhanced through the building of an extension, for example, but generally it reduces over time. The increase in the value of residential property which is a feature of all modern industrial economies is a consequence of increasing land values, not increases in the value of houses themselves. Other factors do influence house prices. The supply of houses of a particular style, or in a certain location, affects prices, as do planning regulations which limit the building of new houses. But each of these factors affects house prices by altering the value of the land they occupy, not the value of the building. The additional wealth enjoyed by the homeowner who sees the price of her house increase, is an addition of rent, not an additional of capital.

In Britain today, there are insufficient homes to meet demand. Millions of people do not have secure housing, and cannot afford to get on the property ladder. Fewer houses are being built than at any time since 1945, and, with the gap between rich and poor steadily widening, the prices of all homes are pulled inexorably upwards and beyond the reach of the least well off. House prices in London have risen to such an extent that the Government is offering subsidies to teachers and nurses who cannot afford to live within commuting distance of their work-places. Most of the houses that are being built are expensive executive homes on *greenfield* sites, from which property developers know they can turn a handsome profit. Very few affordable homes are built on brown-field sites, close to employment opportunities, because they are not profitable. Such homes are usually only built when the government offers financial incentives to property developers in the form of state subsidies. The benefits of a free market, which would otherwise distribute wealth so that sufficient investment capital was made available to fund the con-struction of housing affordable by ordinary people, will not sanction the building of such homes even where great demand exists, because there are other more lucrative opportunities available to developers.

The better-off do very well out of this situation. Many use the unearned wealth in the inflated values of their homes as collateral to borrow money to finance second homes in the country, or abroad, which they use at weekends or for holidays. The impact on the population of rural villages which are the target of such investments is to force up prices to the extent that local people can no longer afford to buy a home. Local shops, pubs, post offices and churches are forced to close, and communities which had survived hundreds of years disappear. There is nothing inherently wrong in owning a second home, as long as it does not prevent other people from owning a home at all. In an equitable econ-omy, where all had access to adequate housing, some may still choose to build or acquire second homes, but this would not affect the ability of others to enjoy this most fundamental of basic needs. Under current con-ditions, the aspirations of the better-off for second homes only serve to widen the gap between the included and the excluded.

The effects of the accumulation of rent extend beyond the housing market: in London, the construction of an extension to the Jubilee Line on the underground system has provided much-needed improvements in transport infrastructure, especially in deprived areas of east London. The project was funded with public money drawn from the taxes paid by wage-earners and enterprises all over Britain. Its effect on the city's economy has been positive, but much of the additional wealth generated has gone straight into the pockets of individuals and companies which happen to own land and buildings along the route of the new line. A recent study commissioned by Transport for London concluded that land values in the vicinity of just two stations along the new line had risen by £2.8 billion as a consequence of the investment.[11] The total cost of the entire extension amounted to only £3.5 billion. The fortunate bene-ficiaries of this uplift in land values made no special contribution to the original investment – it was funded entirely from the public purse; yet their assets now command a grossly inflated rental and resale value, merely because of their location.

The rent problem also reduces the attractiveness of many inner-city areas as places to live and work. In cities around the world, perfectly viable land just beyond the boundaries of the established *central business district* lies derelict and unused, while less than a mile away tiny parcels of 'prime', but otherwise identical, land are acquired for vast sums for the construction of skyscrapers. The distorting effects of rent mean that the ambitious property developer will pay a huge amount for a couple of acres on which he can construct fifty stories, despite the immense cost, because he knows this tiny parcel of land will earn a huge rent for years to come. Location has become so important a factor today that the benefits of wealth creation are concentrated on a relatively small portion of the physical geography of society. *Brownfield* sites, sometimes in prime locations, are left undeveloped, either because the owner is ignorant of the land's value, or because he his speculating on a future increase in its value. In rich countries such sites are an eyesore; elsewhere they become shanty homes to thousands of poor, all desperately competing for a chance to shine the shoes, or otherwise catch the crumbs of those who ride the elevators of these great, rent-dripping, glass towers.

In an economy in which the accumulation of rent promotes a widening gap between the richest and the poorest, other scarce economic assets take on a wealth-generating capacity of their own. Stocks, shares, government bonds and various other financial devices are stores of wealth. They may be limited in supply but, unlike land, their limited supply is not determined by nature, it is determined by the human beings who control the issue of such assets. Nonetheless, just as landownership enables a fortunate minority to sit back and watch their wealth increase with no effort whatsoever, so the speculative trading of surplus wealth enables others to enjoy the same benefits of unearned income. The speculative returns from such trading arise as a consequence of extremes of wealth and poverty, which, in turn, arise from the accumulation of rent in private hands. It follows, therefore, that, if a mechanism was found to share rent more equitably among the population, then ultimately the conditions which encourage the speculative trading of surplus wealth would disappear.

Today, money flies around the world for no other purpose than to make more money on the basis of fluctuations in exchange values. This money is not invested in productive enterprise, but it extracts a large slice of the returns on genuine investments simply through playing the markets in stocks and shares, currencies, precious metals and other commodities. In 1970, 90 per cent of capital flows were used to finance trade or long-term investment and only 10 per cent was speculative. By 1998, 95 per cent was purely speculative. Much of this trade is in financial futures: it is a form of gambling whereby investors take a bet on the likely price of a certain commodity three or six months hence. It has nothing to do with the real economy, the provision of goods and services on which people depend for survival. It is a requirement of the economic system only in so far as those with surplus wealth make it available for productive investment as long as most of the time they can use it to play the casino of global capitalism. In the financial markets, when one set of players wins, another set loses. The winners, generally, are the big-money gamblers of western economies; the losers, generally, the people of economically weaker countries, the currencies and economies of which become prey to speculators.

The gains from speculative investment, like those from rent, are completely unearned. A key aspect of the ethic of universalism is that every individual should have the opportunity to make an economic contribution in return for his or her basic needs. The right to work, and the right to a fair return for the labour effort expended, is fundamental. Conversely, nobody who is able to work, but chooses not to, is entitled to any of the product of the efforts of others. The unearned gains of speculative investment, like the unearned rent enjoyed by landowners, clearly breaches these natural, commonsense rules of equity and justice. This is not to imply that, in an equitable economy, those with surplus wealth should not receive a return for making that wealth available to others for use in tangible economic activities. Why would anybody choose to risk their surplus wealth without the promise of some return? But this is quite different from placing surplus wealth into financial markets, in expectation of a speculative return, when the conditions for successful speculative investment only arise because the economy is already so polarised, and market speculation actively contributes to the further impoverishment of the already poor.

As well as supervising the distribution of wealth among the factors of production, the market mechanism plays an important role in identifying to which, among competing economic opportunities, the available factors of production are applied. This function of the market is also compromised by the effects of the accumulation of rent in private hands. Under conditions of equitable access to land and the resources of nature, where capital serves labour, opportunities for investment would be selected according to their potential for maximising the return to capital and labour in quantities which reflected their relative contributions. Under such circumstances, capital would have to compete for the labour it required by offering wages at a level high enough to persuade sufficient quantity and quality of labour to choose a particular opportunity over any alternative. The profit earned by the supplier of capital would be that which remains once the competitive wages of labour have been paid.

In today's economy, where labour serves capital, and the interests of ordinary people are valued way below those of the owners of land and capital, opportunities for investment are selected by quite different criteria: the likely return to the capitalist, and the speed with which that return will be realised. As a consequence, opportunities to develop genetically modified foods, which guarantee profits for large American enterprises but do little to solve the problem of world hunger, are selected for investment. Opportunities to develop drugs to treat ailments such as heart disease, which result from the sedentary lifestyles of people in rich countries, are selected, rather than the licensing of affordable generic versions of anti-AIDS drugs which might double the life expectancy of a twenty-year-old African. Opportunities to develop clever, but ultimately useless, new electronic gadgets are selected rather than initiatives to build affordable housing for the thousands of families without their own homes. Human well-being, universal needs provision, and improving the prospects of children to live past five years old, are not criteria to which the process of selecting investment opportunities pays any attention whatsoever.

The market fails to select economic opportunities which would improve the well-being of the least well-off precisely because it can only respond to the relative strength of the preferences presented to it by all economic players. Those who control land and capital also control the greater part of the purchasing power in the economy. Those with no land or capital tend to have much less purchasing power. After centuries in which the effects of the law of rent have steadily worked their polarising effect, and the ownership of capital has become concentrated in the hands of a small minority, it is inevitable that a market-driven economy will direct its efforts at satisfying the whims of the privileged few, and largely ignore the basic needs of the many.

Much of the current inequality between nations has its root in historical inequities. The economic effect of the slave trade, for example, set Africa's development back centuries. Just as a population explosion in Europe was creating conditions for the industrial revolution, population growth in Africa was put on hold. It would not begin to grow again until the slave trade was ended, by which time Africa's place as the poor relation in the global economy was decided. But all such historical inequities, be they the consequence of the unjust outcomes of tribal conflict or civil war, or the legacy of imperial conquest and domination, have been reinforced by the cumulative, polarising effects of the accumulation of rent in private hands. Today, with rent-ignorant, western-style development aggressively trailed as the only solution for the poor world, the direct link between economic advance and growing poverty is in evidence wherever you look.

Classical economic theory advocates free trade as an extension of free-market principles. Free trade opens up new markets and therefore additional opportunities for mutually beneficial market exchange. The beneficial effects of free trade are described by the *law of comparative advantage*, according to which countries find themselves particularly well suited to the production of certain goods. By each country focusing on production of that which it can most efficiently produce, all nations, through trade, are able to benefit from exchange access to the most cost-effectively produced goods of all types. However, as David Ricardo pointed out, the law of comparative advantage only works under conditions of capital immobility between nations.[12] If citizens or firms of one country are permitted to employ their capital in the economies of other countries, then free trade equilibrium is upset, and stronger countries can quickly attain a position of *absolute advantage* over weaker ones. Just as the rent problem undermines the equity-promoting function of the market, so capital mobility compromises the capacity of free trade to ensure equity in international exchange.

Under conditions of international economic equity, where the accumulation of rent was mitigated and the market was able to distribute wealth equitably, however, the export of capital would not necessarily be problematic. Much of the capital exported today is used to acquire land, or the right to exploit the resources contained within it – rent-earning assets which further enhance the wealth of capital-holders in rich countries. The problem is exacerbated by political relations which dictate that poorer countries regularly cede control over land and natural resources to foreign interests at prices well below their true value. This compounds pre-existing inequity and ensures the continued under-development of poor-country economies. It does not necessarily mean we need to limit capital mobility, but it does strengthen the argument that we should dispense with national borders as economic boundaries. Given the volume of global trade and capital movement today, they are already quite arbitrary; their abolition would facilitate the implementation of economic arrangements which address the rent problem and bring the law of comparative advantage back into play. The benefits of free trade could then be enjoyed by the citizens of all countries.

Many jobs are now being exported to countries like China and India where wage levels are much lower. With globalization, for the first time a global labour market is being created with the effect that wages in the richer countries are pushed down, whilst incomes for people in traditionally poorer countries begin to rise. As these poor-country economies develop, and as more of the land which has traditionally been used for subsistence farming comes under the ownership of powerful individuals or big corporations, it is likely that rising wage levels in these countries will eventually stabilise, but at levels considerable below those enjoyed by workers in the established industrial economies. As jobs continue to be lost in the rich countries, in order that the standard of living to which many people in the West have become accustomed is sustained, ways of preventing the loss of jobs overseas have to be found. As Kevin Watkins explains, rich-country governments are quick to intervene when the free workings of the global labour market prove unfavourable to their economies: 'Developing countries exporting to the industrialized world today face trade barriers four times higher than those applied by rich countries to each other. Bangladesh pays the United States $314 million annually in import taxes, about the same as France.'[13] The United States and Europe subsidize their agricultural sectors to the tune of $1 billion a day, six times what they provide in aid.[14] The United States is planning to increase farm subsidies by $18 billion a year over the next ten years.[15]

George Monbiot reveals just how cynical rich-country attitudes to trade are. He points out that some of Europe's biggest corporations were founded in Switzerland between 1850 and 1907, and the Netherlands between 1869 and 1912, when neither country recognized patents. 'In both countries the situation appears to have contributed to massive economic growth and innovation', he says. Many of the descendants of these firms now lead calls for patent laws to be strengthened. Companies which owe their success to the absence of patent laws for substantial periods now argue that such regulations should be imposed to protect their position and deny the opportunity for economic progress in poorer countries. If western countries can no longer secure the markets, resources and labour they require for global dominance through military might, then they turn to other more subtle but equally unjust mechanisms. As Monbiot concludes, 'When it suits the rich countries to impose free trade they do so. When it suits them to impose protectionism they argue that it is the only path to development.'[16] Kevin Watkins concurs: 'Europe and the US developed their economies by pursuing policies that are being outlawed in developing countries.' He also points out that 'poor countries are hindered from closing the technology gap at the heart of global inequalities by the fact that northern based companies account for 90 per cent of world patents'.[17]

Under prevailing arrangements, there is no chance of creating the level economic playing field which poor-country development demands. The immense political and economic power of the rich countries, coupled with the effect of capital mobility, the law of rent working within and across national boundaries, and the hypocrisy of rich nations in loading the dice of international trade so heavily in their favour, means that, as we exhaust new market opportunities under a system which excludes growing numbers of people from the economy, the economic security of most people in rich and poor countries alike will be steadily eroded.

The global economic playing field is currently tilted so far in favour of the rich nations that any process of change towards a more equitable economy would require a transitional period in which poor countries' economies are protected until they are able to recover from their initial disadvantage. But, once the playing field has been levelled, free trade is essential, not only to a dynamic economy, but also to variety and diversity. We may not be able to travel to experience the wonders of all other cultures *in situ* but we can certainly enjoy their exported products in our own countries. Britain may no longer import butter from New Zealand once, thanks to sensible political and economic arrangements, it is able to produce equally good butter at a competitive cost. But all those things which can only be produced in certain places will be traded fairly and to everyone's benefit, both economic and cultural.

We have the tools at our disposal to reverse and remedy cumulative historical inequities for all time, to make the most of the huge opportunities offered by free and fair trade between nations, and to create a genuinely level economic playing field which allows poorer countries to take responsibility for their own economic development and their political and cultural regeneration. If we do nothing, we face a future of increasingly uncontrollable migration, growing unemployment, and a divide between rich and poor – within and between nations – which will stretch the social fabric to breaking point, and could bring on the collapse of civilization.

Migration is already a hot political issue. While the focus of debate centres on how best to identify true asylum seekers from purely economic migrants, the reality is that growing numbers are seeking economic opportunities in other countries because of the lack of opportunities at home, and because powerful media images suggest that a better life awaits them elsewhere. With wages at the lower end being driven relentlessly downwards, and the effect of technological displacement, many of the worst-paid jobs in cities like London and Paris are taken up exclusively by immigrant labour. Some of these in-comers work legally; many do not. There is little doubt that migrant labour provides much of the foundation effort upon which the rest of the economy is built. The requirement for a steady supply of people prepared to work at miserable jobs, in dreadful conditions and for poor pay, is a key feature of the contemporary economy.

Without migrant labour, these jobs would not be filled. Our hotel beds would go unmade, our airport lavatories uncleaned; the shellfish which go into our seafood salads would remain unpicked. As long as economic opportunities in poorer countries are restricted by huge global economic imbalances, then even jobs which do not pay a living wage in Frankfurt or Amsterdam will attract desperate in-comers. Most economic migrants are not brazen opportunists; they simply see the life-chances available to many people in rich countries, contrast them with their own, and conclude that they have nothing to lose. If people with the courage, determination and ingenuity of many such migrants were given genuine opportunities to participate constructively in their home economies, they would do so with enthusiasm and success.

One thing rich and poor countries have very much in common is the problem of unemployment and underemployment. According to a report by Alliance Capital Management in early 2004, those without sufficient work opportunities now number one billion worldwide, up from 800 million in 1995.[18] The manufacturing sector is losing jobs at a frightening rate. In just six years, the United Kingdom has lost 12 per cent of factory jobs, the US economy 10 per cent. China, among the fastest growing of the emerging economic powers, lost 15 per cent of its manufacturing jobs in the same period. Within the next 50 years, another 150 million manufacturing jobs may well be lost. Many of these jobs disappear as technology is developed to replace human labour. It is anticipated that many white-collar jobs will also be lost; machines to handle information and crunch numbers are just as easily and cheaply developed as machines to build cars or package food.

In his analysis of these frightening statistics, Jeremy Rifkin ignores the contributory role of the rent issue; nonetheless he says,

> If dramatic advances in productivity can replace more and more human labour, resulting in more workers being let go from the workforce, where will the consumer demand come from to buy all the potential new products and services? We are being forced to face up to an inherent contradiction at the heart of our market economy that has been present since the very beginning, but is only now becoming irreconcilable.[19]

It is the accumulation of rent in private hands, conspiring with capital in the form of continuous technological innovation, which is threatening the long-term capacity of the economy to provide for the majority of the population. Before long, the small minority who control economic assets, or possess knowledge and experience which sets them apart from others, will be the only group for which the economy does provide. There are already signs of a fundamental restructuring in the distribution of wealth in society, with the most successful among middle-class professionals succeeding, mainly through the increasing value of their homes, in keeping up with the most wealthy, while the bulk of the middle class are, in terms of their economic power, pushed down towards the situation of the traditional working class. It seems possible that this emerging one-third, two-third split could become a permanent fixture of rich-country economies. If it does, we will have a serious problem: a minority of economically active individuals cannot possibly support a majority of inactive ones.

We can slow down this process of polarisation by tinkering with the market and forcing a degree of social equity through policies of re-distribution. But, until we recognize that, as long as we allow the private appropriation of rent, the only possible outcome is growing economic inequity; there can be no reduction in poverty or improvement in social justice.

The Enlightenment teachings of classical economics provide a clear explanation for our ongoing failure to solve the problem of social and economic injustice. Henry George used these teachings to explain why, a century later, despite immense technology-inspired economic advance, and an exponential increase in the ability of human beings to generate wealth from the resources of nature, we were no closer to ending poverty. A century further on from George, many more people share his moral ambition, but few understand why we are still unable to make practical progress in respect of the economic question. Even worse, many econ-omists fail even to realise that there is an explanation. It is buried, not especially deeply, in the texts of Adam Smith, David Ricardo and the other philosopher-economists of the Enlightenment. Although many of their books are still in print, the fundamental truths contained within them are ignored by mainstream neo-classical economics, and by the politicians who follow its prescriptions in the formulation of social and economic policy.

Classical economic theory makes it absolutely clear that there is no solution to the problem of poverty, and the exclusion of many millions of people from the economy, until the effects of the accumulation of rent are addressed. More positively, it also makes clear that, if we can successfully address the rent problem, we have at our disposal an understanding of economic laws which not only promises an inclusive, equitable and dynamic economy, but also a form of social organisation which holds out the promise of reconciling the two great competing fundamental human values: individual freedom and social justice.

10

Freedom and Justice

THE MORAL DEMAND for social justice arises from the recognition that the interests of all people should be considered equally. Demands for improved social justice have grown in volume since the Enlightenment, and some considerable progress has been made, particularly in the aftermath of World War II. But it is another child of Enlightenment thinking, the value of individual freedom, which has assumed paramount importance in western culture. Whereas Enlightenment thinkers attempted to reconcile these two apparently opposing values, much of the subsequent debate has pondered their relative merits, and been shaped by the assumption that they are quite irreconcilable.

Today, individualism is often blamed as the principle cause of social injustice. A society which permits and encourages the individual to do as he pleases, it is often suggested, is antithetical to a more inclusive social order. We need to draw a distinction between genuine, or cooperative, individualism, the variety that is vital to progress, and competitive individualism, the form that currently drives social and economic advance.

Genuine individualism is possible only when a person is sufficiently psychologically secure to be able to form independent opinions and attitudes which, although shared by others, are not adopted simply because they are held by others. The starting point for genuine individualism is developing the capacity for independent thought. The individual must aspire to independence of thought in order to be able to distinguish truth from fiction, and reality from the various world views that are peddled by those whose interests lie in perpetuating myths about the inevitability of injustice and inequality. Only in this way can people choose for themselves to commit to the principles of universalism. From the moment an individual subordinates his capacity for autonomous thought to the dictates of one corporate entity or another, his relationship with all other humans is changed irrevocably, from one of equality and an identity of interests, to one of group membership which necessarily conflicts with the interests of other groups. Most of us allow ourselves, quite unconsciously, to be assimilated into corporate interest groups. Very few of us are able to stand as individuals, free of such corporate chains.

Genuine individualism brings with it a fully conscious and informed attitude to social responsibility in which the reality of social relations is self-evident; it comes with certain duties and obligations. Principal among these is the obligation not to act in any way that prejudices the equal autonomy of any other human being. In such a populous and complex world, this means that we must work cooperatively towards our common ends. This realization cannot be the product of indoctrination into the beliefs of a particular interest group. All such groups are, by definition, exclusive and competitive; they deny the universality of material and psychological needs. Only as autonomous individuals can we grasp the reality of our collective unity, learn to value individual uniqueness and potential, and accept that, far from being irreconcilable, these two great truths are essential to one another.

In the United States, the ideal of individual freedom has been used to promote the belief that a stable and thriving society depends not on cooperation, and agreement on common standards of behaviour, but on competition and freedom from any form of regulation. It ignores the very obvious fact that the actions of the free individual can very easily conflict with the like freedoms of others if they are not carefully considered. In no society is any individual completely free to do as he pleases; in most, there are legally enforced limitations on the degree to which one individual can exploit another for his own gain, which only a century ago would have been routinely ignored. There are thousands of laws and regulations covering behaviour in public, and governing business practice, commercial transactions and all manner of social relations. These regulations are impositions by the collective on all individuals; they reduce the freedom of the individual and this is generally regarded as a good thing.

Today, individual freedom appears to consist of one particular freedom: the freedom of a few individuals to amass huge wealth and indulge in ever greater personal consumption in ways which are available only from an economic system which distributes wealth inequitably. We may enjoy other freedoms: a free press, freedom of thought and speech, the freedom to gather and protest, but these freedoms are secondary and subordinate to the freedom to acquire as much material wealth as one is able, and the licence to do so without any sense of responsibility as to the consequences for wider society. Movement to a more inclusive and equitable society inevitably implies the moderation of this freedom. It must be exchanged for a greater freedom: that to exist as an autonomous and independent individual in a society where all human lives are valued equally and where the objective of social cooperation is the economic security of all.

Curbing the right to amass excessive wealth does not imply equal pay for all people regardless of their contribution. In fact, the only limit on reward at the top of the scale is the requirement to reward those at the bottom with sufficient to meet their basic needs. This implies a reduction in the gap between the best- and least-well rewarded, but does not imply equality. Universalism seeks only to guarantee the basic needs of all those willing to work. It makes no judgement about absolute limits on individual wealth. Indeed, if it turns out that universal needs provision is best achieved under new economic arrangements which mean considerable disparities in wealth, then so be it, as long as these disparities do not result in anyone being denied the opportunity to work to provide for his or her basic needs, or threaten the long-term viability of the planet's ecology.

Among all freedoms, the most liberating and life-enhancing is the freedom consciously and autonomously to choose to value the lives of other human beings as highly as one's own. It is the most difficult freedom to attain. It is not available as a right; it is an immense struggle, particularly when faced with a world in which many people are quite unable to share that aspiration. True individual freedom consists of nothing more than the capacity to care for all our fellow humans, and it promises a world that exposes the pathetic and illegitimate freedoms of today for what they really are.

If it is to be worth possessing, freedom must be felt by the individual as positive and beneficial: something which enhances the quality of life; something which, if taken away, would have the effect of reducing happiness and the perception of well-being. It is quite obvious that the ability to enjoy freedom is entirely dependent on a degree of economic security. Economic opportunity and security are vital prerequisites to the enjoyment of the value in individual freedom. Without the possibility of economic security, individual freedom counts for nothing. If you do not have the opportunity to work to feed, house and clothe yourself and those closest to you, then your notional freedom is worthless. People cannot begin to value the interests of others as equal to their own until they have some confidence in their own long-term security. Today, in a western culture which is rapidly being exported to all corners of the world, we make great play of the rights and freedoms enjoyed by all people, but we fail to create conditions for universal access to economic opportunity. The value to be found in a life of individual freedom is thus denied to the majority of the world's people. Those who defend the ideal of individual freedom without reference to the economic realities which dictate its value, assume a purely ideological position which is quite meaningless.

The corruption of the value of individual freedom, and the fact that it feeds off an economic system which inherently favours the accumulation of wealth by a minority, suggests that social justice and individual freedom can only be reconciled through changes in the way we organise the economy. We know the economic conditions which restrict opportunities, and cause the gap between rich and poor steadily to widen. The conditions we allow to prevail today, and which are supposed to embody and promote the value of individual freedom, in reality prevent the extension of that freedom to most of the world's people.

If, as we have concluded, it is the consequences of the private appropriation of rent which deny economic opportunities to so many, then only by finding a means to address the rent problem is there any chance of extending the benefits of individual freedom to greater numbers. Henry George examined various options by which the problems that arise from concentrated land ownership and the accumulation of rent in private hands could be addressed. He controversially concluded that 'we must make the land common property' but he did not mean it in the sense we understand today. George explicitly rejected state ownership of land, or state management of access to it, arguing that only if all the factors of production are subject to private ownership can the market mechanism operate effectively. But how could the land be made common property if its ownership was to remain in private hands?

The answer requires a distinction to be drawn between the right of a landowner to occupy and make use of his land, to let it out for use by others or to sell it, and the right of the landowner to enjoy the rent it earns. The first is a legitimate right, any gains the landowner makes through the use of his land should be his to keep. The second is not a legitimate right; it is the inevitable consequence of the variable quality of land, its fixed supply, population pressure and the advantages of location which emerge in a complex industrial economy. The landowner has no right to keep the rent earned by his land for it is not a reward for his effort, it is a reward for the collective effort of all who engage in economic activity. Recognising the true source of rent in the collective effort of all who make an economic contribution, George's solution was to relieve the private landowner of the unearned income he enjoys by levying a tax on rent at a rate equal to its full annual value.

This tax on rent was not to be an additional tax. George argued that it should replace all other forms of taxation: those on incomes, profits and trade. He believed the variety and weight of taxes which bear down upon production to be a major constraint on economic activity. Following a long tradition of belief in the sanctity of private property, George argued that nobody has the right to appropriate any part of the labourer's share, neither the capitalist who employs him, nor the state which, through taxes on his income and purchases, further diminishes the wealth which he has rightfully earned. For George, the provider of capital was equally entitled to keep all that he earned as reward for his initiative in acquiring and applying capital, or the risk he bears in making it available to others.

At first glance, the suggestion of a tax on rent appears to penalise the landowner in ways that the wage labourer and the provider of capital are not penalised. Surely the landowner is entitled to an income? But a tax on rent does not imply that the landowner's entire revenue be appropriated. Typically, a landowner enjoys three forms of return. He receives wages as reward for any labour effort he applies to his land, including the administrative supervision of his land, and he receives profit as reward for any capital investment he makes in his land. It is only the landowner's third source of income, the rent he receives simply as a consequence of his ownership which, under George's scheme, would be taxed. Most landowners make capital investments which increase the value of their land. The installation of an irrigation system which turns barren land into cultivable land constitutes an investment of labour and capital for which the landowner should be justly rewarded; the construction of industrial premises from which a tenant can conduct a manufacturing business, likewise. Revenues arising from such improvements to land which increase its productive value would not be taxed as they are part of the landowners wages and profit; they are not rent.

George pointed out that a tax on rent has no disincentive effect on economic enterprise, unlike traditional forms of taxation which penalize hard work, which often tax the most enterprising and innovative members of society most heavily, and which reduce the amount of capital available for investment. As he said in *Progress and Poverty*,

> Taxes may be imposed upon the value of land until all the rent is taken by the state, without reducing the wages of labour or the reward of capital one iota; without increasing the price of a single commodity, or making production in any way more difficult.[2]

Adam Smith made the same point in *The Wealth of Nations* when, speaking of the landowner's dubious entitlement to keep rent, he said, 'Though a part of this revenue should be taken from him in order to defray the expenses of the state, no discouragement will thereby be given to any sort of industry.'[3]

George also explained how a tax on rent would actually increase production by addressing the problem of speculation, whereby landowners often withhold viable land from use because they are more interested in realising a speculative gain from it in the future. If land was taxed at or near its full potential rent, then no landowner could afford to hold land out of use. More economic opportunities would be created and output would increase.

If the land belongs to the entire community, in as much as the rent it earns is rightfully common wealth, then the landowner is under an obligation to maintain his land in its original condition. If land is allowed to deteriorate, then its productive potential is diminished. As it is an asset which 'belongs' to the entire community, and as the community's interests are best served by maintaining the quality of the land, it is incumbent upon the occupier to do so. Of course, it is also in the landowner's own interest to maintain his land in good condition. Although, under a Georgist tax regime, he would not get to keep the rent which is maximized on well-maintained land, his application of labour and capital would provide him with greater returns if the land were kept in good condition than if it were not, and these returns are his to keep.

For George, a tax on rent was the only legitimate form of tax because it targets only that part of the wealth generated by economic activity which is not a direct reward for individual effort or initiative. As he said,

> The tax upon land values is the most just and equal of all taxes. It falls only upon those who receive from society a peculiar and valuable benefit, and upon them in proportion to the benefit they receive. It is the taking by the community, for the use of the community, of that value which is the creation of the community.[4]

George described his proposed tax on rent as a tax on the value of land. In the modern-day language of business, commerce and neo-classical economics, the term *land* is generally used to mean land and all the improvements made to it: buildings, drainage, the provision of electricity and gas, among others. All such improvements – indeed any feature of a plot of land which did not exist prior to human intervention – is, in terms of classical economic theory, capital. The term *land value taxation* thus causes confusion among conventional economists, who assume that a tax on the value of land will also impact on the return earned by any improvements upon it. Of course, further linguistic confusion arises over the popular understanding of the word 'rent'. Today, we use 'rent' to describe payments for the temporary use of capital assets (buildings, plant and machinery) more often than we do to describe such payments for the use of land.

The measurement of rent – in the classical sense – for the purposes of establishing tax liability, is not simply a matter of assessing the annual appreciation in land values. Whilst rent is largely responsible for increases in land values, calculating the true value of the rent earned by a piece of land, for purposes of levying a tax upon it, would require different methods of accounting than those currently used. If it is to be successful, a tax on rent must be seen to be just; it must be seen to tax only the unearned aspect of the landowner's income. It is therefore imperative that, before any such tax regime is introduced, clear, intelligible and transparent formulae for the calculation of rent be established. Much research has already been done to this end, and, in terms of the methods applied by accountants and economists, it proves much easier than current approaches to the valuation of economic assets and the collection of taxes to which they are subject. In Denmark, a full valuation of all property, distinguishing between the land element and the capital value of improvements, is carried out annually. For the Danes at least, the collection of the data necessary to implement a full tax on rent is perfectly viable.

The *Single Tax*, as it became known, was not anti-capitalist. George agued as forcefully for the interests of capital as he did for those of labour. A tax on rent would have the effect of levelling the playing field between capital and labour, and ensuring that the output remaining after rent is paid was distributed between labour and capital in proportion to the contribution of each. Once land ownership was no longer a source of unearned wealth, the ownership of land would likely be spread among many more people. If this were to happen, and the capacity of landowners to use their unearned wealth as collateral to acquire additional capital was removed, the excessive accumulation of capital by a small minority would be prevented. It is the unbalanced accumulation of capital, working in conjunction with a pool of landless labour, which allows the capitalist to dictate the terms and conditions under which labour must work. With a more 'natural' distribution of both land and capital, the market would work in favour of greater equity, everyone would enjoy better access to economic opportunities, and all who labour would earn a fair wage.

If rent were to be collected by the state, the return to the provider of capital would still be that which remains after wages and rent have been paid, but this reward would be proportionate, representing the extra value his addition of capital brings to the process of production – that is to say, how much extra wealth is created above that which the labour effort expended could generate without the help of the capital applied. And it would be right and proper that the capitalist receive such a reward because, unlike today, when the motivation and outcome of most capitalist enterprise is to secure a disproportionate reward, capital applied under such arrangements of equity would make a positive contribution to the well-being of all involved: it would increase the reward to labour, and further swell the pot of rent to be collected in tax. Capital would be the servant of labour, and labour would be quite happy to pay capital for its contribution, recognising the value that the application of capital adds to its work effort.

George's *remedy*, as he called it, is radical indeed, but is it necessarily a tax? Among its various definitions, *The Oxford Dictionary* describes tax as 'an oppressive or burdensome obligation'. This, undoubtedly, is the way traditional taxes are viewed by the majority of those who have no choice but to pay them. Tax is widely perceived as the principal means through which individual freedom is undermined by the state. That the motive of much taxation is to raise revenues to address problems of social injustice does little to reduce the sense among many people that tax penalises them for working hard, especially when efforts at improving the lot of the poorest in society, or at providing decent public services, often appear less than successful.

Redistributive taxation causes resentment, not only because it is at odds with the autonomy and freedom we all crave, but also because, in an economy which appears designed to favour the interests of a small minority, middle- and low-income groups feel the burden of taxation more heavily. The wealthiest may pay a higher rate of tax on their income, but it does not bring them noticeably closer to the breadline. And they are often adept at finding legal loopholes which enable them to avoid their full tax liability. The poorest in society often pay tax when their earnings are insufficient to live off. Even when their income falls below the tax threshold, they still have to pay taxes on many of their purchases. And, indirectly, the poor pay a sizeable chunk of the tax liability of the rich: a top-earning executive may pay a higher rate of tax on his income, but his employer treats his inflated salary as an additional cost which is generally passed on to the consumer in the shape of higher prices.

A tax on rent penalises no one for his effort. It does not demand of individuals a share of whatever income they earn through their own hard work and initiative. It only appropriates the rent which is the inevitable product of economic advance and arises from the collective effort of all members of society. The replacement of traditional, unjust, forms of taxation with a tax on rent would not only address the perception that tax constitutes an unwarranted constraint on individual freedom, but it would also create conditions in which economic security, the essential prerequisite to the enjoyment of the value in that freedom, is available to all people. Under such a tax regime, the economy would return to its natural state: maximum efficiency would be encouraged, the generation of wealth would be maximized, and its equitable distribution would be assured. Further, the means by which certain individuals set themselves apart from the majority, and enjoy the power to exploit the labour of others, would be removed. We would still enjoy all the benefits of modernity, but we would also enjoy a new sense of social justice which would flow from these revised economic arrangements.

As a society, we would also find ourselves the beneficiaries of a huge state-administered fund of wealth, to be invested and applied for the collective good. Deciding how these revenues are to be spent would be a matter of democratic choice. In a society in which economic security was extended to all people, it is less likely that the democratic process would be hijacked by one section of the population in defence of its particular interests. Democracy would encourage decision-making by consensus rather than by simple majority. So how large is this rent fund likely to be, and how might we spend it?

The amount of rent collected would depend on the success of economic activity. In an economy in which the polarising effects of rent were addressed, not only would the market mechanism be able to get on with the job of maximising efficiency, but output would also increase as economic opportunities were taken up by all who wished to work. The wealth earned by individuals or enterprises would remain in the hands of its rightful owners, who would have the choice either to spend, save or invest it. Whatever the use to which it is put, it would contribute to the ongoing process of wealth-creation. Currently, this huge fund of rent remains in the hands of a minority, where much of it squandered on non-productive speculative investment, or to furnish the excessively luxurious lifestyles of the super-rich. Under these alternative arrangements, private wealth would remain in private hands and drive the economy forward, while the collective wealth which accrues in rent would be used to fund whatever beneficial schemes and services the electorate deemed appropriate.

There are various criteria by which we might decide how to spend a public fund of rent. Certain economic activities are impossible to run at a profit, or are profitable only in the very long term. Sometimes it is difficult to measure the profitability of an investment or enterprise because the benefits are distributed very widely among the population. Transport infrastructure is a good example. A safe, clean and efficient public transport system makes an immense contribution to any economy by increasing the efficiency and profitably of many enterprises which have no direct stake in it. Such infrastructure projects are usually too expensive, and the returns too disparate and long-term, to make them viable for private investment. Public transport, therefore, is an ideal candidate for funding from the public purse.

Such public investments need not be a drain on the public purse as they are at present. Returning to our earlier example of the Jubilee Line extension in London: had this project been funded in the manner proposed by Henry George, while the state would still have had to finance the initial investment from tax revenues, and the improvement in transport infrastructure would have the effect of increasing land values along the route of the line, instead of that benefit falling into private hands, it would be collected by the state and, assuming the investment had been well considered, would replenish the public purse at a rate well in excess of the initial investment. This is an example of the self-financing economic development that becomes possible when rent is collected. The more successful the economy, the more rent that is collected. It can then be used to further improve the economic infrastructure, the economy steps up another gear in terms of efficiency and output, and the public purse is replenished with 'interest' added. The greater the rate of growth in the economy, the greater the potential for improvements in collective well-being, unlike the current situation where economic success only deepens poverty at the bottom, and increases the gap between the haves and the have-nots. The appropriation of rent for public revenue would become a steadily increasing income stream to be continually reinvested in new public goods and infrastructure projects, so reinforcing the equitable nature of economic activity, and promoting opportunity and security for all.

Any initiative that provides an obvious and considerable benefit in terms of improving human well-being is a candidate for funding from public revenue, even where it does not hold out the promise of profit. Indeed, a key target for such public investments will be those opportunities which offer clear improvements in collective well-being but do not attract sufficient private investment. Libraries, parks, swimming pools, municipal sports facilities, evening classes, policing and fire services all meet these criteria for public funding.

In rich countries, public health services cannot be run at a profit because, with an ageing population, and increasingly expensive new treatments, the only way to generate a profit is to set prices so that provision is rationed to those who can afford to pay a premium. This is what happens in the private system in the United States, where the share of GDP spent on health care is the highest in the world, but where the proportion of the population with access to decent health care provision is smaller than in any other industrialized country. In poor countries, far too few people can afford to pay for health care to make private provision viable. Health care can be profitable, or it can be universal; it cannot be both. But under conditions of economic equity, where rent was collected and part of it used to fund well-resourced and efficient health services, universal access to high quality health care would be quite achievable.

The economic value of a fit and healthy population is obvious. High quality health care services, which focussed as much on prevention as on treatment, would not just have a benefit for the individual who enjoys access to them; they would have a wider economic benefit. A population which is fit in body and mind would be likely to work harder and more effectively in pursuit of their personal ambitions. As a result, productive efficiency will improve, people will be better-off, and the fund of collected rent will swell.

Similarly, access to high quality education brings benefits at both the individual and collective levels. Not only would a well-educated and independently-minded populace be more likely to support equitable social and economic arrangements, but it would also add considerably to the pool of dynamism and creativity on which economic activity can draw. Investment in health and education services promises collective returns at least as great as the returns to each individual. It seems sensible, therefore, that they are funded from public wealth, so that everyone can enjoy the same quality of service provision. In a free society, there is no obstacle to people choosing to take up private options for health care or education if they are willing to pay for it out of their (untaxed) earnings, but it seems unlikely that they would make such a choice if they had access to high quality, publicly funded services.

The debate about health care and education often centres on the people who staff these institutions: principally doctors, nurses and teachers. Doctors are well paid compared with their health service colleagues, but not when measured against similarly qualified people in the commercial sector. Nurses and teachers are very poorly paid in comparison with many professionals in the private sector. Currently, these people are paid from the proceeds of redistributive taxation, the burden of which currently falls most heavily on middle- and low-income earners. Everyone is entitled to make use of these services, yet the less wealthy pay more for the privilege, relative to their earnings. The most well-off not only get relatively cheap access to a universal service, but they also get to enjoy the benefits of untouched rent. Ironically, our current system of funding public goods through taxation redistributes earned income from the less wealthy to the more wealthy, whilst leaving the unearned income of the rich completely untaxed!

The comparatively poor incomes of doctors, nurses and teachers are further reduced by the imposition of taxes on their earnings. Under a tax regime which targeted the unearned wealth in rent, the salaries of these essential workers would be paid from the public fund of collected rent, and, like all earnings, would be untaxed. It is difficult to imagine a more just arrangement for paying the wages of those who staff a valuable public service than to use wealth that arises from the collective efforts of all members of society. It is the obvious and natural way to fund essential public goods.

Various estimates have been made of the proportion of the wealth generated by a modern industrial economy that goes in rent and ends up, untaxed, in private hands. Further research is required, but, given the degree to which current arrangements constrain economic activity and reduce efficiency, it seems possible, at the very least, that a tax on rent could raise sufficient revenues to fund all necessary public services and infrastructure projects. Indeed, apart from environmental constraints – which we shall address shortly – the only limit to the size of the fund of rent is our facility for driving the economy forward.

Under such a tax regime, there would be only one way to increase the fund of collected rent. If we wanted to see improvements to the health service, or smaller class sizes in our children's schools, we would not cast hopeful votes for political parties which make unrealistic promises because they fail to understand the essential laws of economics; we would simply have to work harder and smarter, to increase economic efficiency and output, and thus cause the public purse to swell. What a contrast with the current situation where even progressively-minded governments are forced to reduce public expenditure to keep economic output steady, and where even a 'successful' economy is not able to find sufficient funds to invest adequately in health or education.

There is one very real moral use to which part of a public fund of rent should be applied: the provision of economic goods to those people whom, through no fault of their own, are unable to make an economic contribution. We have discussed how innate differences in individual ability and potential are currently exaggerated by the socialization and education processes. Nonetheless such differences do exist, and they leave some unable to work to provide for their basic needs, even in an equitable economy. This is where the primacy of a moral end, the need to guarantee universal provision of basic needs, takes precedence over the general economic means to that end, free markets under conditions of equitable access to the economy.

This moral imperative demands the creation of a social safety net, funded from the public purse, which provides for the needs of those unable to make a sufficient contribution through work to cover their basic needs. It seems reasonable that such 'welfare' payments be at the average level of economic well-being found in the community, for who is to say that somebody with an economically disadvantaging disability would not have attained an average level of economic success had they been spared their ill-fortune? Many people with disabilities are only pre- vented from realising their full economic potential by the barriers the rest of us create to their entry. The demands of universalism suggest that we should do everything possible to create conditions in which people with disabilities have full economic choices but, where their disability is too great, those of us able to work are under a moral obligation to support them.

Adequate provision for the seriously ill and disabled, for the elderly and for those who take on the responsibility of childcare, would be the sign of a mature society. The immense contribution to society and the economy of high-quality childcare, whether it be provided by natural parents or professional carers, is immense; it should be recognized in the way that effort is valued and rewarded.

The reality of an ageing population also needs to be factored into economic equations. If longer lives mean individuals are able to contribute to economic activity for longer, then all well and good; but, if we extend the post-retirement portion of our lives, the economy will have to make adequate provision for the care of more people living longer. If the public purse is to finance such provision, and if the quantity of funds available is determined by the efficiency of economic activity, then it should be possible to calculate how hard and long we have to work to ensure sufficient provision.

There is a limit to the number of non-workers which can be supported in even the most efficient economy. Today, advances in medical technology are enabling us to live longer, but without necessarily extending the economically active period of our lives. On current trends, it is possible that those unable to work through infirmity or decrepitude could become the majority in industrialised nations. With advances in technology, it may be possible for a third of the population to provide for the needs of the other two thirds, but it will depend on how we decide to spend our wealth. If it is spent on medical research and the development of treatments for extending the lives of the wealthy retired, then reconciling the aspirations of the young for economic benefits similar to those enjoyed by their parents' generation will prove impossible.

Transition to arrangements of equity and freedom in economic matters will require a great deal of careful planning and management. The process of transition would involve the gradual eradication of existing inequalities in wealth and potential which have social, political and cultural causes rather than innate ones. The moral argument for such a period of carefully managed transition is the same as that for change itself. Following from the findings of Lawrence Kohlberg's research, we can point to an innate preference for an inclusive and equitable social order which emerges in all human beings under the right conditions. This is the source of our universal ethic and the root of moral arguments for economic transformation. An economy of equal access promises conditions in which all people may come to identify the interests of others as equal to their own.

Current approaches to the problem of social injustice which rely on redistributive taxation may be better than leaving rent in private hands and doing nothing at all. But such arrangements will always take money from those who are fortunate to find economic opportunities and make the most of them, to support those to whom such opportunities are denied. The values underlying the argument for redistribution should instead inform the argument against the dominant economic model and its inherent contradictions and immorality. Equity in the apportionment of the rewards for work in an economy of equal opportunity, which guards against the concentration of excessive wealth, would remove the need for redistributive taxation. The economy as currently constituted, making no allowance for the effects of the law of rent, cannot deliver on the goal of universal basic needs. Government intervention to ameliorate its worst effects restricts the generation of wealth, and suppresses the creative spirit so vital to progress. A tax on rent may be perceived by some as an unjust form of redistribution, but the redistribution of unearned wealth from the pockets of a privileged few for the benefit of the entire population is of a kind which redresses a prior inequity. What happens to rent is the principal determinant of the degree to which society is inclusive and just.

As we have seen, under special circumstances, such as in the period after 1945, state intervention in the economy can prove successful; it can even go some way to redressing the economic imbalances caused by the rent problem. But under more typical circumstances such policies are unable to reconcile the dual imperatives of wealth-generation and distributive equity. Only by implementing a system which appropriates rent as public revenue, and makes it available to fund those aspects of economic activity which cannot be realistically provided by private enterprise, could we create conditions in which the market mechanism is able to operate in a benign environment, rather than one of artificial scarcity, and supervise the equitable distribution of wealth among all those who contribute to its creation. In time, the public appropriation of rent may come to be seen not as a tax, but as the means by which the common wealth of society is collected and distributed for the benefit of all.

If the private appropriation of rent means that economic advance leads inevitably to deepening poverty, and a widening of the gap between richest and poorest, then how are we to account for the very visible spread of wealth among the wider population that has occurred in many countries since the industrial revolution? There are a number of explanations for this apparent anomaly.

First, despite the market funnelling a disproportionate share of wealth into private hands as rent, capital and labour still earn some return, albeit less than they should. During periods of continuous technological revolution, opportunities for industrial labour are created which did not previously exist. For frequent and sometimes sustained periods over the last two centuries, capital accumulation has drawn heavily on the assistance of labour, even though it has held power over it and been able keep the level of wages down. From very early on, the ambitious entrepreneur realised that, in order to maximise his own income, he needed to operate on a scale that required the involvement of many wage-labourers. Whilst the effects of the law of rent restricted the general level of wages, the most successful of the new industrialists were never averse to paying a little above the going rate in order to attract the best quality labour and thus secure an advantage over their competitors.

Only recently have we begun to invent machines which can operate themselves and largely liberate the capitalist from the requirement to employ labour. The immense economic transformation of the industrial revolution, supported as it was by the securing of colonies which provided low-cost sources of raw materials, and ready markets for increasing industrial output, whilst accelerating the accumulation of rent, also created many new opportunities which ensured a gradually increasing return to labour, and had the effect of spreading wealth further down the social scale than would be the case under more typical conditions.

During the nineteenth century, these special conditions helped provide labour with some bargaining power in its constant struggle with capital. The emergence of trade unions and the principle of collective bargaining ensured the gradual recognition of the right of labour to a living wage. But the capacity of organized labour to extract wider social benefits from economic expansion reaches a natural limit as capital attains a position of absolute power. This position has now been reached, and is why the historical gains of economic advance for the general population are now beginning to reverse.

Second, in changing the economy from an agricultural to an industrial base, the industrial revolution also brought about changes in the pattern and distribution of land ownership. Compared with agriculture, new industry was able to generate great wealth from the occupation of relatively small quantities of land, and for a while was able to offer higher wages than were to be had working on the estates of traditional land-owners. Over time, the land-owning aristocracy was forced to sell off its grand estates, and this led to the ownership of land being spread more widely. Nonetheless, rent still remained in the hands of landowners; and whether the land is owned by a few thousand, or a few hundred thousand, individuals, the operation of the law of rent still leads to the economic subordination of the labouring majority.

The third, and by far biggest, cause of the spread of wealth among the wider population has little to with economics and everything to do with moral concerns, politics and the emergence of democracy. State intervention to supplement the incomes of the poorest, or to create employment through the creation and subsidy of state enterprises, had the effect of widening economic access where the market failed to do so. Government action, prompted by moral repugnance at appalling poverty in the midst of unprecedented wealth creation during the nineteenth century, and continuing to the present day, has been the principal cause of the spread of well-being among the wider population. Similarly, charitable efforts to provide for the needs of the poorest not only alleviate immediate suffering, but sometimes lead to individuals previously excluded from the economy being provided with the means to take up economic opportunities.

Karl Polanyi described the inevitability of government and charitable interventions to ameliorate the worst effects of economic polarisation following the liberalisation of markets in nineteenth-century Britain. In his *Theory of the Double Movement*[5], he suggested that polarizing economic reforms are routinely countered by political reforms to prevent social breakdown.

It was not the free market which extended the benefits of economic advance during and after the industrial revolution, it was the exceptional gains of empire, and the moral courage of legislators and social welfare reformers in their determination to address the dreadful poverty which economic transformation left in its wake. By the same token, the move to greater inclusion in the period following 1945 had nothing to do with free markets and everything to do with the determination of politicians to avoid a return to the conditions of the 1930s. The welfare state is the ultimate symbol of this well-intentioned project, but the conditions favourable to a planned approach to the economy which pertained after World War II could not last forever, in part because it was funded primarily by taxes on the incomes of the middle and lower classes.

There has, indeed, been a spread of wealth down the social scale, but this has been the consequence of atypical circumstances and heavy government intervention which have countered the effects of the private appropriation of rent, and ensured that a degree of equity has been maintained. What improvements in social justice we have enjoyed have little to do with the wealth generating benefits of the free market. We know that the conditions in which the market mechanism can promote equity have been prevented by our collective acceptance that a small minority are entitled to own most of the land and keep the rent it earns. The traditional *Keynesian* remedies which kept society steady during the post-war period are no longer practicable. We are left with a global economy in which markets are less regulated than at any time in history, but in which the accumulation of rent in private hands goes completely unchecked, with entirely predictable results.

If Keynesian remedies have had their day, then the policies of more formal socialism seem equally unlikely to promote progress. It is important to distinguish between the commitment to social justice which drives many socialists, and the often counter-productive policies implemented in the name of socialism over the last century. At its worst, socialism attempts to remove the market mechanism from economic activity, ignorant of its utility and of the means by which its inherent equity is compromised. It tends to centralize control over economic assets and leave decisions over their use to politicians. It allocates economic tasks among the population in ways which cause the immense creative potential of individual human beings to be extinguished. And, perhaps most harmfully, it appears only to be fully implementable if the media are controlled by the state, and if freedom of expression is suppressed.

In contrast, an economy modelled on the insights of Henry George would extract from the owners of land the wealth they receive simply as a consequence of their ownership, and create conditions in which the generation of wealth is maximized and in which its distribution reflects the relative contributions of labour and capital to its creation. It would tax unearned income, and lift taxes on legitimately earned income. It would permit and encourage the extension of individual freedom, it would demand independence of thought, it would encourage initiative, and it would capitalise on the creative potential of all people. In ensuring that the collective wealth that arises in rent was used for the benefit of the entire population, it would address arbitrary, unjust imbalances in access to economic opportunities, and ensure that economic outcomes reflect natural levels of potential, ability and ambition.

Although Karl Marx was keenly aware of the implications of leaving land and the rent it earns in private hands, and of the possibility of using rent to fund public services, many socialist thinkers and policymakers have hampered the struggle for economic justice by targeting free markets and capital accumulation as the root of all economic evils, and largely ignoring the land issue. They have thrown out the baby and kept the bathwater. The accumulation of capital, and the spirit of entrepreneurship it encourages, are crucial to wealth-generation. The use of the market mechanism under conditions in which it can work its 'magic' must be better than leaving the tasks of matching supply and demand to planners and bureaucrats.

But if many socialists have got it wrong, then the arguments of conventional advocates of market deregulation, inspired as they are by the incoherent principles of *neo-classical* economics, are even less well-founded. They suggest that government interference with the free workings of the market is the primary reason capitalism fails to promote a more equitable distribution of wealth. They suggest that by cutting public expenditure we could reduce the tax burden and therefore create conditions more conducive to economic expansion. Reduced taxes on business profits and private consumption may well have such an effect, but the additional wealth generated would not find its way to those at the bottom of society who benefit most from public expenditure. Were people who so argue really concerned with improving economic justice, they would recognize that capitalism's failure lies in the maldistribution of wealth that occurs when rent is treated as private income, and argue for a solution based on Henry George's remedy. Contemporary capitalism is not a system which generates wealth and assures its equitable distribution through the judicious use of capital and the *invisible hand* of the market mechanism, as Adam Smith had hoped; it is a system in which those potential benefits have been crippled by the granting of exceptional and perverse privileges to landowners, and the consequent funnelling of rent into private hands. If both socialist and neo-classical theorists had better understood the realities of economics, in particular the effects of the accumulation of rent in private hands, their various experiments may have met with more success.

Neither the traditional policies of socialism, nor the deregulatory policies which flow from the false reading of economics offered by neo-classical thinking, have any chance of promoting progress towards a more inclusive society. All the variations thus far tried place constraints on the freedom of the individual: socialism by telling people what to do, and capitalism by leaving many so poor that their nominal freedom becomes worthless. That said, if the choice was between a free-market economy which left rent in private hands and made no public provision for the economically excluded, and the redistributive approach currently applied in all market-based economies, only the latter assures social stability and avoids intolerable levels of poverty and suffering.

Given that technology has enabled us to solve the problem of basic needs scarcity, we must conclude that the rent/land issue is the root cause of poverty. Many other factors serve to consolidate the position of the wealthy and to keep the poor down, but they all have their foundation in concentrated land ownership and the accumulation of rent in private hands. Henry George wrote *Progress and Poverty* as a wake-up call more than a century ago. Economic advance was failing to deliver social justice precisely because the findings of classical economic theory were being ignored. His book, like this one, was an effort to alert the world to the fact that there is an explanation for our failings, and within it the seed of a possible solution. By 1906, *Progress and Poverty* had sold more than two million copies; at that time only the Bible had sold more. So whatever happened to Henry George?

Mason Gaffney has documented the role of *neo-classical* economics in the marginalization and discrediting of George's ideas, which had formed a central plank in the policies of the British Liberal Party from 1891 to 1921, and were vocally supported by Winston Churchill, George Bernard Shaw and Leo Tolstoy among others. But George's conclusions constituted a direct threat to the mechanism by which the distribution of wealth heavily favoured the landowner and, to a lesser extent, the entrepreneur. His remedy would ensure that the product of economic enterprise was divided among those who contributed to its creation in proportion to their contribution, and so redress a gross inequity. It was a beautifully simple solution, one that carried immense and obvious moral weight, and was based on sound economics. It had to be stopped at all costs, and the discipline of economics rallied to the task.

The principal theoretical weapon of the neo-classical assault on George was to blur the distinction between land and capital as factors of production. As both could be valued in monetary terms, it was argued, why should the economist, let alone the businessman, bother to distinguish between them? George's assailants ignored the fact that land is fixed in its supply and that, as a result, the degree of concentration of its ownership determines precisely the extent to which the economy is able to provide opportunities for all. But this theoretical assault worked: in mainstream economics, land and capital were united; the essential truths of classical theory were to be ignored.

Even J.K. Galbraith, the leading historian of economics, was apparently convinced that George was wrong, arguing that it was discriminatory to tax returns on land above the rate which returns on other forms of investment are taxed. But, as Gaffney points out, Galbraith failed to recognize the differing nature of asset appreciation in land and other investments: 'The asset which appreciates in railroads, steel mills and other property is the land, not the rolling stock, mill or other property which depreciates'.[6] The owner of land cannot lose: that is the unjust advantage which George set out to remedy. His failure and the forces that ranged against him give us an indication of the difficulties faced by anyone who attempts to reform the economic system for the greater good.

How are we to reverse this coordinated, systematic, anti-intellectual struggle to discredit George and his ideas? I have argued throughout this book that progressive social change depends on changes in the attitudes, values and understanding of many millions of people. The true reading of economics bequeathed in classical theory, and consolidated by George, provides a practical framework for a new economy which reflects and incorporates universalist values. Such an economy cannot precede the spread of universalism, but knowledge of an alternative which has a sound basis in economic theory must help. Determining the precise nature and content of reforms which can effectively build on this sound theoretical base will require considerable further research. The measures we decide upon are unlikely exactly to mirror the recommendations that George made more than a century ago – the world has moved on, as has our understanding – but we have unearthed a valuable new weapon. It is the multi-dimensional aspect of George's remedy that we should hold on to: not only did he indicate the cause of, and a solution to, poverty, but he also provided a mechanism for the sustainable financing of the necessary functions of the state which enhances economic productivity rather than constraining it, and which promises to involve all members of society in the economy. We should bear in mind, however, that, as we approach our task with added intellectual impetus, the reaction of those who defend the status quo will become more desperate. It is difficult to avoid the conclusion that many in the economics establishment have allowed the integrity of their discipline to be compromised in the interests of minority power and privilege. If the discipline of economics is going to be of any help in the pursuit of progress, then it will require root-and-branch reform.

In the next chapter, we shall consider the role of political and democratic institutions in bringing about change, but one thing is already clear: those who support established political viewpoints which take no account of the land/rent issue are going to have to re-evaluate their beliefs. Those on the left will have to get over their resistance to free markets; they must let go of their fear of private property, and they must certainly give up on the idea that any good can come from the taking into state control of 'the means of production, distribution and exchange'. Those on the right must come to realize that there is a place for government in society, that certain public goods are not suited to provision by private enterprise, and that the valid functions of the state have to be funded from wealth generated by the economy. They must also be persuaded that the presumed right of some people to amass unlimited quantities of wealth, in a world in which many starve, is not a right which the rest of us are prepared to grant.

The capacity to revise deeply ingrained ideological beliefs will vary from person to person, but it will require a new breed of reality-engaged, truth-seeking politician to lead us towards a politics which is just and inclusive. Ricardo's essential truth, and George's remedy, should appeal to anyone committed to the principle of economic equity and social inclusion, to anyone able to keep an open mind, and to everyone who wishes to see an end to the growing conflict and suffering which is the daily experience of so many. Still, we should remember that new ideas always meet with great resistance. As John Maynard Keynes said, 'The difficulty lies, not in the new ideas, but in escaping the old ones, which ramify, for those brought up as most of us have been, into every corner of our minds.'[7] Only if people learn that new ideas better describe reality than old ones, will progress be possible.

Nobody can enjoy the value in individual freedom without a degree of economic security. This being so, the cherished freedom of each one of us is now under serious threat from our failure to halt and reverse the damage we are doing to our planet's ecology. Some environmental campaigners who oppose the prevailing order argue that it is our obsession with economic growth that threatens the life-sustaining capacity of the planet. These opponents of growth are right to the extent that growth in economic output created by the unsustainable exploitation of finite resources, and the unchecked pollution of the natural environment, is wrecking our planet's life-sustaining capacity. But this does not necessarily mean that growth, *per se*, is the problem, only the means by which we are pursuing it, and our failure to distribute its benefits equitably. Much of the harm we are doing the environment occurs at the margins, where desperate poverty forces the overuse of poor agricultural land, or the excessive clearance of forests, both of which lead to desertification and the loss of valuable ecological resources for all time. Much of this overuse of marginal lands is only made necessary because, under current arrangements, it is often to the advantage of landowners to withhold perfectly viable land from use.

In addressing the challenge of an environmentally sustainable economy, we must accept that 'sustainable' does not mean forever. At some point in the future, finite resources will be exhausted and our planet will no longer make a suitable home for humankind. This is inevitable, but we do have control over how soon it happens. It is quite realistic to suppose that, through considered use of nature's resources, we can maintain our planet-home in a suitable condition for many generations to come. On the other hand, if we continue with our current approach to economic management and resource overuse, we could easily bring about the end of human civilization within a few hundred years. As we have seen, some forecasts regarding the effects of pollution-induced global warming suggest the possibility of catastrophic climate change within a few decades. Nothing can guarantee the viability of the planet in perpetuity, but it is possible to make the requirement to maintain the environment in a stable state for the foreseeable future a key criterion when assessing the relative merits of economic alternatives.

We need to balance the requirement to continue to generate wealth and distribute it equitably with the need to protect the natural environment. This is perfectly achievable, especially if we remember that improved economic security tends to reduce population growth. The replacement rate of fertility is about two children per woman. With more opportunities for all people in an inclusive economy – and that means many more opportunities for women – perhaps fewer will choose parenthood as a life option. The global population could stabilize at, or slightly below, current levels. Given our capacity for discovering new technological devices to aid economic enterprise, a steady or slowly decreasing population need have no detrimental impact on the economy.

It should be remembered that the objective of growth is to create wealth for those who have too little. Growth currently fails in this objective because, with economic expansion, an increasing proportion of the wealth generated goes in rent to the owner of land. Were rent to be treated as public revenue, and poverty eliminated, it is possible to foresee a time when the relentless pressure for growth *per se* will be replaced by an emphasis on improved quality of life, beyond the material. Under conditions in which the needs and wants of all are satisfied, and people are no longer driven to amass ever greater wealth as a defence against insecurity, *per capita* economic output may even stabilize. Until this happens, however, the environment certainly places limits on the nature of economic growth, if not the rate; but in Henry George's solution, we have a framework in which sustainable growth might finally be achieved.

The threat to our planet's ecology and the implications for the economy and our survival are simply not addressed by prevailing neo-classical economics because it fails to count them as a cost in economic calculations. Indeed, as Herman Daly points out, the conventional measure of growth, Gross Domestic Product (GDP), sees output as a function of only two inputs, labour and capital; it completely ignores the contribution of natural resources. This is why neo-classical economics believes it is wrong to tax land and resource use: why would you tax anything that makes no economic contribution? Daly puts this gross oversight down to the fact that 'economists have traditionally considered nature to be infinite, relative to the economy, and consequently not scarce, and therefore properly priced at zero.' But, as he points out, 'nature is scarce and is becoming more so everyday'.[8] Even Henry George argued against the preservation of natural resources for their own sake. But today, aware of the finite extent of natural resources as we are, we sense a moral obligation to preserve nature, not for its own sake, but for the sake of future generations. Smith, Ricardo and George can all be forgiven this oversight

– it was simply not an issue in their time; contemporary economists have no such excuse.

By failing to include resource costs – be they caused by the consumption or destruction of nature's goods or by harm to the environment through pollution – Daly suggests that, 'growth in GDP has begun to increase environmental and social costs faster than it increases production benefits.'[9] By measuring only our gains, and ignoring the costs to the natural environment incurred in securing those gains, we see only half the picture. If we included these resource costs, the rate of growth would be negligible or even negative. Conventional measures of growth reflect our neglect of the contribution of nature. Those who get wealthier are those who can most easily apply their labour to natural resources; their benefits make up the lion's share of the growth as measured by GDP. Those who see no benefits of growth are those denied access to the resources of nature. The lack of wealth or 'illth' of the poor majority is not reflected in our measurement of economic output.

Economic efficiency and ecological sustainability demand that the cost of nature's contribution should be charged to the user of it. As Henry George argued, this is the only way to ensure that the most efficient use is made of the resources of nature. For George, this is desirable regardless of how scarce or otherwise a resource may be. But he also provides a mechanism though which revenue generated by charging for the use of natural resources can be used to slow down the depletion of finite resources and reduce pollution. Nature and the atmosphere are common property; the revenue charged for their use, like rent, should go to the public purse.

Charging for the use of natural resources implies a complete shift in the target of taxation from the value we create through our application of labour and capital, onto the resources we use. It means extending the concept of rent beyond the privilege of occupying a part of the earth's surface, to include all resource use and pollution. Once these *external costs* are taxed at levels which reflect their true value, the market mechanism can once again get to work on increasing economic efficiency, assuring equitable distribution *and* helping to manage the sustainable use of natural resources. For example, once the exploitation of oil reserves is taxed so as to reflect its true long-term cost, then the relative cost of research and development into alternative, renewable sources of energy will fall. Such ventures, promising at least comparable returns, will attract the investment necessary to make their wide-scale use more cost-effective than the over-exploitation of finite fossil fuels.

Jurgen Backhaus sees George's solution, and the economic analysis underlying it, as the basis for an all-encompassing tax constitution, which 'provides incentives for an optimal use of environmental resources in the interests of both present and future generations', and in which 'the automatic adjustment of rents, as a consequence of technical progress, constantly pushes economic agents to make the most judicious use of environmental resources. This implies that the Georgian system actually encourages the reversal and change of production methods involving natural resources.'[10]

There is much debate among ecological economists and Georgists as to how such taxes on resource use and pollution could most effectively be implemented. It goes without saying that they will not and cannot be implemented until the economic logic of Ricardo's law, the inherent social justice of George's remedy, and the urgent need to protect natural resources for future generations, are understood and embraced by mainstream politics and economics. Sufficient pressure for that to happen is unlikely to come from these praiseworthy, but still marginal, strands of academia. It is encouraging that Georgists and ecological economists are now finding much common ground, but only when their arguments help frame the economic and environmental understanding of many millions of people will we be able, through our democratic institutions, to generate the political commitment for change.

Like the works of the great economists who preceded him, Henry George's *Progress and Poverty* is more than an economic text. It contains an explicit moral philosophy which, although couched in different language, and addressing the specific problems of a different time, precisely mirrors the ethic of universalism outlined in this book. George talked in terms of *natural laws* and *natural justice*. In 1877 he said,

> You will see that the true law of social life is the law of love, the law of liberty, the law of each for all and all for each; that the golden rule of morals is also the golden rule of the science of wealth; that the highest expressions of religious truth include the widest generalizations of political economy.[11]

He argued that, by extending the concept of private property, the right of all free people, to land, to which all people should have equal access, and by lumping the two together and then enshrining ownership rights in law, societies and governments were in breach of such natural laws.

Use of terms such as 'natural law' and 'natural justice' were very much the language of late nineteenth-century philosophy, a philosophy heavily influenced, as we have seen, by Darwin's theories of evolution. But George's meaning is quite different from that widely interpreted from Darwin and explicitly used by Herbert Spencer, with his notion that, through a competitive economic free-for-all, only the fittest would survive and the well-being of all somehow be achieved. George's natural laws are nothing to do with a nature *red in tooth and claw* over which human beings have no influence. Taking his lead from the *Enlightenment*, he used the term to describe essential truths of human social organization. For example, under conditions in which land is regarded as private property, and the rent it earns considered private income, an expanding economy inevitably leads to greater poverty and deprivation. This is a natural law in as much as it is unalterable. We can ignore such laws and condemn millions of people to destitution and premature death, or we can change the conditions in which these laws operate, so the market can distribute the product of economic endeavour equitably. As long as society is willing to countenance the continuation of the status quo, progress will remain elusive. Only if large numbers of people come to realise that poverty is no more an essential part of the economy than, for example, slavery, will progress be possible. This truth needs to be spread far and wide.

Recognising the implications of Ricardo's thought, and the solution promised in George's remedy, brings the reconciliation of individual freedom and social justice within reach. Under arrangements of economic equity, everyone prepared to work would be able to choose the manner of their contribution; the market mechanism would determine the required quantity and quality of effort required of each of us. Some may choose to work long hours and enjoy benefits in excess of their essential needs, others may choose to work less and spend more time on creative pursuits or leisure activities. People would be free to make decisions over what they do with their lives, and this freedom will be compatible with the like freedom of all others. The most ambitious may still choose to set themselves apart, but their success would not have negative implications for the rest of us. The only group which stands to lose from such arrangements is the small number who today constitute the wealthy and privileged elite, and who currently dictate the terms by which the rest of us have to live. But even their loss would be relative: the only pain they need suffer is psychological; and, as a psychology which drives people to accumulate immense wealth from a grossly inequitable economic system is pathological, the power of these people must be challenged articulately and vociferously. Thankfully, in our democratic institutions, we have the means to make such a challenge.

In suggesting that free markets operating under conditions where the rent problem is addressed would promote equity of distribution, we are not echoing the claim apportioned to Adam Smith that the *invisible hand* of the market automatically reconciles the self-interested behaviour of individuals with the wider social good. No such reconciliation is possible as long as self-interest is allowed to extend to the accumulation of vast wealth by certain individuals, denying access to basic economic opportunities to millions of others. It will take an immense leap forward in moral awareness and commitment on the part of many people, worldwide, for the necessary changes in economic arrangements to be introduced. And, if we were to succeed in this task, it would require close adherence to the moral spirit of the new arrangements on the part of all players for it to work. There is no solution in economics for failings on the part of individuals to make the moral commitment necessary to ensure the economy delivers on the objectives of justice and equity.

The essential truths of classical economics offer a means of reconciling the moral demands of universalism with intrinsic aspects of human culture and psyche. We crave autonomy and freedom; we wish to live in peace and harmony with others; we believe that all people are entitled to keep the full reward for their work effort; we claim the right to enjoy private property; we feel that a large state bureaucracy is not best placed to take decisions which affect all our lives; we believe in the democratic process in respect of collective decisions which require the consideration of the equal interests of others, but otherwise prefer to be left to our own devices; we value creativity and diversity, not sameness and stultifying cultural uniformity; we like to think we can leave the world a better place than we entered it, and that the experience of life for our children will be an improvement on our own. A world in which individual freedom and social justice are not only reconciled, but in which each also actively enriches the other, is now within our grasp.

It is impossible to predict how widespread internalization of universalism, and the new economic order which would flow from it, would impact on the motivation of individuals. It seems reasonable to assume, however, that more people would be better motivated under arrangements which promise opportunity and rewards for all, than under the current system which guarantees security only for a minority. If so, the sum total of creativity and dynamism available to humankind must surely increase, and be spread more widely among the population. The fact that, historically, many great technological advances have been a consequence of the efforts of key individuals, does not mean similar future advances might not be the product of collaborative efforts between many people. Indeed, this is already the case in parts of the academic community, where many scientists have realized that the fastest route to progress, especially in an arena of scarce resources, is through cooperation. It is also clearly in evidence in the collaborative efforts and successes of the global *open source* software community, the high-quality free products of which are already challenging the Microsoft monopoly, in part because consumers value the ethos that motivates those who contribute to the project.

We do not need to imagine alternatives by which people might be motivated in the absence of a competitive culture, for there are many examples in all societies and cultures of individuals working cooperatively towards common ends. Many intelligent, experienced and well-qualified individuals choose to work for non-profit organizations: charities, local authorities, or in the public health or education sectors. Rates of pay and working conditions are often poor compared with those for similar jobs in the private sector, yet many people choose to earn less than they otherwise might out of a sense of public service, or from a desire to work for organizations which help the struggling and under-privileged. Our divisive and competitive culture is already failing to catch a sizeable chunk of the population in its net: people who reject the values of mainstream society and who actively seek out opportunities which give them a sense of working for a better world. If so many people are already sufficiently motivated to act with a degree of altruism in their career choices, then imagine what progress might be possible were the values which shape society revised in favour of these ends.

The psychology underlying the realization by an individual of co-operative incentive and motivation will only be revealed as we create the conditions in which it can flourish. Such change would represent a distinct third phase in the development of humankind. The first phase was characterized by largely unconscious behaviour directed towards the survival of the collective: this we might term the *survival phase*. This mode of existence may have continued indefinitely had evolution not provided us with the capacity for conscious and deliberate thought which made us into cultural beings.

Once we acquired culture, we discovered economic surplus, and the fetish of material wealth. Still only semi-consciously, over the last ten thousand years we have built a world driven by the quest for wealth and property. This was the second phase. It differs from the first in that it cannot last forever: we will destroy our planet and ourselves in the relent-less pursuit of wealth and novelty. But this time, evolution gives us no help with the next great leap forward. For two thousand years we have been increasingly aware of the inequity and suffering that this mode of existence brings in its wake. For just two hundred years have we been able to articulate why change is necessary, and begun to understand how it may happen. Yet over the last twenty years the possibility of emergence into the third phase necessary to sustain our species and planet seem as far away as ever. Perhaps the recent dominance of right-wing ideology represents the last hurrah of this *material phase* of human existence.

So what form might the third phase, which we could call the *human phase*, take? How will society be arranged? How will the experience of life within it be different from life today? The key difference will be the objectives and values we apply. The ultimate accomplishment of universal needs provision will relieve much of the stress and dissatisfaction we currently experience and pave the way for a universal cultural expansion which, as well as guaranteeing the survival of our planet, our species and culture, and providing for the well-being of all, will also replace the drive towards expanding material consumption with the objective of sustainable material provision. This cultural leap will redefine the boundaries of human experience and creativity.

We now have the ethical, social-psychological and economic ingredients we need to create a more inclusive and sustainable society. It is not something to be imposed by an idealistic minority upon an ignorant majority, neither will it be the result of violent revolution or the overthrow of one class by another. It should appeal to people at all points of the political spectrum, save the sociopathic ideologues of the extreme left and right, for it promises the ideals of the socialist, the dynamism of the free market, fair shares for all who wish to work, and the chance to save the planet for future generations.

The only obstacles to progress are cultural, psychological, political and economic, each of which are within our individual and collective conscious powers to overcome. We know what needs to change: we have formulated a set of moral principles to guide us in the pursuit of progress, and we have rediscovered a true theory of economics which embraces the dynamism of capitalism and ideals of socialism, but which avoids the pitfalls of each. As Henry George said, his solution offers the possibility of a transition to a true economy of free people.

> We should reach the ideal of the socialist but not through government repression. Government would change its character, and would become the administration of a great cooperative society. It would become merely the agency by which the common property was administered for the common benefit.[12]

There is no possibility of progress until we address the effects of the private enjoyment of the rent of land to which David Ricardo alerted us nearly two centuries ago, but this must be achieved through the only legitimate vehicle of social change. We need a new, fully conscious, articulate democracy, one which recognises that the primary function of politics is to ensure conditions in which the natural workings of the economy can satisfy the moral requirements of justice, freedom and sustainability.

II

The Politics of Progress

PROGRESS TOWARDS a more just and inclusive social order requires a just and inclusive process of change. Change will need to be perceived by most people as fair and ultimately beneficial to themselves, their families, their communities *and* the wider community of human beings. It will require a transformation of the structures and institutions that shape our world, which will need to be synchronized with, and complemented by, the evolving values, perceptions and aspirations of ordinary people. In terms we understand from today's politics, if governments have to pass laws which the majority of people refuse to accept or fail to understand, then policymakers are moving too fast, or the policies are plain wrong; either way, the cause of progress will be undermined.

It should be possible to tell if we are on the right track by assessing progress against the criteria outlined at the beginning of this book: improved life expectancy where it is lowest, economic security for growing numbers, and reversal of the damage inflicted on our planet's ecology. A further indicator of success will be the numbers of people expressing themselves happy with the direction and pace of change. Opinion pollsters may even enquire of citizens whether the changes in global political and economic arrangements are in line with their personal aspirations for the world. Success will depend on people having such global aspirations alongside their desires for themselves and those closest to them. Change will be gradual and it must take people with it. The consequence of changes in our democratic consciousness should ultimately be to move us away from an adversarial politics of competing interests towards a more consensual politics in which all people, whatever their experience and however they label themselves, come to identify their personal interests with those of all others.

Might this process have already begun? We may have started to prepare the ground, but against a background as anti-progressive and threatening to our collective future as any since 1945. The interests of rich countries are currently defended through a combination of military might, economic power and political browbeating, much of which is quite antithetical to the essence of universalism. There are, however, signs of recognition among some rich-country governments that a world run in the interests of a minority of powerful, wealthy states is neither morally acceptable nor politically sustainable, and could ultimately undermine the particular contribution of western civilization to the next phase of history. For all its many failings, and despite its foundations being laid in centuries of imperial conquest and domination, western culture has much to offer. It is inconceivable that a better world could emerge from any chaotic collapse of the structures and institutions of western civilization.

Is it realistic to assert that the prospects for progressive social change depend upon large numbers of people seriously engaging with economics, and, through gaining an understanding of economic truths, bringing about change through established democratic institutions? It may seem ambitious, but if, in a democracy, ordinary people are trusted to elect politicians on the basis of the policies they offer, and if much of what politicians do is make decisions about how the economy should be structured, then it is not unreasonable to expect the electorate to have a solid grasp of basic economic realities. If the majority of the electorate are not well-informed about such issues, a democratically elected government is unlikely to be a good government, or one that governs in the interests of all citizens. As Leon MacLaren said, 'A voter who votes in ignorance forges the chains which bind him.'[1]

Whilst economic laws like the law of rent always operate, their impact can be either moderated or exacerbated by the decisions of politicians. This is nowhere better illustrated than by Karl Polanyi in *The Great Transformation*, which describes how the rapid changes of the industrial revolution promoted massive inequalities and dreadful poverty. Polanyi described several pieces of legislation which had the effect of creating free markets in labour and land. This legislation severed the link between people and the land they worked; it was a re-run of the systematic separation of people and land that occurred in the early civilizations of antiquity. Although people could still work, there was no certainty that they would find land on which to work. Both the labour effort of individuals and the land they depended on became economic commodities subject to open trade. It was therefore inevitable that land and labour would quickly come under the control of those with most wealth. The commodification of land and labour had, to that point, been largely prevented by earlier legislation designed to relieve poverty. These new reforms were pushed through by politicians supporting the interests of the emerging industrial middle class, the members of which were frustrated in their entrepreneurial ambitions by government-imposed restrictions on the free workings of the economy.

Polanyi blamed the creation of free markets in labour and land for the poverty that rapidly consumed large parts of the working class. But as we now know, free markets only lead to extremes of wealth and poverty if land ownership confers the right to keep rent, which in turn leads to the concentration of land ownership. In the mid-nineteenth century, by repealing legislation designed to protect the poorest members of society, politicians created conditions in which the effects of the private appro-priation of rent were exacerbated. They might instead have sided with the poor, and decided not to repeal these laws, but that would have restricted the wealth-generating capacity of the new industrial economy at a time when population growth was outstripping the capacity of the land to feed everyone. The only way for the benefits of the industrial revolution to be shared among the entire population would have been for visionary politicians, armed with knowledge of the implications of the law of rent in a deregulated economy, to put in place measures to address the rent problem.

Unlike earlier social transformations, the establishment of free mar-kets in land and labour without any consideration of the consequences for the poor majority, was a conscious and premeditated project to make minority wealth and privilege an integral part of the social structure and, with the assistance of ideology, to justify and legitimize this change. By treating land as a commodity like any other, fully subject to the workings of the market, most of the extra wealth generated would go to land-owners; and, by treating labour similarly, the owners of land and capital would be able to dictate the level of wages. The abolition of slavery stopped short of putting an end to the *wage* slavery that this process introduced, and which remains with us to this day.

The wealthy minority have long been aided in their project by the inability of people to consider their lives in economic terms. People relate to culture: it is through culture that they define their identity and their relationship with society. People have a sense that, at the very least, being a member of society will provide them with access to the material means to survival. What else is society for? Why should people have to think in abstract economic terms? The fact that economics functions at several levels removed from people's perception and understanding leaves them unable to identify the true cause of their perpetual dis-advantage and the disruption in their lives. They blame a breakdown in culture, custom and the social fabric for their plight, when that very breakdown is the principal means through which the powerful continu-ally realign the economy in their favour.

Politicians may be able to influence the extent to which the accum-ulation of rent in private hands leads to deepening poverty, but they cannot repeal the law of rent. The law of rent, like the law of gravity, was in operation before the emergence of politics, and long before Ricardo explained it. Its operation is inevitable given the variable quality of land, its fixed supply, the tendency for population to increase, and the benefits of location which inevitably arise as society becomes more complex. Policies to deregulate markets which leave rent untouched can only reinforce its effect. They may make markets more efficient, but the additional output which arises from improved efficiency mostly translates into increased rent. Policies designed to reduce poverty through redistribution do reduce rent, but only by compromising the efficiency of the market and reducing output so that everyone suffers a loss. Henry George explained that the only solution to poverty was to liberate the economy from the effects of the private appropriation of rent, leaving the market free to work on reconciling the preferences of all economic players.

If politicians, and those who elect them, misunderstand the impact of the policies they propose because they are ignorant of economic laws, and this ignorance leads to policies which exacerbate poverty and inequality, then there is no solution until that ignorance is remedied. In Victorian times, before the universal democratic franchise, parliament was an institution through which the wealthy ensured their interests were protected. Today, everyone has a vote, so these long-standing privileges could finally be withdrawn from the minority which enjoys them, by democratic will. It is only ignorance of economic realities which prevents this.

Changes in the attitudes, values and beliefs of those with power and influence, or their replacement with people who hold different values, is imperative. Although it is far from clear how much influence the professed values of politicians have on ordinary people, in their failure to talk up the possibility of a more inclusive and just world, they ensure progressive change is kept firmly off the agenda. This silence on the possibility of progress from politicians, many of whom claim to be working for improved social justice, does immense harm and must be overcome.

Many of us grow up believing that our political leaders possess a degree of personal integrity and a sense of public service. They certainly want us to believe this about them. But there is another view of politicians. As Kenneth Gergen argues, 'political participation represents a socialized form of aggression.' He goes on: 'the competitive nature of politics provides ample opportunity for the projection of one's own forbidden aggressive impulses onto others, and the democratic value of political involvement enables one to easily rationalize political involvement'.[2] If there is any truth in what Gergen says, it is clear that many of those who attain political office are part of the problem.

Whatever the psychology and motivation of individual politicians, it is clear that those who currently lead the rich nations all acquiesce in a system at odds with progressive values. Under current conditions, their stock solution to growing social injustice – to increase public spending to fund initiatives aimed at reducing poverty or increasing economic opportunities – generally subjects the economy to forces which undermine economic performance. This is not because increasing public expenditure necessarily causes these outcomes, but because national economies are held to ransom by the international money markets which are only interested in short-term financial returns and the ability to play competing economies off against one another. At the first sign of increased public investment, international investors will reduce their holdings of the national currency, of government stocks and bonds, and of shares in private companies within the country. These actions are bad for the economy, and poor economic performance hits the poor and underprivileged first, hardest and with the most lasting consequences. Even a government genuinely committed to reducing poverty and insecurity can do little without incurring the wrath of the financial markets in ways that will completely offset the benefit of increased public investment.

But can our democratically elected leaders really be as impotent over the global economy as they claim? In 1995, before being elected Prime Minister, Tony Blair said: 'The determining context of economic policy is the new global market. That imposes huge limitations of a practical nature – quite apart from reasons of principle on macroeconomic policies.'[3] While in office, Blair has said and done nothing to suggest he has changed his opinion. This is the leader of the fourth largest economy in the world, a man of great power and influence. Where does he think this determining context which so constrains his policymaking originates? Does he not see that it is the creation of politicians just like himself? Are we really expected to believe that, as someone who professes an ambition to bring about a more just world, he has no inkling that this determining context is deliberately sustained to protect the interests of corporate power and the wealth of a small minority? If Blair truly believes in social justice, then he needs to begin arguing for a new context in which progressive economic policies can be tested. At the very least he needs to start arguing that the context is the problem, and advocating the merits of its abandonment; by failing to do so he makes a rod for his own back. In Britain today, there is widespread discontent with the quality of public services; there is concern about pension provision in an ageing population, and general dissatisfaction with the pressures of being successful in an increasingly competitive society.

These are all inevitable symptoms of the determining context which Blair feels himself quite unable to challenge.

The professed impotence of politicians over the functioning of the global economy derives from their refusal to countenance the existence of a real alternative. There are, in fact, two alternatives to the present order, both of which would reduce poverty, but only one of which is viable in the long term. We could take measures to return the economy to the post-war, Keynesian model, based on consensus and a recognition of common interests. This would bring greater equality, but of the kind in which everyone becomes equally poor. It would, however, demonstrate a moral determination to address the problems of poverty and inequity which have no solution under the prevailing economic model. The second alternative is that proposed in the previous chapter: to acknowledge that there is no solution to poverty, or possibility of universal basic needs provision, until rent is recognised as common rather than private property, and introduce a tax system which appropriates rent as public revenue and applies it for the benefit of all. The key point is that alternatives do exist, and that the current determining context is human-made. It can be dismantled or reconfigured by democratically elected politicians just as it was created by them. The apparent ignorance, and moral weakness, of politicians is cause for considerable concern. It confirms the thesis that a grasp of economic realities first requires a degree of moral maturity, and this is rarely found in those who aspire to lead us. A better informed electorate is the vital ingredient for a properly functioning democracy, one that yields political leaders with the moral ambition and authority necessary to oversee transformative social change.

Increasing democratic participation was a feature of the twentieth century in all the rich industrialized countries. Democracy is one of the most widely held values. It is seen by proponents of the current order as the principal means for sustaining and justifying prevailing economic arrangements: if we have a democracy then our economic arrangements must reflect the will of the people. Opponents of the current order argue that democracy is the means by which an economy which works principally in the interests of minority wealth is kept in check, and the welfare of the general population is protected against the tendency towards economic and social polarization.

That democracy emerged as a counterbalancing force is beyond doubt. At the same time as industrialization was creating immense wealth and distributing it inequitably, great attention was being given by democrats to education. If economic expansion was to be sustained and more people were to be involved in the economy in a rewarding and life-sustaining manner, then greater numbers would require a formal and practical education. But decent education causes people to think about all manner of things, not just what they need to know in order to drive the economy forward.

Although improved access to educational opportunities has so far encouraged few people to think seriously about economics, it has caused growing numbers to question the continuing failure to apportion the rewards of economic advance more equitably. If we enjoyed a healthy democracy, these concerns would be reflected in the policies of the governments we elect. A vibrant, informed and fully functioning democracy must, by definition, push politicians towards more inclusive policies. Who among an insecure majority is going to support the status quo if they can comprehend a viable alternative which would improve their situation?

There is a huge difference between genuine democracy and the ideological form which holds sway today. Modern capitalism has made expert use of democratic ideals in its struggle to colonize the world. Multi-party democracy on the western model has been a condition of loans to poor countries under the IMF's structural adjustment programmes. The quite different conditions and context of these countries are not considered. In industrialized nations, democracy evolved as a reaction to social and economic changes; it was never imposed by an external authority. It was also the inevitable outcome of a more educated and socially aware population, and arose within well-established nation states in which a degree of cultural homogeneity had emerged. In most less-developed countries, none of these conditions pertain.

Imposed western-style democracy need not be an unmitigated disaster, and it has already been seen to despatch some of the vile despots who emerged to lead many newly independent states. But western democracy currently serves the interests of wealth and privilege more than at any time in the last century, and it is being imposed on the poor nations as part of a package of measures which heavily favour those interests. Superficial democracy may survive in these emerging societies, but it will do little for the plight of the poor and dispossessed, and everything for the tiny elites who, in league with their western counterparts, will work to ensure that democracy continues to provide the illusion of inclusion and participation in the face of a reality marked by polarization, and quite antithetical to genuine progress.

Progress can only be achieved through democratic means, but the mere existence of democratic institutions will not facilitate social change. Much has to change before democracy can deliver on its promise to represent the interests of all people.

A fully functioning democracy requires an improved understanding of economics among many people. But this is not simply, or necessarily, a question of greater intelligence, or of a better education. Many of the most 'intelligent' and best-educated people appear wholly ignorant of the economic truths we have uncovered, and many of these are economists. It seems that western culture encourages a cognitive incapacity in respect of economics – not dissimilar to that we identified in respect of racist attitudes – and it is this which prevents otherwise decent and thinking people from seeing economic reality.

In psychological terms, this incapacity acts as a defence mechanism. The prospect of coming fully to terms with economic reality, and the implications of many people so doing, discourages such engagement. Even among people who profess to desire a more just and inclusive world, the fundamental change implicit in proposals to address the rent issue through a George-inspired tax on land ownership and resource use is just too radical to contemplate. It taps into a deep-seated fear of change which has great power in preventing the human mind from embracing new ideas. But, as Albert Einstein observed, 'The world cannot get out of its current state of crisis with the same thinking that got it there in the first place.'

Clearly, in order to understand the economic ideas we have discussed, a degree of intelligence is required; but, in order to accept the implications of this new understanding, an advanced level of moral development or maturity is necessary. If intelligence provides the practical means to greater understanding, it is moral maturity which provides the motivation to seek out that understanding. A deep understanding of classical economic theory, and the type of solution prescribed by Henry George, provides the conduit between the moral maturity essential to progress and the practical possibility of achieving progressive social change. If many more people can achieve that level of moral awareness and motivation, and also grasp the essential truths of economics, then our established democratic institutions will finally be able to fulfil their essential purpose of shaping a society in which the interests of all people are served.

The escalation in international terror over the last few years has explanations in politics which go beyond matters of international economic justice; that said, the threat of terror will not recede until we begin to address its root causes in poverty and injustice. Economic insecurity breeds physical insecurity, from which nobody in the rich countries is any longer safe. The threat will remain until we begin to resolve the problems that drive the perceptions in so many people that rich and powerful western interests care nothing for their situation. We know that the tendency to acts of collective and political violence is rapidly reduced in societies which provide economic opportunities to growing numbers. Only when we succeed in extending economic opportunities to greater numbers of people in all countries, will the madness that inspires acts of insane terror be denied an environment in which to breed.

Whilst the ideas and ideals of freedom, justice and democracy exist independently of any particular economic structure, it is impossible to enjoy these freedoms without a degree of economic security. Current arrangements deny the value in those freedoms to the majority of the world's people, but do nothing to dampen their aspirations for them. It is these aspirations which could form the driving force for a new democracy which might overturn the stifling economic order under which so many struggle. But, instead of confronting the gravity of the situation, and accepting the need for new thinking, politicians pursue a quite different approach: they spend much of their time thinking up new ways to persuade us that, contrary to our observations and gut feeling, we are in fact making considerable progress as a society.

To this end, governments in many western countries have made it a goal to increase the proportion of young people going into higher education, the theory being that the better educated an individual, not only the better their chance of attaining security and satisfaction in life, but also the better it is for the economy as a whole. Not only are far greater numbers getting into higher education, but also at the same time standards are rising – or so we are asked to believe. In Britain, many more young people are scoring consistently higher in pre-university A-level examinations than their counterparts a generation ago. Can this really be possible after twenty-five years of underinvestment in education, with teachers whose pay relative to other professions has steadily declined and whose status in society has fallen? Can a school system in such a sorry state really be able to turn out the most academically successful young people our society has known, at the same time as growing numbers of parents are working longer hours and having less time to devote to assisting with homework or taking an interest in their children's education? A generation ago, the academic elite among young people got university places; today, in some areas, up to 50 per cent of youngsters remain in education beyond eighteen. There can be only one explanation: standards have been purposefully allowed to fall in order to give the impression that we are progressing as a society.

At some universities, special classes in basic essay-writing skills are offered to first-year students whose exam results get them places but whose writing ability is below the standard necessary to participate in undergraduate study. At the University of York, where undergraduate students in electronics sit a maths test before they begin their course, between 1985 and 2001 average scores on the same 50-question multiple-choice test fell from 39 to 19. Back in 1985, 30 was considered an adequate score. Between 1991 and 1998 the average marks in end-of-year exams for students with an A grade in maths A-level fell from 70 to 60 per cent; for those with a B, it fell from 62 to 40 per cent.[4] Across academia, where the same tests are applied to different generations of students, similar evidence of a fall in standards emerges.

The reason for this huge fraud is that politicians, like the public, have a sense that it is an entirely good thing that more people enjoy the benefits of a high-quality and extended education. The problem is that social and economic conditions do not allow an expansion of education so that greater numbers can enjoy the quality of educational opportunity historically enjoyed by a small minority. It would cost far too much, and would require changes not only from the early years of education, but also to the whole processes of nurturing and socialization. Universal access to educational opportunity would be the finest project our society could undertake but, like all the other challenges our politicians try to address, it is impossible without fundamental changes to the structure of society and the economy.

The scope and scale of the change required to bring about a more inclusive global society is immense, but the impact on the lives of ordinary people need not be that great. A successful programme of change will depend on the moral commitment of many millions people; and that commitment will only come once we learn to manage the fear of change which most of us feel. Change need not imply huge sacrifices on the part of those of us who currently enjoy the security and privileges that come with membership of the educated, middle-class, western club. The values, attitudes and world view that currently inform our materialistic way of life certainly require comprehensive revision, but the potential sacrifice we perceive is only relative; it can be overcome. We all stand to benefit from a more inclusive society. Most of the pain we feel is psychological: few of us need suffer materially; we will all enjoy an improvement in our economic security.

Improvement in our collective economic security depends on our accepting that the culture of mass-consumerism which now dominates western society is bad for humankind, and disastrous for the planet. We need to end our love affair with non-essential material consumption, and learn to be happier with less. Not only will this help preserve the resources of nature, and thus extend the life-sustaining capacity of the planet, it will also encourage a redirection of economic activity away from resource-hungry non-essentials for people who already have more than enough, and towards the provision of basic needs for those who have too little. As virtually every study in the industrialized world has found that perceptions of well-being have fallen as we have become materially better off, then in theory at least, giving up some non-essentials should not be difficult. In practice, it is one of the greatest obstacles to progress.

Currently, economic expansion depends on the creation of additional effective demand in a world where growing numbers have no purchasing power. Those who do have disposable income, or are able to obtain credit, must therefore be persuaded to spend more. Human beings have enormous appetites for novelty goods which excite for a short time, before becoming routine or outdated and requiring replacement. The marketing of products which consumers neither need, nor even contemplated before they were persuaded that life would be incomplete without them, is the principal means by which the economy sustains itself. In those tiny pockets of the poor world where wealth is concentrated, demand for the continually refined ephemera of modern life is even greater. Most production of such non-essentials is energy-intensive and resource-hungry, and much of it is useless junk.

It is not in the pursuit of basic needs that we are destroying the planet, rather in the relentless need to stimulate our bored minds with new and whizzier gadgets. As George Monbiot says, 'When people already possess all the goods and services they need, growth can be stimulated only by discovering new needs. Advertising creates gaps in our lives in order to fill them. We buy the products but the gaps remain.'[5] The marketing people might be responsible for pushing these unsolicited products on us, but they do not have to try very hard. Change will depend on our ability, as individuals, to come to terms with our insatiable appetite for novelty, and to begin to dismantle the mechanisms – cultural, educational, and mass media – which succeed so effectively in turning us into willing accomplices in the life- and soul-destroying onward march of consumerism.

In a competitive economy, where the market mechanism makes its adjudications on the basis of the relative strength of the preferences presented to it, the effects of the market in forcing optimal efficiency in production can be negative. The poor wages of so many force the production of low-cost goods without any consideration given to quality, durability, sustainability or the demands of communities for social cohesion. The high streets of Britain, which only twenty years ago were populated by a wide variety of shops which served the needs of the entire community, are now full of 'Pound Shops' selling generic, poor quality merchandise, or charity shops selling second-hand goods to the poor. Many long-established family businesses and branches of national chain stores have been closed down by the relentless demand to reduce costs. The commercial centres of towns and villages, which had for centuries constituted the social and cultural hub of communities, have become virtual ghost towns, breeding depression and despair.

People in all stratas of society become caught up in this relentless push for ever-lower prices. We think we are getting better value, but we measure that value only in terms of the prices we pay for goods, and seldom make the connection with the enormous external costs wider society pays for our personal savings. We return from the supermarket pleased to have taken advantage of the latest 'two for the price of one' offer, but we neglect to consider that, in the process of increasing their market share to two thirds of the food we buy, not only have super-markets driven thousands of small retailers out of business, but they are also forcing farmers to accept prices for their produce which do not cover their costs. We are pleased to pay lower prices but ignore the fact that instead we pay more in taxes so that the government, or the European Union, can subsidize farmers in order that supermarket chains can maintain profit levels, whilst we labour under the illusion that our food represents ever-greater value for money.

An economy which allowed a natural and just distribution of wealth, in line with the ambitions of the great classical economists, would help reverse these trends. Given the preference of most people for a vibrant, clean and safe local community with full amenities, and the ambition of so many to be masters over their own economic destiny, there would be great potential for the organic regeneration of run-down commercial centres. This would satisfy both the demands of customers for high-quality, value-for-money goods, and the demands of frustrated entre-preneurs for opportunities for self-employment. Britain is no longer a nation of shopkeepers, it is a nation of checkout operators!

Many of the problems of rich-country economies are now being exported to poorer countries through globalization. It is not the whole of human experience that becomes subject to the process of global-ization, it is that part of human experience which is about consumption, and it is about the consumption of those items which are most easily turned into commodities for which a demand can be created across cultures. Globalization is the end-game in the two-century-long process of extending an economic system constructed on a flawed theory of economics to all corners of the planet. It is a project with the specific goal of ensuring the world economy is arranged so that the already rich and powerful nations are able to maintain and consolidate their advantage. It can only accentuate pre-existing divisions in society and widen the gap between the rich and the rest. Globalization is already proving disastrous in poorer countries, where it is adopted reluctantly and absorbed falteringly, into cultures hopelessly unable to deal with its consequences.

The globalization project is sold on the basis that it will increase wealth, improve its distribution and spread development. We know this is impossible because the current model of the economy is based on a false understanding of economics. Those who claim globalization holds the key to greater economic equity do so either because they are ignorant, or because it suits their interests. But the power and influence of those who support the dominant model is quite out of proportion to their numbers. The exclusive, materialistic values which drive such beliefs are consciously held by very few individuals. The vast majority of people in rich countries indicate a preference for a world without suffering, hunger and poverty. At the same time, most people are unable to recognize that the means to their relative affluence and security are also the causes of the poverty and insecurity of others, and that the constant striving to preserve their advantage is why the disadvantaged are continually unable to liberate themselves from poverty. Instead, inequality is ascribed to a number of factors: race, intelligence, lack of effort, bad luck, the misfortune of being born in a country with an extreme climate or corrupt government. Rarely is the link made between the inevitability of many poor in a world of a few rich.

Globalization works at a cultural level through the economy. The products and services which drive the process are those which have been developed and refined in the advanced market economies where large companies have become masters at influencing taste and fashion, and creating new markets where the only demand is for something different. Western culture has become cultureless. If culture comprises the historical accumulation of values and locally developed customs and mechanisms for meeting the needs and aspirations of the population, then in the western world it has all but disappeared. The only culture that remains is the culture of consumption, and the only means to sustaining it is to develop new variations to stimulate our voracious appetites for sweet drinks, bland fast food, flashy gadgets and adrenalin-inducing experiences. It is these appetites which define the new global culture, and it contains no trace of the universalist values on which a more inclusive and culturally diverse world depends. The globalization project succeeds in globalizing only the basest of personal and cultural characteristics because that is where an economy which serves the goal of minority wealth is at its most potent.

As consumers, we potentially have tremendous power to influence economic change. If substantial numbers of us began to buy organic food, or fair-trade goods, or to source the bulk of our purchases from small local enterprises and from those with proven ethical records; if we also made a commitment to reduce our purchases of non-essentials, then the economic system and the shape of society could be rapidly and

radically transformed. This is the reality of consumer power in a democratic society: every time you buy, you cast a vote! All it requires is an
informed commitment from many millions of people.

As society becomes more polarized, not only do we have to work harder
and earn more to keep up, but also, in order to succeed, we need to be
able to acquire more: better homes, flashier cars, more exotic holidays.
It takes more to persuade us that we are successful and maintain a
positive self image. It is in modifying this aspect of our psychology that
we may find the means to negotiate the perception that change requires
sacrifice. Many successful people are frustrated and unhappy with their
situation. They may be wealthy but, in order to maintain their elite position in society, they have to work long hours and spend less time with
their children than they would like. Many express a desire to get off the
treadmill, if only they could find a way out and still ensure the economic
security of their families. The first step in this psychological reversal is
to break the equation we make between economic security and increasing incomes. It is an understandable equation, because under prevailing
arrangements they are inseparable, but this need not be the case.

A comfortable, secure home is a legitimate aspiration for all people,
but one which is denied to millions, even in rich countries, because of
the way the economy is arranged. In cities like London, many homes now
command prices in excess of a million pounds. Such houses do not
attract such a price because that is their intrinsic worth: they attract that
price because sufficient people have earned, inherited or obtained
through investments; sufficient cash, equity and borrowing potential to
finance such a purchase, because such houses are in limited supply in a
particular location; and because of the dictates of taste and fashion. Two
decades ago, when the spread of earnings was much narrower than it is
today, the price of the same property would have been much closer to the
average, and therefore affordable to more people.

Movement to a more equitable housing market need not mean a
reduction in welfare for anyone. In a fairer society, in which the polarizing effects of the law of rent were addressed, we would recognize that
all people aspire to a comfortable, reasonably spacious home in a safe
and attractive area with access to shops and amenities. All homes would
not be the same size, neither would all neighbourhoods have the same
variety of amenities, but each would be sufficient to fulfil the aspirations
of people for comfort, convenience and security. The million-pound
house would still exist, but its price relative to other properties would
not be exceptional, and the desirability of its location would be solely a
matter of taste, not a consequence of poor amenities, rampant crime or
the other symptoms of social breakdown. Under such circumstances,

the aspirations that drive us to earn and acquire more, and which further polarize society, will gradually start to reduce.

The threat of sacrifice embodied in proposals for social change is a creation of the prevailing economy and its accompanying social psychology. Any such threat can only be realized if we lose out, personally, relative to those with whom we choose to identify. If the value of your house is reduced by the building of a new road which does not affect other houses, then the threat is realized, and an injustice between those who own expensive houses has occurred. However, during a period of transition to an economy where these artificial and arbitrary differences are removed, any reduction in the market value of a property would not be a sacrifice: it would simply reflect a realignment caused by the restructuring of the economy. And this is key: in relation to others to whom we compare ourselves, no sacrifice need be felt. If an individual measures his or her self-worth simply on the basis of being five times as wealthy as the average person, and, in a changed economic context, is not able to revise this aspiration, then a sacrifice will be perceived. This perception can only be rectified through a change in the psychology of that individual.

Progressive change does not mean wealthier citizens having to give up their homes and move into something more modest; it does imply the need to accept that the value of some homes, relative to others, will reduce. It will still be the same home in the same location, only it will exist within a society where extremes of wealth and poverty and their consequences are steadily reduced. The threat of sacrifice can be managed through a gradual revision of our attitudes and world view, and we will have much help with this. The values and messages that shape our current perceptions will be reversed, and our aspirations will change: we will still aspire to security for ourselves and our families, but we will gradually discover that we can achieve this security only in harness with all our fellow citizens.

Progressive social change will also have an impact on our working lives, and our perceptions of work. We need to recognize that an economy dominated by large enterprises, which requires most individuals to play a rather minor part, tends to stifle individual initiative, and denies the majority of humans the opportunity to make a constructive contribution to society. We educate and prepare too many people for a minor role and to have low expectations, and then we complain at the lack of initiative and enthusiasm they show, and use this observation to argue that the character of most humans makes a competitive, exclusive economy the only viable form of social organization. Society currently advances on the back of the creative ingenuity of a tiny minority. It would be foolish to say that everyone could be an Einstein, a Darwin, a Freud or a Faraday, but, if conditions existed in which everybody could take up legitimate economic opportunities, the sum of human creative capacity would increase exponentially. Nature provided conditions in which that potential can be tapped; culture, political power and a false understanding of economics have conspired to curtail them. We know what it takes to resurrect them; it is up to us to make it happen.

We need to reassess the meaning and nature of work in a free society. Work will always be the primary means to basic needs provision, but it could also be much more. Throughout much of human history, work and culture were inseparable. Most of what we now value about earlier cultures is the product of skilled work, the like of which is rarely seen today. Much of the 'work' of yesterday we now look upon as art; it is unlikely that future generations will so regard much of today's work. By redefining work so that, as Joseph Milne said, 'it becomes a contribution to life, not just the effort to sustain life',[6] we may succeed in re-embedding the work of many people into culture. Work will have a value beyond that of simply securing economic necessities, and certainly beyond that of the creation of artificial wealth to which most of our efforts today are directed.

Suggestions that there is no place for advancing technology in a more equitable world must be firmly resisted. Technology is not the cause of our problems, it is how we choose to apply it that helps accelerate economic division and environmental damage. At present, technological innovation threatens to decimate conventional patterns of employment – which is not necessarily bad – but it also threatens to exclude large numbers of people from the economy – which most certainly is.

Technology constitutes the principal part of the capital applied in the modern economy and, where labour serves capital, it is inevitable that the further introduction of new technologies will cause greater economic polarization. Much traditional work is now done more cost-effectively by machines. This could, and should, be a good thing in relieving people of the tedious, dirty or dangerous tasks which undermine the creative energy of all who have no choice but to perform them. But, if the alternative for those whose jobs become mechanised is exclusion from all economic opportunities, then it is disastrous. In a more inclusive society, technology could play a crucial role in achieving the goal of universal needs provision, and enhancing the life choices of individuals by liberating millions from mundane, mind-numbing work.

Technology must be applied so that its benefits are felt by all people, and so as to halt the damage we are doing to the environment. Without the technological revolution, we would not have experienced the immense economic division in global society, but it is equally true that, having been through that process, the possibility of a return to a more eqitable world is dependent on our prudent and judicious use of technology. Technology is not the cause of economic polarization – that is the dubious boast of the fragile human psyche and the culture it has created – but it is currently an essential lubricant to the process.

Inequitable access to the benefits of technology widens the gap between nations, and, as technology becomes more easily exported, it widens the gaps between people within countries. This is especially true in respect of the information revolution. As long as half the world's people have no access to a telephone line, let alone an internet-ready computer, then the information revolution – despite the best intentions of those who champion the internet as a tool for social and cultural change – must widen the gap between the haves and have-nots. It is yet another medium of value through which opportunity is denied to at least half the world's people.

If we are to slow the damage we are doing the environment, we will require new eco-friendly technologies to take advantage of the immense opportunities that nature offers for sustainable and renewable supplies of energy. Had all the public investment and subsidies that have been poured into nuclear energy research and development, oil exploration and coal mining over the last fifty years been channelled instead into alternative energy sources – solar energy, wave and wind power – most of our energy requirements would now be cost-effectively sourced from these environment-friendly sources. The potential dangers, and the financial cost, of nuclear energy would be avoided, and fossil fuels could be used in a measured way to fill the gaps where renewable sources are not practical. But such investment was not favourable to the market: oil, gas and coal promised high, short-term returns; and nuclear energy challenged the pathological human desire to control and dominate nature. It is not too late: renewable energy options are only expensive because, through misguided investment and huge public subsidy, we have made fossil fuels so cheap. In many poor countries, solar-powered refrigeration has been found to be the most cost-effective means of storing vaccines where electricity is unavailable. If renewable energy is a viable option in countries with tiny budgets, then it can surely work elsewhere. A tax regime which charged for the use of natural resources at their full cost would automatically direct investment towards economic opportunities which were less harmful to the environment.

Technological innovation has an impact not only on the nature of work, but also on the scale of enterprise. The question of optimal scale was examined by E.F. Schumacher in his classic work, *Small is Beautiful,* published in 1973. Many thinkers have questioned the sense in humankind adopting institutions and practices, the scale of which are beyond the capacity of the individual to relate to or identify with. The need to restore *Human Scale,* to use the name of the book by Kirkpatrick Sale, is paramount. People take more satisfaction from their contribution to society and the economy if they can make it in a context in which they feel to be an important and valuable part, rather than a minor and expendable cog. Larger enterprises usually require more of their employees to play an insignificant role. The consequences of increases in scale, the ongoing division of labour and the effect of constant technological innovation, were of great concern to Adam Smith, who feared the impact on morale and motivation, as well as individual happiness, if growing numbers of people were required to perform routine and repetitive tasks. Smaller productive units, applying and further developing sustainable technologies would, argued Schumacher, better serve the requirements of the needs economy, and give more people greater control over, and responsibility for, their work.

There will always be a need to reconcile the benefits of economies of scale, whereby improvements in efficiency derive from conducting productive activity in larger units, with the need for human scale. Addressing the rent issue through the type of solution outlined by Henry George suggests a possible means. Once there is no intrinsic value in owning a disproportionate share of land, it is likely that the distribution of both land and capital will gradually be spread more evenly among people, and will reflect the capacity of certain individuals to make the best possible use of a particular site. With the incentive and means to excessive concentration removed, owners of land and capital would still have the option to pool resources where they identified mutually beneficial opportunities; but this would not threaten the interests of anyone who desired to keep his economic endeavour small-scale and independent, and such ambitions would not be thwarted by the inflated start-up costs which result when land is overpriced. In an equitable economy, the size of productive units would vary, tending to that which promises greatest efficiency of production and equity of distribution, but it would also be determined by the requirement to satisfy the similar aspirations of all members of society. Some would choose to participate in a collective venture, others might choose self-employment; neither group need be penalized for their preference.

In a just society, there would sometimes be a need for the rationing of certain commodities and privileges, and this might entail some real sacrifices. The need for rationing arises from the limits imposed by our planet's ecology. Air travel is a good example. We cannot reduce our output of damaging carbon dioxide without reducing the amount of air travel we currently undertake. Unless we can find non-damaging means of powering aircraft (and we are currently struggling to solve this problem even for cars) then we have to cut back on air travel. Demand for air travel is currently growing at five per cent annually, and by 2030 it is estimated that the current 1.3 billion annual passenger flights will grow to more than four billion. Air travel will then contribute 15 per cent of all emissions of carbon dioxide, as well as deposits of water vapour and other gases which contribute to global warming, into the high atmosphere.[7]

An average distance flight of 500km generates a fifth more carbon emissions per passenger than an equivalent journey by car, and thirty-two times as much as rail travel. A single long-haul flight to the United States causes as much pollution per passenger as the average annual car use of a British driver over a whole year.[8] There seems little point in trying to tackle pollution through reduced car use when western governments are encouraging the rapid expansion of air travel. Huge subsidies are enjoyed by airlines which have to pay no tax on aviation fuel. Further, the Kyoto agreement, which seeks to limit harmful emissions, specifically excludes international air travel. If we still wish to have a planet worth living on a century from now we have no choice but to restrict and ration air travel.

We need to reduce the perceived need for air travel and to reduce aspirations and expectations for it. It is not something we can collectively afford, so it is not a right we can individually demand. Very little air travel is necessary, and it will become less necessary as other, less harmful, technologies provide alternatives. The reason for much business air travel is the belief that face-to-face meetings are essential to effective business communication and decision-making. This becomes less true as communications technologies improve. The expectation of using air travel for pleasure must also be revised. Many of us love to travel and explore other countries and cultures, but this is a privilege which it is quite impossible to extend to all humans. A mechanism to ration the luxury of air travel is clearly required.

Imagine a global society in which the basic needs of all were met, everyone enjoyed economic security and, as a consequence of all people being fully engaged in productive employment, considerable surplus wealth was created. Under such circumstances, those who chose to work in excess of the level necessary to cover basic needs would enjoy rewards greater than others who did not so choose. This additional wealth could then be exchanged so that those who desired to travel by air could do so. The amount of travel would be restricted to that level which the best science tells us can sustainably be supported by the environment. This would mean that, if demand for air travel exceeded supply, prices would rise, and some people would be discouraged from spending their surplus wealth on flights, choosing instead one of a range of other non-essentials to treat themselves. Not all non-essentials would be rationed in this way, only those where unregulated use would undermine the capacity of the planet to sustain life in the long term. Now, if this all sounds like a great deal of central planning and control, it is in fact nothing but the market working to allocate scarce resources according to the laws of supply and demand. Only here the market is required to factor in a sustainable rate of pollution and resource use.

We can come to terms with the perceived sacrifices that transition to a just and equitable society implies by changing our perceptions of sacrifice. There is no point asking people to use their cars less to reduce global warming when there are no viable alternatives to car use, and such a request is not part of a strategy to transform society by addressing the root causes of our reluctance to give up our cars. But hold up the possibility of a different world, and explain how all these perceived sacrifices are only sacrifices in the context of an unchanging, competitive and insecure society, and we might begin to make progress towards real change. The fact that growing numbers already show concern about the long-term prospects for life on earth, suggests that we might surprise ourselves with our capacity to embrace new and radical ways of thinking, and to recognize perceived sacrifices as opportunities for individual and collective transformation.

A frequent defence against arguments for greater social justice is that, if we were all equal, life would be rather dull, devoid of variety and difference. We would become a society of like-minded automatons, it is suggested, and much of what we value in human diversity and the immense variety it provides would be lost. Such arguments must be strongly refuted. We are not facing a choice between a world of gross inequity, a growing economic divide and immense suffering, and an alternative in which everybody looks, thinks, acts, lives and earns the same. Universalism does not argue for uniformity across of all spheres of human experience. Quite the opposite: it argues for diversity, tolerance, variety and innovation, but it argues for these values in a world in which everybody has the opportunity to feed, clothe and house themselves and those they care for. It also argues that everybody should have the opportunity to do something creative and personally rewarding with their lives. Imagine six billion people deciding for themselves what they want to do and how they want to live, once they have each put in the economic effort required to secure their basic needs. Such a world would bear no comparison to our current one in which only a few hundred million have any such control over their lives, and where many secure their economic and social privileges by denying the same to others.

The argument for a more inclusive society is not an argument for material equality, only that all people have the opportunity to provide for their essential needs. If everyone did, billions more people would be able to contribute to the creative mosaic that is global human culture. Neither does movement to a more equitable world imply that people must think alike on all issues. Once there is consensus on what it takes to give everybody a fair chance in life, and acceptance of the limits that places on individual and collective actions, the rest is quite open. Many existing customs, opinions, ideas, aspirations, tastes and hopes are quite compatible with universalism. Compare this with the current situation in which the immense diversity of customs, tastes and ideas that existed pre-globalization is being lost to global aspirations for fast food, fizzy drinks, designer jeans, and expensive running shoes for non-athletes.

Change is not about making impossible choices; it is about creating conditions in which such choices can be avoided. Consider the plight of the endangered tiger. These beautiful creatures will soon be extinct unless we take urgent steps to protect their habitat. That habitat is threatened by the unregulated commercial activities of poor, desperate individuals and communities, often working under the auspices of large corporations which clear forests for timber, or because poor people have no land on which to build homes or grow crops. In reflective moments we are disturbed by the tiger's plight: it saddens us to contemplate a world without the tiger, and it frustrates us that we seem unable to live in harmony with other animals. But the tigers' fate is not linked to human progress *per se*, only to the current mode and method of human progress. Tigers are dying out because our economic system neglects the needs and interests of most people in those parts of the world where tigers live. The circumstances which threaten tigers also threaten the local and global environment. Progressive social change means solutions which address a multitude of problems by attacking root causes which have multiple consequences. By moving towards a cooperative and inclusive mode of economic organization, not only can we better provide for the needs of poor people, but we can also create conditions in which they can meet their basic needs without driving the tiger to extinction, and without destroying local natural resources. Species extinction, ecological damage and human deprivation all have their roots in the way the economy fails to address the basic needs of so many; and they have a single common solution.

The choice is not between peasants feeding their families and the survival of the tiger. We can only address both issues in concert. We do not need sentimental motives to save the tiger. We save it not because it is beautiful to look at, but because in doing so we encourage conditions which secure the planet for future generations and which encourage equitable social relations. In elevating the value of all human lives, we automatically elevate the long-term viability of our planet as a home for all sentient beings and a diverse variety of non-sentient life. The only choice to be made is that between providing for the needs of all humans and animals in perpetuity, or providing for the inflated material needs of a minority of humans now. By choosing the latter course, we condemn many people to short lives, many species to extinction, and future generations to an extremely precarious existence.

Too many people aspire to a different kind of world for the notion to be wholly unrealistic. However, any claim for the possibility of progress must be able to defend itself against charges of utopian idealism and naive optimism. It would be helpful to cast out the images we hold of utopia which suggest a vastly different world from the one we inhabit today. Ever since Thomas More's *Utopia* was published in 1516, these have suggested a return to a pristine state of existence in which technology is largely absent and humans live peacefully amid plenty with rather a lot of leisure time. This is not the kind of world we are talking of building. For those of us who already enjoy a degree of economic security, life, in its practical aspects, would not change very much. We may not have to work so hard to pay for enormous mortgages on our overpriced homes. We will feel less anxiety about having to compete to survive. We will be free to make of our lives what we desire. With the context of our existence so altered, it is hard to imagine what form that freedom and the realization of those desires might take, but it is not difficult to imagine the immense scope for progress and improvement.

For the majority of the world's people, those who enjoy no such economic security, and for whom life is a constant struggle, gradual change in their lives will bring a sense of growing security. It will not be a case of rushing all nations and peoples through a rapid industrial revolution so they catch up in technological terms. Gradually, as security and confidence improves, societies at different levels of development will find new ways – perhaps as yet unimagined ways – of social and economic development. If the move towards transition requires a leap of faith, then envisioning the possible outcomes in terms of the way we live and organize our societies requires an even greater leap of imagination.

In response to the charge of naive optimism, I would contend that realism about the weaknesses and failings of human nature and culture, and an accurate assessment of their relative influence, along with recognition of the desire of many human beings to live cooperatively and to create a world which matches our moral aspirations, does, on balance, leave one optimistic. We have come so far: the abolition of slavery, the successes of civil rights movements, the democratization of society and the emancipation of women are all immense successes, born of a recognition of the essential unity of humankind, and the belief that nobody should be denied an equal chance to enjoy a comfortable and fulfilled life. The last two hundred years have seen great moral advances and considerable social gains. Similar gains in the next two centuries would see us well on the way to an equitable society. Belief in this possibility is no more or less naive than that of the first abolitionists.

We can only speculate about the state of the world a hundred years hence, but the choice available to us is uncertainty with security or uncertainty without. If global society continues to develop along current lines, then a century from now pockets of privileged, wealthy individuals across the planet will be working together to devise schemes for protecting themselves from a growing disenfranchised majority. As minority materialism becomes irredeemably entrenched, relentless acquisition will become the only means to survival. Those who float to the top will demand more and more, faster and faster; they will leave less and less for the struggling majority. In the process they will transform themselves into a race less than human, and will rapidly denude the planet of the means to support life. But they will, for a short while, be in control of most of the viable land, and virtually all the productive assets, and therefore be best placed to protect themselves from the consequences of acute ecological breakdown. For the majority, life will become more miserable, shorter and brutish until it becomes insupportably insecure: it will become a race to die, the only element of uncertainty being whether one falls victim to violence, hunger or disease.

This may sound exaggeratedly pessimistic, but it describes the reality of life for a sizeable minority of people alive today; it can only be a matter of time before it becomes the experience of most humans. It is difficult to envisage how any of us might insulate ourselves from falling absolutely into one camp or the other. If we wish to survive and be reasonably comfortable, we will have to conform to the values of minority materialism. We may have the option to live among the excluded out of a sense of solidarity, but we will be afforded few protections.

This, then, is one view of the future, but not the only one. The alternative, an inclusive global society built on universal principles and organized in the interests of all humans beings, is within reach. Through our advanced moral aspirations we have already laid the foundation, in the United Nations, for a form a global governance which could ensure that the interests of no group of people is given priority over any other, or over the interests of any individual. Whilst international institutions like the UN require radical reform to turn them from agents for the interests of the rich and powerful into agents for the interests of all, their mere existence is a sign of hope. This alternative vision of society is one in which increasing numbers are born into a world which offers them opportunity and security; a world in which people can expect a life free from exploitation and oppression, and in which they will be free to use their time as they wish, providing they do not impinge on the rights of others to do the same; a life of true individual freedom, the kind that is only possible with the taking of full social responsibility. Once this goal is realized, the true potential of humankind will begin to unfold. It is too good an opportunity to pass by.

We began this enquiry with an investigation of evolutionary science in order to establish that human beings are not prisoners of their genes. Ian Robertson puts evolution and genetic science in its rightful place: 'Evolution's gift to us is that we are no longer slaves to our biology. Very few of the important things we do are pre-programmed and pre-ordained in our genes. The cultures we create through the meetings of human minds, the societies that emerge from these cultures – these are what make us do what we do.'[9] Biological evolution will continue in some shape, but our technological and cultural interventions mean that its influence will be negligible. Cultural evolution will take up those aspects of biological evolution which have a place in a sustainable, inclusive and just society. Through our evolving culture we will learn to manage the negative traits of our evolutionary legacy. We should remain on our guard however. Culture can very quickly embrace the basest and most destructive aspects of our evolutionary heritage. It would only take a couple of generations of forgetting what it takes to build a sustainable and inclusive society for humankind to revert, disastrously, to type.

Previous generations, lacking a critical mass of individuals with the moral maturity and insight to see a way forward, were unable to capitalize on the gains of economic advance. The possibility of progress was sacrificed to the immature human psyche, and to temptation and greed. While we should not underestimate the immensity of the task, or the timescales involved, the progress we have already made is clear proof of possible progress to come. Belief in the possibility of progressive social change is the starting point; action in pursuit of that end must quickly follow if we are not to lose the chance of attaining the social maturity that so many have dreamed of. Perhaps humankind has now reached the point at which, in the face of the immense threat to the life-sustaining capacity of our planet, sufficient numbers can be persuaded of the moral argument for change. If so, it is not unrealistic to imagine a world in which poverty is eradicated, in which everyone has the chance to fulfil their full potential, and in which we are able to live in harmony with nature for generations to come. A world of which we can all be truly proud.

Bibliography

Adams, E.M., *A Society Fit for Human Beings* (Albany, State University of New York Press, 1998).

Adams, Mark B. (ed), *The Evolution of Theodosius Dobzhansky* (Princeton, New Jersey, Princeton University Press, 1994).

Albrow, Martin, *Weber's Construction of Social Theory* (London, Macmillan Education, 1990).

Amin, Samir, *Capitalism in the Age of Globalization: The Management of Contemporary Society* (London, Zed Books, 1997).

Archibald, Peter, *Social Psychology as Political Economy* (London, McGraw-Hill Ryerson, 1978).

Bahro, Rudolf, *Avoiding Social and Ecological Disaster: The Politics of World Transformation* (Bath, Gateway Books, 1994).

Banks, Ronald, *Costing the Earth* (London, Shepheard-Walwyn, 1989).

Barthlemy-Madaule, Madeleine, *Lamarck, the Mythical Precursor: A Study of the Relation Between Science and Ideology* (Cambridge, Massachusetts, MIT Press, 1982).

Baum, Gregory, *Karl Polanyi on Ethics and Economics* (Montreal, McGill-Queen's University Press, 1996).

Bellah, Robert et al, *Habits of the Heart: Individualism and Commitment in American Life* (London, Univerity of California Press, 1996).

Bentham, Jeremy, *An Introduction to the Principles of Morals and Legislation* (London, Athlone, 1970; first published 1789).

Bernstein, John Andrew, *Progress and the Quest for Meaning* (London, Associated University Presses, 1993).

Bevan, Aneurin, *In Place of Fear* (London, Quartet, 1978).

Bloom, William, *Money, Heart and Mind* (London, Viking, 1995).

Bock, Kenneth, *Human Nature and History* (New York, Columbia University Press, 1980).

Bolton, James, *The Medieval English Economy 1150-1500* (London, Dent, 1980).

Bottery, Mike, *The Morality of the School* (London, Cassell, 1990).

Bowlby, John, *Attachment and Loss*, Vol 1 (London, Hogarth Press, 1969).

Bowlby, John, *Attachment and Loss*, Vol 2 (London, Hogarth Press, 1973).

Bowlby, John, *Childcare and the Growth of Love* (Harmondsworth, Penguin, 1965).

Bowler, Peter, *Evolution: History of an Idea* (Berkeley, University of California Press, 1984).

Bowler, Peter, *The Invention of Progress* (Oxford, Blackwell, 1989).

Bowler, Peter, *The Mendelian Revolution* (London, Athlone, 1989).

Breakwell, Glynis (ed), *Social Psychology of Political and Economic Cognition* (London, Adademic Press, 1991).

Breuer, Georg, *Sociobiology and the Human Dimension* (Cambridge, New York, Cambridge University Press, 1992).

Bronk, Richard, *Progress and the Invisible Hand: The Philosophy and Economics of Human Advance* (London, Little Brown, 1998).

Brown, Andrew, *The Darwin Wars* (London, Simon & Schuster, 2000).

Burgess, Ronald, *Public Revenue without Taxation* (London, Shepheard-Walwyn, 1993).

Caufield, Catherine, *Masters of Illusion: The World Bank and the Poverty of Nations* (London, Macmillan, 1997).

Cavalli-Sforza, Luigi & Francesco, *The Great Human Diasporas* (Reading, Massachusetts, Perseus, 1995).

Chomsky, Noam, *Profit over People: Neoliberalism and the Global Order* (New York, Seven Stories Press, 1999).

Chossudovsky, Michel, *The Globalization of Poverty* (London, Zed Books, 1997).

Cole, Michael, *Cultural Psychology* (Cambridge, Massachusetts, Belknap Press, 1997).

Coleman, D.C., *The Economy of England, 1450-1750* (London, Oxford University Press, 1977).

Daly, Herman E., *The Economics of Sustainable Development* (New York, Beacon Press, 1996).

Damon, William (ed), *Moral Development* (San Fransicso, Jossey-Bass, 1978).

Darrough, M./Blank R., *Biological Differences and Social Equality* (London, Greenwood Press, 1983).

Darwin, Charles, *On the Origin of Species* (London, John Murray, 1902; first published 1859).

Darwin, Charles, *The Descent of Man* (Amherst, Prometheus Books, 1998; first published 1871).

Daunton, Martin, *Progress and Poverty: An Economic and Social History of Britain, 1700-1850* (Oxford, OUP, 1995).

Dawkins, Richard, *The Selfish Gene* (Oxford, Oxford University Press, 1976).

Degler, Carl, *In Search of Human Nature* (New York, Oxford University Press, 1991).

Deutsch, Morton, *Distributive Justice: A Social-Psychological Perspective* (Newhaven, Yale University Press, 1985).

Donaldson, Peter, *Economics of the Real World* (Harmondsworth, Penguin, 1978).

Doyal, Len/Gough, Ian, *A Theory of Human Need* (Basingstoke, Macmillan, 1991).

Dyer, Kenneth, F., *The Biology of Racial Integration* (Bristol, Scientechnica, 1974).

Elfstrom, Gerard, *Ethics for a Shrinking World* (London, Macmillam, 1990).

Elliott, Larry/Atkinson, Dan, *The Age of Insecurity* (London, Verso, 1998).

Elliot, Robert (ed), *Environmental Ethics* (Oxford, Oxford University Press, 1995).

Etzioni, Amitai, *The Moral Dimension: Toward a New Economics* (New York, Free Press, 1988).

Flugel, J.C., *Man, Morals and Society* (Harmondsworth, Penguin, 1955).

Fowler, James W., *Stages of Faith* (San Fransicso, HarperCollins, 1981).

Fried, Morton, *The Evolution of Political Society* (New York, Random House, 1967).

Fromm, Erich, *Escape from Freedom* (New York, Henry Holt & Co, 1965).

Fromm, Erich, *Man for Himself: An Enquiry into the Psychology of Ethics* (New York, Henry Holt & Co, 1947).

Fromm, Erich, *On Becoming Human* (New York, Continuum, 1997).

Fromm, Erich, *The Anatomy of Human Destructiveness* (New York, Henry Holt & Co, 1992).

Fromm, Erich, *The Art of Loving* (London, George Allen & Unwin, 1957).

Fromm, Erich, *The Sane Society* (London, Routledge, 1991).

Gaffney, Mason, *The Corruption of Economics* (London, Shepheard-Walwyn, 1994).

Galbraith, J.K., *A History of Economics* (Harmondsworth, Penguin, 1989).

Galbraith, J.K., *A Short History of Financial Euphoria* (London, Penguin, 1993).

Galbraith, J.K., *The Affluent Society* (London, Penguin, 1999).

Galbraith, J.K., *The Culture of Contentment* (London, Penguin, 1992).

Gellner, Ernest, *Nationalism* (London, Weidenfeld & Nicolson, 1997).

George, Henry, *Progress and Poverty* (New York, Robert Schalkenbach Foundation, 1979; first published 1879).

George, Susan, *Ill Fares the Land* (London, Penguin, 1990).

George, Susan/Sabelli, Fabrizio, *Faith and Credit: The World Bank's Secular Empire* (London, Penguin, 1994).

Gilligan, Carol. *In a Different Voice* (Cambridge, Massachusetts, Harvard University Press, 1982).

Goldberg, David (ed), *The Anatomy of Racism* (Minneapolis, University of Minnesota Press, 1990).

Gorringe, Timothy, *Fair Shares: Ethics and the Global Economy* (London, Thames & Hudson, 1999).

Grant, Verne, *Organismic Evolution* (New York, W.H. Freeman, 1977).

Gray, John, *False Dawn* (London, Granta, 1998).

Greene, John, *Science, Ideology and World View* (London, University of California Press, 1981).

Grieder, William, *One World Ready or Not: The Manic Logic of Global Capitalism* (London, Allen Lane/The Penguin Press, 1997).

Grof, S./Russell, P./Laszlo, E., *The Consciousness Revolution* (Shaftesbury, Element Books, 1999).

Gunder Frank, Andre, *World Accumulation 1492-1989* (London, Macmillan, 1978).

Hallpike, C.R., *The Principles of Social Evolution* (Oxford, Clarendon Press, 1986).

Harris, Marvin, *Cultural Anthropology* (New York, HarperCollins, 1991).

Harris, Marvin, *Cultural Materialsm: The Struggle for a Science of Culture* (New York, Random House, 1979).

Haste, Helen/Torney-Porta, Judith (eds), *The Development of Political Understanding* (San Fransicso, Jossey-Bass, 1992).

Hastings, Adrian, *The Construction of Nationhood* (Cambridge, New York, Cambridge University Press, 1997).

Hatch, Elvin, *Culture and Morality* (New York, Columbia University Press, 1983).

Hawkins, Mike, *Social Darwinism in European and American Thought 1860-1945* (Cambridge, Cambridge University Press, 1997).

Heilbroner, Robert L., *Behind the Veil of Economics* (New York, W.W. Norton & Co, 1998).

Heilbroner, Robert L., *The Nature and Logic of Capitalism* (New York, W.W. Norton, 1985).

Herrnstein, Richard/Murray, Charles, *The Bell Curve: Intelligence and Class Structure in American Life* (New York, Free Press, 1994).

Hertz, Noreena, *The Silent Takeover: Global Capitalism and the Death of Democracy* (London, Heinemann, 2001).

Hick, John, *An Interpretation of Religion: Human Responses to the Transcendent* (Basingstoke, Macmillan, 1989).

Hirsch, Max, *Democracy versus Socialism* (New York, Robert Schalkenbach Foundation, 1966; first published 1901).

Hobbes, Thomas, *Leviathan* (London, Dent, 1953; first published 1660).

Hobsbawm, Eric, *Industry and Empire* (London, Penguin, 1999).

Hofstadter, Richard, *Social Darwinism in American Thought* (New York, G. Brazillier, 1959).

Holbrook, David, *Evolution and the Humanities* (Aldershot, Gower, 1987).

Holmes, Jeremy, *John Bowlby and Attachment Theory* (London, Routledge, 1993).

Hosking, G./Schopflin, G. (eds), *Myths and Nationhood* (London, Hurst, 1997).

Hudson, Michael/Miller, G.J./Feder, Kris, *A Philosophy for a Fair Society* (London, Shepheard-Walwyn, 1994).

Hutton, Will, *The State We're In* (London, Vintage, 1996).

Jenkins, Richard, *Rethinking Ethnicity* (London, Sage, 1997).

Johnston, R.J., *On Human Geography* (Oxford, Blackwell, 1988).

Jones, Steve, *In the Blood* (London, Flamingo, 1997).

Kaye, Howard, *The Social Meaning of Modern Biology* (London, Yale University Press, 1986).

Keegan, William, *The Spectre of Capitalism* (London, Radius, 1992).

Kennedy, Paul, *Preparing for the Twenty-First Century* (New York, Vintage, 1994).

Keynes, John Maynard, *The General Theory of Employment, Interest and Money* (London, Macmillan, 1936).

Kohlberg, Lawrence, *The Meaning and Measurement of Moral Development* (Worcester, Massachusetts, Clark University Press, 1981).

Kohlberg, Lawrence, *The Philosophy of Moral Development: Moral Stages and the Idea of Justice* (San Francisco, Harper & Row, 1981).

Kohlberg, Lawrence, *The Psychology of Moral Development: The Nature and Validity of Moral Stages* (London, Harper & Row, 1984).

Kohlberg, Lawrence/Levine, Charles/Hewer, Alexandra, *Moral Stages: A Current Formulation and a Response to Critics* (New York, Karger, 1983).

Kuper, Adam, *The Invention of Primitive Society* (London, Routledge, 1988).

Kurtz, Paul, *Forbidden Fruit: The Ethics of Humanism* (Buffalo, Prometheus, 1988).

Landes, David, *The Wealth and Poverty of Nations* (London, Little Brown, 1998).

Lappe, Frances Moore/Collins, Joseph, *Food First: The Myth of Scarcity* (London, Souvenir Press, 1980).

Lappe, Frances Moore/Collins, Joseph, *World Hunger: Twelve Myths* (London, Earthscan, 1998).

Lapsley, Daniel, *Moral Psychology* (Boulder, Westview Press, 1996).

Lasch, Christopher, *The True and Only Heaven: Progress and Its Critics* (New York, Norton, 1991).

Leakey, Richard, *The Origin of Humankind* (London, Weidenfeld & Nicolson, 1994).

Lewis, Alan/Webley, Paul/Furnham, Adrian, *The New Economic Mind* (Hemel Hempstead, Harvester/Wheatsheaf, 1995).

Lewontin, Richard, *It Ain't Necessarily So: The Dream of the Human Genome and Other Illusions* (London, Granta, 2000).

Lewontin, Richard, *The Doctrine of DNA* (London, Penguin, 1993).

Lopreato, Joseph, *Human Nature and Biocultural Evolution* (London, Allan & Unwin, 1984).

Lovtrup, Soren, *Darwin: Refutation of a Myth* (Beckenham, Croom Helm, 1987).

Lunt, P./Furnham A. (eds), *Economic Socialization: The Economic Beliefs and Behaviours of Young People* (Cheltenham, Edward Elgar, 1996).

MacLaren, Leon, *Nature of Society* (London, Martlet Press, 1952).

Malinowski, Bronislaw, *A Scientific Theory of Culture* (New York, Oxford University Press, 1960).

Malthus, Thomas, *An Essay on the Principle of Population* (Harmondsworth, Penguin, 1970; first published 1798).

Mandel, Ernest, *Long Waves of Capitalist Development* (London, Verso, 1995).

Marx, Karl/Engels, Frederick, *The Collected Works* (London, Lawrence & Wishart, 1975).

May, Larry/Friedman, Marilyn/Clarke, Andy (eds), *Mind and Morals* (Cambridge, Massachusetts, MIT Press, 1996).

Maynard Smith, John, *Did Darwin Get it Right?* (London, Penguin, 1993).

Mayr, Ernst, *Evolution and the Diversity of Life* (London, Harvard University Press, 1986).

Mayr, Ernst, *One Long Argument* (London, Allen Lane, 1992).

McKim, Robert/McMahan, Jeff (eds), *The Morality of Nationalism* (New York, Oxford University Press, 1997).

McMichael, Philip, *Development and Social Change: A Global Perspective* (Sage, London, 1996).

McMurthy, John, *The Cancer Stage of Capitalism* (London, Pluto, 1999).

Megarry, Tim, *Society in Prehistory* (Basingstoke, Macmillan, 1995).

Midgley, Mary, *Can't We Make Moral Judgements?* (Bristol, The Bristol Press, 1991).

Midgley, Mary, *Heart and Mind* (Routledge, London, 2003).

Midgely, Mary, *The Ethical Primate* (London, Routledge, 1994).

Miliband, Ralph, *Socialism for Sceptical Age* (London, Polity, 1995).

Mill, James, *Elements of Political Economy* (London, H.G. Bohn, 1844; first published 1821).

Mill, John Stuart, *On Liberty* (Penguin, London, 1985; first published 1859).

Montesquieu, Baron de, *De L'Esprit de Lois* (Berwick, R.Taylor, 1770).

More, Thomas. *Utopia* (London, Dent, 1985; first published 1518).

Mulberg, John, *Social Limits to Economic Theory* (Routledge, London, 1995).

Niebuhr, Reinhold, *Moral Man and Immoral Society* (New York, Touchstone, 1995; first published 1932).

Noyes, Richard (ed), *Now the Synthesis: Capitalism, Socialism and the New Social Contract* (London, Shepheard-Walwyn, 1991).

O'Hear, Anthony, *Beyond Evolution* (Oxford, Clarendon Press, 1997).

Ormerod, Paul, *The Death of Economics* (London, Faber & Faber, 1994).

Ortner, Donald (ed), *How Humans Adapt: A Biocultural Odyssey* (Washington DC, Smithsonian Institution, 1983).

Parkin, Frank, *Durkheim* (Oxford, Oxford University Press, 1992).

Peel, J.D.Y., *Herbert Spencer: Evolution of a Sociologist* (London, Heinemann, 1981).

Piaget, Jean, *Judgement and Reason in the Child* (London, Routledge, 1969; first published 1928).

Piaget, Jean, *The Moral Judgement of the Child* (New York, Norton, 1965; first published 1932).

Plattner, Stuart, *Economic Anthropology* (Stanford, Stanford University Press, 1989).

Plomin, Robert, *Behavioural Genetics* (New York, Freeman & Co, 1997, 3rd edition).

Polanyi, Karl, *The Great Transformation* (Boston, Beacon Press, 1957).

Rachels, James, *Created from Animals: The Moral Implications of Darwinism* (Oxford, Oxford University Press, 1991).

Raphael, D.D., *Moral Philosophy* (Oxford, Oxford University Press, 1981).

Rasmussen, David (ed), *Universalism versus Communitarianism* (Cambridge Massachusetts, MIT Press, 1990).

Rawls, John, *A Theory of Justice* (Oxford, Clarendon Press, 1972).

Redclift, Michael, *Sustainable Development* (London, Methuen, 1987).

Renshon, Stanley (ed), *Handbook of Political Socialization* (New York, Free Press, 1977).

Rescher, Nicholas, *Distributive Justice* (Washington DC, University Press of America, 1982).

Resnick, D./Devlin, B./Roeder, K./Feinberg, S. (eds), *Intelligence, Genes and Success: Scientists Respond to the Bell Curve* (New York, Springer, 1977).

Reynolds, Vernon, *The Biology of Human Action* (Reading, W.H. Freeman & Co, 1976).

Ricardo, David, *Principles of Political Economy and Taxation* (Harmondsworth, Penguin, 1971; first published 1817).

Richter, Melvin, *The Politics of Conscience: T.H. Green and his Age* (Bristol, Thoemmes Press, 1996).

Robertson, Ian, *Mind Sculpture: Unleasing Your Brain's Potential* (London, Bantam, 1999).

Rodney, Walter, *How Europe Underdeveloped Africa* (London, Bogle l'Ouverture, 1988).

Rose, S./Lewontin, R.C./Kamin, L.J., *Not in Our Genes: Biology, Ideology and Human Nature* (London, Penguin, 1984).

Rose, Stephen, *Lifelines* (London, Penguin, 1997).

Rosen, Allen D., *Kant's Theory of Justice* (Ithaca, New York, Cornell University Press, 1993).

Rostow, W.W., *The Stages of Economic Growth: A Non-Communist Manifesto* (London, Cambridge University Press, 1971).

Rousseau, Jean Jacques, *A Discourse on Inequality* (London, Penguin, 1984).

Rousseau, Jean Jacques, *The Social Contract* (Penguin, London, 1968).

Ruse, Michael (ed), *Sociobiology: Sense or Nonsense* (Boston, D. Reidel, 1979).

Ruse, Michael (ed), *The Philosophy of Biology* (Amherst, New York, Prometheus Books, 1998).

Rustin, Michael, *The Good Society and the Inner World* (London, Verso, 1991).

Sagan, Eli, *At the Dawn of Tyranny* (London, Faber, 1986).

Sagan, Eli, *Cannibalism: Human Aggression and Cultural Form* (New York, Harper & Row, 1974).

Sagan, Eli, *Freud, Women and Morality* (New York, Basic Books, 1988).

Sagan, Eli, *The Honey and the Hemlock: Democracy and Paranoia in Ancient Athens and Modern America* (Princeton, New Jersey, Princeton University Pess, 1991).

Sahlins, Marshall, *Culture and Practical Reason* (Chicago, University of Chicago Press, 1976).

Sale, Kirkpatrick, *Human Scale* (London, Secker & Warburg, 1980).

Sanderson, Michael, *Education and Economic Decline in Britain, 1870 to the 1990s* (Cambridge, Cambridge Univerisity Press, 1999).

Saul, John Ralston, *The Unconscious Civilization* (London, Penguin, 1997).

Saunders, Peter, *Capitalism: A Social Audit* (Buckingham, Open Univeristy Press, 1995).

Schneiderman, Leo, *The Psychology of Social Change* (New York, Human Sciences Press, 1988).

Schumacher, E.F., *A Guide for the Perplexed* (London, Abacus, 1997).

Schumacher, E.F., *Small is Beautiful* (London, Blond & Briggs, 1972).

Schwartz, Barry, *The Battle for Human Nature* (New York, Norton, 1986).

Scitovsky, Tibor, *The Joyless Economy: The Psychology of Human Satisfaction* (New York, Oxford University Press, 1976).

Scruton, Roger, *Kant* (Oxford, Oxford University Press, 1982).

Seabrook, Jeremy, *Children of Other Worlds: Exploitation in the Global Market* (London, Pluto, 2001).

Seabrook, Jeremy, *The Race for Riches* (London, Green Print, 1990).

Selznick, Philip, *The Moral Commonwealth* (Berkeley, University of California Press, 1994).

Sen, Amartya, *Development as Freedom* (New York, Oxford University Press, 2001).

Sen, Amartya, *On Ethics and Economics* (Oxford, Blackwell, 1987).

Sennett, Richard, *The Corrosion of Character* (New York, W.W. Norton, 1998).
Singer, Peter, *A Darwininan Left* (London, Weidenfeld & Nicolson, 1999).
Singer, Peter, *How Are We to Live? Ethics in an Age of Self-Interest* (Oxford, Oxford University Press, 1997).
Singer, Peter, *Practical Ethics* (Cambridge, Cambridge University Press, 1993).
Singer, Peter, *The Expanding Circle* (New York, Farrar, Strauss & Giroux, 1981).
Smith, Adam, *The Wealth of Nations*, Books I-III (London, Penguin, 1986; first published 1793).
Smith, Adam, *The Wealth of Nation*, Books IV-V (London, Penguin, 1999; first published 1793).
Smith, Anthony D., *Nations and Nationalism in a Global Era* (Cambridge, Polity, 1995).
Spencer, Herbert, *The Man versus the State* (London, Watts, 1940; first published 1884).
Spencer, Herbert, *The Principles of Sociology* (London, Macmillan, 1969; first published 1896).
Sprigge, T.L.S., *The Rational Foundation of Ethics* (London, Routledge, 1988).
Stewart, Michael, *Keynes and After* (Penguin, Harmondsworth, 1967).
Strange, Susan, *Casino Capitalism* (Oxford, Blackwell, 1986).
Strange, Susan, *Mad Money* (Manchester, Manchester University Press, 1998).
Sumner, William Graham, *Social Darwinism: Selected Essays* (Englewood Cliffs, New Jersey, Prentice Hall, 1963).

Tawney, R.H., *Religion and the Rise of Capitalism* (Harmondsworth, Penguin, 1926).
Tawney, R.H., *The Radical Tradition* (Harmondsworth, Penguin, 1964).
Trainer, Ted, *Developed to Death* (London, Green Print, 1989).
Trainer, Ted, *Towards a Sustainable Economy* (Oxford, Jon Carpenter, 1996).
Trigger, Bruce G., *Sociocultural Evolution* (Oxford, Blackwell, 1998).
Turiel, Eliot, *The Development of Social Knowledge* (Cambridge, Cambridge University Press, 1983).

Veblen, Thorstein, *The Theory of the Leisure Class* (London, Penguin, 1994).

Wallerstein, Immanuel, *Capitalist Civilization* (London, Verso, 1995).
Wallerstein, Immanuel, *Historical Capitalism* (London, Verso, 1995).
Warburton, Peter, *Debt and Delusion* (London, Penguin, 1999).
Waters, Malcolm, *Globalization* (London, Routledge, 1995).
Watkins, Kevin, *The Oxfam Poverty Report 1995* (Oxford, Oxfam, 1995).
Weil, Simone, *The Need for Roots* (London, Routledge, 1978).
Wilk, Richard R., *Economies and Cultures* (Boulder, Westview Press, 1990).
Wilson, Edward O., *Consilience: The Unity of Knowledge* (London, Vintage, 1999).
Wilson, Edward O., *On Human Nature* (London, Harvard University Press, 1978).
Wilson, Edward O., *Sociobiology: The New Synthesis* (Cambridge, Massachusetts, Harvard University Press, 1975).
Wilson, Edward O., *The Diversity of Life* (London, Allen Lane, 1993).
Wilson, Edward O./Lumsden Charles J., *Genes, Mind and Culture: The Coevolutionary Process* (Cambridge, Massachusetts, Harvard University Press, 1981).
Wilson, James Q., *The Moral Sense* (New York, Free Press, 1993).
Winfield, Richard Dien, *The Just Economy* (New York, Routledge, 1988).
Wright, Robert, *The Moral Animal* (London, Abacus, 1994).

Young, John, *Economics is for Everyone* (Eastwood, John Young, 2002).

References

1 Science and Humankind

1. Soren Lovtrup, *Darwin: Refutation of a Myth* (Beckenham, Croom Helm, 1987).
2. John Maynard Smith, *Did Darwin Get it Right?* (London, Penguin, 1993), p.180.
3. Hoyle, Fred/Wickramasinghe, Chandra, *Evolution From Space* (London, J.M. Dent & Sons, 1981).
4. John Greene, *Science, Ideology and World View* (London, University of California Press, 1981), p.123.
5. Howard Kaye, *The Social Meaning of Modern Biology* (London, Yale University Press, 1986), p.23.
6. Tim Megarry, *Society in Prehistory* (Basingstoke, Macmillan, 1995), p.39.
7. Mary Midgely, *The Ethical Primate* (London, Routledge, 1994), p.125.
8. Howard Kaye, *op. cit.* p.24.
9. Quoted in: Richard Hofstadter, *Social Darwinism in American Thought* (New York, G. Brazillier, 1959) p.87.
10. Carl Degler, *In Search of Human Nature* (New York, Oxford University Press, 1991), p.12.
11. Charles Darwin, *The Descent of Man*, in: Paul H. Barret (ed), *The Works of Charles Darwin*, Vol 21 (London, William Pickering, 1989; first published 1879), p.204.
12. Carl Degler, *op. cit.* pp.15-16.
13. John Greene, *op. cit.* p.121.
14. Tim Megarry, *op. cit.* p.44.
15. Howard Kaye, *op. cit.* p.55.
16. *Ibid.* p.54.
17. Edward O. Wilson, *On Human Nature* (London, Harvard University Press, 1978), p.16.
18. Quoted in: Kenneth Bock, *Human Nature and History* (New York, Columbia University Press, 1980) p.79.
19. Marvin Harris, *Cultural Materialism* (New York, Random House, 1979), p.125.
20. John Maynard Smith, *op. cit.* p.82.
21. Marvin Harris, *op. cit.* p.134.
22. Georg Breuer, *Sociobiology and the Human Dimension* (New York, Cambridge University Press, 1992), p.223.
23. *Ibid.* pp.252-3
24. Tim Megarry, *op. cit.* p.41.
25. Mayr, Ernst, *One Long Argument* (London, Allen Lane, 1992). p.7.

2 Evolution and Culture

1. Richard Leakey, *The Origin of Humankind* (London, Weidenfeld & Nicolson, 1994), Preface, p.xiv.
2. *Ibid.* p.79.
3. Luigi & Francesco Cavalli-Sforza, *The Great Human Diasporas* (Reading, Massachusetts, Perseus, 1995), p.124.
4. Stanley Ambrose, reported and quoted on BBC Online, 8 September 1998.
5. Quoted in: Tim Megarry, *Society in Prehistory* (Basingstoke, Macmillan, 1995), p.99.

6. Vernon Reynolds, *The Biology of Human Action* (Reading, Freeman, 1986).
7. Eli Sagan, *At the Dawn of Tyranny* (London, Faber, 1986), p.232.
8. *Ibid.*
9. Eli Sagan, *Cannibalism: Human Aggression and Cultural Form* (New York, Harper & Row, 1974), Introduction, p.xx.
10. *Ibid.* pp.140-1
11. Michael Hudson, 'Land Monopolization, Fiscal Crises and Clean Slate "Jubilee" Proclaimations' in: *A Philosophy for a Fair Society* (London, Shepheard-Walwyn, 1994), p.42.
12. *ibid*, p.44.
13. Erich Fromm, *The Anatomy of Human Destructiveness* (New York, Henry Holt & Co, 1992), p.186.
14. Eli Sagan, *Cannibalism*, pp.106-10.
15. Marvin Harris, *Cultural Materialism* (New York, Random House, 1979).
16. *Ibid.* p.62.
17. *Ibid.* p.105.
18. *Ibid.* p.106.
19. Eli Sagan, *Cannibalism*, Introduction, p.xvi.

3 Economics and Morals

1. Frances Moore Lappe/Joseph Collins, *World Hunger: Twelve Myths* (London, Earthscan, 1998).
2. World Bank Devopment Indicators 2003 (Washington DC, World Bank, 2003).
3. Eric Hobsbawm, *Industry and Empire* (London, Penguin, 1999) p.35.
4. Martin Daunton, *Progress and Poverty: An Economic and Social History of Britain, 1700-1850* (Oxford, Oxford University Press, 1995), p.87.
5. William Keegan, *The Spectre of Capitalism* (London, Vintage, 1993).
6. Ted Trainer, *Developed to Death* (London, Green Print, 1989), p.14.
7. *Ibid.* p.14.
8. *The Guardian Weekly*, 29 August 2002.
9. *Ibid.* 2 May 2002.
10. *The Observer*, 18 January 2004.
11. *The Guardian*, 2 December 2003.
12. *Ibid.* 12 August 2002.
13. BBC News Online, 18 October 1999.
14. *The Guardian Weekly*, 28 August 2002.
15. BBC News Online, 18 October 1999.
16. *The Guardian Weekly*, 7 March 2002.
17. *Ibid.*
18. *Ibid.* 29 August 2002.
19. *Ibid.*
20. Quoted in: Rudolf Bahro, *Avoiding Social and Economic Disaster* (Bath, Gateway Books, 1994), p.20.

4 The State of the World

1. United Nations Fund for Population Development, www.unfpa.org.
2. Ernest Gellner, *Nationalism* (London, Weidenfeld & Nicolson, 1997), p.17.
3. *Human Development Report 2003* (NewYork, UNDP, 2003).
4. *New Internationalist*, June 2002.
5. *The Guardian Weekly*, 20 September 1998.
6. *Ibid.* 17 May 1998.

7. *World Development Report 2003* (Washington DC, World Bank, 2003).
8. *The Guardian Weekly*, 31 January 2002.
9. *Ibid.* 22 August 2002.
10. *Ibid.*
11. *Ibid.*
12. *Ibid.* 6 June 2002.
13. *Ibid.* 20 September 1998.
14. *Ibid.* 22 August 2002.
15. *Ibid.* 11 July 2002.
16. *Human Development Report 1995* (New York, UNDP, 1995).
17. *The Guardian Weekly*, 3 September 1995.
18. *Ibid.* 9 May 2002.
19. *Ibid.* 6 December 2001.
20. *Ibid.* 11 July 2002.
21. *Ibid.* 13 December 2001.
22. *Ibid.* 6 June 2002.
23. *Ibid.* 11 July 2002.
24. *The Economist*, 17 April 2004.
25. *Ibid.*
26. *The Guardian Weekly*, 11 July 2002.
27. World Food Programme, www.wfp.org.
28. *The Guardian Weekly,* 13 June 2002.
29. *New Internationalist*, May 1995.
30. *Ibid.*
31. *Ibid.*
32. *The Guardian Weekly*, 9 August 1999.
33. *New Internationalist,* May 1995.
34. United States National Institute of Diabetes & Digestive & Kidney Diseases, www.niddk.nih.gov.
35. *The Guardian Weekly*, 13 June 1998.
36. *Ibid.* 20 August 1995.
37. *Ibid.* 11 Oct 1998.
38. *Ibid.* 13 January 1999.
39. *Ibid.*
40. *Ibid.* 22 August 2002.
41. *Ibid.* 19 May 1999.
42. *Human Development Report 2003* (New York, UNDP, 2003).
43. *The Guardian Weekly*, 28 March 1999.
44. *Ibid.* 9 December 1999.
45. *Human Development Report 1995* (New York, UNDP, 1995).
46. *The Guardian Weekly*, 17 May 1998.
47. *New Internationalist*, March 1999.
48. *The Guardian Weekly*, 27 February 2002.
49. *Ibid.* 21 October 1999.
50. *New Internationalist*, May 1999.
51. *The Guardian Weekly,* 20 May 1998.
52. David Moberg, *Silencing Joseph Stiglitz,* Global Policy Forum (www.globalpolicy. org), 2 May 2002.
53. *The Guardian Weekly*, 16 July 1995.
54. *Ibid.* 17 December 1995.
55. Kevin Watkins, *Oxfam Poverty Report 1995* (Oxford, Oxfam, 1995).
56. John Ralston Saul, *The Unconscious Civilization* (London, Penguin, 1997).
57. Paul Kennedy, *Preparing for the Twenty-First Century* (New York, Vintage, 1994).
58. *New Internationalist*, January 1995.
59. *Ibid.*

60. *The Guardian Weekly*, 25 January 1998.
61. Michel Chossudovsky, *The Globalization of Poverty* (London, Zed Books, 1997).
62. *The Guardian*, 22 September 2003.
63. BBC News Online, 16 December 2002.
64. *Ibid.*
65. *The Guardian*, 22 August 2000.
66. *Ibid.* 9 April 2002.
67. *New Internationalist*, June 2002.
68. *The Guardian,* 9 April 2003.
69. *The Guardian Weekly*, 8 July 1999.
70. *The Guardian*, 22 August 2000.
71. *The Guardian Weekly*, 18 July 2002.
72. *Ibid.*
73. *Ibid.*
74. *Ibid.* 17 December 1995.
75. *Ibid.* 3 January 2002.
76. *Ibid.* 9 May 2002.
77. *Ibid.* 3 September 1995.
78. *Ibid.* 18 January 1998.
79. *Ibid.* 22 February 1998.
80. Organisation for Economic Cooperation and Development, www.oecd.org.
81. Richard Sennett, *The Corrosion of Character* (New York, W.W. Norton, 1998), p.82.
82. www.helpusa.org.
83. *The Guardian Weekly,* 26 February 1995.
84. *Human Development Report 2003* (New York, UNDP, 2003).
85. *The Guardian Weekly*, 26 July 1998.
86. *The Guardian,* 10 February 1995.
87. *The Guardian Weekly*, 6 October 1999.
88. *Ibid.* 21 March 1999.
89. *Ibid.* 12 April 1998.
90. Richard Sennett, *The Corrosion of Character* (New York, W.W. Norton, 1998), p.54.
91. *Statistical Abstract of the United States* (United States Department of Commerce), various years.
92. *Ibid.*
93. *The Guardian Weekly*, 21 July 2000.
94. *Statistical Abstract of the United States* (United States Department of Commerce), various years.
95. *The Guardian Weekly*, 21 June 1998.
96. *Ibid.* 21 June 1998.

5 A Universal Ethic

1. Richard Dien Winfield, *The Just Economy* (New York, Routledge, 1998).
2. J.K. Galbraith, *A History of Economics* (London, Hamilton, 1987), p.18.
3. Reinhold Niebuhr, *Moral Man and Immoral Society* (New York, Touchstone, 1995; first published 1932), p.27.
4. Allen D. Rosen, *Kant's Theory of Justice* (Ithaca, Cornell University Press, 1993), pp.173-208.
5. *Ibid.* p.206.
6. Jeremy Bentham, *An Introduction to the Principles of Morals and Legislation* (London, Athlone, 1970; first published 1789).
7. Richard Bronk, *Progress and the Invisible Hand* (London, Little Brown, 1998), p.100.
8. Reinhold Niebuhr, *op. cit.* pp.25-7.
9. Peter Singer, *The Expanding Circle* (New York, Farrar, Strauss & Giroux, 1981).

10. Gregory Baum, *Karl Polanyi on Ethics and Economics* (Montreal, McGill-Queens University Press, 1996), p.42.
11. Reinhold Niebuhr, *op. cit.* Preface to 1960 edition.
12. *Ibid.* Introduction, p.xxiv.

6 Perception and Reality

1. Bernie Devlin/Stpehen E. Feinberg/Daniel P. Resnick/Kathryn Roeder (eds), *Intelligence, Genes and Success: Scientists Respond to the Bell Curve* (New York, Springer, 1977).
2. *Ibid.* p.162.
3. Richard Jenkins, *Rethinking Ethnicity* (London, Sage, 1997), pp.9-10.
4. *Ibid.* p.10.
5. Ernest Gellner, *Nationalism* (London, Weidenfeld & Nicolson, 1997).
6. Adrian Hastings, *The Construction of Nationhood* (Cambridge, Cambridge University Press, 1997), p.169.
7. Steve Jones, *In the Blood* (London, Flamingo, 1997).
8. Christopher Lasch, *The True and Only Heaven* (New York, W.W. Norton, 1991), p.35.

7 Psyche and Society

1. Jeremy Holmes, *John Bowlby and Attachment Theory* (London, Routledge, 1993), p.18.
2. *Ibid.* p.35.
3. *Ibid.* p.38.
4. *Ibid.* p.42.
5. *Ibid.* p.70.
6. *Ibid.* p.88.
7. *Ibid.* p.174.
8. *Ibid.* p.174.
9. *Ibid.* p.200.
10. *Ibid.* p.206.
11. Ian Robertson, *Mind Sculpture* (London, Bantam, 1999), p.271.
12. *Ibid.* p.173.
13. *Ibid.* p.202.
14. *Ibid.* p.192.
15. *Ibid.* p.264.
16. *Ibid.* p.270.
17. *Ibid.* p.172.
18. *Ibid.* p.223.
19. Richard Sennett, *The Corrosion of Character* (New York, W.W. Norton, 1998), p.89.
20. *Ibid.* p.9.
21. *Ibid.* p.26.
22. *Ibid.* p.31.
23. *Ibid.* p.118.
24. Max Hirsch, *Democracy versus Socialism* (New York, Robert Schalkenbach Foundation, 1966; first published 1901), p.168.
25. Erich Fromm, *The Art of Loving* (London, George Allen & Unwin, 1957), p.44.
26. *Ibid.* p.44.
27. *Ibid.* p.45.
28. *Ibid.* p.46.
29. *Ibid.* p.48.
30. *Ibid.* p.162.
31. Christian Bay, 'Political and Apolitical Students' in: *The Journal of Social Issues*, 1967, Vol 23, p.76.

32. Robert McKim/Jeff McMahan (eds), *The Morality of Nationalism* (New York, Oxford University Press, 1997), p.79.
33. *Ibid.* p.83.
34. *Ibid.* p.178.
35. Peter Russell/Ervin Lazslo/Stanislav Grof, *The Consciousness Revolution* (Shaftesbury, Element Books, 1999).
36. *Ibid.* p.130.
37. John Ralston Saul, *The Unconscious Civilization* (London, Penguin, 1997), p.51.
38. *Ibid.* p.56.
39. Eli Sagan, *At the Dawn of Tyranny* (London, Faber, 1986) p.376.

8 Moral Development

1. Jean Piaget, *Judgement and Reason in the Child* (London, Routledge, 1969; first published 1928).
2. *Ibid.*
3. Daniel Lapsley, *Moral Psychology* (Boulder, Westview Press, 1996).
4. *Ibid.* p.91.
5. *Ibid.* p.80.
6. Eli Sagan, *Freud, Women and Morality* (New York, Basic Books, 1998), p.160.
7. *Ibid.* p.163.
8. *Ibid.* p.164.
9. *Ibid.* p.167
10. *Ibid.* p.168.
11. Christian Bay, 'Political and Apolitical Students' in: *The Journal of Social Issues*, 1967, Vol 23, p.76.
12. Richard Jenkins, *Rethinking Ethnicity* (London, Sage, 1997), p.64.
13. Kwame Anthony Appiah, 'Racisms' in: Goldberg, David (ed), *Anatomy of Racism* (Minneapolis, University of Minnesota Press, 1990).
14. Eli Sagan, *Freud, Women and Morality* (New York, Basic Books, 1998), p.206.
15. *Ibid.* p.207.
16. Gregory Baum, *Karl Polanyi on Ethics and Economics* (Montreal, McGill-Queens University Press, 1996), p.26.
17. Reinhold Niebuhr, *Moral Man and Immoral Society* (New York, Touchstone, 1995; first published 1932), p.28.

9 A True Economics

1. *The Guardian,* 16 February 2004.
2. See www.paecon.net – The Post Austistic Economics Review.
3. Adam Smith, *The Wealth of Nations*, Book IV (London, Penguin, 1999; first published 1793), Introduction.
4. *Ibid.* Chapter 1.
5. Richard Bronk, *Progress and the Invisible Hand* (London, Little Brown, 1998), p.98.
6. *Ibid.* p.90.
7. *Ibid.* p.95
8. David Ricardo, *Principles of Political Economy and Taxation* (Harmondsworth, Penguin, 1971), p.49
9. *Ibid.*
10. Henry George, *Progress and Poverty* (New York, Robert Schalkenbach Foundation, 1979; first published 1879), p.6.
11. *Land and Property Study: Assessing the Change in Land and Property Values Attributable to the Jubilee Line Extension* (London, Jones Lang LaSalle, 2004).

12. Herman Daly, 'Sustainable Development: Definitions, Principles, Policies', speech to World Bank, 30 April 2002 (www.earthrights.net/docs/daly.html).
13. *The Guardian Weekly,* 5 September 2002.
14. Kevin Watkins, 'Farm Fallacies that Hurt the Poor' in: *Development Outreach,* July 2003 (www1.worldbank.org).
15. *The Guardian,* 5 June 2002.
16. *The Guardian Weekly,* 11 April 2002.
17. *Ibid.* 5 September 2002.
18. *The Guardian,* 2 March 2004.
19. *Ibid.*

10 Freedom and Justice

1. Henry George, *Progress and Poverty* (New York, Robert Schalkenbach Foundation, 1979; first published 1879), p.328.
2. *Ibid.* p.413.
3. Adam Smith, *The Wealth of Nations,* Book V (London, Penguin, 1999), Chapter 2.
4. Henry George, *op. cit.* p.421.
5. Karl Polanyi, *The Great Transformation* (Boston, Beacon Press, 1957).
6. Mason Gaffney, *The Corruption of Economics* (London, Shepheard-Walwyn, 1994), p.22.
7. John Maynard Keynes, *The General Theory of Employment, Interest and Money* (London, Macmillan, 1936), Preface.
8. Herman Daly, 'Sustainable Development: Definitions, Principles, Policies', speech to World Bank, 30 April 2002 (www.earthrights.net/docs/daly.html).
9. *Ibid.*
10. Jurgen Backhaus, 'The Quest for Ecological Tax Reform: A Schumpeterian Approach to Public Finance', paper prepared for presentation at the Fifth Conference of the International J.A. Schumpeter Society, August 1994.
11. Henry George, 'The Study of Political Economy', a lecture delivered before the students of the University of California, March 9, 1877, and published in: *The Popular Science Monthly,* March 1880.
12. Henry George, *op. cit.* p.456.

11 The Politics of Progress

1. Leon MacLaren, 'The Function of Economics' (transcript of lecture, 1951).
2. Gergen, K./Ullman, M. in: Renshon, Stanley (ed), *A Handbook of Political Socialization* (New York, Free Press, 1977).
3. *The Financial Times,* 22 May 1995.
4. *The Guardian Weekly,* 11 October 2001.
5. *The Guardian,* 27 August 2002.
6. Joseph Milne, private correspondence.
7. The Intergovernmental Panel on Climate Change (IPCC), *Special Report on Aviation and the Global Atmosphere* (1999).
8. *The Observer,* 12 May 2002.
9. Ian Robertson, *Mind Sculpture* (London, Bantam, 1999), p.280.

Index

abortion 107, 184
adultery 117, 184
Africa
    cradle of humankind 23-5
    misconceptions about tribes 30
    causes of differential development 46-7
    effects of slave trade 61, 227
    increasing mortality rates 78
    reduction in household incomes 81-2
    number of doctors 82
    impact of AIDS 83
    nature of food shortages 85
    falling literacy rates 87
    impact of natural disasters 98-9
    child soldiers 100
    effect of cold war 131
    pace of urban cultural change 153
agrarian states 34
agricultural surplus
    impact of discovery 67
agriculture
    emergence of 34-6
    conditions for expansion of 47
    technological versus sustainable forms
        85
    economics of agricultural society
        209-15
    and land ownership 210, 247
AIDS 80-2
    impact on children 83
    economic effects 83
    successes in combating 84
    inequitable access to drugs 227
air travel
    need for rationing 278
    projected growth in 279
    as a cause of global warming 279
alcohol abuse
    effect on unborn infant 138
alcoholism
    in Russia 96
Alliance Capital Management 231
Ambrose, Stanley 28
American revolution 4
ancient Greece
    acceptance of slavery 113
    contemporary relevance of Greek
        thought 107
    separation of ethics and economics 107

anthropology 31-2
    use in defence of racist attitudes 45
anti-capitalist movement 239
Appiah, Kwame Anthony 197
Aquinas, Thomas 110
archaeology 29, 31
archaic civilizations 36-7
Aristophanes 108
Aristotle 106-7, 110
Armenian genocide 144
arms race 131
Asian Tiger economies 92-4
Atkinson, Dan 104-5
attachment theory 158
    societal implications of 158
Augustine, Saint 110, 184
Auschwitz 195
australopithecines 23
Aztecs 40

Backhaus, Jurgen 255
Balkans 41, 99, 144
Bankruptcy Act (1861) 62
Barthes, Roland 139
basic needs
    definition of 55
    universality of 55
    global capacity for provision of 56, 79
    connection with economic growth 70,
        73
    threat from ecological breakdown 71
    ethics and 119, 125
    human rights and 121
    capitalism and 125
    competition and 171-2
    cooperation in procurement of 211-12
    case for social provision of 244-5
Baum, Gregory 198
Bay, Christian 177-8, 195
Behavioural Genetics 19-20
Bentham, Jeremy 113, 115
biological humanists 14
biological psychology 162
biology 3
    and evolutionary theory 5-8
    and human needs 45
    and individual development 138
Blair, Tony 265-6
Boethius 110

Botswana
    decimation of population 80
    scale of AIDS epidemic 83
Bowlby, John 156-9
brain development
    education and 160-1
    evolution and 23-4
    infant nurturing and 159
    irreparable failure in 159
    pre-natal environment and 138
    Piaget's theories of 185
Brazil 91, 134, 145
Bretton Woods Conference (1944) 63
Breuer, Georg 19, 20
Brezhnev, Leonid 97
Britain – *see* Great Britain
Bronk, Richard 114, 207
Bronowski, Jacob 14
brownfield development 224-5
Brown, Gordon 204
Buddhism 108, 115
Bush, George Snr. 104
Bush, George W. 72, 104
Byzantium 45

Canada 28
cannibalism
    causes of 39-41
    modern-day reaction to 44
capital
    accumulation of 221
    applied sustainably 85
    in ancient civilizations 37, 42
    in classical economic theory 215-20
    as enhancer of labour efficiency 221
    as factor of production 209-12
    flows across borders 69, 93-4, 228
    reward to owner of 209
    and technology 75, 276-7
capitalism
    as a determining context 265
    enlightened form 64
    failure to address poverty 70-1
    foundations in economic theory
        205-7
    and growth 68-70
    positive contribution of 74-6
    relation with culture 125-6
    and the third way 204
    tycoon model of 96
    impact on work patterns 170-1
carbon emissions 71-4, 278
Caribbean 83
cash crops 43
categorical imperative 111-12
Cavalli-Sforza, Luigi Luca 27
centralized states
    emergence of 36

charity
    example of John Rockefeller 12
    role in ensuring social stability 76, 248
Chicago School 66
child labour 100-1
children
    and competition 173-4
    and education 164-8
    importance of attachment 156-8
    inherited intelligence in 136
    irreparable failure in brain development
        159-60
    orphaned through AIDS 83
    poverty in rich nations 103
    Piaget's theory on development 185-6
    preventable deaths of 80
    education in Third World 86
    victims of war 99-100
child soldiers 100
China 36, 134, 144
    demise of great civilization 47-8
    AIDS predictions for 83
    Unemployment 231
Chossudovsky, Michel 95
Christianity
    and symbolic sacrifice 40
    influence on ethics 109-10
Churchill, Winston 251
civil rights, 118, 282
classical economics 208-11
    eclipsing by neo-classical theory 206
    and free trade 228
clean-slate proclamations 42, 90
Clinton, Bill 104
cognitive incapacity
    in respect of economics 268
    in respect of racism 197
cold war 88, 145
collective bargaining 220, 247
collective unconscious 181
colonial expansion 6
Columbus, Christopher 45
commodification
    of land 57, 262
    of labour 262
common descent, theory of 8-9
communism 54, 96-7
    perceived threat from 65, 131
communitarianism 126-7
comparative advantage, theory of 228
competition
    in children 173-4
    in early societies 33, 35
    economic 150-1, 170-2, 217-18
    in evolutionary theory 10-11
    non-economic 172
complex society 37-40, 45
Confucius 108, 119

conscience 189, 193-4
  universalized social form 200
consciousness
  economic 129-30
  non-ordinary states of 181
  need for revolution in 182-3
  as unique to humankind 21, 180
consensus
  on evolutionary theory 13
  post-war economic 64-7
consumer culture
  and globalization 152, 273
  need to moderate 271-2
consumer democracy 274
Crete 36
Crick, Francis 14
cultural change 15, 18
  relation to economic advance 44, 125-7,
    152-3
  negative impact of 39
cultural diversity 151-3, 280
  economic implications 120
  misplaced belief in value of 178
cultural evolution 30-2
  distinguished from biological form 14-17
  and cannibalism 39-41
  reasons for differential rates 45-8
  and economics 48-51
cultural materialism 45, 46
cultural traditions 97, 100, 152
culture
  and ethnicity 140
  and globalization 273
  and myth 150-1
Cuomo, Mario 104
customs 273, 281
  valuable versus negative 152

Daly, Herman 254-5
Darwin, Charles 3
  and common descent 8, 31
  and eugenics movement 12, 142
  theory of natural selection 5-8
  and social Darwinism 9-11
  survival of the fittest 20-1
Darwin, Erasmus 4
Declaration of Independence 11
Degler, Carl 12
democracy 266
  and consensus 241
  counter to economic failings 76, 248
  failures in contemporary form 276-8
  paramount value of 267-8
Denmark 73, 239
deregulation 249
determining context of global economy
    265-6
development goals 204

discrimination 132-3, 149, 153
division of labour
  and economic advance 208
  emergence of 36, 57
  dependence on trust 211
DNA 25-6, 162
  impact of discovery of 14
Dobzhansky, Theodisius 13
dollar standard 64
double movement, Polanyi's theory of 248
drug abuse 138

Earth Summit, Rio (1994) 72
economic development
  historical nature of 42-3, 57-8
  uniformity in modern times 152
  classical theory underlying 209-19
economic growth 68
  beneficiaries of 70
  conditions for 69
  constraints upon 70
  and the environment 93, 253-4
  and improved social justice 70
economic insecurity 49, 268
economic justice – *see* social justice
economic migration 230-1
economic polarization 42-3, 87, 103
economics
  moral corruption of 251
  disembedding from culture 125
  separation from ethics 107-8
  engagement by ordinary people 262
  and politics/democracy 263-4
economic surplus 35
  and emergence of politics 35-6
  effects of discovery of 36, 48-51, 57
economies of scale 278
education
  and brain development 160-1
  and values of competitiveness 164
  and democratic participation 267
  equitable means of funding 243-4
  and moral development 190
  claims for rising standards 269-70
  objectives and outcomes of 163-7
effective demand 68, 70, 85, 91, 271
egoist movement 111
Egypt 36, 65, 209
Einstein, Albert 268, 275
Elliott, Larry 104-5
El Niño 98
embeddedness
  economic concept of 35, 44
emotional intelligence 160
endangered species 281
energy
  dependence on oil 71
  renewable options 73, 277

energy—*contd*
  means to sustainable use of 155
enlightened capitalism 64, 66
Enlightenment, the
  causes and principles 3-4
  and education 164
  ethics and economics 67, 107, 232-3
  and rationality 127
  reaction in romanticism 142
environment
  and economic growth 93, 253-4
  and economic security 253
  protective economic mechanism for
    254-6
  severity of threat to 71-4
  protective economic mechanism for
    254-6
  varying impact of breakdown in 98
epigenetics 162
equal consideration of interests 119, 121-2
essential goodness, notion of 151
ethics
  and enlightenment thought 67, 107, 113,
    232-3
  exclusion of economics 107-8
  history of 108-13
ethnicity 139-40
  and Enlightenment thought 127
  and economic exclusion 132
  and intelligence 137-8
  and socialization 196-7
eugenics 12-15
Euripides 108
European Union 72, 84, 102, 272
evolution
  biological theory of 5
  biological versus cultural 3, 6-8, 14-20
  human 23-5
  social and cultural 29-34, 43-4, 259
evolutionary biology 5-6
evolutionary psychology 18
evolutionary synthesis 13
export credit guarantees 90

factors of production 209
fair trade 230
Faraday, Michael 276
fear of change 268-70
feminist movement 131
fertility
  rates in poor countries 79
  and population growth 80-1
  replacement rate of 254
feudalism 47, 58-9
food
  as a basic need 55
  in classical economics 210-12
  and consumer culture 272-3

food—*contd*
  provision in early societies 32-3
  global production of 57
  and population growth 80-1
  causes of shortage 84-5
forager societies 31-6
forced marriages 153
fossil fuels 74, 255, 277
Fowler, James 176
France 3, 47, 144, 179, 229
fratricide 16
free market
  and economic growth 69
  as an economic mechanism 206-8
  and investment opportunities 226-7
  as a political ideology 70-1
  role in allocating wealth 211-12
free trade 228-9
Freud, Sigmund 155-6, 175, 185
Friedman, Milton 66, 94
Fromm, Erich 43, 174-6
full employment 64, 67

Gaffney, Mason 251
Galbraith, John Kenneth 107, 251
Galton, Francis 12
Gandhi, Mohandas 51, 195, 198
Gellner, Ernest 80, 143-5
Genes 3, 7-8, 14-21, 162
  and intelligence 136-8
genetic inheritance 7, 16, 51
  as component of heritability 136
genetic variation 7, 13, 27
Genghis Khan 52
genital mutilation 153
George, Henry 219-22, 232
  and tax on rent 238-40
  suppression of ideas 251
  and efficient resource use 254-5
  and morality 256
  on government 260
Gergen, Kenneth 264-5
Germany 13, 144, 179
Ghana 192
Gilligan, Carol 191-2, 200
Gleick, Peter 86
globalization 125, 128, 281
  and traditional cultures 152-3
  and moral relativism 121
  objectives and outcomes of 272-3
  opportunities provided by 203
global warming 71-2
  and natural disasters 98-9
  and carbon emissions 279-80
golden rule 119, 147, 256
Goodall, Jane 30
Gorbachev, Mikhail 96
Gray, John 97

Great Britain
    causes of industrial revolution 59-61
    child poverty 103
    education system 166-7
    gap between rich and poor 102
    homelessness 102
    malnutrition 103
    social morality under feudalism in 124-5
great society programme 65
Great Transformation, The 124, 262
Greene, John 10, 13
greenfield developments 224
Grof, Stanislav 180-2
Grotius, Hugo 114-15
gypsies 146

Hammurabi 108
Hapsburg Empire 145
Harris, Marvin 16, 18, 45, 47
Hastings, Adrian 146
health care services 55
    viable means of funding 242-4
Hegel, Georg 145
Herder, Johannes 142, 180
heritability
    of acquired characteristics 7
    genetic versus environmental 136
Herrnstein, Richard 135-6, 138
Hinduism 108, 115
Hiroshima 195
Hirsch, Max 171-2
historical materialism 123
Hitler, Adolf 13, 51, 53, 63, 179, 187
Hobbes, Thomas 4, 110-11
Hobsbawm, Eric 60
Holmes, Jeremy 156, 158
holocaust, the 14, 63, 65, 75, 102, 187
homelessness 77, 98, 102
Homer 108
homo erectus 23-5
homo habilis 23
homo sapiens 23-7
Hong Kong 92
horiculturalist societies 35-8
housing
    as a basic need 55-6
    in poor countries 81
    causes of rising house prices 223-4
    reform of housing market 274
Hoyle, Fred 9
Hudson, Michael 42-3, 46
humanism 14, 110, 176
human nature
    as a constraint on progress 123
    flexibility as defining characteristic 51
    and sociobiology 15
human rights 114, 120-2
human sacrifice 39, 40-1, 44

human scale 278
human species 21-3, 26, 30
Hume, David 111
hunter-gatherer society 15, 29
Hutcheson, Francis 111
Huxley, Julian 13-14
hydraulic states 46-8

ideology 93, 123-4, 278
IMF 89, 90-1, 94, 95, 168, 267
incentive 258-60
inclusive fitness 16
India
    threat from AIDS 83-4
    early economic success 48
individual freedom 6
    legitimate constraints upon 112-13, 123, 234
    paramount value in western culture 233
    value in 235, 253
    reconciled with social justice 219, 233-6, 249
    to amass great wealth 234, 257
individualism 234
individuation 38-9
Indonesia 88, 99, 145
industrial revolution 58-62
    impact on ethics 113-14
    and distribution of wealth 247-8, 263
inequality 103
    between nations 227-8
    emergence of 135-7
    explanation in economics 210-16
infanticide 16
infant mortality 182
inflation 49, 64-7, 105
information revolution 277
instrumental needs 55
intelligence
    causes of variation in 135-8, 161
    and brain development 159-60
    and economic understanding 268
invisible hand (of the market) 114, 207, 250, 257
IQ 135-8, 190
isolated speciation 8
Italy 101, 110, 144

Jainism 108
Japan 63, 144
Jefferson, Thomas 11
Jenkins, Richard 139, 196-7
Jews 146, 187
Johnson, Lyndon 65
Jones, Steve 146
Jung, Carl 181-2
justice – *see* social justice
just war
    concept of 141

Kant, Immanuel 111-13, 115, 123, 189
Kaye, Howard 10, 14
Keegan, William 64
Kennedy, Paul 93
Keynesian economics 64-6, 248-9, 266
Keynes, John Maynard 65, 254
King, Martin Luther 195
Kohlberg, Lawrence 187-93, 196-7, 199, 246
Kosovo 146
Kyoto protocol 72, 279

labour
    as factor or production 209
    in competition with capital 217
    in classical economic theory 221-4
    conditions for equitable reward of 211-12
    subordination in early societies 58
    of women and children 100
laissez-faire 5-6, 9, 11, 107
Lamarck, Jean-Baptiste 4-5, 7-8, 14
land
    tenure in antiquity 33
    emergence of rights over 34-7
    as factor of production 209
    cause of maldistribution of 220
    limited in extent by nature 210-20
    separation of people from 41-3, 61
    and law of rent 214-15
    impact of variable quality 215
land enclosure 61, 209, 220-21
landowner 217-18, 236-9
    unearned income of 220-1
land tax 238, 268
land values 223
Lapsley, Daniel 187
Lasch, Christopher 149
Laszlo, Ervin 180, 182
law of rent 210, 214-15, 219, 221-3, 262-4
Leakey, Richard 24, 26
Leibniz, Gottfried 4
less-developed countries – *see* Third
    World
liberal democracy 200
life expectancy x
    in early societies 29
    falling in poor countries 80, 83
    in Russia 96
limited liability 62
Litchenberg, Judith 180
Locke, John 185
London
    comparative murder rate 104
    effect of law or rent on 224-5
love
    as a universal need 45, 177
    forms of 174-6
    impact of absence 194-5
Lovtrup, Soren 7

MacLaren, Leon 262
macromutations 8
malnutrition 56, 78, 103, 122
Malthus, Thomas 11, 219, 221
    on population growth 79-81
Mandela, Nelson 52, 83, 90, 198
Mandeville, Bernard 111
market mechanism 59, 248-9
    in classical economic theory 207-8
    in operation 217
Marshall Plan 63, 71
Marx, Karl 123, 129, 149
Maynard Smith, John 8, 17
Mayr, Ernst 13, 21
Meacher, Michael 72
meat eating
    effect on human evolution 23
Megarry, Tim 10, 13, 21
mercantile system 208
merchant capitalism 62
Mesopotamia 36, 42, 108
Mexico 40, 92, 46
Midgely, Mary 10
migrant labour 230-1
migration
    and human evolution 23-5, 134, 139
    economic form in contemporary
        world 230
Milne, Joseph 276
Milosevic, Slobodan 52
mitochondrial eve theory 25
Monbiot, George 71-2, 85, 229, 271
monetarism 66
Montesquieu 3, 4
moral aspirations 116, 127-8, 130, 282-3
    out of synch with reality 202
    universal compatibility of 187
moral development 199-200
    Kohlberg's stage theory of 188-93
    as condition for economic cognition
        268
moral freedom 118
moral generalization 48, 198
moral law 109-11, 117-19, 122
moral learning 118, 185
Moral Man and Immoral Society 109, 127
moral reasoning 190-4, 196-7, 200
moral relativism 120, 121, 127
moral selectivism 10
moral stages 188-93
More, Thomas 116, 282
mortality rates 78, 80, 88
Mother Theresa 52
motivation
    to economic understanding 267-8
    in an equitable society 258-60
    to moral action 111
    of neo-classical economists 206

Mozambique
    dubious benefits of economic growth
      69
    reduction in economic security 87
Mozart, Wolfgang Amadeus 148, 198
multi-party democracy – *see* democracy
multi-regional hypothesis 24-5
Murray, Charles 135-6, 138
myth
    of common ancestry 140
    historical function of 150
    contemporary forms 151-2

Napoleonic Wars 145
National Academy of Science 72
nationalism 177, 180
nationhood 142-6
nation state
    as condition for democracy 267
    relation to ethnicity 146
    emergence as political unit 142-4
native Americans 46
natural disasters 97-9
naturalistic fallacy 190
natural justice 256
natural laws 256-7
natural resources
    and basic needs provision 55-6
    destruction by humans 74
    and land ownership 220-1
    international access to 228
    sustainable use of 254-6
natural selection
    theory explained 7-8
    and social behaviour 15-16
    and human evolution 26
Nazis 13
Neanderthal 26
needs economy 49-50, 55-6, 278
neo-classical economics
    as outshoot of classical form 206
    and the environment 254
    campaign against Henry George 251
    ignorance of law of rent 210
    compared with socialist theory 249-50
neurosis 155-6, 158, 179, 195
New Deal, Roosevelt's 63
New Right 66, 193
New Zealand 230
Niebuhr, Reinhold 107, 108, 116, 127, 201
Nietzsche, Friedrich 145
Nightingale, Florence 52
Nixon, Richard 65
non-essentials
    consumption of 270-1, 279
nurturing
    and intelligence 138
    importance for attachment 158

nurturing–*contd*
    and brain development 159
    and educational achievement 176-8
    social implications of failures in 179
nutrition 32, 81-2, 138, 184

odious debts 90
oil crisis 88
oil reserves 71, 255
On the Origin of Species 3, 10
OPEC 65
open source software 258
oppression of homosexuals 131
optimism 282
    and the Enlightenment 3
original sin 184
Ottoman Empire 145
out of Africa hypothesis 24-5

parenting
    and education 167-8
    and intelligence 137
    quality of 157-9
patents 229
Pelé 198
Petrarch 110
Philippines, The 83
philosophical biologists 14
Piaget, Jean 185, 186, 188
Plato 106, 109, 110-11, 128
Polanyi, Karl 118
    and individual freedom 123
    theory of double movement 148
    on ethics and economics 124-5
    societal change 155
    great transformation 262-3
    opaqueness in modern world 199
political hierarchy 33
politicians
    psychological motivation 264
politics
    emergence in early society 35-8
    impotence re economics 265-6
    in ancient Greece 107
    and social provision 248
    and economic laws 263-4
pollution 71-4, 254
popular science 18
population
    forecast growth in 78
    effect in law of rent 214
    Malthus' theory of 79-80
    sustainable level 254
pornography 184
Portugal 47, 144
post-war consensus 64-6
poverty 81, 84, 92
    emergence in early society 36

poverty–*contd*
   and economic growth 70
   explanation in economics 220-1
   and education 168
   futility of current responses 205
   and globalization 274
   and industrial revolution 61-3
   and political interventions 262-4
   evidence of worsening 102-3
prejudice 160, 178, 197
   and economic exclusion 132-3, 148-9
prestige economy 35-8
preventable diseases 80, 91
Principles of Political Economy and Taxation
   209
printing press
   impact of invention 44
private property
   emergence of 42
   condition for market efficiency 236
   land as 236
   effects of rent teated as 218-19
privatization 89-9, 96, 204
profit
   in classical economics 209-11
   in competition with wages 218-19
   not the cause of poverty 249
   not reduced by tax on rent 237-8
Progress and Poverty 219, 237, 250, 251, 256
Protagorus 109, 120
psychic unity, doctrine of 4, 52, 124, 142
psychoanalysis 155, 156
psychological development 157-8, 177, 183
   195
psychological health 124, 183
public investment
   in renewable energy 73
   without undermining economy 237
   as a self-financing income stream 242
public services
   need for 241
   sustainable means of funding 242-4
Putin, Vladimir 97
pygmies 27

race and intelligence 135-8
racism 18, 131, 177, 197
rape 87, 99, 103
   as a weapon of war 40
rationality 115-16, 195-6
rationing
   of life chances 168
   forced by ecological imperative 278
Rawls, John 114-15
Reagan, Ronald 66
recession 65, 68-9, 88, 204
redistribution
   of wealth through taxation 246

reformation, the 59, 60, 183
relativism – *see* moral relativism
religion
   contribution to ethics 108
   and universalism 124, 147-8
Renaissance 110
renewable energy 73-4, 255, 277
rent
   Ricardo's law of 210-19
   private appropriation of 220-1, 236-7
   in classical economics 209
   as source of public finance 239-42
   in today's world 222-5
Reynolds, Vernon 30
Ricardo, David 11, 209-10, 221, 232, 252,
   256-7
Rifkin, Jeremy 73, 231
Robertson, Ian 159-61, 284
Rockefeller, John 11, 12
Romanticism 142
Roosevelt, Franklin D. 63
roots
   perceived need for 177-80
Rosen, Allen D. 112
Rousseau, Jean-Jacques 113, 185
Russell, Peter 180-2
Russia
   impact of AIDS 83
   health of population 96
   economic collapse 96-7

Sagan, Eli 38, 39, 44, 50, 179, 183, 194-8, 200
Sale, Kirkpatrick 278
Sartre, Jean-Paul 118
Saul, John Ralston 182, 183
scarcity
   in ancient societies 33-5, 58
   perception of and competition 172, 218
   not cause of poverty 221
Schmitt, Carl 180
Schumacher, E.F. 277, 278
scientific method 1-3, 22
sea level
   effects of rises in 72
second homes 224
self-awareness 24, 29
self-esteem 175
self-interest
   and individual freedom 112
   legitimate versus excluding 208
self-love, positive form 175-6
Sennett, Richard 165, 169, 170
September 11, 2001 104
sexual selection 7
Shaftesbury, Lord 111
shanty towns 99, 225
Shaw, George Bernard 251
sibling rivalry 16

Sierra Leone 82, 99
Simpson, George 13
Singapore 92
Singer, Peter 116
single tax 239
Six Day War 65
skin colour 27, 119, 178
slavery 91
slave trade 227
Small is Beautiful 277
Smith, Adam 5, 108, 206-7, 209-10, 219, 221,
    232, 237, 250, 257, 278
social aggression 50
social conscience 200
social contract 113, 188
social Darwinism 9-13, 15
social evolution 9-14, 43-5, 53
socialism 171, 249, 250, 260
socialization of debt 89
social justice 256-8, 264-5, 280
    in Kant's thought 112
    and individual freedom 233-6
social morality 58
social safety net 95, 244
social science 3, 14, 19, 20, 193
social stratification 33
sociobiology 14-15, 17-19
sociology 11, 19, 155
Socrates 109, 128
South Africa
    impact of AIDS 83
    inherited debt 90
    incidence of rape 87
South Korea 92-3, 95
sovereign debt 88
Spain 47, 90, 144
speculative investment 226, 241
Spencer, Herbert 5-6, 9-12, 20, 22, 26
Stalin, Josef 52, 97
Stoics, the 110, 115
structural adjustment 89-91, 267
structuralism 155
subjectivism 117
Sumner, William Graham 11, 12
survival of the fittest 6, 10, 20
sustainability xi, 52, 166, 205, 255, 260, 271
sustainable agriculture 50, 85
Switzerland 82, 229
Syria 65

Taiwan 92-3
taxation 240
tax on rent
    no disincentive effect 237
    moral justification for 236-7
    ease of collection 239
    in place of other taxes 236
    as source of public revenue 241-4

technological advance
    and capitalism 75
    as force for cultural change 46-8
    and the industrial revolution 58-9
    and opportunities for progress 277-8
    and unemployment 231-2
territoriality 33
terrorism 268-9
Thailand 83, 84, 93-5
Thatcher, Margaret 66
theory of forms, Plato's 109
third way 204
Third World
    impact of AIDS 83
    economic progress in (1965-84) 69
    population explosion 78-9
    nature and extent of poverty 80-9
    structural adjustment and debt 89-91
tiger, endangered 281
Tolstoy, Leo 251
trade barriers 229
trade unions 220, 247
Trainer, Ted 69
trickle-down effect 70-1
Tsirkunov, Vladimir 97
Tuvalu 72
tycoon capitalism 96

Uganda 83, 84
unemployment
    among young and old 101
    in global manufacturing 230-1
    structural nature of 66
United Kingdom – *see* Great Britain
United Nations
    development goals 204
    trailblazer for global governance 283
    and human rights 115, 121-2
United States
    post-war development aid 63-4
    education and employment 165
    and eugenics 13
    murder rate 103-4
    poverty 65
    and social Darwinism 12
    and trade barriers 229
    as example of western model 104
Universal Declaration of Human Rights 115
universal democratic franchise 155, 264
universalism
    and conscience 194-5
    and culture 258
    definition of 123-5
    and individual freedom 233-5
    and group identity 177-8, 197
    and moral relativism 187
    and religion 147-8
    and social provision 244-5

utilitarianism 113-14
Utopia 116
utopian idealism 282

veil of ignorance, Rawls' 114
Venezuela 91
Versailles 146
Vienna Conference (1815) 145
Vietnam war 65
    global cultural effects of 131

wages
    in classical economics 209
    in competition with profit 218-19
    equitable where rent is taxed 239
    forced down by law of rent 218-19
    reduction in Mexico 92
    subordinate to rent and profit 222
    of teachers and health workers 243-4
Wallace, Alfred 8
Wall Street 64, 94
Ward, Lester 11
water
    as a basic need 55
    role in social advance 46-7
    threat of global shortage 86
Watkins, Kevin
Watson, James 14
wealth
    in classical economics 209-10
    equitable distribution of 249-50
    impact of redistributive tax on 246
    cause of excessive concentration of 218

Wealth of Nations, The 206, 237
Weber, Max 139
welfare state 156, 248
western civilization 115, 262
Wickramasinghe, Chandra 9
Wilson, Allen 25
Wilson, Edward O. 14, 15, 70
Wolfensohn, James 204
women
    impact of AIDS upon 83
    status in early societies 32
    notions of inferiority 146-7
    and moral reasoning 191
    as principal workers 100
    scope for men to learn from 191
work
    burden of in poor countries 100-1
    changing patterns of 169
    division in early societies 32
    and education 165
    value beyond subsistence 276
working lives
    length of 275
World Bank, The 70
World War I 99, 144-5, 179
World War II 63, 145, 187, 233, 248

Yeltsin, Boris 97
Yom Kippur War (1973) 65

Zeigler, Wolfram 74
Zeno 115